THE SOPHISTS

THE SOPHISTS

An Introduction

Edited by
Patricia O'Grady

B L O O M S B U R Y
LONDON • NEW DELHI • NEW YORK • SYDNEY

Bloomsbury Academic
An imprint of Bloomsbury Publishing Plc

50 Bedford Square
London
WC1B 3DP
UK

1385 Broadway
New York
NY 10018
USA

www.bloomsbury.com

Bloomsbury is a registered trade mark of Bloomsbury Publishing Plc

First published in 2008 by Gerald Duckworth & Co. Ltd.

Editorial arrangement © Patricia O'Grady 2008

Patricia O'Grady has asserted her right under the Copyright, Designs and Patents Act, 1988, to be identified as Editor of this work.

British Library Cataloguing-in-Publication Data
A catalogue record for this book is available from the British Library.

ISBN: PB: 978-0-7156-3695-4
ePUB:978-1-4725-2120-0
ePDF:978-1-4725-2119-4

Library of Congress Cataloging-in-Publication Data
A catalog record for this book is available from the Library of Congress.

Contents

To Mary Skaltsas,
dear friend,
ever supportive and encouraging.

Contributors

Doug Al-Maini is Professor, Department of Philosophy, St Francis Xavier University, Canada.

George Arabatzis is Research Associate, Research Centre on Greek Philosophy, Academy of Athens, Greece.

Dirk Baltzly is Senior Lecturer, School of Philosophy, Monash University, Australia.

Bevin Boden is Technical Support Officer, Flinders University, Australia.

Geoff Bowe is Assistant Professor, Philosophy, History and Politics, Thompson Rivers University, Canada.

Craig Cooper is Professor of Classics, University of Winnipeg, Canada.

Trevor Curnow is Reader in Philosophy, University of Cumbria, UK.

Sabatino DiBernardo is Instructor in Religion, Philosophy and Humanities, University of Central Florida, USA.

Christine Farmer is Writer and Illustrator, University of Birmingham, UK.

Louis Groarke is Associate Professor, Department of Philosophy, St Francis Xavier University, Canada.

Paul Groarke is Assistant Professor, Department of Criminology and Criminal Justice, St Thomas University, Canada.

Colin Higgins is Instructor in English, University of Louisiana Lafayette, USA.

Jonathan Lavery is Assistant Professor, Philosophy and Contemporary Studies, Wilfrid Laurier University, Canada.

Patricia O'Grady is Adjunct Research Associate, Department of Philosophy, Flinders University, Australia.

Glenn Rawson is Assistant Professor of Philosophy, Rhode Island College, USA.

Steven R. Robinson is Associate Professor and Chair, Philosophy Department, Brandon University, Canada.

Andrew Shortridge is Tutor, School of Philosophy and Bioethics, Monash University, Australia.

Daniel Silvermintz is Assistant Professor of Humanities, University of Houston-Clear Lake, USA.

Seamus Sweeney is Special Lecturer and Senior Registrar in Psychiatry, St Vincent's University Hospital/University College, Dublin, Ireland.

Acknowledgements

It is with pleasure that I acknowledge friends and associates for their ongoing assistance and advice. I am grateful to Rodney Allen, Allan Chalmers and Ian Ravenscroft for advice in a number of areas and for each reading one or more of my chapters and offering suggestions for improvement and clarification. I especially thank Daniel Silvermintz for researching and writing a first-rate chapter, 'The Double Arguments', at short notice. My thanks to George Couvalis for wise advice, to Michael Tsianikas, George Frazis, Maria Palaktsoglou of the Modern Greek Section of the Department of Languages at Flinders University for continued support, to Suzanne Roux for her interest and loyalty, and to the ever-patient administrative assistants, Julie Elkson, Lis Jansson, Mary Skaltsas and Maureen Taylor. My thanks to the library staff of Flinders University for whom no query was too difficult, and to Bevin Boden, Technical Support Officer, also of Flinders University for unravelling the mysteries of contrary computers. A special thank you to my loyal family.

Special thanks, also, to Deborah Blake, Editorial Director at Duckworth, for patience and understanding.

I am grateful to the Flinders University of South Australia for providing the necessary resources which enabled me to embark on this project. Without that support this book would not have come to fruition.

Sincere thanks to all the contributors, those dedicated scholars of the philosophy of ancient Greece, for their valuable, thought-provoking work, often slotted in between the demands of teaching, marking, administrative duties and family crises.

Thank you, everyone, for making another dream come true.

Introduction

Patricia O'Grady

The impetus for this book came from the realisation that there is no available book on the sophists written in a straightforward uncomplicated style suitable for students and non-specialists studying fifth- to fourth-century BC Greece. Study of the politics, society and education of Athens in the fifth to fourth century would be shallow and incomplete without knowledge and understanding of the sophists.

This book is an introduction to certain unique individuals who influenced the political and social structure of Greece, particularly Athens, to such a marked degree that they stand out from the traditional more general category of sophists (wise men, poets and teachers), becoming a topic of study on their own account.

The period under discussion was vibrant with activity in literature, architecture, music, poetry, sculpture, politics, and philosophy. At the same time the Athenian empire was being established and expanded. We know of many notable and talented men, and a few women, from this time. We hear of the playwrights Aeschylus, Euripides and Aristophanes, of the philosophers Anaxagoras, Socrates and Democritus, of the politicians Aristides, Cimon, Themistocles, Alcibiades, Pericles and his mistress, perhaps wife, Aspasia, to mention just a few of the outstanding figures of the time. Plato was born in about 429 and Xenophon a year or two later; they both attained distinction early in the following century. Glorification of Athens following destruction during the Persian Wars was under way: construction of the Parthenon began in 447, directed by the brilliant architect Ictinus and the sculptor Phidias. And we add to this illustrious list the names of the sophists who form the subjects of this book.

Our story of the sophists commences in about 450, when Athenians were still basking in the euphoria of their victory over the Persians, almost to a point of hubris. The first chapter is devoted to defining the word 'sophist', and shows how, in the literature and orally, and especially in the works of playwrights, it became a derogatory term, a usage which it retains, to some extent, to this day.

Chapter 2 outlines the background and sets the scene for the advent of the sophists. The early kings did not exercise total control. It would be a foolhardy king who failed to heed the shouts of opinion from his men in the assembly. Freedom of speech was no longer the birthright of the privi-

1

leged. The world's most famous democracy was evolving, and the theatre and the market place became important meeting places for conversation and debate, just as in the courts and the assembly.

A slight digression may be permitted here while we ask, 'Why were the sophists so successful, and so sought after?' The answer lies partly in the sum of just two obols. It seems extraordinary that the course of western civilisation could be so affected by the payment of two obols a day. Let us establish how this came about.

Pericles, the incorruptible statesman, who was selected by the people fifteen times to be chief archon (the most powerful judicial and executive position) of Athens was, by about 450, the most powerful person in Athenian politics. In his attempt to broaden democratic government and curry favour with the lower classes of citizens, Pericles introduced a payment of two obols a day[1] as compensation to enable farmers and tradesmen to attend the law courts and participate in the business of government. This payment was enough to enable poorer citizens to leave their work to attend to the business of government. It was not the recipients of the two obols who were the clients of the major sophists – their fees were too large for an ordinary workman to afford – but their attendance at the courts and assemblies brought them into close contact with people and events in Athens. They might be very good farmers, but they were inexperienced, and lacked the ability to take part efficiently in the management of the affairs of state; they were untrained in the processes of government. If a man sought success, that is wealth, power and authority, he needed skills in communication, especially in persuasive speech. He needed to be able to participate effectively in debate, to prepare a speech, and to defend or attack a proposal. A citizen could not be represented by an advocate, meaning that he needed to learn to protect himself against possible charges. Words became a very powerful tool, and skill in the art of persuasion held the prospect of success. A citizen could attract authority, approval and admiration, but also envy and malice.

Enter the sophists, most of whom came from other city-states where they had already developed the necessary skills that were now much sought in Athens, a city of ever-increasing opportunity. The sophists would happily teach these desirable skills to others for a fee, often a very high fee. The Athenians were ripe for the picking. Non-Athenians were metics, that is Greeks but not Athenians, so therefore foreigners, and while this debarred them from participating in the business of the assemblies and the law courts, they were immensely influential in training Athenians to embrace their new-found roles in politics, society and education and as speech writers to those who needed to acquire such expertise. Words became a valuable commodity; well chosen words were powerful, and learning the technique of choosing the right words, the persuasive words, was costly.

The chapters on the sophists commence with Chapter 3 on Protagoras, perhaps the most famous of them all, and continue with eleven named sophists and a chapter on the minor sophists. The date of Protagoras' arrival in Athens is not known, but he heralded the advent of the sophists. We know that he was already well known because the young Hippocrates, son of Apollodorus, sought to become one of his pupils in order to learn how to become a sophist (Plato, *Protagoras* 310b-312a). Protagoras is most famous for his declaration, 'man is the measure of all things'; with that profound statement he unleashed one of the most constant debates in the history of ideas. He also held a view about the gods, another weighty statement that is open to different interpretations. And he professed to make his students better, day by day, in this way declaring his intent.

Gorgias is the subject of Chapter 4 and, as we shall see, one of the most controversial of the sophists. From Diodorus Siculus (XII.53.2-3; Sprague 1972, 32), we learn that he was highly regarded as a most powerful speaker. He represented his city, Leontini, as an ambassador to Athens, and 'by his style he amazed the Athenians' (Diodorus Siculus XII.53.2-3; Sprague 1972, 32).

In Chapter 5 we read about the multi-talented Hippias, the most versatile of the sophists and probably the richest. We will see that he certainly knew the value of a well-prepared speech and it seems that he deprecated foolish talk – he regarded discussions such as he and Socrates had engaged in as 'petty arguments', 'mere words' which could make one appear a 'fool' (Plato, *Hippias Major* 304a-b). It comes as no surprise to learn that he represented Elis as an ambassador. Hippias is credited with discovering the quadratrix, an outstanding advance in geometry. He promoted his view that all citizens should regard themselves as a brotherhood of mankind and act accordingly. This was a fine ideal, but it came to nothing.

Prodicus, the subject of Chapter 6, appears in *Protagoras* in the company of Hippias, and numerous other followers of Protgaoras. Prodicus is one of several sophists also to address the public assembly (Plato, *Hippias Major* 282b c). He appears as a character in Aristophanes' *Clouds* (361), where the chorus listen to him because of his wisdom. Prodicus is noted as a grammarian, who insisted on precision in the language, and considered as most important 'the truth about the correctness of words' (Plato, *Cratylus* 384b; Sprague 1972, 75), and is reported to have said 'first one must learn about correctness of words' (Plato, *Euthydemus* 277e; Sprague 1972, 77).

In Chapter 7 we come to Antiphon, whoever he may be and whether he is one person or an amalgam of the several Antiphons of the time. Almost as if to compensate for that lack of knowledge, we are most fortunate in having some fragments of papyri, retrieved from the dry preserving sands of Egypt at Oxyrhynchus. (Part of the papyrus of Antiphon adorns the cover of this book.) In the chapter, Antiphon's ideas are analysed, but they are not fully developed; they were new and the sources are meagre.

Thrasymachus, the subject of Chapter 8, is a major figure in Plato's

Republic, in which he and Socrates disagree, almost coming to violence. Thrasymachus is defending his thesis about justice in conflict with Socrates' own views. In a particularly disputatious episode at the beginning of the *Republic* (336b) Plato has the 'frightened' Socrates describe how Thrasymachus 'hurled himself upon us as if he would tear us to pieces'. Thrasymachus believed that the gods had no concern for the affairs of mankind He is also important for his contributions to the theory of rhetoric.

Chapter 9: Callicles is known only through Plato's depiction of him in *Gorgias*. Some regard him as an imaginary figure, but Plato certainly portrays him as very real. He is a sophist of a different class; he was rich and had no need to charge fees. He saw the power of persuasion as most important. This places him far from the pursuits of philosophy. Callicles was outspoken, without restraint and believed that he was reflecting human values, but was he evil? It seems that in 'creating' Callicles, Plato aimed to bring to notice the evil traits that Callicles embodied, perhaps expecting that they would then be rejected. However, far from obliterating them, he promoted them, later influencing immoralists such as Nietzsche and others.

Critias, the topic of Chapter 10, was an Athenian of a privileged family that traced its ancestry back to the time of Solon. He was well educated in the traditional manner, and surely destined to become a distinguished politician in Athenian life. He is one of the speakers in Plato's *Protagoras* and this placed him in the company of sophists as well as with Socrates and Alcbiades. Following a difference with Socrates, he formed a close bond with the notorious Alcibiades: together they caused great harm to Athens. As history records, he became the brutal, merciless despot of the reign of terror of the Thirty Tyrants.

In Chapter 11, we reach another low point in the history of the sophists, with the two elderly brothers, Euthydemus and Dionysodorus. Plato's dialogue, *Euthydemus*, depicts the brothers delivering an exhibition of verbal trickery. They consider themselves to be 'the finest and speediest teachers on human excellence in the world' (*Euthydemus* 272e-273d). Their purposes were in total contrast to those of Socrates, whose pursuit of the definition and attainment of virtue had engaged much of his life. He knew that virtue was a quality neither easily nor quickly acquired.

In Chapter 12 we meet Isocrates (436-338) who lived to a great age, encompassing the life of Plato. Isocrates gained his fame as an orator, being acclaimed as one of the Ten Attic Orators, excelling in display (epideictic) speeches which may have provided amusement, but also illustrated his skill in oratory. Isocrates was critical of the sophists, believing that they made excessive claims which were unachievable. He was an accomplished rhetor who does not fit comfortably into the category of philosopher or entirely into that of sophist.

Chapter 13 discusses *The Anonymus Iamblichi* and *The Double Argu-*

ments. *The Anonymus Iamblichi* was compiled in the fifth or early fourth century by an anonymous writer from sources who are not identified. It is a guide book to living a good life as distinct from a life of pure enjoyment. Prominent in the treatise is that wide-ranging word, virtue, a quality not easily or hurriedly attained. Anonymus lists the qualities that are essential attributes in the effort to reach a virtuous state. The attainment of virtue requires hard, consistent work over a long period. The longest section is the discussion on law – not how to evade it but of the value to be gained by upholding the law, both for individuals and for the polis. Anonymus acknowledges that the necessary characteristics are supreme and matchless and really beyond the capacity of men.

The Double Arguments is another anonymous work named after the two words with which it begins, *dissoi logoi*. The anonymous author is interested in giving both sides of a debate. The examples of double arguments that the anonymous writer recorded are uncomplicated, indeed simplistic, but they conceal the complexity and importance of double arguments that are inherent in them. So to the final sentences of the chapter: 'The sophist is proven to be the wise man who is capable of navigating the cultural norms so as to know the right way to act in any given situation (*Dbl. Arg.* VIII.1-2). As the author of this chapter writes: 'With knowledge of all things, the sophist is the one best equipped to advise both individuals and cities.' The words, 'knowledge of all things' would guarantee total involvement in endless seminars. *Double Arguments* warrants careful study, certainly very much more than it now receives.

Chapter 14 focuses on 'Minor Sophists', regarded as 'minor' because there is so little preserved about them. To retrieve them from the literature, the author of the chapter has delved deeply into the ancient literature, frequently with scant rewards. Often the information is so inadequate that it is difficult to know whether a named person was a sophist or not. Two of the earliest sophists are The Sicilians Corax and Tisias. Also hailing from Sicily was Polus who was a pupil of both Gorgias and Licymnius. Some of these names are mentioned in earlier essays, but who is Licymnius? He may have been a pupil of Gorgias, but it may have been that Gorgias was the pupil of Licymnius. We do not have sufficient information to be able to say. The writer of this chapter resurrects many men about whom we know almost nothing apart from their names. We are unlikely ever to learn more about them or their contributions, but they receive some slight acknowledgement in having their names recorded again, regardless of their place in the history of the sophists.

The next seven chapters are devoted to discussion and analysis of issues that arise naturally from the chapters on the named sophists. They develop questions which even today generate lively debate between academics in various fields, notably philosophy, politics and law. Most of the topics were crucial issues of the times, such as 'Can Virtue be Taught?' and

'The Case against Teaching Virtue for Pay'. One chapter title asks the question, 'Was Socrates a Sophist?' another is a statement, 'Plato the Sophist'. Law versus nature was a perennial concern of the sophists. In 'The Sophists and Natural Theology' we find interesting and original ideas about religious phenomena. And the question is asked: 'Were the Sophists Philosophers?'

The final chapter discusses the relevance of the sophists today. What is their legacy to us? The sophists generated intellectual ferment in Athens. Without their influence Socrates may not have realised his mission, and Plato would have had no need to defend Socrates. Plato, and through him, Socrates, remain of immeasurable influence. It was once thought that excellence was the birthright of the aristocracy, an inborn quality that was therefore unteachable, but the sophists claimed to be able to teach this virtue and set about trying to do so. Virtue – excellence, goodness – was a topic of general interest. Socrates sought to define the nature or essence of virtue. It whipped up lively debate then, and continues to do so now. The sophists were the first professional teachers. The progress made in the dissemination of knowledge springs from advances in education, and these rely on professional teachers. It is true, as the author of the chapter states, that 'we live, in this quite pragmatic sense, in a world created by the sophists'.

The sophists practised rhetoric, the art of making a convincing case, of presenting a winning argument. It is the art of persuasive speech for which they charged a fee. Plato displayed marked hostility to the sophists. He scorned them, ridiculed them and, almost certainly, maligned them. By writing dialogues in their names, Plato immortalised numbers of sophists whom we now consider, on his authority, to be the most prominent, richest, destructive, fraudulent, false and dishonest of men: *Protagoras, Hippias, Gorgias, Euthydemus*. Other sophists about whom chapters have been written for this book figure prominently, as we shall see, in these and other dialogues.

The sophists were the catalyst that drove Socrates on his mission and activated debates which Plato 'recorded' in his dialogues. It is paradoxical that the entire works of Plato remain available to us today – paradoxical because Plato was the most vehement critic of the sophists and also our major source. Was Plato right when he criticised and derided the sophists so intensely?

Plato's purpose was to praise Socrates, his beloved mentor, for his wisdom, courage and honesty, his untiring devotion to establishing the nature of virtue for mankind's well being. It is mainly owing to the writings of Plato that Socrates is immortalised. For this he deserves our unending gratitude.

The sophists initiated a 'new intellectual ferment' (Guthrie 1969, 4). They raised unusual controversial questions, many of which are still zealously discussed and argued about today. The sophists were the learned men of their time, but were they smart rather than wise?

*

Apart from the chapters I have written I do not claim responsibility for the views expressed by the other contributors. Although I have edited the work I have tried to avoid imposing my own views. The sophists were so controversial, and remain so in modern times, that opinions of them are likely to vary. Those expressed in this book may not necessarily be my views, or yours. That is part of the appeal of studying the sophists. They were individuals, not a school of common thought, and they varied considerably in their theories and interests, which, as we shall see, were wideranging. One of their primary interests was linguistics, the development of language, perhaps because this was their stock in trade. In a general comment, Cole (1967, 70) remarked that 'Language provides the essential medium through which the formation and consolidation of society takes place'. The sophists would have agreed.

The contributors to this book share my desire to introduce the sophists to a broader range of readers. Presenting complex arguments in an uncomplicated style requires special skills. Not everyone has those necessary skills, but the contributors to this book have acquired them and implemented them to attain the desired result.

Our aim is to inform and delight. If we are able also to inspire readers to delve more deeply into a particular sophist or theory that they may have found intriguing, or puzzling, that will be an added bonus.

Note

1. The date of this innovation is not known. It may have been any time between 465 and 450 BC. Cimon was ostracised in 461 and Ephialtes died in 462, leaving Pericles the most powerful man in Athens. The sum was raised from two to three obols in 425 (see Roberts 1984, 60-1) after the death of Pericles. An obol was a reasonable amount, being about one third of a drachma, and was 'a good day's pay for a skilled workman in fifth century Athens'. Commodities were then cheap but luxuries, such as payment to a sophist, were costly and out of reach of wage earners (Dillon and Gergel 2003, 339n.1).

Bibliography

Cole, Thomas, *Democritus and the Sources of Greek Anthropology* (Cleveland: Case Western Reserve University, 1967).

Dillon, John and Gergil, Tania, *The Greek Sophists* (London: Penguin, 2003).

Diodorus Siculus, trans. Francis R. Walton, vol. II, Loeb edition (Cambridge, Mass.: Harvard, 1957).

Guthrie, W.K.C., *A History of Greek Philosophy*, vol. III (Cambridge: Cambridge University Press, 1969).

Homer, *The Odyssey*, trans. A.T. Murray, Loeb edition (London: Heinemann, 1919).

Homer, *The Iliad*, trans. A.T. Murray, Loeb edition (London: Heinemann 1921).

Plato, *Hippias Major*, trans. H.N. Fowler, Loeb edition (London: Heinemann, 1963).

Plato, *Protagoras*, trans. W.K.C. Guthrie (Harmondsworth: Penguin Classics, 1956).

Roberts, J.W., *City of Sokrates* (London: Routledge & Kegan Paul, 1984).

Sprague, Rosamond Kent (1972), *The Older Sophists* (Columbia: University of South Carolina Press).

1

What is a Sophist?

Patricia O'Grady

'Words, words, words. Is there no end to the tricks you can make them perform?' (Harris 2006, 402). The sophists pushed this question to the limit and were condemned for their alleged trickery. Let us examine the use of the word 'sophist' from its early beginnings to the time when it was used to describe those Greeks who developed certain trends of thought which set them apart. Our discussion will show how the meaning of the word changed as it accommodated the new breed of sophists.[1]

The word 'sophist' (*sophistês*) is derived from the Ancient Greek *sophos* meaning 'wise', 'skilful', 'clever'. The associated noun, *sophia*, indicates 'wisdom', 'skill' and 'knowledge'.[2] In an unqualified meaning, a sophist is a person who has wisdom, skill and perhaps knowledge, a person who is wise, skilful and clever. But there are degrees of such qualities as wisdom and skill and cleverness, and a wide range of purposes to which such capabilities may be applied, from the most worthy to the utterly despicable. In the following chapters we will recognise sophists who used their wisdom and cleverness in commendable teaching and activities, and sophists whose behaviour was contemptible and whose purposes were morally dissolute. Even so, the line between the two is not always clear. A despicable person may have some fine qualities, and the most admirable people invariably lack some quality or another. There are many sophists about whom we know so little that it is not possible assess their qualities.

In the earliest Greek literature a sophist was a teacher, poet and wise man. This is the way 'sophist' was used by Homer and Hesiod, who were writing their poetry in the eighth/seventh centuries BC. It comes as no surprise to locate the earliest use of the word in their writings. They were the first sophists: poets, teachers, and men of wisdom. From these early writers the Greeks learnt their history, genealogy, social customs and ethics. They also learnt their place in relation to the gods and in society. In the *Iliad* (IX.432-43) we read of Achilles who had been sent to Phoenix to be taught 'to be both a speaker of words and a doer of deeds'.

The word 'sophist' could convey skill or expertise in a craft or practical art. This is what Homer intends when he writes of a 'cunning workman' (*Iliad* XV.412). When Homer and Hesiod used the word to describe a person, it was a complimentary term. When it was used of the Seven Wise Men of Ancient Greece it was an accolade.

We refer to Solon, the statesman who was a wise man, a poet and teacher, a sophist in the best, that is, the traditional sense of the word. In about 594 BC Solon, being considered to be 'the justest and the wisest (*phronimôtaton*) of all', and because he was aware of the hardships suffered by the oppressed classes, was chosen as chief archon (chief magistrate) and commissioned to alleviate the privation of the underprivileged classes, to 'set free the condemned debtors, divide the land anew, and make an entire change in the form of government' (Plutarch, *Solon* XIV). He was doomed to failure: for the disadvantaged he did not go far enough while the landed classes felt he had gone too far.

We turn to Pindar, the acclaimed lyric poet, who was born in about 518 BC, still in the archaic period. His odes are specifically written to extol the victors and celebrate their victories at the Games. He makes frequent use of *sophos* to highlight their skills and cleverness. He wrote a victory ode to a certain Arcesilas of Cyrene, who won the Pythian chariot-race of 462 BC. Pindar praises Arcesilas as a skilful (*sophos*) charioteer (Pindar, *Pythian Ode* V.115). This high praise was the appropriate honour for the victor of the race. Winners at the Games were honoured and indulged as heroes, just as they are today. In similar vein Pindar wrote of the true poet who 'knoweth much by gift of nature' in contrast with those who have only learnt the lore of song, and chatter like intemperate crows (Pindar, *Olympian Ode* II.86). Here we see the early recognition of a sophist in comparison to a philosopher.

The main involvement in this work is with the sophists of the fifth and fourth centuries BC. As we proceed into the chapters, the areas in which a sophist of the fifth century differed from a sophist to whom the word was applied in the traditional sense will become clearer, but it is likely that different readers will glean different views from the authors of the chapters.

With Herodotus (*c.* 490-425/420 BC), we move into the Presocratic period. Herodotus employed 'sophist' to mean 'teacher' (Herodotus 1.29.1; 2.49.1; 4.95). Diogenes Laertius writes that a philosopher was a lover of wisdom, and a professor, one who had attained a state of 'mental perfection; sophists was another name for the wise men, and not only for philosophers but for the poets also. And so Cratinus [*c.* 484-*c.* 419 BC] when praising Homer and Hesiod in his *Archilochi*, gives them the title of sophist' (Diogenes Laertius, *Lives of Eminent Philosophers* I.12).

Euripides (*c.* 480-460) has the Muse Terpsichore apply the word 'sophist' unfavourably to Thamyris, a Thracian bard, who 'full oft had mocked our [the Muses'] skill', a most unwise thing to do, for which the Muses blinded him (*Rhesus* 924). The word was already developing a fine nuance of a pejorative sense.

In a general sense the noun 'sophist' denoted wisdom and skill, and was usually a term of praise. So how did this once complimentary term acquire the pejorative connotations that it developed and even now, to a considerable extent, still carries?

1. What is a Sophist?

In the early 1870s Henry Sidgwick described the sophists as:

> ... a set of charlatans who appeared in Greece in the fifth century, and earned an ample livelihood by imposing on public credulity: professing to teach virtue, they really taught the art of fallacious discourse, and meanwhile propagated immoral practical doctrines ... they were there met and overthrown by Socrates, who exposed the hollowness of their rhetoric, and triumphantly defended sound ethical principles against their pernicious sophistries.[3]

Just fifteen years later, in 1888, Friedrich Nietzsche expressed a totally opposing opinion: '... every advance in epistemological and moral knowledge has reinstated the sophists' (Nietzsche 1964, 348). George Grote (1904, ch. LXVII), the respected philosopher/historian, was another influential commentator who provided more realistic analyses of the sophists.

What is one to make of such differing views? Who is right? And who were the sophists? What did these professors profess? Why not call them philosophers? Could a sophist also be a philosopher, and could a philosopher be a sophist? What distinguishes a sophist from a philosopher?

Many eminent scholars have attempted to define and explain the word 'sophist', with varying success.[4] Of the most well-known sophists, who can or should be classified as a sophist? Is it desirable to be so designated? Is Protagoras a philosopher at the same time as he is a sophist? How should we designate Gorgias and, indeed, is Socrates a sophist?

As our most prolific source for the sophists, Plato must be given careful attention. At the same time it is necessary to bear in mind that he is a hostile witness who is frequently unfair to the sophists. He was not the first to pillory the sophists, but he was the most influential and all his works survive. They are readily available and constantly read and analysed. Later chapters will show the extent to which Plato influenced judgements about the sophists, but we will not be able to judge the degree to which Plato relied on original writings of the sophists, how much was anecdotal, or how much he was exercising his fertile powers of imagination, exaggerating the inadequacies of the sophists for his own purposes and depicting them as unprincipled opportunists.

In his dialogue entitled *Sophist*, Plato has the Elean Stranger (from Elea in Italy)[5] concede that the word 'sophist' is difficult to define, 'troublesome and hard to catch' (*Sophist* 218c). A sophist 'demands its pay in cash' (223a). A sophist is an entertainer, a juggler, an imitator of realities (235a), in 'a baffling classification where it is hard to track him' (236d). A sophist 'is very far from being wise, although his name implies wisdom' (221d). Again, the Stranger states that a sophist hunts 'for pay, is paid in cash' by 'rich and promising youths' (223b). '[Sophists] promise to educate men to enable them to argue about laws and public affairs' (232d). Plato has the Stranger utter an all-embracing condemnation of the sophists:

11

'The sophist is nothing else, apparently, than the money-making class of the disputatious, argumentative, controversial, pugnacious, combative, acquisitive art, as our argument has again stated' (226a). Despite the concession of the Elean Stranger that the word is hard to define, Plato finds no difficulty in denouncing the sophists at length, putting into the mouth of the Elean Sranger explicit pejorative language.

A very simple definition of sophists, and one that is devoid of Plato's dogmatism and malevolence, is this: sophists were freelance, mostly non-Athenian, independent teachers who travelled throughout Ancient Greece from city to city making their living out of the new demand for education. This demand in Athens came about mainly as a result of changing social circumstances.

This brings us the great Athenian statesman, Pericles, who was born in 495 BC. By about 450 he was the most powerful man in Athens. He was an empire builder, and under his control an Athenian Empire grew in size, wealth and power. Pericles increased the number who could attend the assembly and, as was shown in the Introduction, made a daily payment which enabled the poorer citizens to leave their fields and trades and take part in the business of state. Every citizen, and that meant every free man born in Athens, had an opportunity to participate in the political life of the city and, indeed, was expected to take part in this famous democracy. It therefore became necessary for a man to be able to compose a speech, to deliver it effectively and persuasively, to mount a case, to support or denounce a proposal, to be able to defend himself against charges and to build and maintain the standing of his family. There was no avenue for appeal and, except for a very brief period, no laws against libel (see slander, pp. 64-5 below).

Most of the sophists were foreigners, Greeks but not Athenians, so they could not be involved directly in the affairs of the assembly and the law courts, but this motley, controversial set of men had a dynamic influence on the character, culture, politics, literature and education of the city.

> Athens at the time was an exciting place. Culture was flowering. Arts and science blossomed. There existed an unprecedented level of intellectual curiosity, a questioning of superstitions and conventions, and a belief in progress. All of the arts, particularly the literary arts, oration and rhetoric reached their zenith as the masters in the various disciplines competed for fame and honour (Usher 2005, 113).

It was onto this scene that the sophists emerged. The first of the early sophists dealt with here – that is, the sophists of the mid-fifth century BC, men who introduced new curricula which they taught in a new style, sought to develop rhetoric or skills in argumentation, could persuade or convince, and brought new meaning to the word 'sophist', changing it forever – was Protagoras, who hailed form Abdera in Thrace in Northern

1. What is a Sophist?

Greece. In his dialogue *Protagoras*, Plato[6] has Protagoras acknowledge that:

> A man has to be careful when he visits powerful cities as a foreigner, and induces their most promising young men to forsake the company of others, relatives or acquaintances, older or younger, and consort with him on the grounds that his conversation will improve them (*Protagoras* 316d).

Born in Abdera, Protagoras was a foreigner. He is visiting the powerful city of Athens and realises that his teaching will arouse resentment and hostility. He 'admits to being a sophist and an educator' (*Protagoras* 317b), explaining that he found admission rather then denial to be a better precaution against being regarded as a rogue who tries to hide his occupation. This passage indicates that being considered a sophist already incited resentment, perhaps a hint of danger even before such well known figures as Protagoras appeared on the scene.

Protagoras was a wordsmith who seemed to think that more was better: we find him chided by Hippias: '... and Protagoras should refrain from shaking out every reef and running before the wind, launching out on a sea of words till he is out of sight of land' (*Protagoras* 338a). Protagoras lived to a great age, and spent many years in Athens. He knew the value of words, and his skill rewarded him with great wealth.

Some of the other sophists also amassed fortunes through charging high fees for their instruction, whereas Plato and others regarded teaching for money as insupportable. It was one of the practices of the sophists that so inflamed Plato that he referred to the earnings of the sophists on at least thirty-one occasions.[7]

Plato also derided the sophists for claiming to be able to teach virtue, but he identified as one of their worst aspects the fact that they showed no discrimination. They would teach anyone who had the money to pay. Plato and the privileged aristocrats believed that education was for the upper classes and that an educated citizenry was a danger to the very foundations of the aristocracy on which Athens had been built. Plato came from a wealthy, privileged family; from such an elite position it is all too easy to be critical of lesser mortals who need to work for their living.

The word 'sophist' implies skill and wisdom. Skill entails ability or aptitude in crafts, the making of things, such as boat-making or sculpture, or of performance such as horsemanship or public-speaking. The sophists were skilful. They were teachers of higher education, and this might commence at the age of about fourteen.[8] Between them they provided instruction in a wide range of subjects, including history, genealogy, mathematics, geometry, linguistics, grammar, and the correct usage of words and names.

The sophists delivered lectures, seminars and demonstration speeches known as '*epideixeis*', which were exhibitions or displays presented both to the general public and privately (Plato, *Hippias Major* 282b-c). The *Protagoras* is set in the house of the rich Athenian Callias, who was a considerable financial supporter of the sophists (Plato, *Apology* 20a). In addition, Callias was well connected, being related to Pericles through marriage. Listed among those present are the names of a significant number of men, including Prodicus of Ceos (*Protagoras* 314c), who follow Protagoras as he walks in the portico. Another group of Athenians sits around Hippias of Elis, who occupies a 'seat of honour' (315c), and also in the crowd (315d) are a number of foreign followers. Two days after the meeting in the house of Callias, Hippias was to present a display in 'Pheidostratus' schoolroom' (*Hippias Major* 286b).

The tragedian Aeschylus (*c.* 525-*c.* 456 BC) notes the demarcation between wisdom and knowledge when he writes that a wise person is one who knows useful things, rather than many things (Aeschylus, fr. 218). One should accept that the sophists were knowledgeable. Although they knew many things, they also knew useful things. The sophists were skilful and learned but, apart from Hippias of Elis, they were not described as wise.[9] They practised and taught speech-making or rhetoric, the art of clever speech, designed to sway an argument or convince an opponent. A sophist is a 'master of the art of making clever speakers' (Plato, *Protagoras* 312d). The goal of the sophists was winning: philosophers are seekers of the truth.

A man might be described as a sophist, meaning that he was wise. Plutarch tells us that Damon, a teacher of Pericles, was a consummate sophist who concealed his real power from public knowledge by posing as a teacher of the lyre. Under the teaching of Damon,[10] Pericles' great natural talent as a speaker flourished. Further, Plutarch tells us that Damon was ostracised for being a great schemer and a friend of tyranny. In reference to tyranny, it is interesting to note that in a play, *Chirones*, the comic playwright Cratinus (*c.* 484-*c.* 419) described Pericles as 'a tyrant exceedingly great'. These may be the extravagant words of a poet, but Pericles did wield exceptional power, being voted archon for fifteen years (Plutarch, *Pericles* 161). He was a fine orator, as one may perceive by reading, in particular, the funeral oration which is reported by the historian Thucydides (II.35-46). We will never know precisely what Pericles said, but Thucydides attributes to him a powerful, impassioned and eloquent funeral oration glorifying Athens, and those Athenians who died in 431 in the first campaign of the Peloponnesian War (431-404 BC). Pericles was a persuasive orator, enthralling his audience by heaping honour upon the mothers of sons who died in battle and speaking to the dead heroes who proved their manly courage and stood stoutly to their task.

A new discipline was established by the sophists when they gave instruction on learning how to assess situations and how to argue, but they were condemned for making weaker arguments stronger, regardless of the

14

merit of the argument. Rich fathers were prepared, and indeed quite willing, to pay large amounts of money to have their sons taught the art of making clever speeches, in order that they would become successful, i.e. rich and influential. Plato's dialogue *Protagoras* opens with a young man, Hippocrates, son of Apollodorus, knocking on Socrates' door before day-break. He has heard that Protagoras is in town and wants Socrates to take him to meet the great sophist so that he can learn how to become a sophist (310b).

Antagonism towards the sophists developed when their skills were put to winning, rather than to discovering truth. Even the porter at the home of Callias, where Protagoras and other sophists are staying, refuses entry to Socrates and Hippocrates, thinking them to be sophists. There are already so many sophists and visitors in the house that the porter is irritated with them. It is not until Socrates refutes the accusation that the porter allows them to enter (*Protagoras* 314d).

It was claimed of Protagoras that he could make the weak argument the stronger. Aristotle writes of 'making the worse appear the better argument' adding that 'men were justly disgusted with [this] promise of Protagoras' (Aristotle, *Rhetoric* 1402a). Aristotle lived from 384-322 and wrote *Rhetoric* in about 330 BC, but he is describing a view of the sophists that was commonly held in Athens a century earlier. The once complimentary term came to be applied in a derogatory way, a usage which it retains to a considerable extent to this day.

Our earliest remaining written reference to making the weaker argument the stronger is in Aristophanes' play, *Clouds*, which was presented in 423. Other references to making the weaker argument the stronger appear in reports written later. Aristophanes was born in about 457 BC to a well-to-do family whose interest was in maintaining the status quo. Perhaps no one describes Athenian feelings towards the sophists and their methods better than he does in *Clouds*.

When analysing *Clouds*, it is necessary to keep in mind that Socrates was regarded as a sophist, and any Athenian who was asked to name a sophist would almost surely name Socrates. He was an aggravating man, asking all and sundry tricky, 'unanswerable' questions, such as 'What is virtue?' and 'What is justice?' and humiliating those who could not answer. They could name a virtuous person, or describe an act of justice or injustice, but they could not define virtue or justice; they did not know the *essence* of virtue or justice. These are ideals, almost impossible to attain, being in the nature of the divine. So Socrates showed them to be ignorant when they thought that they were knowledgeable.[11] *Clouds* heaps ridicule upon Socrates as a sophist, regarding him as a corrupt teacher of rhetoric. Obviously the references must have had meaning to the audience: that was how the playwright got his laughs.

Clouds involves a spoilt young Athenian, Pheidippides, the son of a farmer, Strepsiades, and of a wealthy mother who indulges him. However, he has incurred debts for which his father is liable. The father wants his son to go off to join a school in Athens where he can be taught how to make the weaker argument the stronger, and how to outwit his creditors, to defraud them and evade payment. But Pheidippides will have none of this: 'I know them. Those rank pedants, those pale-faced, bare-footed vaga-bonds.[12] That Socrates, poor wretch, and Chaerephon' (*Clouds* 111). He will never be able to face his friends again after associating with such people. Socrates is portrayed as a sophist, and any stick will do to beat him.

There is a lot of hilarious discussion about getting a witch to swing on the moon to hold it in place so that it cannot advance to being a new moon which is the time for paying accounts. Also discussed are such 'crucial' questions as how far a flea can jump and which end of a mosquito makes the buzz, questions which are brought in to ridicule the sophists and, of course, to make the audience laugh, because the play, after all, was an entry in a competition. Now the Clouds, who are goddesses, promise to make Strepsiades the best speaker in all Greece, so that he will be able to prevail in the Assembly (*Clouds* 432). This is more ambitious than Strep-siades desires. 'But I wish to succeed, just enough for my need. And to slip through the clutches of law.' He wants only to find the solution to his predicament, that is, to defeat his creditors. Aristophanes may be pointing here to Strepsiades' grasping of this new skill and his lack of any intention of applying it for anything but his own dishonest purposes. This is a reference to making the weaker argument the stronger, developing the art of persuasion for immoral purposes, and is associated with the teachings of the sophists, with whom Socrates did associate, and is associated. Strepsiades implores Socrates to take Pheidippides in hand and Socrates agrees to turn Pheidippides into a 'splendid sophist' (*Clouds* 1111).

In *Clouds* all the prejudices held against the sophists are rolled into this one character, Socrates, one of the best known men in Athens. He was everywhere, asking his interminable questions, an unattractive fat man with a snub nose and bulging eyes. *Clouds* reflects the general conception of the sophists, presented in a slapstick, exaggerated and boisterous way. It is interesting to note that it won only third prize in the City Dionysia. Today it is still hilarious, a 'laugh out loud' play, but it is iniquitous and defamatory. Aristophanes was a superb playwright, a weaver of words, a trickster who certainly knew how to make a winner out of a weak argument.

Because Socrates, through Plato, recognised the influence that Aristo-phanes brought to bear by his mockery, it is important to mention Plato's *Apology* (*Defence of Socrates*) in which Socrates defends himself against charges of impiety and of misleading the youth of Athens. Plato has Socrates refer to his accusers as dangerous men:

> … who gained your belief since they got hold of most of you in childhood, and accuse me without any truth, saying: There is a certain Socrates, a wise man, a ponderer over the things in the air and one who has investigated the things

beneath the earth and who makes the weaker argument the stronger. These, men of Athens, who have spread abroad this report, are my dangerous enemies (*Apology* 18b).

Socrates is unable to name these men 'unless one of them happens to be a playwright' (*Apology* 18d). The trial of Socrates took place in 399 BC, twenty-four years after *Clouds* was first presented, but it is clear to Plato that the influence of the play was forceful and compelling. Plato was present at the trial of Socrates (*Apology* 38b) and was thirty years old when Socrates was executed. Aristophanes had some fourteen years to live, dying in about 385 BC.

In the *Apology*, Plato has Socrates use the word wisdom many times, 'What kind of wisdom is this? Just that which is perhaps human wisdom? For perhaps I really am wise in this wisdom' (20d). Socrates equates human wisdom with the 'gift of nature' about which Pindar had written fifty years earlier. Socrates, this most moral of men, was a true wise man. His name and spirit are immortal and his teachings are of endless influence.

Were the sophists charlatans, as Sidgwick claimed? And were they guilty of everything that Plato heaped upon them? Certainly, Euthydemus and Dionysodorus, who could argue both ways relentlessly and effectively, and Thrasymachus with his belief that justice is rightly for the stronger, held dangerous views and taught their students their insidious ideas.

Most of the sophists were engaged in the development of language, of vocabulary, of gender in nouns, and of speech in general. This, of course, enhanced their exhibition speeches and their teaching, but had more lasting benefits. Several of them acted as ambassadors for their states, no doubt because of their expertise in rhetoric and their knowledge of language. A number of them discussed justice and argued the virtues of natural law as compared with man-made law. This is a topic which engaged sophists and philosophers alike.

The sophists were mainly foreigners, itinerants who plied their trade where the opportunities were greatest, the pickings the highest and this was primarily Athens. Being itinerant, they seemed to have no allegiance to any city. This would be viewed most unfavourably by Athenians who were euphorically proud of their city-state, more so since their magnificent victories against the Persians and the peace of 449/8 BC.

The sophists were the earliest public educators, initiating methods that were the precursor of modern education. They questioned the long established ingrained institutions and, in doing so, they shook Athens. A number of the sophists were certainly philosophers, and while some of them practised dubious rhetoric, perhaps taking advantage of gullible youth, it is not true to state, as Henry Sidgwick did, that they were all charlatans. These are big claims which cannot justly be made against the sophists in general. The passage from Sidgwick quoted above reads as a furious exaggeration and cannot reasonably be imposed on a movement of independent professional men holding individual beliefs and practising different methods.

The sophists were much acclaimed, much maligned, eagerly sought after and tremendously influential with many of them amassing excessive wealth. They were teachers, and they were rhetoricians, practised and successful in the art of persuasive speech, of presenting a winning argument. They developed language skills, and incorporated the most descriptive, convincing words into their speeches for the purpose of persuasion. There is nothing wrong with persuasive speech as long as one does not use tricks that are planned to deceive, but some of the sophists were expert in making words perform tricks. Plato has Socrates explain that 'the man whose rhetorical teaching is a real art will explain accurately the nature of that to which his words are to be addressed, and that is the soul, is it not?' (Plato, *Phaedrus* 270e). The welfare of the soul was not a concern of the sophists. Although they claimed to be able to teach virtue, they did not see Socrates' mission as their course. If they did in fact see, that is perceive and comprehend, Socrates' mission, they would discard it as useless, time-wasting nonsense. They aimed to win arguments, to make the weak argument the stronger and to teach gullible followers how to prevail in the courts, how to outsmart their creditors and to confound and belittle their detractors.

When I claim that the sophists were clever rather than wise, smart rather than genuine, deceitful rather than honest, I am making a generalisation. None of them was entirely bad, though it is difficult to find redeeming aspects in such sophists as Thrasymachus, Euthydemus and Dionysodorus.

Totally opposite to Sidgwick, Nietzsche praised the sophists, but may be seen to extol too much. But did he? Because each word in his quotation warrants careful thought, I repeat it: '... every advance in epistemological and moral knowledge has reinstated the sophists'. As we progress through the book, it will be fruitful to dwell on that clause and consider how far it is true in relation to the sophists who are discussed here. In chapter LXVII of *A History of Greece*, George Grote presents an analysis of the sophists that is rational, insightful and meaningful. The chapter is deservedly famous. It is highly recommended and worthy of attention (Grote 1904, especially pp. 28-80).

The sophists followed a profession, but they were never a school or a guild. They taught their students how to succeed in public affairs, in politics, in business, in their personal lives. Their method was to pour information into their students, like milk into a jug. Although he claimed never to teach anyone, Socrates led his students to recognise virtue, that is, to value the fine and honourable qualities of character, by leading them to resurrect the innate knowledge that he believed all people held within themselves. He harried, teased and debated. While Socrates would never defy the law, the sophists instructed their students in the art of rhetoric, how to get around the law, how to construct and present a winning argument regardless of the rightness of an opinion or an action.

1. What is a Sophist?

The sophists were good and they were bad. In their diversity, they ranged from the worthy to the depraved. There is no typical sophist.

In ensuring the immortality of Socrates, Plato also ensured the immortality of the sophists, so why did he write about them? His writings provided the vehicle through which he could applaud Socrates and preserve and propagate his ideals. He lauded the goodness of Socrates and, while he extolled his hero, he brought to the world, not only the philosophy of Socrates, but the legacy of the sophists, even though he reviled most of them and their opinions and teaching. He could well be saying 'this is what happens when unprincipled people of poor breeding are allowed rights beyond their standing. They denigrate and destroy the tried and true traditions of the polis. This is what should be avoided.'

Without the advent of the sophists, Socrates would have found less to condemn and may not have recognised his mission. Plato would have had no need to defend Socrates as he did. Athenian and western philosophy, society, politics, democracy, and learning in general, would have taken a vastly different path.

The subjects that the sophists taught and the topics that made up Socrates' mission are issues that are as relevant today as they were in ancient Greece. They are still passionately debated. It may be argued that this is the greatest gift from the sophists.

You, the reader, may develop a different view.

Notes

1. Originally, it was planned to follow Guthrie (vol. III, 9n.2; 33n.2) and others, and use the word 'Sophist' with a capital S for the particular sophists who are the main topic of this book. Lower case was to apply to sophists in general. However, it became obvious that the dividing line between the two is often fine and frequently indistinguishable. In some instances it was impossible to decide. It seemed desirable and less confusing to abandon the original idea and use only 'sophist' with a small s.

2. Venturesome students may care to seek the evidence for the use and meaning of *sophia, sophos,* and *sophistes* in the comprehensive *Greek-English Lexicon* of Liddell and Scott (1940). It is quite useful to anyone who wishes to trace the development of the usage of the word by the earliest Greek writers and commentators. The 1980 impression of *An Intermediate Greek-English Lexicon,* founded upon the 7th edition of Liddell and Scott's Greek-English Lexicon (Oxford: Oxford University Press), is worthwhile, simpler and generally adequate.

3. Henry Sidgwick, 'The Sophists', *Journal of Philology* (1872), 288-307 and (1873), 66-80.

4. See especially Plato, *Sophist*; Grote 1904, 31-4; Guthrie 1969, 27-54; Kerferd 1981, 24-41.

5. Apart from 221d which is spoken by Theaetetus, the other lines quoted in this paragraph are delivered by the Elean Stranger.

6. It needs to be borne in mind that Plato was born in 429 or 427 BC, and was writing in the fourth century when the earliest sophists, apart from Gorgias, were already dead. To what extent Plato's dialogues were imaginary or historical is much debated. Even so, it may be feasible to accept that he was writing of affairs with which he had familiarised himself, but also that he was extremely biased against the sophists.

7. Guthrie 1969, 36n.2.

8. The education of younger boys consisted of lessons in language, literature (mainly Homer) and athletics (see Aristotle, *History of Animals* 581a12ff.).

9. It seems that Hippias of Elis was the only sophist called a 'sage' by the Greeks (Pausanias, *Elis* I.XXV.4).

10. Pindar was the teacher of Damon who was the teacher of Pericles.

11. It is of interest to note Aristotle's view: 'The object of our inquiry is not to know what virtue is, but to become good men' (Aristotle, *Nicomachean Ethics* 1103b27).

12. This is an allusion to Socrates, who was the bane of sandal-makers, apparently never wearing shoes but going barefoot in summer and in winter.

Bibliography

Aeschylus, trans. Herbert Weir Smith, vol. II, Loeb edition (London: Heinemann, 1946.

Aristophanes, trans. Benjamin Rogers, vol. I: *Clouds*, Loeb edition (London: Heinemann, 1950).

Diogenes Laertius, *Lives of Eminent Philosophers*, vol. I, Loeb edition (Cambridge, MA: Harvard University Press, 1980).

Grote, George, *A History of Greece*, vol. VII (London: John Murray, 1904).

Guthrie, W.K.C., *A History of Greek Philosophy*, vol. III (Cambridge: Cambridge University Press, 1969).

Harris, Robert, *Imperium* (London: Hutchinson, 2006).

Homer, *The Iliad*, trans. A.T. Murray, Loeb edition (London: Heinemann, 1925).

Kerferd, G.B., *The Sophistic Movement* (Cambridge: Cambridge University Press, 1981).

Liddell, Henry George, and Scott, Robert, *A Greek-English Lexicon,* a new edition revised and augmented throughout by Sir Henry Stuart Jones (Oxford: Clarendon Press, 1940).

Nietzsche, Friedrich, *The Will to Power*, vol. I (New York: Russell and Russell, 1964), nos 348, 428.

Homer, *The Iliad*, trans. A.T. Murray, Loeb edition (London: Heinemann, 1925).

[Pindar], *The Odes of Pindar*, including the principal fragments, trans. Sir John Sandys, Loeb edition (London: Heinemann, 1915).

Plato, *Apology*, trans. H.N. Fowler, Loeb edition (London: Heinemann, 1960).

Plato, *Protagoras*, trans. W.K.C. Guthrie (Harmondsworth: Penguin Classics,1956).

Plato, *Sophist*, trans. H.N. Fowler, Loeb edition (London: Heinemann, 1961).

Plutarch, *Plutarch's Lives*, vol. I, trans. Bernadotte Perrin, Loeb edition (Cambridge, MA: Harvard University Press, 1914).

Plutarch, *Plutarch's Lives*, vol. III, *Pericles*, trans. Bernadotte Perrin, Loeb edition (Cambridge, MA: Harvard University Press, 1916).

Thucydides, *History of the Peloponnesian War*, trans. Rex Warner (Harmondsworth: Penguin, 1954).

Usher, Matthew, 'Thucydides', in *Meet the Philosophers of Ancient Greece*, ed. Patricia O'Grady (Aldershot: Ashgate, 2005).

The Political Background of the Sophists at Athens

Steven R. Robinson

Rhetoric before the 'art of rhetoric'

One of the unique features of ancient Greek civilisation is the pre-eminent role of rhetoric, or persuasive public speech, within its political culture. Even the earliest Greek literature – the heroic epics composed by Homer in the eighth century BC – shows us kings who meet with assemblies of their armies and 'harangue' them this way and that in contentious debate over the best course of action. Though they are described as powerful commanders, these Homeric kings clearly rely on the shouts of approval from their massed troops as a demonstration of their rightness. Any leader who underestimates or dismisses the shouts of his men in assembly is later shown to regret it, as is illustrated by the overall plot structure of the *Iliad* itself.[1] On the very opening page we are given an instance:

> Then all the rest of the Achaians cried out in favour that the priest be respected and the shining ransom be taken; yet this pleased not the heart of Atreus' son Agamemnon ... (*Iliad* I.22-4).[2]

Agamemnon's subsequent denial of common sense and the collective will of his soldiery sets the scene for the unfolding of the tragic plot. Though the world of Odysseus and Achilles is certainly no democracy, it is a world in which leadership relies upon rhetorical persuasion to be effective. Homer's famous dictum is that to be great, a hero must be not only a doer of fine deeds, but a speaker of fine words.[3]

It had not always been that way. This prevalence of public speaking that leaves its traces everywhere in Greek literature indicates a fundamental shift in political consciousness away from a previous deference to powerful elites (who were accountable to no one) and towards the self-conscious rejection of absolute authority by the masses of Greek citizens.[4] It is as if the Greeks had decided among themselves, 'The kings cannot command us; they must persuade us.' With this shift in consciousness had come a shift in power. After all, any leader who can act unilaterally without regard for his people's wishes has no need of persuasion; by resorting to rhetoric he admits that he is dependent upon the cooperation of his audience, and that he cannot compel them.[5]

Even in Homer's day it was those on the receiving end of all the fancy talk – the masses of Greek farmers (basically, the militias) – whose cooperation had to be won before serious political action could be taken. The precise cause of this shift in power is not easy to determine because it happened during the tenth and ninth centuries BC, when writing was not practised in Greece. But that it had happened by the eighth century is clear, and can be identified with the emergence of that distinctively Greek form of social organisation called the *polis* (often translated as 'city-state'). In the Greek *polis*, writes Jean-Pierre Vernant, 'The art of politics became essentially the management of language; and *logos* [i.e. argumentation] from the beginning took on an awareness of itself, of its rules and its effectiveness, through its political function' (Vernant 1982, 50).

But despite having crossed this threshold into the rhetorical politics of the new '*polis*' power structure, Greek political culture did not settle into a stable pattern. From Homer onward we read out of Greek literature a record of steady rhetorical innovation and ideological differentiation. New spokespersons emerge for new groups, new interests, and new political strategies, bringing with them new genres of speech and writing engaged in an ongoing struggle between masses and elites over the 'management of language'.[6] One major bone of contention was *who* should have the authority to address 'the people'. At one extreme stands Homer, who shows us popular assemblies where only kings and holy seers are allowed to speak. An exception proves the rule: in Homer's *Iliad*, Thersites is a common soldier who dares to stand up and speak at an assembly, challenging Agamemnon (*Iliad* II.212-77). His rhetorical question, 'Why must we continue to die here for the greed and lust of you kings?' strikes modern ears as perfectly reasonable. Yet Homer depicts him as grotesque and crippled, and has Odysseus silence him with insults and heavy blows – to the laughter of all assembled. The message to Homer's own audience is clear: Shut up and let your betters do all the talking! At the other end of the spectrum is Plato's depiction of the democratic Assembly in late fifth-century Athens, the city that at that time famously offered the most freedom of speech in all of Greece. (Socrates is speaking):

> I observe that when we convene in the Assembly and the city has to take some action on a building project, we send for builders to advise us; ... This is how they proceed in matters which they consider technical. But when it is a matter of deliberating on city management, anyone can stand up and advise them, carpenter, blacksmith, shoemaker, merchant, ship-captain, rich man, poor man, well-born, low-born – it doesn't matter (*Protagoras* 319b-d).[7]

Between these two examples stretches over three hundred years of political evolution during which the elites' monopoly on public address was slowly eroded in favour of *parrhesia* and *isegoria* – basically, freedom of speech.

Crows and arrows

One phase in this historical development was the dramatic collapse of public faith in elite ideology after about 520 BC, and even more after 490 (i.e. after the battle of Marathon). This was partly the result of a downturn in relations between Greece and Persia. The elites within the Greek cities had always demonstrated their superiority and difference by cultivating close personal ties with the (by common Greek standards) decadent and excessive luxury of Eastern dynasts. But after Persia had begun annexing Greek cities in Ionia, and then attempted the same against Athens at Marathon, the Greek elites started to look like a Persian 'fifth column' within every *polis*. In self-defence it became necessary for those elites to dissociate themselves from the East and instead to try justifying their personal wealth and luxury in terms of its value to the rest of the *polis*. It was at this time that lavish spending by wealthy individuals at the Olympic Games began to be portrayed in a patriotic vein as winning renown for the whole *polis* – not just for the victor. It is also at this time that *epinikion* 'praise poetry' appeared on the scene to advertise publicly the superior worth of these wealthy families and individuals. These praise-poets, such as Pindar, insisted upon a quality of inborn human excellence that justified superior social status and, along with it, a superior facility with words. A common theme was to praise the bloodline of an athletic champion, and to express public gratitude for his family's glorious display of its wealth.

Though not members of the elites themselves, these poets claimed a unique intellectual status from which to speak to their betters, and *of* their betters, on behalf of the *polis* as a whole.

> Many swift arrows have I crooked beneath my elbow in their quiver for speaking to those who understand; but for the masses interpreters are required. Wise is the man with much inborn knowledge; while those who learn by study, like a pair of greedy crows, spout indiscriminate chatter compared to the divine bird of Zeus (Pindar, *Olympian Odes* II.83-9).[8]

Here Pindar distinguishes his own voice from lesser, competing voices, and claims a kinship in wisdom with his 'target' audience, those who understand his words (i.e. his 'arrows') by means of their own inborn knowledge. By contrast, persons who acquire their intelligence not by birth but by study (i.e. social climbers) are to be paid no attention; they are like squawking crows compared to the 'divine' eagle, Pindar himself. It is not hard to see in these 'crows' – greedy, ugly, and chattering – the image of Homer's Thersites once again, but now there is no Odysseus standing by to deliver the blow that will shut them up. Pindar can only encourage his audience not to listen to them.

Whose are those other voices? Who is this 'pair of greedy crows'? A standard reading would have it that Pindar is referring to his competitors in his profession of praise-poetry (i.e. Simonides and Bacchylides), and is alleging that their poetry is just tricked-up hack writing in contrast to his own, which is divinely inspired. But that interpretation seriously under-plays the apparent class-consciousness of these lines. Another suggested reading (which has problems of its own, but is too tantalising to ignore) is that the 'pair of crows' are Corax and Tisias – the inventors of the art of rhetoric (i.e. the first sophists).[9] The name 'Corax' is the Greek word for 'crow'. The most famous story told about these two is that Tisias (who learned the art of rhetoric from Corax) refused to pay his tuition fee. When Corax tried to sue him for the fee in court, Tisias made it his defence that even if the judgement went against him he should not have to pay Corax, because then he would clearly not have received value for his money: his fee was to purchase an ability to win court cases. The court ejected them both, declaring, 'From a bad crow a bad egg has come.'[10] Here indeed was a pair of crows not to be listened to!

What sort of 'indiscriminate chatter' might Pindar have been worried about? More than just competition from his rival praise-poets. As a matter of fact, the honouree of Pindar's above-quoted poem (dated about 476 BC), Theron, Tyrant of Akragas (in Sicily), was about to be violently removed from power and replaced with a democracy (in 472) – as was his friend and ally just down the road, Thrasyboulus, Tyrant of Syracuse, where Corax and Tisias happened to be living and practising their new 'art of rhetoric'. The story goes that Corax achieved his greatest fame after the fall of Thrasyboulus in 467. The tyrant had confiscated lands from many Syracusan land-owners. When democracy was established the deprived landowners were invited to reclaim their lost properties in court, but most of them had no idea how to present legal arguments because they had never been in court before or even spoken publicly. Corax helpfully penned the first-ever manual of rhetoric, one that could instruct his less able fellow citizens how to speak in court with a hope of winning – in exchange for a fee.[11] It was Corax's novel claim that one's skill at speaking could be learned by study instead of being inborn that first made rhetoric into an 'art'. To the elites in Greek Sicily and beyond this would have marked out Corax and Tisias as men who threatened to give an effective public voice to ordinary citizens, thereby further weakening elite control over public address, and hence over government. We might well understand Pindar's defensive reaction against 'those who learn by study, like a pair of greedy crows', whomsoever he was actually referring to in these lines. To judge by events, Pindar and his fellow praise-poets were losing their case in the court of public opinion, and the people were already listening to voices that were expressing very different views of the wealthy tyrants Theron and

Thrasyboulus. At the same time this 'art of rhetoric' seemed to hold out a promise to empower formerly silent citizens who had been marginalised by their inability to compete with the voices of elite speakers, and this radical new type of constitution – democracy – was just the place to put it to use.

Democracy and Athens

Democracy in Greece was a complicated affair which evolved considerably between its earliest appearances (Athens, 507 BC, is usually called the first) and its later forms, all of which were eventually abolished by Philip of Macedon towards the end of the fourth century. The word itself, of course, suggests rule by the people, 'by the majority', but it would be fair to say that democracy always involved something of a sliding scale of inclusiveness and participation. Here, as always, the issues were *who* was to count among the body of citizens that could play a role in the democratic arena (e.g. should landless citizens be included?); as well as *who* was to be allowed to address them and *under what conditions*. Different democracies were more or less radical but at almost no point were elite citizens barred on either count, and in most cases it was their voices that continued to be heard most of all in public – even in Athens. Of course, it was only ever the adult male citizens who were considered: foreigners, slaves, youths, and even citizen women were given no voice at all. However, the trend was clearly towards ever greater inclusiveness of the poor, and at Athens this was taken to the extreme. Democratic institutions were now any regular events or places that brought large numbers of citizens together for the purpose of hearing speeches or reading bans – which meant that the marketplace (*agora*) and the theatre were as much a part of the democracy as the courts or the Assembly. In these circumstances, one's noble birth or wealthy family was no automatic ticket to influence in politics, nor was one's poverty or modest birth necessarily a bar. Rather, democracy provided an opportunity for motivated and able individuals to emerge as leaders regardless of their backgrounds. And once the high-stakes political decisions had been handed over to absolute and direct determination by the vote, a politician's personal rhetorical ability became a much greater factor in politics than it had ever been before. Out of this crucible came some of the greatest orators the world has ever known.

It is therefore no accident that the beginnings of sophistry were bound up with democracy. However, as is well known, sophistry did not begin at Athens. All the famous early sophists would appear to have acquired their skills by means of practical exposure within their own native democracies: Gorgias in Leontini (Sicily), Protagoras in Abdera (Thrace), Hippias in Elis (Peloponnesus), and so on.[12] What drew these men to Athens was not primarily its freedom of speech but its wealth and its large population – the sheer number of its citizens who were willing and able to pay for rhetorical training. Moreover, the infamous litigiousness of the Athenians

25

and, for a time, their requirement that all sorts of legal hearings from around the empire be held before the peoples' courts in Athens caused a disproportionate amount of forensic rhetoric to be practised there. The sophists were, after all, in business; they were not themselves from elite families nor independently wealthy by birth. They needed to earn a living and they did so very well by travelling around Greece teaching the skills that men needed to succeed in politics and law – especially rhetoric. Naturally the greatest demand for these services was at Athens.

There might, however, appear to be a paradox here. As noted above with regard to Corax and Tisias, the invention of the 'art of rhetoric' was potentially a blow to elite control of the *polis*, because it allowed ordinary citizens to master techniques of public speaking with which they might effectively speak up for themselves and contradict the dominant voices of ideologues such as Pindar. Moreover, these new rhetorical techniques began to be marketed at about the same time as ordinary citizens across Greece were revolting against their wealthy rulers and first establishing democracies. But were the poor really availing themselves of this new art? Certainly, Corax's deprived landowners would appear to be a case in point, though we don't know how poor they really were – they had to pay his fee. And while Plato's claim that any and every citizen was welcome to speak up at an Athenian Assembly is most certainly true, what Socrates does not tell us there is that they almost never did, and instead continued to let their 'betters' do most of the talking.[13] There is evidence that some sophists offered a variety of courses in rhetoric, including some at low cost, but it is clear that they were ever drawn to the big money. The fact is that their 'art of rhetoric' was very valuable, and those who could afford to pay the most tended to monopolise the learning. Some sophists even bragged about how much they had been paid. As a result, though the art of rhetoric was antithetical to Pindar's elitist exclusivity of public address and would appear to have thrived only in a democratic context, it nonetheless continued to privilege the voices of wealthier speakers – since only they could afford to pay for it.

But was that sort of privilege necessarily undemocratic? Many have assumed that it was and that as a result Athens was a democracy only in name, since the wealthy used rhetoric simply to 'hoodwink' the masses and thus continued to make all of the important decisions themselves.[14] However, that cynical picture is far too simplistic and understates the significance of the democratic achievement in Greece, in Athens in particular. Participation in democracy was not restricted to the use of one's own voice; it also included *the regulation of the conditions under which all democratic speech was conducted.* That was a job for the audiences. Neither the sophists nor the elites determined those conditions; only the people did. Josiah Ober has sought what he calls the 'key to Athens' success in maintaining a political system unique in its own time and labelled an impossibility in ours'. That key, he concludes, was:

the mediating and integrative power of communication between citizens – especially between ordinary and elite citizens – in a language whose vocabulary consisted of symbols developed and deployed in public arenas: the peoples' courts, the Assembly, the theatre, and the agora. This process of communication constitutes the 'discourse of Athenian democracy' (Ober 1989, 34-5).

In other words, the practical conduct of affairs in these public arenas had effectively nullified the expression of elite ideology in public contexts. Elite *voices* could be allowed to continue dominating Athenian institutions precisely because they had already been forced, by the people, to make their speech conform to democratic parameters: language, voting, and transparent shared assumptions. Under these conditions, the art of rhetoric became less about hoodwinking the people than about demonstrating that one had recognised and accepted the criteria of real collective judgement.

If Ober is correct that ordinary Athenians exerted their control over political rhetoric not by speaking up themselves, but as active auditors who imposed strict demands upon speakers,[15] then the fact that the sophists taught their art of rhetoric mostly to the rich is not a paradox after all. Rather, the sophists can be understood more like 'tutors in democracy' to the rich; they coached potential speakers in how to address a random crowd of citizens so as to persuade them more effectively. The rich, like everyone else, needed to learn that. Pindar had bragged that he shot his poetry over the heads of the masses who therefore 'required interpreters' to understand him; by contrast, the sophists understood that Pindar's strategy was a sure way to lose votes, and advised low-balling to the crowd instead. Not bad advice once the people had taken control! So far from being subverters of democracy, the sophists were actually enablers of democracy who helped their elite clientele to adjust to the realities of politics under the new regime. Meanwhile that genuine sort of self-conscious elite ideology – the kind that laid claim to a higher level of understanding than the majority could share in – had lost its appreciative *public* audience, and so disappeared into private conversations behind closed doors. It went underground.

Walking a fine line

To understand the politically charged contexts of sophistic teaching and oratory, then, we need to distinguish between two groups of elites within the Greek democracies. On one hand there were those wealthy citizens who flocked to the sophists in order to learn how to succeed in democratic politics; on the other, were those who merely posed as participants in democracy while actively plotting in secret to overthrow the constitution. The two groups look very much alike on the surface and must have been difficult for even their own fellow citizens clearly to distinguish; no doubt some individuals shifted back and forth between the two groups. While both resented the power of the people and looked down contemptuously upon the 'stupid masses', only the latter group could actually be called 'enemies of the people'. But these enemies did exist, and occasionally even succeeded in acting to restrict or overturn the franchise. Such were the leaders of the oligarchic coup in Athens in 411 BC and the brutal regime of the 'Thirty Tyrants' in 404.[16] While in reality (and with hindsight) we can say that Athenian democracy was very stable, still there seems never to have been a time when at least some of 'the people' were not afraid that an overthrow of the constitution was being plotted. Both the wealthy politicians and those foreign interlopers who taught them (the sophists) had to be on constant guard against being mistaken for anti-democratic subversives.

Plato's *Protagoras* is, among other things, a tour-de-force depiction of the political sensitivities involved in being a sophist in fifth-century Athens. We see Protagoras at the peak of his fame, yet arriving in Athens *without* public fanfare only to be cloistered within one of the wealthiest homes in the city, packed in behind closed doors with the cream of elite Athenian youth (including Alcibiades and several others who would later be convicted for attacking the constitution). Protagoras points out to Socrates that 'jealousy, hostility, and intrigue on a large scale are aroused' by his practice of sophistry (316d); moreover, he says, 'I have given thought to other precautions as well, so as to avoid, God willing, suffering any ill from admitting I am a sophist' (317c). When faced with Socrates' subsequent challenge – that if Protagoras really can teach true political expertise to his wealthy students, then why do we live in a democracy? – a lesser sophist might have begun to sweat, but Protagoras is in his element. Socrates, after all, was just pointing out the seeming paradox that we noted above. Protagoras' lengthy and eloquent response – that really he is teaching nothing else than what the majority already believe – is essentially the same solution of that paradox as Ober has proposed. Still, the sense of insecurity in this scene is almost palpable and is reinforced by Plato's putting together in the same room three top sophists with several soon-to-be-revealed 'enemies of the people'. Though Protagoras himself might very well be democratic in outlook, he still has a great deal to fear from how he appears to others. And in the world of sophists, as he himself so famously taught, appearances are everything.

Notes

1. Latacz 2004, 182-94, provides an excellent recent overview of this structure of the *Iliad* in relation to broader historical themes.

2. Homer quotations are in the translation of Lattimore 1951.

3. There are many expressions of this principle in Homer, but a classic statement is from Achilles' tutor Phoenix at *Iliad* IX.438-43.

4. Detienne 1996 and Vernant 1982 treat this transition in political consciousness at length.

5. See Lincoln 1994, esp. 'Constructing Authority', pp. 1-13.

6. Morris 1996 provides a fascinating overview.

7. Plato quotations are in the translation of Lombardo and Bell 1992.

8. My own translation of this much-contested passage.

9. This reading of Pindar goes back to the nineteenth century, but see also Cole 1991, 81.

10. This tradition about Corax's rhetoric derives from a variety of fragmentary sources dating back as far as the late-fourth-century BC Sicilian historian Timaeus. See Kennedy 1963, 59.

11. This second main tradition about Corax's rhetoric derives from Aristotle through Cicero's *Brutus*; again, see Kennedy 1963, 60; also Robinson 2007, 113-16.

12. See Robinson 2007.

13. For a discussion of the relative degrees of participation in public speech by elites and non-elites at Athens, see Ober 1989, 104-18.

14. This is a quite common opinion, but Osborne 2004, 114, sums it up nicely: '[The sophists] taught clever talk designed to enable their pupils to manipulate public opinion in their favour, and thereby maintain their plutocratic advantage in a system that was only nominally democratic.'

15. See Ober 1989, 104, for an evocation of the reciprocal nature of democratic public speech at Athens.

16. See Chapter 10, pp. 115-17 below for a brief discussion of the Thirty Tyrants.

Bibliography

Cole, Thomas, 'Who was Corax?', *Illinois Classical Studies* 16 (1991), 65-86.

Detienne, Marcel, *The Masters of Truth in Ancient Greece* (New York: Zone Books, 1996).

Homer, *Iliad*, trans. Richmond Lattimore (Chicago: University of Chicago Press, 1951).

Kennedy, George, *The Art of Persuasion in Greece* (Princeton, NJ: Princeton University Press, 1963).

Latacz, Joachim, *Troy and Homer: Towards a Solution of an Old Mystery* (Oxford University Press, 2004).

Lincoln, Bruce, *Authority: Construction and Corrosion* (Chicago: University of Chicago Press, 1994).

Morris, Ian, 'The Strong Principle of Equality and the Archaic Origins of Greek Democracy', in Josiah Ober and Charles Hedrick (eds), *Demokratia: A Conversation on Democracies, Ancient and Modern* (Princeton, NJ: Princeton University Press, 1996).

Ober, Josiah, *Mass and Elite in Democratic Athens: Rhetoric, Ideology, and the Power of the People* (Princeton, NJ: Princeton University Press, 1989).

Osborne, Catharine, *Presocratic Philosophy: A Very Short Introduction* (Oxford: Oxford University Press, 2004).

Plato, *Protagoras*, trans. Stanley Lombardo and Karen Bell (Indianapolis, IN: Hackett, 1992).

Robinson, Eric W., 'The Sophists and Democracy Beyond Athens', *Rhetorica* 25 (2007), 109-22.

Vernant, Jean-Pierre, *The Origins of Greek Thought* (Ithaca, NY: Cornell University Press, 1982).

Protagoras

Jonathan Lavery

Protagoras was among the most versatile, nimble and innovative thinkers in ancient times. He was the first person to teach argumentation, oratory and rhetoric for a fee, the first to declare that every argument can be opposed by a counter-argument, the first to draw important – and now familiar – linguistic distinctions between verb tenses (past, present, future), nouns by gender (masculine, feminine, neuter), and grammatical moods (interrogative, declarative, command, etc.), and the first to call himself a sophist openly. Not only was he in the advance guard of fifth-century intellectuals, he maintained his pre-eminence for decades as the sophistic movement grew in size and influence. It is, therefore, a shame that so little of his work survives – fewer than a dozen fragments, various testimonia from some hostile but credible sources, and accounts of his life that were written centuries after his death. Perhaps no other ancient figure has been so ill-served by the scribes, copyists, compilers, librarians, book collectors, doxographers, historians and others who have preserved the texts of ancient philosophy. Still, what has survived to the present is suggestive, and from these remnants we get revealing hints of his significance.

Consider a few of the thematic links between some of the best attested fragments of Protagoras' thought. These follow on p. 31. Together [F1], which declares that 'man' is the measure of all things, and [F3], which expresses doubts about human knowledge of divine matters, give the impression of Protagoras as a secular humanist who should be understood as an agnostic rather than an atheist on theological questions. [F2], [F7] and [F8] are all about education and give the impression of Protagoras as a thoughtful teacher and educational theorist. Finally, [F4] and [F5] on practical argumentation situate him at the centre of fifth-century developments in rhetoric and public debate. When I imagine this engaged, wide-ranging and original thinker as a contemporary, I see him occupying an endowed chair of humanities at a prestigious university, writing ground-breaking books for scholarly publishers, contributing op-ed columns to prominent newspapers, and winning accolades for his teaching. Such was the scope of Protagoras' influence: Other intellectuals in several fields had to reckon with him as a specialist, political leaders solicited his advice on matters of state, and droves of students sought to enter his circle.

Bearing in mind this broad-brush picture of Protagoras as a Hellenic public figure, let us try to fill in some details about his life and thought. Admittedly, much of our information is uncertain or problematic. Some details are uncertain because the evidence we have is inconclusive. Others are problematic either because the evidence we have is ambiguous or because our ancient sources are not consistent with one another. But if we are alert to the difficulties presented by the sources at our disposal, we can discern what made Protagoras such a fascinating and influential person in his day.

Textual materials

I shall begin by reviewing the fragments and testimonia that are reasonably well attested or that come from sources closest to Protagoras' lifetime.[1] Then I shall turn to the interpretation of these materials, both individually and collectively. I distinguish fragments (F), which purport to be in his own words, from testimonia (T), which attempt to capture the substance of his thought along with some interpretation; fragments that are more likely to be paraphrases than direct quotations are in italics.

Fragments

[F1] Of all things the measure is man (*anthrôpos*), of things that are that they are, and of things that are not that they are not.

[F2] Teaching needs endowment and practice. Learning must begin in youth.

[F3] Concerning the gods, I cannot know either that they exist or that they do not exist, or what form they might have; for there is much to prevent one's knowing: the obscurity of the subject, and the shortness of a man's life.

[F4] *Protagoras was the first to say that there were two opposing arguments about everything.*

[F5] To make the weaker cause the stronger.

[F6] *It is impossible to contradict.*

[F7] Art without practice, and practice without art, are nothing.

[F8] Education does not take root in the soul unless one goes deep.

Testimonia

[T1] Plato, *Protagoras* 318a: (Protagoras is speaking to a prospective student) 'If you associate with me, young man … then you will be able, at the end of your first day in my company, to go away a better man; and the same will happen on the next day, and each day after that you will continue to grow better and improve.'

[T2] Plato, *Protagoras* 318d: (Protagoras is responding to a question from Socrates as to what it is in relation to that his students make such steady progress) '... he won't have the same experience as he would have had by associating with one of the other sophists. These others are a curse on young men. Just when they have escaped from *technical subjects* (*technai*), they bring them back and throw then once again into technical subjects – arithmetic, astronomy, geometry, music – ... but with me he will learn only the subject which he came to learn and no other. The course of instruction is *good planning* (*euboulia*) both of his own affairs, to the end that he would best manage his personal estate, and of the *city's* (*polis*), to the end that he would be in the strongest position to conduct, in speech and action, the common business of the city.'

[T3] Plato, *Protagoras* 320c-323a (Protagoras' 'Great Speech' responds to a challenge from Socrates to explain how human virtue is both teachable and not natural). 'There once was a time when there were gods, but no mortal creatures. And when the time came which was decreed by fate for their creation also, the gods figured them within the earth, compounding them of earth and of fire, and of everything which is mixed with fire and earth. And when they were ready to lead them towards the light, they charged Prometheus and Epimetheus that they should furnish and distribute powers to each as it should be fitting. But Epimetheus begged Prometheus and asked that he might himself make the distribution, saying, "Let me first distribute; afterward examine my work." And when he had persuaded him with these words he began to make distribution. And as he distributed, to some he added strength without speed, while the weaker he furnished with swiftness. And some he armed, while to others he gave an unarmed nature, devising for them instead some other power for their safety. For whichsoever he confined and made small of stature, to these he distributed a refuge of wings or a dwelling under the earth; but whichsoever he made great of stature, by their very greatness he kept them safe. And so, in like manner, he made just an equal distribution, devising these things as a precaution lest any kind might vanish from the earth.

'But when for each he had prepared a refuge from the others against destruction, next he devised comfort against the seasons sent by Zeus, clothing them about with thick fur and tough hides sufficient to keep out the winter and able to resist the scorching sun, and in order also that when they took themselves to their rest, these things might supply to each its own natural covering for the night. And some he shod with hooves, and others with tough and bloodless hide. Next he supplied for them varied nourishment – to some the plants of the earth, to others the fruit of trees, and to others roots. And to some he granted other creatures for their subsidence, adding to these meagreness of progeny, but to their prey abundant fruitfulness, supplying their kind with a means for their preservation.

'But because Epimetheus was not exceeding wise, he exhausted all the powers upon the brute beasts and noticed it not. Yet still humankind was left unfurnished, so that he was perplexed what he should do. And being thus perplexed behold there came to him Prometheus to examine his distribution. And he found the other animals diligently provided for, but man without clothing, without shoes, without coverings for the night, without weapons. And already the allotted day was at hand in which man must come out of the earth into the light. Being thus sore perplexed as to what safety he should find for man, Prometheus stole from Hephaestus and Athene *practical wisdom* (*entechnê sophia*) together with fire – for without fire no man may acquire or make use of this – and he bestowed them upon man. In this way man acquired *wisdom* for his sustenance, but he did not have *citycraft* (*politikên*). For it lay with Zeus. Nor was it any longer permitted to Prometheus to approach the citadel where Zeus had his habitation; and moreover, the guardians of Zeus were fearsome. But he came in stealth to the common habitation of Hephaestus and Athene, in which they practised their *skills* (*technê*) and stealing the *skills* of Hephaestus – which is working with fire – and of Athene, he gave them to men, so that it came to pass that man had abundant means for his sustenance. Afterwards Prometheus was charged with theft, as it is told, because of Epimetheus.

'Since there was a part of man which was divine, he alone of all living things began, because of his kinship with the gods, to believe in gods and to build altars and images of gods. And then soon, by his skill, he began to speak and to use words; he invented dwellings and clothing and shoes, coverings for the night and nourishment from the earth. Being thus equipped, men were scattered at the beginning, and there were no cities, so that they were destroyed by wild animals because they were weaker in all things. And though the skill of their hands was sufficient for their sustenance, for warring against the beasts it was not sufficient. For they did not yet have *citycraft*, of which *warcraft* is a part. At first they thought to gather together for their safety by founding cities. But when they were gathered together, they *committed injury* (*adikein*) one upon another, since they had not the skill of citycraft, so that they were scattered anew and began once more to perish. Whereupon Zeus, being afraid concerning our kind, that it might perish utterly, sent Hermes unto mankind with *justice* (*dikê*) and a *sense of shame* (*aidôs*), to bring order to their cities and common bonds of amity. And Hermes asked Zeus in what manner he ought to give justice and a sense of shame to man, saying: "Am I to distribute them even as the practical skills have been distributed? For thus have they been distributed: one man skilled in medicine is sufficient unto many who have not the skill, as it is also with other men of skill. Am I in like manner to distribute justice and a sense of shame among men, or am I to distribute among all?" "Among all," Zeus replied, "and let all have them in common. For there could be no cities if but a few had them, as it is with the other skills. And lay down this law from me: if any man be not able to share justice and a sense of shame even as other men do, they must kill him as a pestilence to the city." '

33

[T4] Plato, *Protagoras* 328a: (near the end of the same speech as [T3]) 'I believe that I am one of these [people who are] better than others at helping men on their way to becoming noble and excellent, worthy of my fee, if not more, as my pupils agree. That is why I have adopted the following method of charging. Any student may, if he wishes, pay me my fee in cash. But if not, he can go to a temple, make a sworn declaration of what he believes to be the true value of my instruction, and deposit that sum.'

[T5] Plato, *Protagoras* 329b: (Socrates is speaking) '... Protagoras here is equally competent at delivering long splendid speeches, as we have heard for ourselves, and at answering a question briefly, and when he has asked a question himself, at waiting to hear other people's replies – a rare attainment.'

[T6] Plato, *Protagoras* 335a: (Protagoras is responding to a request from Socrates to keep his answers brief, so that Socrates can follow them): ' "Socrates," he said ... "I have debated many men in my time; and if I had argued by the rules of debate laid down by my opponent, as you demand, I should have proved no better than the next man, and the name of Protagoras would not be celebrated throughout Greece." '

[T7] Aristotle, *Metaphysics* 997b34: 'But on the other hand astronomy cannot be dealing with perceptible magnitudes nor with this heaven above us. For neither are perceptible lines such lines as the geometer speaks of (for no perceptible thing is straight or round in the way in which he defines "straight" and "round"; for a hoop touches a straight edge not at a point, but as Protagoras used to say it did, in his refutation of the geometers) ...'

[T8] Aristotle, *Metaphysics* 1007b18: 'Again, if all contradictory statements are true of the same subject at the same time, evidently all things will be one. For the same thing will be a trireme, a wall, and a man, if of everything it is possible either to affirm or to deny anything (and this premiss must be accepted by those who share the views of Protagoras).'

[T9] Aristotle, *Metaphysics* 1009a6: 'From the same opinion proceeds the doctrine of Protagoras, and both doctrines must be alike true or alike untrue. For on the one hand, if all opinions and appearances are true, all statements must be at the same time true and false.'

[T10] Aristotle, *Metaphysics* 1047a4: 'And similarly with regard to lifeless things; nothing will be either cold or hot or sweet or perceptible at all if people are not perceiving it; so that the upholders of this view will have to maintain the doctrine of Protagoras.'

[T11] Aristotle, *Metaphysics* 1053a35: 'But Protagoras says "man is the measure of all things", as if he had said "the man who knows" or "the man who perceives"; and these because they have respectively knowledge and perception, which we say are the measures of objects.'

[T12] Aristotle, *Metaphysics* 1062b13: 'The saying of Protagoras is like the views we have mentioned; he said that man is the measure of all things, meaning simply that that which seems to each man also assuredly is. If this is so, it follows that the same thing both is and is not, and is bad and good, and that the contents of all other opposite statements are true, because often a particular thing appears beautiful to some and the contrary of beautiful to others, and that which appears to each man is the measure.'

[T13] Aristotle, *Rhetoric* 1402a23: '... This sort of argument illustrates what is meant by making the worse argument seem better. Hence people were right in objecting to the training Protagoras undertook to give them. It was a fraud; the probability it handled was not genuine but spurious, and has a place in no art except Rhetoric and Eristic [disputatious argumentation].'

[T14] Aristotle, *Rhetoric* 1407b7: 'A fourth rule is to observe Protagoras' classification of nouns into male, female, and neuter; for these distinctions also must be correctly given.'

In addition to these texts, there is further discussion of Protagoras' thought in Plato's *Euthydemus* (286b-287a), *Cratylus* (385e-386a), and *Theaetetus* (151e-152c, 161c-e, 166c-167d). Further, several late ancient authors, such as the sceptic Sextus Empiricus (*c.* AD 200), consider Protagoras' views in passing.

Life

Diogenes Laertius (third century AD) gives a biographical account of Protagoras in his *Lives of the Eminent Philosophers* (book IX, chapters 51-3), as does Philostratus (second/third century AD) in his *Lives of the Sophists* (book I, chapter 10). Isolated biographical evidence can be found in Plato's dialogues (*Hippias Major* 282d-e; *Meno* 91d), Plutarch (*Life of Pericles* 36), Eusebius, and other ancient authors. In every case, we must be careful about accepting a source as authoritative. None of these authors wrote for the purpose of faithfully setting down the historical record, and often they are not consistent with one another. Nevertheless, we must attempt to separate reasonably reliable information from pure conjecture, and to piece together a life story from all the anecdotes and gossip attached to Protagoras' name.

Protagoras was born in Abdera in the north Aegean coastal region of Thrace, whence the atomist Democritus also hailed.[2] He was born between 490 and 484 BC, and according to Plato's *Meno* (91d) lived to be seventy years old. According to Philostratus, his father was a very wealthy associate of the Persian king, Xerxes (519-465 BC), and through this connection enjoyed the privilege of studying with Zoroastrian priests. Diogenes Laertius attributes much humbler origins to Protagoras, for he says that Protagoras served as a porter at one point. Either account of his early life could be correct, but – it must be acknowledged – both could be false. The porter story may derive from a report that he invented a special strap for carrying wood, but, of course, he need not have been a manual labourer to have invented such a device. To be safe, we should say that, apart from being born in Abdera, Protagoras' origins and early life remain uncertain. In any case, his career as a sophist spanned forty years (Plato, *Meno* 91d). During that time he travelled widely throughout Greece, and, if we accept Philostratus on his connection to the Persian monarchy, he travelled to Asia Minor too.

Protagoras visited Athens at least twice, and he seems to have enjoyed an ongoing association with the city over the course of many years. Evidently he was intimately acquainted with the most prominent politician of the Athenian golden age, the democratic leader Pericles (495-429 BC). Plutarch reports that Protagoras and Pericles once spent an entire day debating a question as to the responsible party when a misdirected javelin killed a spectator at an athletic event.[3] What was the cause of this person's death – the javelin, the athlete who threw it or the officials overseeing the games? This is just the sort of moral-practical issue that fell within the sophists' purview.

A more telling sign of the depth of Protagoras' connection to Pericles and Athens is the role he played in founding a pan-Hellenic colony at Thurii (in southern Italy) in 443 BC. Both Spartans and Athenians supported this enterprise, and the venture was overseen by Pericles. Protagoras was assigned responsibility for drafting the city's constitution of laws, which must be seen as an indication of the very high esteem with which the most powerful statesman of the age regarded the famed sophist. Even if Protagoras' fame was based on his reputation as a teacher, this connection to Pericles suggests that his influence extended directly into affairs of state.

Still, it was as a teacher, more than anything else, that Protagoras was unrivalled during his lifetime. In *Protagoras*, for example, Plato also casts Hippias and Prodicus, but Protagoras is acknowledged by everyone to be the pre-eminent sophist present. [T3] is the beginning of a long episode in the dialogue now known as 'The Great Speech' of Protagoras. The entire speech is a showcase for his rhetorical virtuosity, and it is possible that a large portion of it is based on Protagoras' own words, especially [T3].[4] [T2] and [T4] suggest that he was not afraid to promise results for his students, that he was prepared to guarantee satisfaction.

The unorthodox payment scheme described in [T4] appears to be corroborated by an anecdote about Protagoras and one unscrupulous former student named Euathlus. According to Diogenes Laertius (IX.56), Protagoras trained Euathlus in forensic oratory with the understanding that payment for this instruction was not due unless Euathlus won his first court case; in the event that Euathlus lost his first case, he owed Protagoras nothing. After completing his studies, Euathlus attempted to defer the question of payment indefinitely by never going to the law to prosecute a case – an ingenious stratagem to avoid both paying Protagoras' fee and risking the humiliation of public defeat. Eventually, Protagoras forced the issue by suing Euathlus, arguing in court as follows: If you decide in my favour, then Euathlus must pay me as the judgement determines; however, if you decide against me, then Euathlus must pay me according to the terms of our original agreement. As legend has it, Euathlus replied with a clever argument of his own: If you decide in my favour, then I am released from the obligation to pay Protagoras according to your judgement; however, if you decide against me, then I have no obligation to pay Protagoras according to our original agreement. There are no reports of how the case was decided; moreover, it is possible that the entire story was fabricated as a joke at the sophist's expense or as a dig at Protagoras' claim to improve the moral and political character of his students (see [T2] especially).

Protagoras' fame was sufficient to make him a worthy subject for literature. In 421 BC he was a central character in Eupolis' comic play *Spongers*. The play was very successful, for it won first prize in the Dionysian Festival competition. Only fragments of this comedy are extant, but enough remains to establish its setting as Athens, in the luxurious house of Callias, son of Hipponicus (*c.* 450-367 BC). Protagoras was one of the spongers in the play who surrounded Callias and lived off his large inheritance. Apparently the play alluded to an actual occasion (probably in 422 BC). This visit by Protagoras must have created quite a buzz in Athens, especially as an emblematic symbol of the relationship between a subsection of the city's wealthy citizens and the sophists. The occasion is also depicted in Plato's *Protagoras* (see [T1]-[T5]), a work that was written approximately twenty to twenty-five years after Protagoras' death.

Protagoras' views also figure prominently in Plato's *Theaetetus*, *Cratylus* and *Euthydemus*, although in these dialogues other people discuss his ideas without him being present. In these works, the focus is not so much on the man, as *Protagoras* is, as it is on the man-measure doctrine expressed in the most famous and controversial fragment of his work, [F1]: man is the measure of all things, which in these dialogues is glossed as a denial of objective knowledge. It is, in fact, his signature doctrine, which we shall consider further in the next section.

The agnosticism of [F3] is similarly controversial, so much so that Philostratus reports that its publication precipitated Protagoras' death. According to this biographer of the sophists, when Athenians heard that Protagoras said that it was not possible to know anything about the gods (even whether they existed), they banished him for impiety, then they chased him out to sea. In his flight from pursuing Athenians, his small vessel sank and he drowned. This story, however, does not square with Plato's *Meno*, in which Socrates says that Protagoras died with a good reputation (91d). Since Philostratus wrote about the incident hundreds of years after Plato, it is difficult to give much weight to the biographer's romantic account of an old man's demise at the hands of religious fanatics. Philostratus' story also does not accord with that of another biographer,

Diogenes Laertius, who says a work named *On the Gods* was the *first* work Protagoras read publicly; if, as is likely, [F3] is from this work, then it is difficult to imagine how it could have induced such violent zealotry so many years later. Nevertheless, Diogenes Laertius (IX.55) also reports Protagoras drowning at sea, so this may well be how he died, even if he was not being pursued by enraged Athenians at the time.

Thought

Owing to the paucity of primary source evidence, it is difficult to get a clear picture of Protagoras' career as a writer, and as a result it is difficult to assess his accomplishments as an intellectual and a theorist. Diogenes Laertius lists several titles of books he is supposed to have authored, covering a broad range of subjects. Not one complete work has survived intact. It is possible that these were never 'books' in a sense that we would recognise. [F1] is attributed to a work entitled *Truth*, for example. But this book does not get mentioned in the one surviving work that paints the man in full, Plato's *Protagoras*. When Plato considers this passage in *Theaetetus*, nothing else from *Truth* is quoted, even though the *meaning* of the doctrine is central to the dialogue. We should expect [F1] to be glossed in light of other passages from the same work. Instead Socrates asks his interlocutors what they might imagine the dead man to say if he were to pop his head out of the grave and join their discussion of his doctrine. Plato treats [F1] as if it were expected to stand alone, as an aphorism. Perhaps that is all it ever was – a gnomic utterance that was designed to provoke thought, not an axiom at the centre of a stable system of ideas. The same might be said of all the other memorable fragments, too.[5]

Let us concentrate a little longer on [F1], now known as the *homo-mensura* (man-measure) principle. This passage presents difficulties both for translators and for interpreters. As a translation, our text uses 'man' to translate the Greek noun '*anthrôpos*'. Some translators use 'human being' here. McKirahan, for example, translates the line as 'A human being is the measure of all things ...' (see McKirahan 1994, 379). A translator must make difficult choices with this passage, for every trans-lation from Greek to English forces us to accept compromises in rendering the structure, meaning and rhetorical economy of the original line.[6] These features we certainly want to retain as much as possible in translation. But there are some important – perhaps intentional – ambiguities in the Greek text, and these we ought to preserve in translation, too. And finally, we want to avoid other ambiguities that come out in translation that are not present in the original line.

The Greek text of [F1] reads as follows: '*Pantôn chrêmatôn metron estin anthrôpos, tôn men ontôn hôs ouk estin*'. This seminal humanist principle is expressed with great compression in only eleven words. Our translation uses more than twice as many words, primarily because certain relations that are conveyed implicitly in the Greek sentence must be expressed explicitly in words in English. One virtue of our translation (which comes from Michael J. O'Brien in Sprague 1972, 18) is that it very closely replicates the structure of the original sentence. 'Man' also captures a fundamental ambiguity in Protagoras' use of *'anthrôpos'*. Is the singular *'anthrôpos'* being used generically (as in 'the lion is a carnivore') to say something about humanity collectively, or is it being used individually (as in 'each person is the source of judgements about all things') to say something about the subjectivity of human beings passing judgement? Both in the original text and in our translation, it's left undetermined whether all things are measured 'relative' to humanity considered collectively or by each individual person 'subjectively'.[7]

If we interpret *'anthrôpos'* in [F1] as pointing to generic restrictions on judgement that apply to human beings as a species, then Protagoras is voicing a generic humanist thesis: that is, there is no privileged, transhuman point of view from which objective, authoritative judgements on any question can be pronounced. But if we interpret *'anthrôpos'* as pointing to individual differences in judgement between different people, then Protagoras is voicing a stronger humanist thesis, i.e. subjectivism: there is no way to overcome differences of *individual* judgement on any question. Several testimonia from Aristotle's *Metaphysics* ([T9], [T10], [T11] and [T12]) adopt the second interpretation, i.e. the subjectivist reading of [F1]. The same wind may appear cold to you and warm to me, and there is no 'real' warmth or coldness in the wind itself to determine that one of us is correct and the other incorrect. Plato reads [F1] this way in *Theaetetus*, and indeed this interpretation may be faithful to Protagoras' own intentions; Aristotle follows Plato's lead in [T9], [T10], [T11] and [T12], focussing on subjective perceptual impressions. All the same, it would be best to use a translation that keeps the 'relativist' interpretation in view as an open possibility; Plato and Aristotle may be our best sources for Protagoras' thought, but we need to be careful to separate the evidence they provide for the content of Protagoras' ideas from their critical responses to those ideas.

Again, in [F3] Protagoras is drawing a sharp distinction between (a) a conception of the world as it is manifested to a human being that *is* subject to certain cognitive limitations and (b) another conception of it from the perspective of a being that *is not* subject to these limitations. Not only does [F3] discourage speculation about the gods, it encourages us to confine our inquires to subjects that are not obscure, i.e. those which are accessible to human modes of apprehension. In this way, [F3] appears not to be irreligious or radically sceptical, even if it rules out speculative theology. Religion, as a social institution and important anthropological phenomenon, need not be rejected by Protagoras.[8] In fact, in the Great Speech in Plato's *Protagoras*, he uses a version of the ancient Prometheus-Epimetheus myth to explain the source of human virtue [T3], and he reports that students can pay what they think his instruction is worth after swearing an oath as to their opinion of its true value [T4].[9]

The doubts expressed about speculative theology in [F3] may have wider implications, even if they do not extend as far as radical, global scepticism. The implied injunction that human beings eschew 'obscure' subjects would exclude all speculative sciences, including physics, geometry and mathematics. In [T2] he complains about rival teachers who force their students to study technical subjects such as arithmetic, astronomy, geometry and music.[10] By contrast, his own programme of education fosters 'good judgement' in practical affairs. Abstract theory and scientific speculation are, for him, idle enterprises. In epistemology he is best characterised as a pragmatist who emphasises the value of direct experience rather than a sceptic who denies the possibility of knowledge. Presumably, this was the approach he adopted in his 'refutation' of the geometers who claim that a round line touches a straight line only at one point: anyone can see that a hoop touches a straight edge at more than one point [T7]. Experience – not the interplay of carefully defined abstract concepts and theoretical postulates – settles the matter for Protagoras.

Similar considerations inform the principles of argumentation and debate that have come to be associated with Protagoras. As [F4] says, any argument on a question can be contested by an opposing argument. Since there are no independent standards to which one may appeal for an objectively decisive answer, all questions are contestable. How then are such disputes to be decided? The contrast between Protagoras and Socrates is instructive here. In many of Plato's dialogues we find Socrates eliciting from an interlocutor his opinion about what justice is (or virtue or piety, etc.). Socrates then follows up with a series of questions, moving one step at a time, until arriving at a direct contradiction of the opening statement about justice (or virtue or piety, etc.). The contradiction is crucial, for it is by this that Socrates' interlocutor is forced either to formulate another account of the subject matter or admit that he does not know the answer to Socrates' original question. Perhaps Socrates was animated by the hope that all false opinions may be eliminated, one at a time, until only true opinions remain. Protagoras, however, could not entertain hopes for such a procedure, for according to [F6] the crucial step, arriving at a contradiction, is impossible. This should not be very surprising, given the important role played by experience in Protagoras' epistemology and the fact that a logical contradiction is exactly the sort of abstract principle he refused to abide.

As the Great Speech illustrates ([T3], [T4]), Protagoras was a charismatic orator who was capable of winning audiences with masterful rhetoric. But he enjoyed a reputation for excelling at the cut and thrust of debate, too [T5]. So he could be persuasive either with set-pieces and speeches or with ingenious repartee. No doubt, the tricks of the trade that he discovered and deployed to attain this success were central to the curriculum he passed on to students. But since they were not set down in a handbook or formulated as a set of rules (e.g. always begin with a joke, communicate your principal message by repeating it in a mnemonic slogan, etc.), it is not possible to know exactly how he argued in these situations. The closest we come to such a principle is in Plato's *Protagoras*, when he refuses to adapt his arguments to suit Socrates' demands for brevity: his considerable reputation as a debater was built, Protagoras says, by ensuring that such disputes are assessed according to his own standards, not those of his opponent [T6]. Presumably, making the weaker cause the stronger [T5] must have consisted in shifting the terms of the debate in such a way as this.[11]

While Protagoras' sophistic programme of education was clearly aimed at adults and youths on the cusp of maturity, clearly he thought about the educational process as a continuum from the inculcation of moral guidance in earliest childhood to oratorical and rhetorical training in fully-fledged citizens. [F2] stresses the need for moral education to begin in youth, and [F7] emphasises a need for the ongoing practical reinforcement of these lessons. Neither of these claims is controversial, but it is worth noting how they anticipate some of Aristotle's account of moral development in book II of his *Nicomachean Ethics*. Aristotle's account concentrates on the importance of habit, but since habits are reliable patterns of action there are significant conceptual overlaps between this appeal to habit and Protagoras' appeal to practice. These links are reinforced by a shared contention that the purpose of moral education is psychological (as opposed to the merely behavioural).[12] In Aristotle this purpose is expressed as an account of the virtues as psychological states of character, whereas Protagoras expresses it in [F8] as assertion that education must 'take root in the soul'.

Where Protagoras and Aristotle part company is in their diverging accounts of the later stages of moral development. According to Aristotle, the highest form of wisdom and maturity is marked by theoretical knowledge. The central issue being investigated in book X of his *Nicomachean Ethics* concerns whether the best kind of human life is (i) that life which is guided by rationally justified habits towards political action or (ii) that life which is directed towards a purely theoretical apprehension of the highest principles of reality. The first kind of life is practical, but guided by abstract principles which are discovered in an exercise of speculation that goes beyond immediate experience; the second kind of life is oriented around speculation as an enterprise with its own intrinsic purpose. It is difficult to imagine Protagoras praising either kind of life, given his implicit commitment to pragmatism and explicit aversion for speculation (see [T7]). The endorsement of general knowledge as 'art' (*technê*) in [F7] is inextricably tied to practice. And even if a fuller account of Protagoras' conception of political virtue could be reconciled with Aristotle's portrayal of the highest kind of political life (see (i) above), the sophist would never feel the pull exerted by the theoretical life (which Aristotle extols as being divine and 'higher than human', book X, chapter 7).

Since so little of our evidence of Protagoras' thought comes to us 'in his own words', we have been forced to examine that thought indirectly. Plato provides dramatic and vivid testimony as to the content of his thought in *Protagoras*, but does so in a way that is designed to emphasise the differences between Protagoras and Socrates. Since Socrates occupies a special place in Plato's own philosophical development, we must be wary of partisan distortions in this presentation, even if it is on the whole complimentary. Aristotle is more openly hostile towards Protagoras, especially when he considers Protagoras' denial of the principle of non-contradiction in [T8] and [T9] and the disputatious orientation of Protagoras' rhetoric in [T13]. Still, it should be taken as a sign of respect that Protagoras received such intense critical attention from the two authors whose works now dominate our picture of ancient philosophy. It shows how seriously *they* took the sophist's challenge to theoretical philosophy and what a powerful influence he exerted in his own time and upon subsequent generations of humanist thought. We would do well to follow their examples and take him seriously, too.[13]

Notes

1. The two most prominent sources are Plato (who was born *c.* 429 BC while Protagoras was still alive and knew people who had met the sophist) and Aristotle (who was born a generation later in 384 BC). Neither of these authors is a sympathetic representative of the Protagorean doctrines they cite, but there are no strong grounds to believe that they misrepresent his thought. Passages cited from Plato's *Protagoras* are from *Plato's Protagoras*, edited and translated by B.A.F. Hubbard and E.S. Karnofsky (London: Duckworth, 1982). All other citations of Plato are from *Plato: Complete Works*, edited by John M. Cooper (Indianapolis: Hackett, 1997). All passages cited from Aristotle's *Metaphysics* come from *Metaphysica*, translated by W.D. Ross in *The Basic Works of Aristotle*, edited by Richard McKeon (New York: Random House, 1941). Passages from Aristotle's *Rhetoric* are from *Rhetoric & Poetics*, translated by W. Rhys Roberts and Ingram Bywater, Introduction by Friedrich Solmsen (New York: Modern Library, 1954). Translations of fragments from Protagoras come from Michael J. O'Brien in *The Older Sophists*, edited by Rosamond Kent Sprague (1972, 18-24). Wherever possible, standard pagination and line numbers are provided for readers who may want to consult other translations. In a few cases, I have made minor alterations to the text quoted from these sources.

2. Diogenes Laertius cites the comic poet Eupolis as reporting that he was from the island of Teos. W.K.C. Guthrie adequately explains how the attribution of Protagoras' origins to Teos is erroneous (1971, 262n.1). Speculation by Philostratus and Diogenes Laertius that Protagoras was a student of Democritus is implausible, since Democritus was probably 20-30 years younger.

3. Plutarch's source (Stesimbrotus of Thasos) was a fifth-century contemporary of Protagoras and Pericles, and it may be that this was a real event, since the victim is named (Epitimus of Pharsalus). Also, if such a debate did take place, we

should not dismiss it as idle quibbling. Athenians took prosecution of the law very seriously; since the cause of a crime was considered 'pollution' (miasma), it was imperative that the cause (even if it is an inanimate object, such as the javelin) be identified, and, after due process, expelled.

4. My opinion is that the version of the Prometheus myth in [T3] and the payment scheme in [T4] are drawn from Protagoras himself, but that other parts of the speech exhibit signs that Plato is using Protagoras as a *dramatis persona* to be manipulated for the author's own purposes rather than as a historical figure whose words must be recorded faithfully. For instance, in [T4], Zeus bestows 'justice (*dikê*) and a sense of shame (*aidôs*)', but immediately after this he declares the basis of political life to be 'justice (*dikaiosunê*) and moderation (*sôphrosunê*)' (324a, not quoted above). The older terms of [T4] are here replaced by newer, more abstract nouns, which become central to the systematic account of virtue provided by Socrates in *Republic* IV, so it appears that Plato is here nudging the dialogue towards his own views.

5. For a helpful discussion of Protagoras' style of writing and teaching, and further exploration of the hypothesis that his thought was expressed aphoristically (rather than in a series of extended arguments), see Schiappa 2003, 157-60.

6. 'Of all things (*pantôn chrêmatôn*) the measure is man (*metron estin anthrôpos*), of things [that are that they are] (*tôn men ontôn hôs*), and of things that are not [that they are not] (*ouk estin*).' That which is found in square brackets in our translation is implicit in the Greek.

7. 'Man', for all its limitations as a gender-neutral term, carries forward this suggestive ambiguity much better than McKirahan's 'a human being', which rules out the relativist interpretation entirely; McKirahan's indefinite article 'a' is the problem, since neither a definite nor an indefinite article is found in the Greek. Alternatively, and all other things being equal, 'humanity' might be used to translate *anthrôpos*, but it rules out the subjectivist interpretation. 'Man', which might refer to one arbitrarily selected instance of humanity or to each individual member of the class, seems to capture a crucial ambiguity that haunts the Greek text.

8. The spirit of Protagoras' humanism is very much captured by Alexander Pope's lines in *An Essay on Man*: 'presume not god to scan, the proper study of mankind is man'.

9. For further discussion, see Schiappa 2003, 143-8.

10. Note how this list corresponds with the propaedeutic mathematical subjects advocated by Socrates in Plato's *Republic* VII (522b-532a).

11. Aristotle, in particular, has no patience for Protagoras' denial of the principle of non-contradiction (see [T8], [T9], [T10], [T12] and [T13] especially). It is a fascinating question whether this shifting perception of the cause from being weaker to being stronger constituted an unscrupulous act of deception or a medical rehabilitation of the putatively weaker cause so that it is made stronger. Again, readers seeking further elaboration should consult Schiappa 2003, 103-13.

12. Later in the Great Speech, the *dramatis persona* of Protagoras provides accounts of punishment as deterrence and early moral education as action guiding. I suspect that here Plato is diagnosing what he detects as a tension within Protagoras' thought (i.e. between [F8] and the behavioural account of punishment and early moral development), not reporting his thought verbatim. It is for this reason that [T3] includes only the opening pages of the speech.

13. I want to thank Evan Habkirk and Katharine Hashimoto for help in preparing this chapter. I also want to thank Patricia O'Grady for inviting me to contribute to this book.

Bibliography

Ancient textual and biographical sources:

Aristotle, *Metaphysica*, trans. W.D. Ross in *The Basic Works of Aristotle*, ed. Richard McKeon (New York: Random House, 1941).

Aristotle, *Nicomachean Ethics*, trans. W.D. Ross in *The Basic Works of Aristotle*, ed. Richard McKeon (New York: Random House, 1941).

Aristotle, *Rhetoric & Poetics*, trans. W. Rhys Roberts and Ingram Bywater, introduction by Friedrich Solmsen (New York: Modern Library, 1954).

Diogenes Laertius, *Lives of Eminent Philosophers*, trans. R.D. Hicks, Loeb edition (London: Heinemann, 1925).

Philostratus, *Lives of the Sophists*, trans. W.C. Wright, Loeb edition (London: Heinemann, 1921).

Plato's Protagoras: A Socratic Commentary, trans. with commentary and notes by B.A.F. Hubbard and E.S. Karnofsky (London: Duckworth, 1982).

Plato, *Theaetetus*, trans. with notes M.J. Levett, rev. M. Burnyeat (Indianapolis, IN: Hackett Publishing Company, 1992).

Contemporary sources and commentaries:

Guthrie, W.K.C., *The Sophists* (Cambridge: Cambridge University Press, 1971).

Kerford, G.B., *The Sophistic Movement* (Cambridge: Cambridge University Press, 1981).

McKirahan, Richard D., *Philosophy Before Socrates* (Indianapolis, IN: Hackett Publishing Company, 1994).

O'Brien, Michael J., 'Protagoras', in Rosamond Kent Sprague (ed.), *The Older Sophists*, (Columbia, SC: University of South Carolina Press, 1972), pp. 3-28.

Schiappa, Edward, *Protagoras and Logos: A Study in Greek Philosophy and Rhetoric*, 2nd edn (Columbia, SC: University of South Carolina Press, 2003).

Waterfield, Robin, *The First Philosophers: The Presocratics and the Sophists* (Oxford: Oxford University Press, 2000).

Wheelwright, Philip, *The Presocratics* (New York: Macmillan, 1964, repr. 1985), ch. 8.

4

Gorgias

Colin Higgins

Of all the early sophists, Gorgias (483-375 BC) is the most controversial and polarising. He was condemned by some for what was interpreted as his nihilist or relativist philosophy (just as many of the sophists were condemned for different aspects of their work), and praised by others for his wisdom, style and eloquence. While it is an exaggeration to say that he introduced rhetoric to Greece, his efforts were instrumental in its evolution as an art. He was also responsible for the development of the Attic dialect of ancient Greek, advances in poetics (and what is called the 'prose spectacle' – a highly ornate and poetic prose style) and even philosophy. The influence of Gorgias can be seen in the sceptic philosophical movement known as Pyrrhonism which erupted in the third century BC and again four hundred years later.

Life

Gorgias, son of Charmantides, was born in Leontini in Sicily. Little is known of his family, but the historian can assume that they were cultured and intellectual; his brother Herodicus was a physician. Gorgias was a student of Empedocles (492-432 BC), an important Presocratic philosopher and physician responsible for the four-element theory of matter (air, water, earth and fire) and represented by some scholars as the inventor of rhetoric. Gorgias may also have been influenced by Zeno of Elea (490-430), a philosopher famous for his mathematical paradoxes (see Aristotle's *Physics* VI). It is assumed that prior to his arrival in Greece, Gorgias' scholarly concerns were limited to physical science and eristics (disputations).

For much of the fifth century Leontini had been an independent city-state, but it was eventually threatened by the increasing power of its rival, nearby Syracuse. This led to a military alliance of the Chalcidian cities in 433. Chalcidice was an area on the Greek mainland north of Athens, and Leontini was originally a Chalcidian colony. Athens refused to commit to this alliance, however, and this set the stage for a diplomatic mission in 427 to be led by Gorgias, who, according to Diodorus Siculus was 'in power of speech by far the most eminent of the men of his time' (Diodorus Siculus XII.53, I, 2; Sprague 1972, 32). Upon arriving in Greece, Gorgias delivered a series of speeches that dazzled the Athenian audiences and won him fame and admiration. As an early advocate of *panhellenism* (an effort to unite all Greeks into one democratic political body), he implored the Athenians to come to the aid of Leontini. Nevertheless, his mission ended in failure in 425, and the issue would remain unsettled until the Athenian 'Sicilian Expedition' of 415 launched in the midst of the Peloponnesian War. After sustaining heavy losses in a series of battles against the Syracusans, the Athenians ultimately abandoned the island of Sicily altogether.

Gorgias then travelled throughout Greece as a teacher of rhetoric and as an orator, and spoke at the pan-Hellenic festivals. He was seen in Boeotia and at Argos, where a ban was imposed on attending his lectures (Untersteiner 1954, 93). Plato remarks that Gorgias wandered to Thessaly where he turned the 'Thessalians into lovers of wisdom' (*Meno* 70a-b).

The constitutional reforms which began at Athens in 462/461 BC brought into being what some regard as full or unmixed democracy (Kerferd 1984, 16). It became possible for an individual with money and connections to obtain an important political office within the courts or the assembly. Formal education in rhetoric became a prerequisite for obtaining and holding such political positions, and this created an opportunity for the early sophists. These men were considered professional educators with an important specialised skill, or *technê*. They depended upon the patronage of the statesman Pericles (495-429), who was sympathetic towards their efforts (the tenth-century Byzantine encyclopaedia, the *Suda*, tells us that Gorgias was one of Pericles' teachers) (*Suda* A 2a; Sprague 1972, 32). Many of them set up schools and charged fees in return for instruction, and Gorgias was no exception. He was the teacher of the orator Alcidamas (fourth century BC) and Antisthenes (446-366), the latter considered by many to be the first cynic philosopher. According to Quintilian and others, Gorgias was also the teacher of Isocrates (436-338), and Plato identifies Meno (*Meno* 76aff.) among Gorgias' students.

Philostratus (*Lives of the Sophists* I.9.I) tells us that Gorgias began the practice of extemporaneous oratory, and that he had the boldness to say '*suggest a subject* ... he was the first to proclaim himself willing to take the chance, showing apparently that he knew everything and would trust the moment to speak on any subject'. This ability to speak with authority on any issue became a kind of advertising vehicle, or manifesto for Gorgias. In Cicero's *De Inventione* (I.5.2) the author states, 'Gorgias of Leontini, almost the earliest rhetorician, thought that an orator ought to be able to speak best on all subjects'. In an effort to prove they were knowledgeable in many areas, the sophists wrote essays on everything from wrestling (Protagoras) and Olympic champions (Hippias), to dreams (Antiphon) and constitutions (Critias) (de Romilly 1992, 8).

Gorgias died at the age of 108 at Larissa in Thessaly at the court of Jason, tyrant of Pherae. Aelian (*Historical Miscellany* II.35) tells us that the exhausted Gorgias' last words were, 'Sleep already begins to hand me over to his brother Death.' He never held citizenship anywhere in Greece, nor did he marry or have children, and contrary to rumours of vast wealth (he charged each of his students 100 minas and supposedly had a solid gold statue built in his own honour), left behind only one thousand staters (Isocrates 155; Sprague 1972, 37). This is despite Isocrates' claim (*Antidosis* 156; Sprague 1972, 37) that Gorgias never paid taxes!

Four primary works are attributed to Gorgias: *On the Nonexistent* or *On Nature*, the *Defence of Palamedes*, the *Encomium on Helen*, and the *Epitaphios* or *Athenian Funeral Oration*. The original text of *On Nature* has been lost, and survives only in two different paraphrases, one in Sextus Empiricus' *Against the Professors* and another in an anonymous work entitled *Melissus, Xenophanes, Gorgias*. There are two different manuscripts of *Palamedes* and *Helen* (the Cripps and Palatine versions), one slightly different from the other.

Gorgias was said to have authored a treatise on rhetoric that included a collection of model speeches, but this has never been found. Two other *encomiums* are accredited to him, one to Achilles and another to the Eleans, and he was also said to have delivered a *Pythian Oration*, but these too have never been recovered (Untersteiner 1954, 95-6).

Oratorical and literary style

Gorgias was one of the orators responsible for the development of what is now called the 'Attic dialect' of ancient Greek. His rhyming style was highly poetic, and he viewed the orator as a man leading a kind of collective 'sacred incantation'. He believed in a liberal application of metaphor and figurative expressions to illustrate his assertions, and frequently used humour as an instrument of refutation. As Aristotle remarks, 'Gorgias said that *the opposition's seriousness is to be demolished by laughter, and laughter by seriousness*' (*Rhetoric* 1419b3). The term *macrologia* (using more words than necessary in an effort to appear eloquent) is sometimes used to describe his oratorical technique (Kennedy 1999, 63). His style was so influential that for centuries scholars would refer to the 'Gorgianic figures', or 'figures in the style of Gorgias'. Examples include: *paronomasia*, in which two or more words that sound alike but have different meanings are brought together to form a kind of pun; *homoioteleuton*, adjacent or parallel words with similar endings; *anadiplosis*, in which the last word from a previous sentence or phrase begins the next sentence; and *antithesis* or *paradoxologia*, in which conflicting ideas or concepts are juxtaposed for rhetorical emphasis. Unfortunately, many of these figures lose their character when translated from the ancient Greek.

Not everyone was impressed with Gorgias' style, however. Aristotle dismisses him as a 'frigid' stylist who indulges in excessive use of compound words such as 'begging-poet-flatterers' and 'foresworn and well-sworn' (*Rhetoric* 1405b34). He also faults Gorgias for his overly poetic language, citing as examples the phrases, 'grass-pale (trembling)' and 'bloodless matters'. And 'you shamefully sowed these and wretchedly reaped' (*Rhetoric* 1406b4). We can perhaps see other examples in Gorgias' description of *logos* as a great dynast or lord and as a 'drug' (*Encomium of Helen* 8-14; Sprague 1972, 52-3), or the sophist's descriptions of orators as 'frogs croaking in water' (Gnomologium Vaticanum 743 no. 167; Sprague 1972, 66). Despite its ostentation, however, this style was heavily imitated to the point where Philostratus was forced to admit that 'in Thessaly, ... *to be an orator* acquired the synonym *to Gorgianize*' (Philostratus, *Epistle* 73; Sprague 1982, 41).

Cicero contends that Thrasymachus and Gorgias were 'the first to have tried these figures [antithesis, parison, etc.], and after them Theodorus of Byzantium and many others whom Socrates in the *Phaedrus* calls *skilled in tricking out a speech*' (*Orator* 12, 39). In Cicero's view, Gorgias immoderately abuses the 'festive decorations' of dithyrambs and balanced opposites, and his style ultimately becomes 'puerile' (52, 176). Nevertheless, we must remember that rhetorical guidelines had changed significantly between the time of Gorgias and that of Cicero. What was considered 'good style' in fifth-century Greece had become extravagant and gaudy by the later years of the Roman Republic.

Philosophical works: *On Nature*

Nowhere is Gorgias' sophistical love of paradox more evident than in the short treatise *On the Nonexistent* or *On Nature*. *On Nature* may have been written (or delivered) before Gorgias left Sicily for Greece in 427, but there is no proof of this. The subject of this work is ontological (concerning nature of being), but it also deals with language and epistemology (the study of the nature and limitations of knowledge). In addition to this, the treatise can be understood as an exercise in sophistical rhetoric; Gorgias tackles an argument that is seemingly impossible to refute, namely that, after considering our world, we must come to the conclusion that 'things exist'. His powerful argument to the contrary proves his abilities as a master of oratory, and some believe the text was used as an advertisement of his credentials. Variations on Zeno of Elea's theories of multiplicity and motion appear in this treatise, and it should be pointed out that Zeno himself also wrote a treatise entitled *On Nature*.

Gorgias begins his argument by presenting a logical contradiction, 'if the nonexistent exists, it will both exist and not exist at the same time' (a violation of the principle of non-contradiction). He then denies that existence itself exists, for if it exists, it is either eternal or generated. If it is eternal, it has no beginning, and is therefore without limit. If it is without limit, it is 'nowhere' and hence does not exist. And if existence is generated, it must come from something, and that something is existence, which is another contradiction. Likewise, nonexistence cannot produce anything. Gorgias then explains that existence can be neither 'one' nor 'many', since if it were one, it would be divisible, and therefore not one. If it were many, it would be a 'composite of separate entities' and no longer the thing known as existence (*Against the Professors* VII.73-4; Sprague 1972, 44).

Gorgias then turns his attention to what is knowable and comprehensible. He remarks, 'if things considered [imagined or thought] in the mind are not existent, the existent is not considered', that is to say, existence is incomprehensible. This supposition is backed up by the fact that one can imagine chariots racing in the sea, but that does not make such a thing happen (*Against the Professors* VII.82; Sprague 1972, 46). The operation of the mind (intellection) is fundamentally distinct from what happens in the real world; 'the existent is not an object of consideration and is not apprehended'. It is helpful to think of apprehension here in Aristotelian terms, as *simple apprehension*, the first operation of reasoning (logic) in which the intellect 'grasps' or 'apprehends' something. Simple apprehension happens when the mind first forms a concept of something in the world, and is anterior to judgment.

Finally, Gorgias proclaims that even if existence could be apprehended, it would be incapable of being conveyed to another. This is because what we reveal to another is not an external substance, but is merely *logos* (from the Greek verb *legô*, 'to say'). *Logos* is not 'substances and existing things'. External reality becomes the revealer of *logos*; while we can *know* logos, we cannot apprehend things directly. The colour white, for instance, goes from a property of a thing, to a mental representation, and the representation is different from the thing itself. In its summation, this nihilistic argument becomes a 'trilemma':

i. Nothing exists
ii. Even if existence exists, it cannot be known
iii. Even if it could be known, it cannot be communicated.

This argument has led some to designate Gorgias as either an ontological sceptic or a nihilist (one who believes nothing exists, or that the world is incomprehensible, and that the concept of truth is fictitious). But the trilemma can also be interpreted as an assertion that it is *logos* and *logos* alone which is the proper object of our inquiries, since it is the only thing we can really *know*. *On Nature* is sometimes seen as a refutation of Presocratic essentialist philosophy (McComiskey 2002, 37). Robert L. Scott (1994, 314) contends that the treatise 'may be interpreted as an attempt to show that man can be certain of no absolute standard'.

Of all the sophists, Gorgias was the most deliberately philosophical. He once remarked that 'those neglecting philosophy and devoting themselves to general studies were like suitors who, though wanting Penelope, slept with her maids' (Gnomologium Vaticanum 743 no. 166; Sprague 1972, 66).

But as George Kennedy asserts (1999, 36), one must be careful not to credit Gorgias 'with an uncharacteristic power of conceptualisation. Gorgias imitated what he found in the philosophers [specifically Zeno] as he did what he found in the poets, not so much as contributions to a theory of knowledge as to a technique of speech'. Gorgias was a rhetorician first and foremost, and this brings us to the next section.

Rhetorical theory and method

Most of what we know concerning Gorgias' views on rhetoric comes from the *Encomium*. This work can be understood as a sophistical effort to rehabilitate the reputation of Helen of Troy. In it, Gorgias attempts to take the weaker argument and make it the stronger one, by arguing for a position contrary to well-established opinion: in this case, the opinion that Helen was to blame for the Trojan War. Gorgias argues that Helen succumbed either to (a) physical force (Paris' abduction), (b) love (*eros*), or (c) verbal persuasion (*logos*), and in any instance, she cannot be blamed for her actions. According to Gorgias, *logos* is a powerful force that can be used nefariously to convince people to do things against their own interests. It can take the form of poetry (metrical language), divine incantations, or oratory. As mentioned earlier, *Logos* is described as a 'powerful lord,' and 'The effect of speech upon the condition of the soul is comparable to the power of drugs over the nurture of bodies' (82b11.8,14; Sprague 1972, 53). This is in contrast to the view of Isocrates that *logos* is a 'chief' or 'commander' (Isocrates, *Nicocles* 5-9). The difference here is subtle, but Gorgias' *dynastic* concept of *logos* clearly turns it into a despotic over-lord, while Isocrates' 'commander' is a leader with delegated authority, an individual who fights alongside his troops. Plato remarks: 'I often heard Gorgias say that the art of rhetoric differs from all other arts. Under its influence all things are willingly but not forcibly made slaves' (*Philebus* 58a).

Examples of persuasive speech, according to Gorgias, are the 'conflicts among the philosophers' arguments in which the swiftness of demonstration and judgment make the belief in any opinion changeable' (82b11.13; Sprague 1972, 53). This is similar to the claim of the Pyrrhonist (sceptic) philosopher Sextus Empiricus that equally convincing arguments can be formed against, or in favour of, any subject. It is the foundation of what would come to be known as the *dissoi logoi*, or two-fold argument, a rhetorical tactic practised by many of the sophists. Life is full of conflicting arguments, but the remedy for this, according to Gorgias, is not to suspend judgement as Sextus Empiricus would, but to act. As Scott (1994, 316) remarks, when one is faced with a difficult decision, 'He must say with Gorgias, *I know the irreconcilable conflicts, and yet I act.*'

Gorgias may have believed in a relative notion of truth that was contingent upon a particular *kairos* (an opportune moment or 'opening'), that is to say, truth can be found only within a given moment. He seems to reject the idea of truth as a philosophically universal principle, and thus comes into conflict with Plato and Aristotle. Nevertheless, the rhetor (orator) is ethically obliged to avoid deception, and it is the duty of the same man both to declare what he should rightly and to refute what has been spoken falsely (Gorgias, *Helen* 11.2; Sprague 1972, 50). Ultimately, Gorgias' opinion concerning truth is difficult to ascertain, but from his writings, we can conclude that he was more concerned with rhetorical argument than the truth of any given proposition or assertion. De Romilly (1992, 9) maintains: 'In the Sophists' intellectual world, where nothing was accepted *a priori* anymore, the only sure criterion was immediate, concrete human experience. Gods, traditions, and mythical memories no longer counted for anything. Our own judgments, our own feelings and interests now constituted the sole criteria.' Zeno of Elea contended that all theories were based upon unprovable hypotheses, even mathematics, and this idea is reflected in the writings of Gorgias.

In the epideictic (exhibition) speech *Defence of Palamedes,* Gorgias uses a mythical narrator (Palamedes) further to illustrate his rhetorical technique and philosophy. Palamedes was reputed to have invented the Greek alphabet, wine-making and currency. In the *Odyssey*, Palamedes was responsible for revealing Odysseus' 'madness' as a fiction, an act for which he was never forgiven. Ultimately, Palamedes was executed for treason, after Odysseus accused him of conspiring with the Trojans. Gorgias focuses on the invention of arguments (*topoi*) necessary to exonerate Palamedes within the setting of a fictional trial, all of which depend upon *probability.* In other words, plausible arguments are used to refute conventional truths (Jarratt 1991, 59). Palamedes could not have committed treason with a foreign power since he speaks no language other than Greek, and no Greek desires social power among barbarians (Gorgias, *Palamedes* 11a6-13; Sprague 1972, 56-7). In the second example, we see that *topoi* 'embody the values of the community, in the sense that they comprise what the community considers important' (Consigny 2001, 84). A fundamental difference between the *topoi* found within Aristotle's *Art of Rhetoric* and Gorgias' *topoi* is that Aristotle's are 'acontextual, while Gorgias places his in the narrative context of the Palamedes myth' (McComiskey 2002, 49). Therefore, we can say that there is a direct relationship between *kairos* and invention. In other words, a given argument cannot be separated from the context in which it is employed.

Gorgias rejects the use of *pathos* (emotional appeal) in his *Defence,* with the assertion that 'among you, who are the foremost of the Greeks ... there is no need to persuade such ones as you with the aid of friends and sorrowful prayers and lamentations' (Gorgias, *Palamedes* 11a33; Sprague 1972, 62). He prefers to use *ethos* (ethical appeal, or arguments from character) and *logos* as his instruments of persuasion.

Only second-hand fragments of the *Epitaphios* or *Funeral Oration* survive. It is unclear whether the oration was delivered in honour of a military event or if it was merely an epideictic exercise. Its ostensible purpose was to praise the Athenians' bravery in war, and in the speech we find excellent examples of Gorgias' liberal use of antithesis: 'For what did these men lack that men should have? What did they have that men should not have? ... For the courage these men possessed was divine, and the mortal part alone was human ... often preferring gentle fairness to inflexible justice.' Later in the oration, Gorgias uses a series of adjectives, each with a second, complementary adjective arranged in parallel groups: 'insolent with the insolent, decent with the decent, fearless with the fearless, terrible among terrors' (Planudes on Hermogenes, *Rhetores Graeci* V.548; Sprague 1972, 49). Here we have complex parallel constructions complete with rhyming elements to form a balanced cadence.

Most funeral orations were full of *commonplaces*, or an assemblage of received ideas from history or mythology – stories, anecdotes, and quotations. Gorgias used these commonplaces within both the *Encomium* and the *Epitaphios* just as any orator would, but he also managed to transform them through juxtaposition, giving them a new poignancy and impact (Loraux 1986, 228). Of the five canons of rhetoric (invention, arrangement, style, memory and delivery), Gorgias was the master of arrangement and style, and if some of his constructions seem bewildering or theatrical, we have to remember that they were meant to be performed. De Romilly (1992, 73) contends that 'Protagoras was concerned with the precise correspondence between thought and expression, while Gorgias was concerned with the effect on the audience.' The dynamic between audience and speaker is central to Gorgias' rhetoric.

Critics and contemporaries

Gorgias' most famous critic is Plato. In the dialogue *Gorgias*, Plato (through his mentor Socrates) expresses his contempt for sophistical rhetoric; all rhetoric is 'a phantom of a branch of statesmanship ... a kind of flattery ... that is contemptible' (Plato, *Gorgias* 463e; Waterfield 1994, 31) because its aim is simply pleasure rather than the welfare of the public. Nor can rhetoric be considered an art (*technê*), since it is irrational (*Gorgias* 465a; Waterfield, 32). The end result of rhetoric is a cosmetic alteration of language that conceals truth and falsity (*Gorgias* 465b; Waterfield, 33). Furthermore, rhetoric is 'designed to produce conviction, but not educate people, about matters of right or wrong' (*Gorgias* 455a; Waterfield, 17). The character of Gorgias in the dialogue is forced to admit that his 'art' deals with opinion (*doxa*) rather than knowledge (*epistêmê*); that its intention is to persuade rather than to instruct, and that rhetoric deals with language without regard to content. Gorgias is portrayed as a man with an ambivalent attitude towards truth, a relativist, who boldly asserts that it does not matter if one truly has knowledge of any given subject, only that he is *perceived* by others to have knowledge, and that 'Rhetoric is the only area of expertise you need to learn. You can ignore all the rest and still get the better of the professionals!' (*Gorgias* 459b; Waterfield, 24). Gorgias lived long enough to encounter Plato's dialogue, and according to Athenaeus remarked, 'How well Plato knows how to satirise!' (Athenaeus XI.505D; Sprague 1972, 37). There is no agreement among historians as to what this statement means, but it offers us a glimpse into the personality of Gorgias. Instead of defending his art against Plato's attacks, he merely shrugs off the philosopher's dialogue as an example of rhetorical satire.

There are several explanations for Plato's antipathy towards sophistic rhetoric. The first is simply philosophical; Plato was not a relativist, nor did he believe rhetoric had a pedagogical value. But there is also a political element to be considered. Bruce McComiskey (2002, 20) points out that Plato believed in an 'oligarchic government' for Athens, while many of the sophists 'favoured the Athenian Democracy the way it was, and their desire for democracy rested on their relativistic epistemologies'. On a more practical level, the Greek city-states also served as a market for those who would *sell* instruction in rhetoric. Some of the sophists (Gorgias included) were criticised for charging large sums of money in return for education. Isocrates, in his *Antidosis* (28-31; Norlin 1968, 203), was required to defend his practice of receiving 'enormous sums of money' in return for instruction in the art.

In Aristophanes' play *Birds*, Gorgias is portrayed as a member of

> ... a nation
>   With its tongue its belly fills;
> With its tongue it sows and reaps,
> Gathers grapes and figs in heaps,
>   With its tongue the soil it tills.
> For a Barbarous tribe it passes,
> Philips all and Gorgiases.
> And from this tongue-bellying band
> Everywhere on Attic land,
> People who a victim slay
> Always cut the tongue away (1695-705, trans. Rogers 1937).

The dramatist may have been disgusted by what he saw as the obsequious begging for patronage and clients on the part of the sophists, or their support of the verbal disputes within the courts. So much so that he hints their tongues should be cut out at the root. In a footnote to this translation, Rogers (1937, 285) writes, 'The Barbarians are the foreign sycophants and sophists who flock to Athens and earn a living by their tongues.' According to Cosigny (2001, 96), 'a sycophant in fifth-century Athens, is a person who criminally abuses the courts by bringing suits for his own personal gain rather than for just cause; and a "barbarian," in Aristophanes' depiction, typically embodies the antithesis of the "Greek" intellectual and moral virtues.' Because Gorgias was not a citizen, he could not bring cases to the courts himself, but his instruction in political rhetoric (deliberative) allowed others to do so.

Conclusion

In 1930 the French philosopher Jacques Maritain remarked (1930, 65-6): 'sophistry is not a system of ideas, but a vicious attitude of mind; ... [the sophists] came to consider as the most desirable form of knowledge the art of refuting and disproving by skilful arguments.' This statement reflects an ancient prejudice against the sophists, and against Gorgias in particular. But the historian, when reflecting upon the depth and originality of Gorgias' thought, cannot but conclude that the sophist was indeed a philosopher, although not in the same vein as Socrates or Aristotle. Gorgias developed and refined the idea of *kairos* (the opportune moment), offered a theory of language, and gave rhetoric a civic and political relevance. He, like many of the sophists, professed himself a master of virtue and claimed to direct his students towards social ends. In this way, as Untersteiner declared (1954, xv), we can say that Gorgias' philosophy anticipates the advent of humanism.

Bibliography

Aelian, *Historical Miscellany*, trans. N.G. Wilson, Loeb edition (Cambridge, MA: Harvard University Press, 1997).

Aristophanes, vol. II: *The Peace, The Birds, The Frogs*, trans. Benjamin Rogers, Loeb edition (London: Heinemann, 1937).

Aristotle, *On Rhetoric: A Theory of Civic Discourse*, trans. George Kennedy (Oxford: Oxford University Press, 1991).

Aristotle, *Prior Analytics*, trans. Robin Smith (Indianapolis, IN: Hackett, 1989).

Cicero, *De Inventione*, trans. H.M. Hubbell, Loeb edition (London: Heinemann, 1949).

Cicero, *Brutus, Orator*, vol. V, trans. E.H. Warmington, Loeb edition (London: Heinemann, 1971).

Cicero, *De Oratore*, trans. H. Rackham, Loeb edition (London: Heinemann, 1942).

Consigny, Scott, *Gorgias: Sophist and Artist* (Columbia, SC: University of South Carolina Press, 2001).

Diodorus Siculus, vol. XII, trans. C.H. Oldfather, Loeb edition (London: Heinemann, 1950).

Isocrates, trans. George Norlin and LaRue Van Hook, Loeb edition (London: Heinemann, 1968).

Jarratt, Susan, *Rereading the Sophists: Classical Rhetoric Refigured* (Carbondale, IL: Southern Illinois University Press, 1991).

Kennedy, George, *Classical Rhetoric and its Christian and Secular Tradition from Ancient to Modern Times* (Chapel Hill, NC: University of North Carolina Press, 1999).

Kerferd, G.B., *The Sophistic Movement* (Cambridge: Cambridge University Press, 1984).

Loraux, Nicole, *The Invention of Athens: The Funeral Oration in the Classical City*, trans. Alan Sheridan (Cambridge, MA: Harvard University Press, 1986).

Maritain, Jacques, *Introduction to Philosophy*, trans. E.I. Watkin (London: Longmans, Green, 1930). There are at least seventeen editions/reprints of this title. The 1930 edition was also published by Sheed and Ward in London. If difficulty is experienced in locating the 1930 edition, try other Sheed and Ward editions. Page numbers may vary slightly, but the citation appears in ch. III, 'The Sophists and Socrates', in the sub-section 'The Sophists'.

McComiskey, Bruce, *Gorgias and the New Sophistic Rhetoric* (Carbondale, IL: Southern Illinois University Press, 2002).

Philostratus, *Lives of the Sophists*, trans. Wilmer C. Wright, Loeb edition (London: Heinemann, 1921).

Plato, *Five Dialogues: Euthyphro, Apology, Crito, Meno, Phaedo*, trans. G.M. Grube (Indianapolis, IN: Hackett, 2002).

Plato, *Gorgias*, trans. Robin Waterfield (Oxford: Oxford University Press, 1994).

Plato, *Philebus*, trans. Benjamin Jowett (Teddington: Echo Library, 2006).

Romilly, Jacqueline de, *The Great Sophists in Periclean Athens* (Oxford: Oxford University Press, 1992).

Sextus Empiricus, *Against the Professors*, trans. R.G. Bury, Loeb edition (London: Heinemann, 1949).

Sextus Empiricus, *Outlines of Pyrrhonism*, trans. R.G. Bury (Amherst, NY: Prometheus, 1990).

Scott, Robert L., 'On Viewing Rhetoric as Epistemic', in Theresa Enos and Stuart C. Brown (eds), *Professing the New Rhetorics: A Sourcebook* (Englewood Cliffs, NJ: Prentice-Hall, 1994).

Sprague, Rosamond Kent (ed.), *The Older Sophists* (Columbia, SC: University of South Carolina Press, 1972).

Suda online: http://www.stoa.org/sol/.

Untersteiner, Mario, *The Sophists*, trans. Kathleen Freeman (New York: Philosophical Library, 1954).

Hippias

Patricia O'Grady

Elegant and justifiably proud, the flamboyant Hippias would have created a sensation as he strolled through the precincts of Olympia, dressed entirely in garments and accessories he had made himself.

This is how Plato has Socrates speak of Hippias' attire:

> 'You [Hippias] said that once, when you went to Olympia everything you had on your person was your own work; first the ring – for you began with that – which you had was your own work, showing that you knew how to engrave rings, and another seal was your work, and a strigil and an oil flask were your works; then you said that you yourself had made the sandals you had on, and had woven your cloak and tunic; and what seemed to everyone most unusual and proof of the most wisdom, was when you said that the girdle you wore about your tunic was like the Persian girdles of the costliest kind, and that you had made it yourself' (Plato, *Hippias Minor* 368b-d).

Despite the scoffing tone of Plato's dialogue, the lines indicate the self-sufficiency Hippias sought (*Suda*, s.v. Hippias) and the versatility for which he is acknowledged (Philostratus, *Lives of the Sophists* I.11.495; Plato, *Hippias Major* 285b-286b). The *Suda* describes Hippias as 'sophist and philosopher', and also records that '[he] wrote a great deal'. I will return to discuss the writings about Hippias but, first, a little background. Hippias was a native of Elis, the name of both a city and a state in the lovely north-western coastal region of the Peloponnese. Today, the once influential city of Elis attracts few visitors. Compared with the glories of Olympia (Pausanias, *Elis* I, XXV.7-8), which lies about twenty-two miles to the south, it has little to offer the tourist but much appeal for philosophers and archaeologists.

Hippias was the son of Diopeithes and the pupil of Hegesidamus. Nothing further is known about his father or his teacher, and the dates of events in his life are uncertain. Plato has Protagoras state that he, Protagoras, might be the father of any one of those present (*Protagoras* 317c). Protagoras was born in Abdera in about 490 BC. I place Hippias' birth in about 470 BC, making him roughly contemporary with Socrates (Dillon and Gergel 2003, 118). It seems that Hippias was still living when Socrates was executed in 399 BC (Plato, *Apology* 19e), but the year of his death is unknown. His life encompassed a magnificent period in the history of Athens, the second half of the fifth century, a period in which art and literature glorified Athens, but which was also the most tragic. He lived through the twenty-eight years of the Peloponnesian War (431-404 BC), 'the greatest disturbance in the history of the Hellenes' (Thucydides I.1); as he was an alien, that conflict would have limited his opportunities for visiting Athens. During brief periods of truce, however, such as the Peace of Nicias in 421, Hippias could have taken advantage of rare chances to visit Athens.

No writings of Hippias survive, but the meagre ancient fragments that remain support the fact that he was a man of many talents and varied interests. A great deal, but not all, of our information about Hippias is derived from three works of Plato: *Hippias Major*, *Hippias Minor* and *Protagoras*. It is not always possible to recognise when Plato is serious. His work is thickly overlaid with sarcasm and acrimony, even bitterness. He is debasing, critical and downright rude but, as much as Plato disapproved of Hippias, he immortalised him through his dialogues. Plato's purpose is to draw a contrast between Hippias and Socrates, to support Socrates' ideals, and to distance Socrates from the teaching and methods of the sophists who not only charged for their services but claimed to be able to teach virtue without comprehending the innate essence of virtue. At least, that is how Plato represents Socrates' opinion of the sophists.

Plato itemises the many areas in which Hippias was proficient and even expert, but he does little more than list them. We are told of Hippias' involvement in mythology, geography, history, literature, law and politics. He was concerned with language and the 'value of letters and syllables and rhythms and harmonies' (*Hippias Major*, 285d; Philostratus, *Lives of the Sophists* I.11.496). We learn about his success, his appeal as a teacher and the vast fortune he made through lecturing. Socrates claimed never to have made money from his teaching, while Hippias proudly declared his wealth (*Hippias Major* 282e).

In Socrates we have an unattractive man, seemingly impoverished, barefoot and in a threadbare coat, hanging around the market place, asking embarrassing 'unanswerable' questions, badgering people and generally making himself unpopular. In Hippias we have a man who is rich, elegantly dressed, popular, sought-after and entertaining. But one could argue that while Socrates was debating with anyone he could accost, 'at the same time, he was cooking up western civilization' (*The Age,* Melbourne, 1999). And one could also point to the fact that the sophists were writers, quite in contrast to Socrates. They were bookish men who 'made a decisive contribution to the development of the book on which the rise and further existence of scholarship depended' (Pfeiffer 1968, 55).

We turn now to a discussion of Hippias and his remarkable accomplishment in geometry.

In his time, Hippias had a superior knowledge of mathematics. Our source for this information is Plato himself: Plato has Hippias assure Socrates that he is skilful and quick in arithmetical calculations, being 'the most powerful and wisest of men in these matters' (*Hippias Minor* 366c). A few lines later, in response to a question from Socrates, Hippias declares that he is an 'expert in geometry also' (367d).

Plato portrays Hippias as excessively boastful, but his pride may be seen as justified for, in about 420 BC, he solved one of the three great problems which the early mathematicians identified and which engrossed them. These were the trisection of an angle, the squaring of the circle, and the doubling of the cube. The feat is recorded by Proclus, the great Neoplatonist philosopher who, apart from Plato and Xenophon, is our most fruitful source on Hippias.

> Hippias of Elis, the famous sophist of the fifth century BC, the inventor of a curve known as the quadratrix which, originally intended for the solution of the problem of trisecting any angle, also served (as the name implies) for squaring the circle (Proclus, *Commentary on Euclid Book I* 272.7).

Proclus provides firm acceptance of Hippias' discovery. Proclus, in the fifth century AD, knew Hippias of Elis as the famous sophist of the fifth century BC, almost nine centuries earlier. As we can see, his report clearly states that Hippias' curve was originally intended for the solution of the problem of trisecting any angle. Its statement that the curve 'also served (as the name implies) for squaring the circle' has led commentators, such as Gow, Heath and others, to the conclusion that Hippias did indeed discover the quadratrix (Heath 1921, vol. I, 182).

Proclus discusses Euclid's ideas on bisecting rectilinear angles, and points out that it is not always possible to bisect an angle; for instance, a horned angle (this an angle which is formed when a curved line meets, or intersects, a straight line) (*Commentary* 271). He adds that it is possible to trisect a right angle using 'some of the theorems that follow, but we cannot thus divide an acute angle without resorting to other lines that are mixed in kind' (mixed lines are curves other than circles). He then introduces geometers who applied themselves to the problem of trisecting a rectilinear angle.

> Nicomedes [*c.* 200 BC] made use of conchoids – a form of [curved] line whose construction he has himself taught us, being himself the discoverer of their peculiarities – and thus succeeded in trisecting the rectilinear angle generally. Others have done the same thing [applied themselves to the problem of trisecting a given rectilinear angle, which is one that is bounded or formed by straight lines], by means of the quadratrix of Hippias and that of Nicomedes, they too using mixed lines, namely, the quadratrices (*Commentary* 272.7).

Proclus then acknowledged the difficulty of these ideas, and stated that he would not pursue the ideas. In a later passage Proclus explained how mathematicians

... are accustomed to distinguish lines, giving the properties of each species. Apollonius [born *c.* 264 BC), for instance shows for each of his conic lines what its property is, and Nicomedes likewise for the conchoids, Hippias for the quadratrices, and Perseus [*c.* 300 BC] for the spiric curves. After the species has been constructed, the apprehension of its inherent and intrinsic property differentiates the thing constructed from all others (*Commentary* 356.6-13).

In these lines Proclus stated, precisely, that Hippias identified the properties of his curve and the features which were unique to it, making it possible to understand that particular curve. It is feasible to assume that Hippias provided the method for constructing the curve, but Proclus does not present it. We turn to other geometricians, such as Geminus, Pappas and Sporus, for enlightenment.

We recall that Proclus (*Commentary* 272) stated that the trisection had been performed by others who had employed the quadratrix of Hippias and of Nicomedes, applying mixed lines. It is feasible to suggest that the notion of the curves discovered by Hippias to develop the trisectrix was extended by the work of Perseus and Nicomedes.

Because Proclus was writing about nine hundred years after Hippias, it is important that we establish the sources that were available to Proclus. Heath argues that the source for Proclus on the curves invented by Hippias was probably Geminus, and the opinions of Heath warrant the greatest respect; he was a mathematician of extraordinary ability and industry.

Geminus is a very important authority on many questions pertaining to the history of mathematics, as is shown by the numerous quotations from him in Proclus' *Commentary on Euclid Book I* (Heath 1921, vol. II, 223).

Geminus was a Stoic philosopher who was probably born on the island of Rhodes. He was a pupil of Posidonius, and was writing in about 73-67 BC (Heath 1921, vol. II, 222-6.) His treatise, numbering at least six volumes, was a classification of scientific topics, including a comprehensive work of almost encyclopaedic proportions on mathematics. He wrote extensively on geometry (Heath 1921, vol. II, 224). This included the classification of curves (*Oxford Classical Dictionary*, s.v. Geminus), making him an authority of great importance. In his *Commentary on Euclid Book I,* Proclus refers to Geminus no less than twenty times (Morrow 1970, 38n.66) and, one presumes, probably many more times that remain unacknowledged. It can hardly be doubted that Geminus was the source for Proclus, and therefore for the geometry of Hippias. Heath cites a passage from Proclus:

Thus Apollonius [of Perga, first half of the thrid century BC] shows in the case of each of the conic curves what is its property, and similarly Nicomedes with the conchoids, Hippias with the quadratrices, and Perseus with the conic curves. ... This suggests that Geminus had before him a regular treatise by Hippias on the properties of the quadratrix (which may have disappeared by the time of Sporus) [and thus by the time of Pappas], and that Nicomedes did not write any such general work on the curve; and, if this is so, it seems not impossible that Hippias himself discovered that it would serve to rectify, and therefore to square, the circle (Heath 1921, vol. I, 226).

Pappas, who was active in about AD 320, compiled a *Collection* or *Synagoge* of classical geometry. One of the many authors about whom he wrote was Dinostratus, and he mentions Dinostratus' brother, Menaechmus (Heath 1921, vol. II, 359), who used the curve of Hippias, '*to which they gave the name of quadratrix* [my italics] for the squaring of the circle' (Heath 1921, vol. II, 359).

Proclus repeats this cogent passage:

For the squaring of the circle Dinostratus, Nicomedes and certain other and later geometers used a certain curve which took its name from its property; for those geometers called it *quadratrix*' (Heath 1921, vol. I, 225).

Pappas applies the quadratrix, but does not mention Hippias. This omission is probably because Hippias did not apply the curve for the quadrature of the circle, but for the trisection of the angle (Waerden 1971, 146).

Sporus (end of the third century AD), just slightly earlier than Pappas, recognised a difficulty in the quadratrix because it necessitates the construction of a curved line and a straight line, both being constructed at the same time, taking 'an equal time' as Sporus says, that is, moving at precisely the same speed (Heath 1921, vol. I, 229). This difficulty is clearly recognised in the construction of the particular trisection of an angle which is attributed to Pappas. Clearly, moving uniformly and *in the same time* are essential for accurate construction, but are almost impossible to attain.

We return to Proclus, *Commentary* 272, and read: 'The thoughts of these men [Hippias and Nicomedes] are difficult for a beginner to follow.' Proclus does not attempt an explanation but directs us to the *Elements* of Euclid. The intrepid reader might care to consult Heath (1956, 265-7), for enlightenment.

In an article on the *MathWorld* website it is claimed that, in 1836, the 'problem [angle trisection] was algebraically proved impossible by Wantzel' (Weisstein 1999). Against this is the fact that an angle can also be divided into three (or any whole number) of equal parts using the quadratrix of Hippias or trisectrix, albeit with a lesser degree of accuracy. The words 'equal parts' then become inappropriate.

Hippias was a giant in mathematics. It is feasible to conclude that he discovered the curve which enabled the trisection of certain angles, and his discovery of the then unique curve now has general acceptance: the curve which he discovered 'is the first named curve other than the circle and line' (Xah Lee 2000). It was from geometers such as Hippias that Greek youths learnt their geometry.

I now turn to a philosophical item of great importance which is reported by Plato and by Xenophon. Hippias proposes a scheme which may be seen as the forerunner of the social contract. In a passage in the dialogue, *Protagoras,* cited below, Plato records a discussion which is probably historically based. It relates a discussion that had previously taken place in the house of Callias. In addition to the Friend, the illustrious gathering included Socrates, Hippocrates (an ambitious young Athenian) Protagoras, Alcibiades, Callias, Critias, Prodicus and Hippias. The dramatic date of the dialogue is about 432 BC, just before the start of the Peloponnesian War. Protagoras was about fifty-eight, already an established educator and held in high esteem: Socrates and Hippias were about thirty-six years old. The topic is the acquisition of virtue. The tenor of the discussion deteriorates to the stage where it becomes tense and unproductive. Callias, the wealthy Athenian who was an important supporter of the sophists, implores Socrates and Protagoras not to break up the debate, but the discussion becomes ineffective, even nasty, and its continuation is threatened. This is borne out by the following words of Prodicus: 'I add my plea, Protagoras and Socrates, that you should be reconciled. Let your conversation be a discussion not a dispute. A discussion is carried on among friends with goodwill, but a dispute is between rivals and enemies' (*Protagoras* 337a-b). This is an astute definition of discussion and dispute. In an effort to calm the situation the wise Hippias speaks:

> 'Gentlemen, who are here present, I regard you all as kinsmen and intimates and fellow citizens by nature, not by law: for like is akin to like by nature, whereas law, despot of mankind, often constrains us against nature. Hence it would be shameful if we, while knowing the nature of things should yet – being the wisest of the Greeks, and having met together for the very purpose in the very sanctuary of the wisdom of Greece [Athens] and in this the greatest and most auspicious house of the city of cities [house of Callias] – display no worthy sign of this dignity, but should quarrel with each other like low churls' (*Protagoras* 337d).

Hippias' appeal is first aimed at bringing harmony to the interlocutors – he directs his appeal at everyone who is present, regardless of their place of origin. A number of those present are not Athenian, including Protagoras of Abdera, Prodicus of Ceos and Hippias himself. The nationality of the Friend is not stated. In addition there are several strangers – fellow-citizens of Hippias and some others (*Protagoras* 315c). Non-Athenian Greeks were designated as metics and did not have the rights of citizens. Hippias seems to regard this as an artificial barrier. He considers them all to be fellow-citizens by nature, not by law, that is, a brotherhood of mankind. He regards law as a despot [absolute ruler, tyrant, oppressor], that is, as a tyrannical restraint forcing citizens to act in accordance with artificial laws which are contrary to natural law. Hippias points to the privileged position that they enjoy, men of knowledge, having the advantage of meeting together in the house of the wealthy Callias in Athens, and showing no gratitude or respect for their honour and privileges.

Hippias is censuring the gathering for their quarrelling which he sees as reprehensible, and far beneath their station. Plato has him use the word *phaulotatous*, 'most paltry', in the superlative, likening the quarrelsome interlocutors to the lowest of churls, totally petty, of no account, to be held in no regard at all. Hippias pointed to a distinction between high and low birth, perhaps expecting that privileged people of high birth would know how to behave. His endeavour is to have all those present recognise their commonality, not based on race or citizenship of a particular place, but on the fact of their humanity. He envisages a unity, an international brotherhood of all Greeks, and he instigated the idea among various Greeks in Athens in the house of Callias. Hippias knew of the frequent wars between the Greek states, and that an amnesty was created before each Olympic Festival. This was an effort to bring about amity, but it was a futile gesture lasting only as long as the Festival itself. He knew of the simmering discord between Athens and Megara (which contributed to the tragedy of the Peloponnesian War of 432-404 BC). Hippias travelled widely, becoming acquainted with the varying customs of different states. He was an ambassador well practised in the art of negotiation. Hippias knew that each man's belief was based on his own opinion. His words were an ethical milestone. He may, in fact, have been the first person publicly to promote such cosmopolitanism. His cosmopolitanism may have been part of the reason for Plato's contempt for Hippias. As Havelock wrote, 'But the operation of dismemberment performed here by Plato upon the doctrine of man's common nature and brotherhood and world citizenship is not quite forgivable' (Havelock 1957, 229). This is alluding to a social contract. Hippias' attitude is cosmopolitan, but we have no evidence to support the idea that he visualised an international social contract.

Xenophon, in his *Memoirs of Socrates,* or *Memorabilia*, relates a discussion about right conduct which he claimed to 'know' that Socrates had had with Hippias. Hippias, who had not been in Athens for long, found Socrates talking:

> ... he was saying that if you want to have a man taught cobbling or building or smithing or riding, you know where to send him to learn the craft: ... And yet, strangely enough, if you want to learn Justice yourself, or to have your son or servant taught it, you know not where to go for a teacher (*Memorabilia* IV.iv.5-6).

Now in the past, Hippias had heard this same tired old discussion and questioning from Socrates, and said so: 'Surely, not again? ... Still the same old sentiments that I heard from you so long ago?' Such a rejoinder is most pleasing to Socrates who replies: 'Always the same and on the same topics too!' (*Memorabilia* IV.iv.6). And this embodies Socrates' absolute belief that questions such as 'What is justice?' have not been answered. While people may state that a certain action is a just action, or a certain decision is a just decision, they do not define 'justice' itself. It can be said that a just man is one who acts justly, but if one does not grasp the essence of 'justice' and if that very essence is not known, then the nature of justice cannot be comprehended or followed. At least, that is Socrates' opinion about justice. Hippias does not recognise his ignorance of the nature of 'justice', or at least his ignorance of the definition that Socrates seeks to extract from his victims. Perhaps Hippias considered that if Socrates *still* had not been able to elicit the essence of 'justice', enough debate had been devoted to the quest and too many years spent on it. Hippias was not concerned with a Socratic definition. To Hippias, justice was a practical issue. To Hippias it would be more productive to proceed, to progress to instances of justice and injustice, and how it was administered, rather than continue the fruitless search for the seemingly indefinable. We may compare this with a comment in Aristotle's *Nicomachean Ethics* (1103b272-9), written about a century later: '... for we are not investigating the nature of virtue for the sake of knowing what it is, but in order that we may become good, without which result our investigation would be of no use ....'

The debate continues and Socrates and Hippias engage in a discussion on 'laws of the state' with Hippias stating that these are 'covenants made by the citizens whereby [the citizens] have enacted what ought to be done and what ought to be avoided' (*Memorabilia* IV.iv.13). Hippias had little regard for man-made laws, because he had observed that 'the very men who passed them often reject and amend them' (*Memorabilia* IV.iv.14). (Man-made laws, of course, are the laws under which Socrates later, in 399 BC, was charged, convicted, and executed.)

Natural laws are universal laws. Socrates and Hippias agree that unwritten laws are divine laws that are ordained by the gods (*Memorabilia* IV.iv.19). Becoming acquainted with gods' standards may be deemed an insurmountable problem, but the ancients 'knew' of instances of divine revelation: Hesiod recorded in his *Theogony* the laws of the gods as they were revealed to him by the muses; the Spartan Tyrtaeus, who flourished in about 640 BC, was aware of the social inequalities and injustices that prevailed in Sparta and proposed a plan to carry out a re-division of the country (Aristotle, *Politics* 1306b36), which was then sanctioned by the god at Delphi. The debate continues and both Hippias and Socrates declare 'lawful and just to be the same thing' (*Memorabilia* IV.iv.18). Hippias agrees that unwritten laws are those that are uniformly observed in every country. These must be natural laws, laws that eventuate, or emerge, or come into being in the natural course of the history of mankind. These are not negotiated or imposed laws for, clearly, not everyone could possibly meet to reach agreement, nor would they all speak the same language if they could meet.

The notion of natural law requires some explanation. Natural law is laid down by the gods, i.e. it is supernatural. So how can natural law be both natural, i.e. in nature, and also ordained by, or come from the gods. There is a sense of natural law that reconciles these two sides. As in much ancient Greek, Roman and medieval philosophy, natural law is in nature in the sense that it is discoverable by human reason reflecting on nature. Humans do not need divine revelation to understand natural law. At the same time natural law can be divinely ordained, in the sense that it would not exist unless God or gods had created it. It may be relevant to note that the ancients saw themselves as part of nature, not standing aside and observing nature.

Thomas Aquinas, building on Aristotle, said there were four sorts of law, two of which are natural laws:

1. Eternal law – the laws governing all things in nature. Eternal law describes the natural tendencies, discoverable by human reason, that God has implanted in all things.
2. Natural law – that part of eternal law that applies to humans. It differs from that part of eternal law that applies to objects in that humans, because of their free will, can disobey it. It is moral law.
3. Human law – laws made by humans. They are neither morally nor legally valid unless they reflect natural law.
4. Divine law – divine revelation.

I think it is the natural, universal, moral law of point 2 that we understand Socrates and Hippias agreed upon, but that humans can disobey. Natural laws are universal laws. As we saw above, Socrates and Hippias agree that unwritten laws are divine laws that are ordained by the gods (*Memorabilia* IV.iv.19). The human law of point 3 consists of man-made laws, laws of the state, which Hippias could not abide, but which Socrates upheld and died for through his allegiance to the Athenian law.

We now leave Plato and Xenophon but continue the discussion of Hippias' ethics and his apprehensions about the distribution of justice, citing two fragments from Plutarch:

> Hippias says there are two kinds of envy – the legitimate, when one envies or begrudges bad men their honours, and the illegitimate, when one envies the good. And envious persons suffer twice as much as those who are not, since they resent not only their own troubles, like others, but also other men's prosperity (Plutarch, *On Calumniating* fr. 155, Plutarch, *Moralia* XV).

> Hippias says that calumny (which he calls *diabolia* [false accusation, slander]) is a dreadful thing because there is no penalty prescribed in the laws for slanderers, as there is for thieves. Yet they steal the best of possessions, friendship, so that violence, damaging though it is, is more honest than calumny, because it is not underhand (Plutarch, *On Calumniating* fr. 156, Plutarch, *Moralia* XV).

64

It is not known when these statements were made but, bearing in mind his social contract theory, they seem to be the sort of sentiments that Hippias would express.

For only a short time in the period under consideration here was slander illegal – playwrights in particular were able to malign and vilify people. Politicians were fair game and the playwrights made great sport of figures such as Pericles, Aspasia, Anaxagoras, Damon and Socrates, to name just a few, in order to get laughs at the theatre. When a decree was passed prohibiting certain comic speech in the theatre, it was short-lived. It held in law for only two years, 440-439 BC (Gagarin 2005, 362-4). It is feasible that Hippias was aware of the damaging effects on Socrates of Aristophanes' *Clouds*, and this ties in well with his views on slander.

Apart from his military service, Socrates never left Athens, the city-state in which he was born. He therefore lacked the opportunities to observe at first hand the way of life, customs and traditions of societies in other states and countries. Hippias was ahead of Socrates in these experiences. He had travelled widely and this opened up many opportunities for him to observe different societies, their customs and the manner in which they dispensed justice. Hippias lectured in Athens, Sicily and Sparta, and was a regular visitor at Olympia where he had never been defeated in the intellectual contests held there (Plato, *Hippias Minor* 364). In all those places, and especially during times of festivals such as the Olympic Games, he attracted eager audiences to hear him deliver his talks. Through his travels and his accomplishments, he became well known and popular. One may accept that he wrote a great deal. If success is equated only with high earnings, Hippias was a successful man. Plato has him boast of his fortune to Socrates, when he claimed to have made 'more money than any other two sophists together'. Even in the small Sicilian town of Inycus, and despite the fact that Protagoras was also in Sicily, he attracted an audience and made twenty minas, which was, apparently, a handsome sum (Plato, *Hippias Major* 282d-e). He frequently visited Lacedaemonia [Sparta] (*Hippias Major* 286a-b) but never received payment from the Lacedaemonians because it was unlawful for them to pay for foreign education or to instigate changes from the Spartan way of life (283c-284c). Hippias told Socrates that the Spartans were not interested in astronomy or geometry. They were not interested in the processes of thought, nor in 'those matters which [Hippias] of all men [knew] best how to discuss, concerning the value of letters and syllables and rhythms and harmonies' (285d). They liked to hear about antiquity, about the genealogies of heroes, and the early history of cities. That is the reason, Hippias explained, why he learnt those things by heart and practised his presentations (285d). One of his visits to Athens provides Plato with the material for *Hippias Major*, which is, in part, an attempt to define 'the Beautiful'. There are just the two characters, Socrates and Hippias. Socrates greets Hippias, commenting on his long absence from Athens. Hippias explains that he was too busy, being frequently engaged by the state of Elis as an envoy, or ambassador, most frequently to Lacedaemonia (286a-b). As the dialogue continues, Hippias reveals that, only recently, he had been highly praised for a presentation which explained the noble pursuits a young man should follow:

> 'I recount how, when Troy has been captured, Neoptolemus asks Nestor what type of noble pursuits could give the one who practises them a fine reputation, even if he is young. And, in response, Nestor laid out for him a whole collection of very noble customs' (268b).

This *epideixis* or public lecture, which is known as the 'Trojan Discourse', was already prepared, having previously been presented at Sparta. Hippias was to deliver a similar *epideixis* again in Athens, where he was visiting at the invitation of a certain Eudicus, the son of Apemantus. We are fortunate in having some material that describes the content of Hippias' teachings and, although we do not know the exact content of the lecture, we may accept that it related to virtue, and was not sophistry.

Hippias continues: 'I say that Homer made Achilles the best man of those who went to Troy, Nestor the wisest, and Odysseus the wiliest' (*Hippias Minor* 364c). Coming from Hippias, this is intriguing, and we may allow ourselves a slight digression. The revered Nestor was the king of Pylos, a region which bordered Elis. Odysseus was the son of Laertes, the king of Ithaca, and husband of Penelope. Ithaca is less than a hundred kilometres north-west of Elis. Achilles was the son of the goddess Thetis, but he was a man, real or imaginary, not a god. His name may have a connection with the river Achelous, which is in mainland Greece, east of Ithaca. One may believe that Hippias would have sought out the stories of Nestor in neighbouring Pylos, and of Odysseus and Achilles in near-by areas. They would have been very real people in his lectures. Hippias surely knew much more than we now do about these characters, and one may envisage lively lectures in which the virtues, vices, strengths and weaknesses of Nestor, Achilles and Odysseus provided examples of the noble pursuits which featured in Hippias' discourses.

Hippias delivers the 'Trojan Discourse', a 'fine display' (*Hippias Minor* 363a), and on the following day the events which are depicted in *Hippias Minor* occur. The 'great crowd' has departed, leaving only Socrates, Eudicus and Hippias. Again the debate revolves around Homer and we see the ironic Socrates feigning ignorance of matters with which he would have been quite familiar, trying to make Hippias appear a bragging know-all sophist.

Socrates then begins to question Hippias about Homer. A discussion ensues about Achilles, the bravest; Nestor, the wisest; and Odysseus, the wiliest. The debate continues and Socrates describes the apparel Hippias claims to have worn on one of his visits to Olympia. These are the lines with which this chapter opened, and they continue:

5. Hippias

'And in addition you said that you brought with you poems, both epics and tragedies and dithyrambs, and many writings of all sorts composed in prose; and that you were there excelling all others in knowledge of the arts of which I was speaking just now, and of the correctness of rhythms and harmonies and letters, and many other things besides, as I seem to remember; and yet I forgot your art of memory, as it seems, in which you think you are most brilliant; and I fancy I have forgotten a great many other things' (*Hippias Minor* 368b-d).

Through the techniques employed in his dialogues, Plato provided significant information about Hippias – we learn of Hippias' many skills, extensive knowledge, varied interests and abilities. Plato praised Hippias to a far greater degree than is at first apparent. We learn that Hippias travelled widely; that he was frequently engaged by Elis to act as an envoy, a role that kept him rather busy; his extraordinary memory, which he seems to have developed through a system of mnemonics; his wealth, in contrast to Socrates who claimed that he had never made money from his teaching; his successful performances in the intellectual contests at the Olympic Games; his knowledge of astronomy and literature. Very important is his familiarity with Homer – he taught the 'noble and beautiful pursuits' that a young man should follow, using as examples the qualities of Homer's heroes, Achilles, Nestor and Odysseus. Hippias knew what ought to be taught – he could identify the 'very many lawful and beautiful pursuits' which, if acquired by a young man, would enable him to become most famous (*Hippias Major* 286a-b). Hippias regarded discussions such as he and Socrates had just been engaged in as 'petty arguments', 'mere words' which could make one appear to be a 'fool' (*Hippias Major* 304b).

We can now look at other sources which add to our understanding of Hippias. Apart from Plato, two other ancient writers refer to Hippias' outstanding memory. Philostratus (born *c*. AD 170) recorded that 'Hippias of Elis, the sophist, had such extraordinary powers of memory, even in his old age, that after hearing fifty names only once, he could repeat them from memory in the order in which he had heard them' (Philostratus, *Lives of the Sophists* I.11.1). Plato may have been the source for Philostratus, but Philostratus gives a little more information about Hippias' enviable skill, so there may have been a source common to them both. Xenophon informs us that Hippias taught Callias 'the art of memorising' (Xenophon, *Banquet* IV.62). (We met the rich Callias earlier, in Plato's *Protagoras*.)

The Messenians of Sicily regarded Hippias so highly that they commissioned him to write elegies to commemorate the choirboys who drowned on a voyage to Rhegium (Pausanias, *Elis* I.XXV.4). The verses were inscribed on bronze statues which were erected at Olympia. The name of the commissioned artist is recorded as Callon of Elis (*c*. 494-436 BC).

Plutarch wrote: 'It is difficult to fix chronology accurately, especially when it is derived from the *List of Olympic Victors*, which Hippias of Elis is said to have published late, lacking any reliable starting point for his work' (Plutarch, *Numa* I.4). But living close to Olympia, being a frequent attendee at the games and a zealous researcher of facts and dates, would have afforded Hippias an advantage. The list of victors has proved to be of inestimable value in establishing the chronology of Greek history. Hippias was the first that we know recorded facts in this way: he was the originator of this sort of history. Other works by Hippias included a *Synagoge*, or *Collection*. Clement of Alexandria quotes the lines which may have been part of the introduction to this *Collection*:

> Some of these things may perhaps have been said by Orpheus, some briefly here and there by Musaeus, some by Hesiod, some by Homer, some by others among the poets, some in prose writings by Greeks or by barbarians. But I will put together the most important and inter-related passages from all these sources, and will thus make this present piece both new and varied in kind (cited in Kerferd 1981, 48).

This valuable passage is rich with promise, and though it warrants closer analysis than space allows here, some comments on it can be made. In 1944 the incalculable importance of the passage was recognised by Bruno Snell in a paper, written in German, which translates as 'The News about Thales and the Beginnings of the Greek History of Philosophy and Literature'. Kerferd writes of Snell's 'remarkable article' and states that 'He [Snell] went on to demonstrate with as near an approach to certainty, I would say, as is possible in questions of this kind, that Hippias was the source that had connected the doctrine of Thales' with the passage of Clement of Alexandria, cited just above' (Kerferd 1981, 48-9).

Hippias' *Collection* must have been wide in scope and content because it was to include Greek sources, and also historical material from barbarian sources. This may be a reference to Hippias' ideal of the commonality of all races, their common humanity. It seems certain that Hippias' *Collection* was the source for Plato's and Aristotle's writings on Thales and other philosophers. Diogenes Laertius (*Lives of Eminent Philosophers* I.24) recorded that 'Aristotle and Hippias of Elis affirm that, arguing from the magnet and from amber, [Thales] attributed a soul or even life to inanimate objects.'

The fragments of the *Collection* record interesting scraps of information, such as that about Thargelia of Miletus who lived at the time of Darius (probably Darius I of Persia, 521-486 BC). Athenaeus preserved the details from Hippias. Thargelia 'had been married fourteen times, and ... was very beautiful in looks as well as clever' (Athenaeus XIII.608). It seems that she attracted influential men and, through her talents, was able to influence her husbands with her pro-Persian ideas. That is political gossip, but no doubt the Greeks were as intrigued by gossip as anyone else. Hippias' book was surely an important work. Again, we see that he instigated the study of history through researching and recording it.

5. Hippias

'Hippias the sophist says that Lycurgus himself was very well versed in war and took part in many campaigns' (Plutarch, *Lycurgus* XXIII.1). Hippias wrote *A Nomenclature of Tribes* (Sprague 1972, 100) and, as part of his studies of geography, devised the names of Asia and Europe from Asia and Europa, daughters of Oceanus. Like Pherecydes, Hippias said that the Hyades are seven in number (Sprague 1972, 103). Hippias, and Ephorus, believed that Homer came from Cumae (Sprague 1972, 103).

Other authors have written about Hippias, but so little remains of these fragments that they fail to divulge any further information of value (see Sprague 1972). It seems that they are mere shreds, probably taken from larger works. They do tell us that Hippias of Elis was worthy of discussion, and they testify to his versatility and wide range of interests. Hippias recorded theories held by ancient philosophers. A remarkable detail about his research is that he did it without the advantage of a school such as Aristotle had at the Lyceum, where he could assign research to his students. And there were no established libraries. Jonathan Barnes (1982, 6) has referred to the 'jackdaw eye' of Hippias; like a jackdaw or a magpie, Hippias was a collector. He recognised worthwhile details and useful information, or perhaps just items of interest, and put them in his collection. It is fair to state that he deliberately sought the information that interested him (and that seems to have been almost everything), and incorporated the facts into his lectures. It is certain that he researched topics for presentation and had lectures available to be presented on request. Hippias had many abilities that identified him as different and set him apart. He ranks among the most talented and versatile of the sophists. He was wise and expert in many skills and in crafts, music, sculpture and other techniques.

Plato treats Hippias as though he was a stupid man. Clearly, Plato despised much that Hippias represented. Plato depicted Hippias as boisterous, boastful, overconfident and puerile, unable to consider and debate, even oblivious to *the beautiful* and *the just,* which were two of the fundamental issues which formed part of Socrates' mission, but this does not equate to stupidity. Hippias was the most versatile, and probably the richest of all the sophists, but to Plato his riches were the ill-gotten gains of teaching rhetoric. It was too easy to be critical of those who worked for a living: Plato had no need to charge for his teaching because he came from a wealthy family; he had 'old' money which makes for respectability, and can engender self-righteousness. But, as Grote remarks, despite Plato's mockery he never portrayed Hippias as 'preaching a low and corrupt morality' (Grote 1904, 640).

Hippias was much more than the vain and arrogant sophist depicted by Plato. He 'was the most many-sided of the sophists, a polymath or encyclopaedist' (Philostratus: translator's introduction, xxvii). Far from being stupid, Hippias was acclaimed as 'the acutest of the sophists' (Ammianus Marcellinus XVI.5.8; Sprague 1972, 100), and was 'called a "sage" by the Greeks' (Pausanias, *Elis* I.XXV.4), a verdict that is amply substantiated by the ancient evidence.

Bibliography

Athenaeus, *The Deipnosophists*, vol. VI, trans. C.B. Gulick, Loeb edition (London: Heinemann, 1937).

Aristotle, *Politics*, trans. H. Rackham, Loeb edition (London: Heinemann, 1959).

Barnes, Jonathan, *The Presocratic Philosophers* (London: Routledge and Kegan Paul, 1982).

Dillon, John and Gergel, Tania, *The Greek Sophists* (London: Penguin, 2003).

Gagarin, Michael and Cohen, David (eds), *The Cambridge Companion to Ancient Greek Law* (Cambridge: Cambridge University Press, 2005).

Gow, James, *A Short History of Greek Mathematics* (New York: Chelsea Publishing Company, 1968).

Grote, George, *A History of Greece*, vol. VII (London: John Murray, 1904).

Guthrie, W.K.C., *A History of Classical Philosophy*, vol. III: *The Fifth Century Enlightenment* (Cambridge: Cambridge University Press, 1969).

Guthrie, W.K.C., *A History of Classical Philosophy*, vol. IV: *Plato: The Man and his Dialogues: Earlier Period* (Cambridge: Cambridge University Press, 1975).

Havelock. Eric A. (1957), *The Liberal Temper in Greek Politics* (London: Jonathan Cape, 1957).

Heath, Sir Thomas, *A History of Greek Mathematics*, vols I and II, *From Aristarchus to Diophantus* (Oxford: Clarendon Press, 1921).

Heath, Sir Thomas, *The Thirteen Books of Euclid's Elements*, translated from the text of Heiberg, with introduction and commentary, vol. III (New York: Dover Publications, 1956).

Kerferd, G.B., *The Sophistic Movement* (Cambridge: Cambridge University Press, 1981).

Pausanias, *Description of Greece*, vol. II, book 5, translated by W.H.S. Jones and H.A. Ormerod, Loeb edition (London: Heinemann, 1960).

Pfeiffer, Rudolf, *History of Classical Scholarship* (Oxford: Clarendon Press, 1968).

Philostratus, *Philostratus and Eunapius, Lives of the Sophists*, trans. W.C. Wright, Loeb edition (London: Heinemann, 1922).

Plato, *Apology*, trans. H.N. Fowler, Loeb edition (London: Heinemann, 1961).

Plato, *Greater Hippias, Lesser Hippias*, trans. H.N. Fowler, Loeb edition (London: Heinemann, 1963).

Plato, *Protagoras*, trans. W.R.M. lamb, Loeb edition (London: Heinemann, 1962).

Plutarch, *Lives: Lycurgus and Numa*, trans. B. Perrin, Loeb edition (London: Heinemann, 1914).

Plutarch, *Moralia*, vol. XV, trans. F.H. Sandbach, Loeb edition (London: Heinemann, 1969).

Proclus, *A Commentary on the First Book of Euclid's Elements*, trans. with introduction and notes by Glenn R. Morrow (Princeton: Princeton University Press, 1970).

Snell, Bruno, 'Die Nachrichten über die Lehren des Thales und die Anfänge der griechischen Philosophie- und Literaturgeschichte', *Philologus* 96 (1944), 170-82.

Thucydides, *History of the Peloponnesian War*, trans. Rex Warner with introduction and notes by M.I. Finlay (Harmondsworth: Penguin, 1954).

Waerden, B.L. van der (1971), *Science Awakening*, trans. Arnold Dresden (Oxford: Oxford University Press, 1971).

Weisstein 1999: http://mathworld.wolfram.com/AngleTrisection.html

Xah Lee 2000: http://xahlee.org/SpecialPlaneCurves_dir/specialPlaneCurves.html

Xenophon, *Memorabilia*, trans. O.J. Todd, Loeb edition (Cambridge, MA: Harvard University Press, 1997).

6

Prodicus

Craig Cooper

Prodicus came from Iulis on the small island of Ceos situated in the Cylades. Like Gorgias, he made his first impression on the Athenians through diplomatic efforts on behalf of his native community. Both Plato and Philostratus indicate that on one particular occasion Prodicus created quite a stir in the Athenian Council. In Plato's *Hippias Major* (282c; Sprague 1972, 72)[1] Socrates indicates that this was not Prodicus' first visit and that he had often frequented Athens on public business. But it was on his most recent visit that he gained notoriety by addressing the Council and giving private displays (*epideixeis*). This must be the occasion that Philostratus (*Lives of the Sophists* I.12; Sprague 1972, 72) has in mind when he states that 'on an embassy to Athens he appeared before the council and showed himself an extremely capable man, though a bit hard to hear because of his low-pitched voice'. Philostratus' information should, however, be regarded as wholly derivative, conflating two separate accounts by Plato: the one from *Hippias Major* and the other in *Protagoras* (315c-d; Sprague 1972, 72), where Socrates comically describes the sight of Prodicus in Callias' house, still lying in bed, wrapped in heavy blankets, surrounded by students. Again, his words were inaudible because of his deep voice. These two Platonic sources are key to dating Prodicus' birth and period of diplomatic activity.

If we accept Socrates' comments in *Hippias Major* (282c) that Prodicus had frequently come to Athens on public business, we can well imagine that the years leading up and into the early part of the Peloponnesian War demanded Prodicus' services on more than one occasion, but the occasion of his most recent visit, which left such a vivid impression on the Council, possibly falls within the period of the Peace of Nicias (421-414 BC).[2] The *Suda* (Sprague 1972, 71) represents Prodicus as a contemporary of Democritus and Gorgias; this, as Guthrie notes, could place his date of birth anywhere between 490 and 460 (Guthrie 1971, 274). A date of 490 for his birth would mean that he was in his seventies during the 420s. But evidence from Plato suggests a date of birth closer to 460. *Protagoras* represents Prodicus as much younger than the dialogue's namesake. This may partly explain why the *Suda* makes Protagoras his teacher, though I suspect it has more to do with the fact that the two sophists shared similar interests in language and rhetoric. At one point in the dialogue Protagoras declares that he has been at his craft (*technê*) for many years and is old enough to be the father of Socrates, Prodicus or Hippias (317bc). The dramatic date of *Protagoras* is sometime before the outbreak of the Peloponnesian War (431 BC), since Pericles and his sons, who died of the plague in 429, are spoken of as still alive (319e; Kerferd 1981, 19). Morrison (1941, 2-3) argues for a date of 433. If we place Protagoras in his mid-fifties (born around 490), that should mean that Prodicus was in his mid-twenties to early thirties, giving a birth date somewhere between 465 and 460 and making him at best a few years younger than Socrates, who was born in 469. At the very earliest, then, his first diplomatic efforts on behalf of his native Iulis date to the years immediately preceding the war, which would mean that already by the late 430s, at a relatively young age, Prodicus had made something of a name for himself to attract the kind of admirers depicted in the *Protagoras*. The scene presents him surrounded by some prominent Athenians. Other sources mention among his students, Callias (Xenophon, *Symposium* IV.62; Sprague 1972, 73), Theramanes (Athenaeus V.220b; scholium on Aristophanes' *Clouds* 361; Sprague 1972, 74-5) and even Euripides (Aulus Gellius, *Attic Nights* XV.20.4; Sprague 1972, 74). We can well imagine then that his diplomatic activities in the years leading up to the outbreak of the war aroused such interest in the Cean sophist that it led to a subsequent invitation to Callias' house and to a growing number of students.

More than once Plato has Socrates speak admiringly of Prodicus and his teaching, commenting about his wisdom (*Protagoras* 341a), addressing him as *sophos*, 'wise' (*Theaetetus* 151b) or *passophos*, 'all wise' (*Protagoras* 316a), indicating that they were on intimate terms (*Hippias Major* 282c), and even going so far as to suggest that he was for a time Prodicus' student (*Meno* 96d). In *Charmides* (163d) Socrates claims to have heard Prodicus on countless occasions speak on the distinctions in the meanings of words. For some, like Guthrie, such comments suggest genuine admiration (Guthrie 1971, 22); for others they are tinged with irony (Willink 1983, 26; cf. Dover 1968, lv). However we take them, they do suggest an almost unrivalled reputation for wisdom that ranked Prodicus among the sophistic triumvirate of Protagoras, Hippias and Prodicus mentioned in the *Apology* (19c); it is this same trio that greets Socrates when he enters Callias' house in the *Protagoras*. The notoriety of Prodicus' wisdom is confirmed by Aristophanes: he is described by a character in *Tagenistai* as one of those chatterers who can corrupt his listener (fr. 506 Kassel and Austin 1984). In *Clouds* (360-2) the chorus inform Strepsiades that they will listen to 'none of the present day astrological sophists (*meteorosophistes*) except Prodicus for reasons of his wisdom and thought'. The rhetorical displays that attracted so much attention of the Athenians were no doubt meant to showcase that wisdom, the so-called 'fifty drachma display' that Socrates mentions (Plato, *Cratylus* 384b; Sprague 1972, 75) could teach one 'the truth about the correctness of words'. Unfortunately for Socrates, he could afford only 'the drachma one', a small sample of which is parodied in *Protagoras* (337a-c; Sprague 1972, 75-6), where we find it greeted with approval by many in the audience. But outside this small circle of the wealthy elite, who obviously admired Prodicus, the general public viewed him with deep suspicion. As Willink (1983, 26-7) notes, the satirical presentation of Socrates in *Clouds*, as a fee-grubbing philological quibbler who holds heretical views of the cosmos, is modelled after the popular view of Prodicus.

Like Protagoras, Prodicus taught and advertised by delivering epideictic speeches, public displays that were meant to showcase his wisdom rhetorically. These displays were delivered by Prodicus in public settings such as the Lyceum (pseudo-Plato, *Eryxias* 397d; Sprague 1972, 84) and in private settings such as Callias' house; we hear of Prodicus charging half a drachma, two drachmas and four drachmas for admission to hear such displays (pseudo-Plato, *Axiochus* 366c; Sprague 1972, 85). A small sample of a display on the correctness of the meanings of words is, as we just noted, parodied by Plato in *Protagoras*.

A better and longer example on the question of the ethical value of education is found paraphrased by Socrates in Xenophon (*Memorabilia* II.1.21-34: Sprague 1972, 79-80).[3] There, we are told that this composition on Heracles was recited to large audiences, and Socrates concludes his rendition of it by saying that 'in some such way as this, Prodicus related the education of Heracles by Virtue but he adorned his thoughts with turns of phrases still more magnificent than I used now'. The speech was obviously of some renown, delivered before a series of audiences, ready and willing to pay admission, perhaps used by Prodicus as a way to attract students to take his more in-depth fifty-drachma sessions. The notoriety of this particular display piece can be gauged from the fact that it was parodied by Aristophanes in *Clouds* (889-1114), which was first performed in 423 BC. The *Contest* of the play, in which Right and Wrong *Logos* advocate to Pheidippides a different choice of education – the former physical exercise that will lead to modesty and moderation, and the latter to a life of indulgent pleasures without any exertion – picks up the language and themes of Prodicus' display (Bowie 1993, 109-10).

Though Xenophon's paraphrase captures some sense of the content of the Prodicean original (Untersteiner 1954, 207), it does not, on Socrates' admission, fully capture its rhetorical eloquence, nor, I suspect, the full rhetorical structure of the original. The speech tells of how Heracles when faced with the decision of what road to choose as he entered manhood, the one of virtue or of vice, retired in seclusion to ponder his choice. There he was confronted by two women, Virtue and Vice; the former is modestly dressed with a modest comportment, the latter is decked out in makeup and plays the role of seductress. Each argues her position in turn, with Vice advocating the road that leads readily and easily to pleasure, and Virtue a road that involves hardship. As Guthrie (1971, 277) notes, the *epideixis* is 'the sort of thing that one would expect a sophist to compose for recital before a popular audience, conveying elementary moral commonplaces through the easily absorbed medium of a fable'. But that is the beauty of it; as Kuntz (1994, 163-81) has shown, Prodicus has taken the familiar heroic figure of Heracles, exploited the status of his myth (his labours), much as Gorgias does the myth of Helen in his *Encomium to Helen*, and reshaped his story, producing an allegory that also derives some of its rhetorical force by exploiting earlier poetical allegories on divergent paths as we find in Hesiod (*Works and Days* 286-92) and Simonides.[4] Both women in their opening speeches and again in Vice's rebuttal continue the metaphor of life's road with which the story begins (Kuntz 1994, 171).

Xenophon's paraphrase suggests that in its original form 'the composition on Heracles' was a highly antithetical display along the lines of the *antilogiai* of Protagoras that allowed the student sufficient ability to argue both sides on any matter (Plato, *Sophist* 232e). In Xenophon's composition on Heracles, each woman presents a contrasting image in appearance, nature, body, expression, bearing and dress, and this contrast continues into the speeches. Commencing with Vice, each argues her case in turn, following up her initial speech with a secondary speech as one would typically find in a private suit from the Athenian court. In her second speech (*Memorabilia* II.1.29) Vice even summarises the positions each women has advocated so far, echoing language from the first set of speeches, but before she can expand further, she is interrupted by Virtue, who gives a lengthy speech in which she first attacks the lifestyle of Vice before extolling her own. Presumably in the Prodicean original Vice also had a longer second speech in which she attacked the life of Virtue and praised her own to correspond to Virtue's rebuttal. In the first pair of speeches the antithesis is more complete and reflected in the language. To create a sense of the ongoing exploration of pleasure that awaits Heracles should he choose her, Vice uses a series of indirect questions expressed with a participle, followed by a pledge. She promises:

> First of all you will have no concern for wars or trouble but will constantly be considering what food or drink you might find satisfying, or seeing and hearing what, you might be cheered, or tasting or touching what, you might be pleasured, and mingling with what boys you especially might be delighted and how most comfortably you might sleep, and how with the least amount of toil you might obtain all these objects (*Memorabilia* II.1.24).

By contrast, Virtue notes that nothing really good or honourable is granted to mortals by the gods without toil and practice. And to reinforce rhetorically the toil involved in acquiring these good gifts, a series of conditional sentences follow in which the protasis (the 'if' clause) expresses Heracles' desire and the apodosis (the consequence) contains a verbal construction that expresses the necessary action that he must pursue to achieve that desire:

But if you want the gods to be gracious to you, you must worship the gods; if you wish to be loved by your friends, you must be kind to your friends; if you desire to be honoured by a city, you must help the city; if you expect to be admired for virtue by all of Greece, you must attempt to benefit Greece; if you want the ground to bear crops abundantly for you, you must cultivate the land; if you want to make money from your cattle, you must tend to your cattle; if you are eager to enhance yourself through war and want to be able to free your friends and subdue your enemies, you must learn the very arts of war from experts and practise how you should put them to use. And if you want to be able in body, you must accustom your body to submit to reason and must exercise it with toil and sweat (*Memorabilia* II.1.28-9).

Whether any of the rhetoric here can be traced back to Prodicus is uncertain. Socrates himself admits that his paraphrase falls far short of Prodicus' rhetorical eloquence. As Untersteiner (1954, 207) notes, the style does not seem to be Prodicus' own but contains echoes of Gorgias' figures of speech. At the very least it gives us a hint of the rhetorical skill of the sophists.

In the scholium on Aristophanes' *Clouds* (361; Sprague 1972, 78), we read that 'The composition on Heracles' formed part of a larger work entitled *Horai*, *The Hours*, which seems to have included encomia of 'the virtues of Heracles and others' (Plato, *Symposium* 177b; Kerferd 1981, 46). Prodicus is also known to have composed a work entitled *On the Nature of Man* in which he discussed the character of phlegm; according to Galen (*On the Physical Faculties* II.9; Sprague 1972, 82), Prodicus named that part of the humours phlegm which has been burned or, as it were, over-cooked, deriving its meaning from the verb 'to burn'; though he used different terminology, he described its substance in the same manner as others. The white coloured substance which all others call phlegm, but which Prodicus labelled *blenna*, is the cold and damp humour found most in the elderly and those who have suffered frostbite. Apparently Prodicus' penchant for fine distinctions in the meanings of terms, for which he was famous in antiquity and parodied on more than one occasion by Plato, was less a matter of simple semantics; it had philosophical bearing on his investigation into the nature of things. Elsewhere Galen (*On the Elements* I.9; Sprague 1972, 2) includes Prodicus, along with Parmenides, Empedocles, Alcmaeon and Gorgias, among those who wrote on nature.[5] On the basis of this comment Untersteiner (1954, 206-7; cf. 212) conjectures that Prodicus wrote a work *On Nature* which he argues was not an independent treatise of its own but formed part of his larger work, *The Hours*. He further suggests that *On Nature* was itself divided into two parts, one of which dealt with *The Nature of Man*. Presumably the other part discussed the nature of all other things. It is possible, as both Untersteiner (1954, 209-27) and Nestle (1976, 425-51) argue, that *The Hours* was a comprehensive work that contained all of Prodicus' teaching on cosmology, the origin of religion, on the nature of things and man, including a discussion of the origin of language, an explication of his doctrine of near synonyms and his teaching on ethics as exemplified by the figure of Heracles. Galen confirms both the doxographical tradition preserved in the *Suda* (Sprague 1972, 71) and what is implied by Aristophanes, who connects Prodicus with Anaxagoras and other astrological sophists, that Prodicus was a natural philosopher and less concerned with rhetoric. His theory of language and his demand for precision in the meaning of terms seems more philosophically than rhetorically oriented.

Only four fragments possibly connect Prodicus with the study of rhetoric. In the first (prolegomena *In Hermogenem* W, VII 9; Radermacher 1951, B VIII 2), Prodicus and Hippias are alleged to have put forward the proposition that rhetoric was 'the strength of words concerning what seems persuasive'. If indeed he had defined rhetoric, we might suppose he taught it or at least illustrated it through arguments in his display speeches. Perhaps closely related to this is a new papyrus fragment first published in 1966:[6]

> A paradoxical judgment derives from Prodicus that 'it is not possible to contradict'. How can he say this? It is contrary to the thought and opinion of all. For all argue, contradict both in their daily lives and in their thoughts. He speaks dogmatically that 'it is not possible to contradict'. For if they contradict, they both speak; and it is impossible for both to speak to the same thing. For he says that only the one who is truthful and is declaring the matters as they stand speaks on it. But the one who opposes him does not speak of the thing ....

This fragment at once reminds us of Protagoras whom Diogenes Laertius (IX.53) notes on the authority of the *Euthydemus* was the first to discuss Antisthenes' argument that it is not possible to contradict and the first to introduce methods of attacking any position (*theses*).[7] Protagoras is also said to have been the first to 'maintain that there were two arguments (*logoi*) on any matter by which he developed arguments by a series of stages' (Diogenes Laertius IX.51, my translation; Sprague 1972, 4). Diogenes next quotes Protagoras' famous dictum, 'man is the measure of all things', which we are told opened one of Protagoras' works. From the *Theaetetus* (161c) we learn that it came at the beginning of his work *On Truth*. This dictum appears to have guided his approach to argumentation and his emphasis on the correct usage of language (such as mood and gender) which he saw as important for effective speeches (Classen 1976, 218-30). As Diogenes (IX.52) notes, Protagoras was the first to distinguish tenses, to set down the importance of *kairos* (the opportune moment of speaking), to create contests of *logoi* and to teach rival pleaders sophistic arguments (*sophismata*). Thus we see Protagoras' philosophical position is closely tied to his approach to rhetoric. According to the papyrus fragment Prodicus held very much the same philosophical position about contradiction as Protagoras, but I am not convinced that it was as closely tied to the study of rhetoric as it was for Protagoras, much as Prodicus' study of language seems less connected to questions of rhetoric than it was for Protagoras.

In the third fragment (Sprague 1972, 75), found in Quintilian (III.1.12), we learn that Protagoras and Gorgias were the first to deal with common-places (*communes locos*),[8] and Prodicus, Hippias, Protagoras and Thrasymachus with questions of emotion. Commonplaces were developed to provide speakers with ready made forms of arguments for their forensic and political speeches. In particular, Gorgias' commonplaces consisted of praise and belittlement, as he believed it was the function of oratory to magnify a thing with admiration and deride it with censure (Cicero, *Brutus* 46). Thrasymachus taught through model speeches how to arouse emotions such as pity and anger (Plato, *Phaedrus* 267c; Sprague 1972, 92), and Prodicus may have done something of the same in his display speeches. In the final text (*Phaedrus* 267b; Sprague 1972, 78), in response to Socrates' comments that both Tisias and Gorgias valued probabilities over truths, could make small things appear great and great things small through the power of speech, and had discovered conciseness in arguments and boundlessly lengthy treatments about all matters, Prodicus is said to have laughed that he alone had discovered what speeches are required by the art, neither long ones nor short ones but ones of proper length. This should suggest that Prodicus, like the other sophists, was interested in techniques of rhetorical argument, but whether he taught rhetoric is a different matter and it is possible that Prodicus was speaking here of his method of teaching (Kerferd 1981, 32-3). At best we can say that if Prodicus did teach rhetoric it was along the lines of Protagoras and Gorgias through *antilogiai* and model speeches that provided their listening audience with methods of argumentation that could be learned by heart (Guthrie 1971, 270; Cooper 2004, 146-7). Perhaps we should agree with the assessment of a later lexicographical tradition preserved in the scholia of Aristophanes (*Birds* 692; Sprague 1972, 75) that Callimachus (*c.* 305-*c.* 240 BC) was incorrect to catalogue Prodicus among the rhetoricians, when clearly compared with them he was a philosopher.

The two areas of Prodicus' teaching of which we have some knowledge involve his cosmology and doctrine of near synonyms, and it is on these two topics that we conclude our discussion of him. Prodicus follows Empedocles in postulating that all life originates with the four elements. According to Epiphanius, the fourth-century AD bishop of Cyprus who wrote a work addressing Christian heresy (*Against Heresy* III.21), Prodicus called 'the four elements gods, then the sun and moon. From these he stated life within all things arose'.[9] From these same primordial elements would have originated primitive man, who, if we can believe Aristophanes (*Birds* 685-7), enjoyed a precarious and nebulous existence, living a 'dim life by nature, like the race of leaves, feeble, moulded from clay, fleeting shadowy tribes, wingless creatures lasting a day, wretched mortals, dreamlike men'. As scholars have noted, Aristophanes' depiction of the origin (moulded from mud, a mixture of the elements) and the primitive state of man derives from Prodicus, as the chorus leader (at 691-2) offers a new theory about the 'nature of birds, origin of the gods, rivers, Erebus and Chaos' to replace the cosmology of Prodicus (Benn 1909, 411-12; cf. Untersteiner 1954, 221n.3; Nestle 1976, 440; Kerferd 1981, 40). Aristophanes' parody makes sense and has comic force only if it plays off Prodicus' own cosmology, elements of which must have been familiar to the Athenian audience (Benn 1909, 411). According to this 'new' cosmology, in the beginning were Chaos, Night, black Erebus and broad Tartarus; as yet there was no earth, air or heaven, and in the boundless recesses of Erebus black-winged Night brought forth a wind-egg from which sprang Eros, who then, mingling with winged Chaos in broad Tartarus, produced the race of birds. There was no race of gods until Eros mingled all things together, and as one thing mingled with another Heaven came into being, the Ocean, the earth and the race of blessed immortal gods (*Birds* 693-703). There is an obvious allusion to the cosmology of Empedocles for whom Love was one of two forces (Strife the other) involved in generation and destruction (Tarrant 1923, 113; Sommerstein 1987, 242). It is quite possible, as scholars suggest, that Prodicus popularised Empedocles' cosmology in his own teaching, some of which Aristophanes has picked up and parodied here (Benn 1909, 413; cf. Nestle 1976, 440). As Epiphanius suggests, Prodicus was indebted to Empedocles for the notion of the divine nature of the four elements.

The surviving fragments suggest that Prodicus described the development of things through evolutionary stages: first the four elements and then the sun and moon. This chronological progression through stages of evolution is also suggested in those fragments that recall his conception of the development of human religion. The first stage sees men call natural phenomena (e.g. the sun, moon), things of nature (e.g. rivers and springs) and anything else that sustains life and is regarded as useful, gods (Sextus Empiricus, *Against the Schoolmasters* IX.18; Sprague 1972, 83-4). The next stage has man granting divine status and honour to persons who first invented shelters and discovered new crops and other useful arts. According to Philodemus (*On Piety*, col. 9.17; Sprague 1972, 83), who quotes the authority of the stoic philosopher Persaeus, Prodicus wrote that the forces that provided food and help were first acknowledged and honoured as gods, and next those who discovered shelters, means of obtaining food or related arts were given names such as Demeter, Dionysus and the like. It is probably at this stage that Prodicus postulated the development of religious rites, sacrifices and mysteries, all of which he claimed derived from agricultural practices (Themistius, *Orations* 30; Sprague 1972, 84). As Themistius rightly notes, it was Prodicus' opinion that the very concept of gods and then the development of their worship both came from agriculture. Prodicus' rejection of traditional belief left him open to charges of atheism by contemporaries such as Aristophanes and by later writers (Sextus Empiricus, *Against the Schoolmasters* IX.51; Cicero, *On the Nature of the Gods* I.37.118; Sprague 1972, 83).

Prodicus' insistence on precision in the language is well known from antiquity (Sprague 1972, 75-8). Within the context of a discussion on the distinction between 'learning' and 'understanding', Prodicus is reported to have said 'first one must learn about correctness of words' (Plato, *Euthydemus* 277e; Sprague 1972, 77). Elsewhere, Socrates remarks that Prodicus' 'fifty drachma display' would teach 'the truth about the correctness of words' (Plato, *Cratylus* 384b; Sprague 1972, 75). The expression 'correctness of words' at once reminds us of Protagoras' 'correctness of diction' (*orthoepeia*), and indeed one late source (Themistius, *Orations* 23.289d) notes that Prodicus himself taught correctness of diction and 'the correct use of words'. Protagoras, however, was interested in correct usage of words as it related to speech composition and effective means of persuasion (Classen 1976, 219-27). Thus in the *Phaedrus* (266-267c; Sprague 1972, 16), among an enumeration of the various elements of an effective speech introduced by the sophists Theodorus, Gorgias, Hippias and others, Protagoras, we are told, emphasised correctness of diction. From the *Protagoras* (339a) we learn that Protagoras regarded as the greatest part of a man's education 'skill in words' by which he meant understanding and distinguishing what has been 'correctly' and incorrectly composed. As such, then, Protagoras was interested in the formal aspects of language that went into the composition of a speech, such as the correct use of moods and genders (Pfeiffer 1968, 37-8).

Prodicus moved from a different philosophical perspective. His insistence on 'correctness of words' may in fact have been a reaction to the scepticism of Democritus and others who maintained that words do not reflect reality (Guthrie 1971, 224-5). His research into language led to the development of new technique called *diaresis*, by which he analysed pairs of near synonyms to distinguish the differences in terms of accident between a pair of words and so apprehend the correct meaning of each word. In *Protagoras* (340a-b) Prodicus is called upon by Socrates to use his 'artistry' (*mouiskê*), which enabled him to distinguish 'wish' from 'desire', to discern the difference between 'becoming' and 'being'. Classen argues that Prodicus never defined words individually but only in pairs, nor it seems did he differentiate the meaning of a word into a subset of meanings, as we find attributed to him by Aristotle (*Topics* 2.6, 112b22; Sprague 1972, 78), where he is said to have subdivided 'pleasure' into 'joy', 'delight' and 'enjoyment' (Classen 1976, 233-5; cf. Taylor 1976, 138-9; Guthrie 1971, 222n.3). The best preserved example of his technique of *diaresis* is found in the *Protagoras* (337a-c). Here Prodicus analyses four pairs of near synonyms: 'impartial' and 'undiscriminating'; 'to debate' and 'to wrangle'; 'to esteem' and 'to praise'; 'to derive enjoyment' and 'to derive pleasure'.[10]

In the first three pairs Prodicus relies on common usage to distinguish the meanings of the pairs. To accord each speaker an 'equal' hearing, though it can convey the sense of listening 'jointly', that is 'impartially', by extension it means 'undiscriminating'. 'To debate' does not necessarily imply hostility between the two parties but 'to wrangle' always does. 'Praise' can often be insincere but 'esteem' that comes from a good reputation never is. In the final pair, the distinction that he makes between 'enjoyment' derived from intellectual activities, like listening and learning, and 'pleasure' derived from physical activities, like eating or some other bodily sensation, may be based on etymology, as *euphrainesthai* ('to derive enjoyment') can be connected to the noun *phronêsis* ('intelligence'; see Taylor 1976, 138 citing Adam and Adam 1909, 145). From Galen (*On the Physical Faculties* II.9; Sprague 1972, 82) we have seen already how Prodicus could resort to such etymologies to distinguish terms; Prodicus' derived the meaning of phlegm from the verb 'to burn'. The fact that he is called upon later in the *Protagoras* (339e-341c) to use his 'artistry' to distinguish 'becoming' and 'being' to clarify the meaning of one of Simonides' poems, suggests that Prodicus on occasion resorted to poetic usage in his *diaresis*.

I have tried to show something of the 'artistry' of Prodicus that won him such renown in Athens, a following of prominent students and a place among the most celebrated sophists of his day. Although his displays were rhetorical showcases that could serve as models of argumentation, and he undoubtedly explored questions of rhetoric, he seems less preoccupied with these matters than some of his contemporaries. The ancient tradition overwhelming characterises him as a natural philosopher in the tradition of Anaxagoras. His study of language, which led him to determine the precise differences of meaning between near synonyms by his method of *diaresis,* may have been aimed at answering the scepticism of his contemporaries about reality and the moral relativism that developed from such scepticism (Momigliano 1930, 129-40; cf. Guthrie 1971, 224-5). As such, then, he has an important place in the history of philosophy. It is quite possible that Prodicus had a profound influence on Socrates himself; his insistence on precisely distinguishing the meanings of near synonyms may have influenced Socrates' own approach to philosophy and his insistence on defining moral terms.

Notes

1. Unless otherwise specified, all the fragments come from the collection by Diels-Krantz, *Die Fragmente der Vorsokratiker* (Berlin 1960-1), an English translation of which is provided by Sprague 1972. All translations are my own.

2. Thucydides recorded at V.25: 'It is true that for six years and ten months they [Athens and Sparta] refrained from invading each other's territory; abroad, however, the truce was never properly in force, and each side did the other a great deal

of harm, until finally they were forced to break the treaty made after the ten years, and once more declare war openly upon each other.'

3. Smith (1903, 80) notes that Xenophon may have heard Prodicus recite his composition of Heracles at Thebes. We are told by Philostratus (*Lives of the Sophists* I.12; Sprague 1972, 72) that Xenophon, when he was a prisoner of war in Boeotia, would be granted bail to hear Prodicus lecture.

4. Just before Socrates reproduces Prodicus' speech he quotes the passage of Hesiod (Xenophon, *Memorabilia* II.1.20); the fact that Prodicus is called upon in the *Protagoras* (339e-341c) to clarify the meanings of certain words in Simonides might suggest that the sophist made recourse to this poet in his displays.

5. Cicero, *On the Orator* III.32.128 (Sprague 1972, 82), also notes that Prodicus, Thrasymachus and Protagoras lectured and wrote 'on the nature of things'.

6. Binder and Liesenborghs 1966, 37-43; repr. in Binder and Liesenborghs 1976, 452-62.

7. The argument in *Euthydemus* (283e-286d) is attributed to Protagoras by Socrates at 286c.

8. Cf. Cicero (*Brutus* 46) who on the authority of Aristotle says the same thing about Protagoras and Gorgias.

9. This fragment is not included in Sprague 1972. For a comprehensive discussion of Prodicus' cosmology see Untersteiner 1954, 209-11, which I largely follow.

10. For a full discussion of Prodicus' method, which I summarise here, see Taylor 1976, 136-40.

Bibliography

Adam, J. and Adam, A.M., *Platonis* Protagoras, 2nd edn (Cambridge: Cambridge University Press, 1905).

Benn, A.W., 'The Cosmology of Prodicus', *Mind* 18 (1909), 411-13.

Binder, G. and Liesenborghs, L. (1966), 'Ein Zuweisung der Sentenz *ouk estin antilegein* an Prodikos von Keos', *Museum Helveticum* 23 (1966), 37-43, repr. in Classen (ed.) 1976, 452-62.

Bowie, A.M., *Aristophanes: Myth, Ritual and Comedy* (Cambridge: Cambridge University Press, 1993).

Classen, C.J. (ed.), *Sophistik* (Darmstadt: Wissenschaftliche Buchgesellschaft, 1976).

Classen, C.J., 'The Study of Language among Socrates' Contemporaries', in Classen 1976, 215-47.

Cooper, C., 'Demosthenes, Actor on the Political and Forensic Stage', in C.J. Mackie (ed.), *Oral Performance and its Context* (Leiden: Brill, 2004), 145-61.

Diogenes Laertius, *Lives of Eminent Philosophers*, trans. R.D. Hicks, vol. II, Loeb edition (London: Heinemann, 1958).

Dover, K.J., *Aristophanes: Clouds* (Oxford: Oxford University Press, 1968).

Guthrie, W.K.C., *The Sophists* (Cambridge: Cambridge University Press, 1971).

Kassel, R. and Austin, C. (eds), *Poetae Comici Graeci*, vol. III.2: *Aristophanes* (Berlin: W. de Gruyter, 1984).

Kennedy, G., *The Art of Persuasion in Greece* (London: Routledge & Kegan Paul, 1963).

Kerferd, G.B., *The Sophistic Movement* (Cambridge: Cambridge University Press, 1981).

Kuntz, M., 'The Prodikean "Choice of Herakles": a Reshaping of Myth', *Classical Journal* 89 (1993), 163-81.

Meiggs, R., *The Athenian Empire* (Oxford: Oxford University Press, 1972).

Momigliano, A., 'Prodico di Ceo e le dottrine del linguaggio da Democrito ai Cinici', *Atti della Accademia delle Scienze di Torino, Classe di Scienze morali, storiche e filologiche* 65 (1930), 129-40.

Morrison, J.S., 'The Place of Protagoras in Athenian Public Life (460-415 BC)', *Classical Quarterly* 35 (1941), 1-16.

Nestle, Wilhelm, 'Die Horen des Prodikos (1936)', in Classen 1976, 425-51.

Pfeiffer, R., *History of Classical Scholarship* (Oxford: Oxford University Press, 1968).

Plato: *Complete Works*, ed. with introduction and notes by John M. Cooper (Indianapolis: Hackett, 1997).

Radermacher, L., *Artium scriptores* (Vienna: Rudolf M. Rohrer, 1951).

Reesor, M.E., 'The Stoic Idion and Prodicus' Near-Synonyms', *American Journal of Philology* 104 (1983), 124-33.

Smith, J.R., *Xenophon Memorabilia* (Boston: Ginn & Co., 1903).

Sommerstein, A.H., *The Comedies of Aristophanes*, vol. II: *Clouds* (Warminster: Aris and Phillips, 1982).

Sommerstein, A.H., *The Comedies of Aristophanes*, vol. VI: *Birds* (Warminster: Aris and Phillips, 1987).

Sprague, R.K (ed.), *The Older Sophists* (Columbia, SC: University of South Carolina Press, 1972).

Tarrant, D., 'Aristophanes, *Birds* 700', *Classical Review* 37 (1923), 113.

Taylor, C.C.W., *Plato: Protagoras* (Oxford: Oxford University Press, 1976).

Thucydides, *History of the Peloponnesian War*, trans. Rex Warner (Harmondsworth: Penguin, 1954).

Untersteiner, M., *The Sophists*, trans. Kathleen Freeman (Oxford: Oxford University Press, 1954).

Willink, C.W., 'Prodikos, "Meteorosophists" and the "Tantalos" Paradigm', *Classical Quarterly* 33 (1983), 25-33.

Antiphon

Andrew Shortridge and Dirk Baltzly

To study the sophists is to study the scant fragments of a once-great intellectual tradition. To Antiphon's pen are attributed many fragments, to his person are attributed many identities. One or more persons named 'Antiphon' wrote books *On Truth*, *On Concord*, *Politicus*, the *Tetralogies*, and a collection of forensic legal speeches. The author (or authors) is said to have been an orator,[1] a sophist, a tragic poet. Who was Antiphon? Which of the works did he actually write? What philosophic position is defended in those writings? Sketching answers below, we shall concentrate particularly on the final question.

Plato, in the dialogue *Menexenus* (236a), has Socrates mention the oratorical skills and teaching of Antiphon, from the Attic deme of Rhamnus. This Rhamnusian was a leader of the oligarchic faction in politics and led the Four Hundred in the oligarchic coup d'état. He was executed by the restored democracy in 411 BC. Thucydides praised his defence speech (VIII.68), while Aristotle praised the magnanimity this Antiphon displayed in the face of his impending execution (*Eudemian Ethics* 1232b6-9). Xenophon, in his *Memorabilia* (I.6), depicts Socrates in conversation with Antiphon 'the sophist': they discuss poverty, wealth, politics, and wisdom. Although there are many other references to individuals named 'Antiphon' the chief question is whether Antiphon of Rhamnus is the individual Xenophon depicts disputing with Socrates.

Did Xenophon mean to differentiate Antiphon the sophist from other individuals of the same name? Unitarians deny that Xenophon meant to distinguish between two separate men. Gagarin (2002, 42) argues that Xenophon calls Antiphon a sophist *perhaps* because he wishes to show the sorts of discussions Socrates had with the sophists, and distinguish his philosophical commitments from theirs. Separatists argue that 'the sophist' and 'the Rhamnusian' are different individuals. Antiphon the sophist is a teacher, but Pendrick (2002, 5) argues that 'the case for regarding Antiphon of Rhamnus as a professional teacher is very weak'. He also argues that Antiphon of Rhamnus would most naturally have been identified either by his demonym, 'of Rhamnus', or his profession of orator (*rhêtôr*). Since Xenophon labels Antiphon a sophist, Pendrick concludes that he does this to distinguish sophist from orator. Guthrie (1971, 286), however, argued that it would be difficult to distinguish a sophist from a *rhêtôr*, 'since in ancient times the word *sophistês* would be applied equally to both', so Pendrick's point is perhaps not decisive. Unless we come to have new evidence, the question seems to admit no definite solution.

Whoever Antiphon was, what did he write? Unitarians can attribute everything to Antiphon of Rhamnus. Thus, Pendrick argues that Antiphon the sophist wrote *On Truth*, *On Concord*, *Politicus*, and a book on the interpretation of dreams. Reading any of the works attributed to Antiphon, it might be tempting to argue from biography to interpretation, or vice versa. For instance, *On Truth* is egalitarian, but Antiphon of Rhmanus was not egalitarian, so Antiphon of Rhamnus did not write *On Truth*. However, given the fragmented condition of Antiphon's works, and the disputed question of Antiphon's identity, this interpretive strategy is best avoided. As Woodruff (2004, 329) counsels, it is best to suspend judgement on Antiphon's identity and focus on the texts themselves. Of the extant works, the most promising is *On Truth*. Kerferd (1981, 49-51) argues that regardless of the identity question, it is the author of *On Truth* whose work is of greatest importance for studies of the history of philosophy. Three substantial fragments from this work examine, respectively, Greeks and barbarians; custom and nature; and legal proceedings. Providing a criticism of human custom, apparently in favour of nature, the fragments are a very early expression of what later became the theory of natural law.

Fragments and reports of the contents of Antiphon's work are scattered throughout a variety of sources, as is common with Presocratic philosophers. In this section, we will concentrate on fragments from Antiphon's work *On Truth*. Here the main source comes from the bits of papyrus unearthed from what was, in essence, the rubbish tip of the Egyptian city of Oxyrhynchus. There is a variety of translations, with a variety of emendations. There is also some dispute about the proper order of the fragments: we will use the translation by Dillon and Gergel (2003). We begin with Antiphon's comments on Greeks and barbarians.

In fragment a, Antiphon suggests that we respect the laws of our own cities, but not those of distant lands, ignorant of the fact that 'as far as nature is concerned, we are all equally adapted to being either barbarians or Greeks' (Dillon and Gergel 2003, 22a, 150). He claims, 'things which are natural and necessary to all mankind ... are available to all in the same way' (22a). He lists breathing using mouth and nostrils, laughing when happy and weeping when sad, and so on, before the fragment breaks off. Barnes suggests (1979, 211) that this is an argument about the natural equality of peoples, which leads Antiphon to a conclusion about the moral equality of people. We think that this suggestion is incorrect.[2] Antiphon suggests only that people are equally suited to be either barbarian or Greek, not that being barbarian or Greek is of equal moral worth. Even if one cannot be a natural slave, Antiphon has no obvious objection to the idea that some cultures might produce subjects who are servile because of the social conventions they follow. While we might equally have been barbarians or Greeks, if we had been born and raised in different cities, it does not follow that Greek and barbarian cities are equal in any way, nor does Antiphon make this claim.

Assuming the widely accepted supplement in the first line, 'We recognise and respect <the laws of nearby communities> ...' (22a), this fragment contrasts law and social convention (*nomos*) with nature (*physis*), as do the fragments that follow. This contrast requires some explanation. The Presocratics, Greek philosophers of an age prior to the sophists, are called by Aristotle 'nature-ologists' (*physiologoi*) because they sought to identify the underlying nature of all things. This underlying nature – whether it be Empedocles' four elements or Anaximenes' air – are universal forces that order the cosmos as a whole (see Guthrie 1971, 55-60; Guthrie 1962; Guthrie 1965). However, Antiphon's appeal to natural necessities seems to be neither derived from a source external to humankind, nor cosmic in scale: '[by] *physis*, Antiphon means primarily human nature ... [including] certain desires, wants, longings and yearnings' (Barnes 1979, 211; see Ostwald 1990, 299). The natural necessities are those of *human* nature, 'physiologically and genetically ingrained in all mankind' (Ostwald 1990, 298). This focus on human nature, and the natural needs of individuals, is a chief focus of the fragment concerning law and nature.

Fragment b, detailing the relationship between law and nature, is the longest and most complex of the three under examination. It begins with a definition: that justice is a matter of not violating the customs of one's own city (22b, Dillon and Gergel 2003, 150). Antiphon apparently thinks that it follows from this fact (*oun*) that it is advantageous to obey the laws in public, but to follow one's own nature when in private. This is because the basis of law is agreement (*homologia*) – a basis that is contrasted with the necessity (*anangkê*) of nature and its demands.

> For the demands of the laws are adventitious, but the demands of nature are necessary; and the demands of the laws are based on agreement, not nature, while the demands of nature are not dependent on agreement (22b).

The different status of law and nature is evident in the consequences of ignoring their demands. Violations of legal justice bring punishment only when other people witness these acts: violating the law when alone brings neither penalty nor shame. Antiphon argues that violating the laws of nature results in a different punishment from the sort incurred by violating the laws of agreement, since 'the injury which he suffers is not a matter of appearance, but of truth' (22b).

The laws seem to be based on a contract – an agreement – of some kind. In Plato's *Republic* (358eff.) Glaucon provides a contractual account of justice that bears some similarities to Antiphon's account. But there are two aspects to Glaucon's contractual theory that appear to be lacking in

Antiphon. First, Glaucon presents the emergence of such a contract among humans as itself the outcome of a *natural process* in which we get a taste of being harmed by others, as well as a taste of the fruits of harming others, and decide that the former is so bad that we should agree to forego the latter, provided that others will do the same. So the existence of laws based on contract is itself natural in this sense. But, second, those things that the law forbids are themselves natural to us. So, in that sense, law is contrary to nature. The fragments of Antiphon, by contrast, are silent on the question of how law comes to be. Nor is it clear that he supposes that what the law forbids is *always* something natural to us.

Antiphon says that 'many of the things that are just according to the law are at odds with nature' (22b). Examples are then given of how the laws constrain natural activities: 'for the eyes, what they may see and what they may not', etc. Looking at things with the eyes is natural, and sometimes beneficial and sometimes not. However, looking at your neighbour's wife at her toilette is unlawful (at least in Athens at the time). Nothing Antiphon says implies that he thinks that such peeping would be necessarily beneficial, simply because forbidden by law. Nor does Antiphon say that peeping is natural because pleasant – only that the eyes naturally see things. What the law commands and forbids may bear no systematic relationship at all to what is natural.

At what does nature aim? Life and death are in accordance with nature, the former advantageous, and the latter disadvantageous. The laws provide advantages of some sort, but they are shackles on nature, whereas 'the advantages prescribed by nature make for freedom' (22b). This section concludes with the claim that, although some might say otherwise, painful things do not genuinely benefit nature more than things that are pleasant, sad things are less advantageous than things that produce joy: 'For the things that are truly advantageous ought not to harm but to help us' (22b).

These sections of *On Truth* are confusing. Antiphon certainly seems to suggest that it is *best* to pursue your own advantage. Perhaps he even thinks that it is psychologically inevitable that we *will* pursue what we take to be our own advantage, though this is not clear from what is said. It is unclear whether his claims are normative or descriptive. Moreover, what things are advantageous? Not all natural things are advantageous – death is natural but disadvantageous. It seems that there are advantages provided by law, but not of the same calibre as those prescribed by nature since the latter, but not the former, contribute to 'freedom'. The fragment insists that painful things – and the context suggests that Antiphon has in mind painful remedies imposed by law – are not more to our advantage than pleasures are. Is Antiphon a hedonist, then? We think this is possible, but perhaps unlikely. The very next line seems to endorse an axiom about advantageous things that it is not easy for a hedonist to accept: things that are truly advantageous must not harm, but rather benefit us. Arguably some pleasures (e.g. too much wine and rich food) harm us. A hedonist *can* say – as Epicurus was later to say – that such pleasures *qua* pleasures are good, but they are not choiceworthy at this cost. But we have no evidence to suggest that Antiphon was a hedonist of this sophisticated sort. Indeed, we think it likely that Antiphon might have had in mind a list of things that were advantageous for a person, but the text breaks off just where he provides this list at the end of fragment 22b. Antiphon might have supposed that pleasure is a *better indicator* of advantage than anything else and so is an important part of *judging* what is, in truth, beneficial to us, but he says nothing substantial about advantage itself, that end at which our every action aims.

We have seen that the dictates of law can be at least *disconnected* from nature. When and how are the laws *contrary* to the dictates of nature? Antiphon's conception of the demands of nature arises out of physiological necessities that everyone, whether Greek or barbarian, experiences. One possible way to understand Antiphon's criticism of the 'adventitious' laws is that the operations of nature involve necessity, but law is haphazard. Inevitably, if I ignore the promptings of hunger for too long, it will prove to my disadvantage. But conforming to conventional law sometimes benefits, sometimes harms, and sometimes does neither. Conventional law shackles the advantages of nature when it demands something that will *inevitably* lead to one's own disadvantage.

Commencing a discussion of the shortcomings of law, Antiphon gives examples of what appear to be good behaviours, each of them 'morally highly commendable' (Ostwald 1990, 299): not starting fights, taking care of bad parents, etc. He claims that these are against nature, since they produce more pain and misfortune than is necessary (22c, Dillon and Gergel 2003, 151). Since the laws demand that we give up our right to retaliate directly against threats and harms, Antiphon argues that they must be unjust, since they cannot guarantee our safety: crime is committed in law-abiding societies, but the laws 'leave the sufferer to suffer and the doer to act' (22c). Further, under Athenian law, the sufferer must persuade a jury that the offence was real, and the aggressor might persuade them otherwise.

It seems that Antiphon operates with what we might call a principle of necessary vindictiveness: people are naturally inclined to harm those who harm them. Much of Antiphon's critique of law revolves around the fact that law requires us to harm those who have not harmed us, as when we give evidence in court against someone, even though he has not harmed us. Antiphon does not say, explicitly, that this is a 'law of nature' – it is up to the character Callicles in Plato's *Gorgias* (483e) to first use the paradoxical phrase '*nomos phuseôs*'. But Antiphon does play with the double sense of the verb '*adikein*', which can mean 'to harm' or 'to commit an injustice', in such a way as to suggest a kind of natural, as opposed to conventional, justice. Naturally, people we harm will want to return the harm. So, naturally, we should avoid doing this.

But the conventional workings of justice are contrary to nature in this regard.

Under the law, we renounce our right to retaliate, we are not guaranteed safety, and the law 'is no more particularly on the side of the sufferer than on the committer of the act' (22c). Hence, the law is against nature.

> If some assistance accrued from the laws to those who give up their rights in such ways [i.e. their right to pursue natural justice and retaliate] ... then obedience to the laws would hold some advantage; but as it is, it is clear that justice in accordance with the law does not give assistance to those who give up their rights (22c).

Is this 'if' a strict counterfactual, meant to apply to all conceivable systems of law and customary justice (Pendrick 2002, 343)? If it is, then Antiphon seems to suggest that the laws are always against nature, and that they cannot be reformed.

While some scholars have argued that we should not reject the possibility of laws that are somewhat advantageous (Reesor 1987, 204-9), others have suggested that the essential point of laws might be that they repress or constrain nature (Barnes 1979, 212-13). Certainly if Antiphon thinks that some laws are not against nature, he says very little about them (Pendrick 2002, 328). Our view is that no set of laws could prescribe conduct that is consistently advantageous for every individual, for the world is too complex. Hence Antiphon's claim is that we should be guided by law just to the point at which it ceases to be advantageous.

Whatever the case, law will not be the source of our actions. Consider some action that is a genuinely advantageous and demanded by nature; imagine, further, that this action was not illegal, but actually and actively promoted by law. At the very least, it would seem that the motivation to act would stem from the fact that some pleasure or advantage accompanied the action, not that the action was commanded by law. This is another sense in which law is imposed, adventitious, ersatz.

Can the laws of nature be violated? A difficult but vital phrase suggests the answer. Dillon and Gergel translate, 'If ... a man – *per impossibile* – violates one of the inherent demands of nature ...' (22b). It is possible, however, to quibble about the translation (Ostwald 1990, 294). Our view is that one cannot renounce the demands of nature for very long. Imagine that a soldier on watch feels tired. The command of nature is that he should rest. Suppose that the punishment for falling asleep at one's post, a serious dereliction of duty, is execution. Since death is a natural disadvantage, the soldier maximises his own advantage by following the law, not nature. However, note that this will involve an immediate penalty: he will feel tired, and the longer he puts off sleep, the more tired he will become. Eventually, he must succumb and slumber, but until then he can follow his orders and keep watch. He can ignore nature, but not beyond what is possible: nature always trumps law in the end.

If this is an accurate account of how nature and law are related, then it also tells us something else about laws. The 'advantages' of law are really only advantageous in situations where the penalty for violating law is worse than that for ignoring nature: the only advantage comes about through a greater disadvantage! Hence, when nature and law conflict in private, one ought to follow nature, since law has no power without witnesses. When in public, obey the law, if failure to do so is of greater detriment than the penalty for ignoring nature. Remember, though, that nature will eventually take its course, from necessity.

Note that when Antiphon considers the disadvantages that follow from conformity to law and convention, he is thinking about disadvantages *for the individual*. At no point does Antiphon say that we, *collectively*, are better off with laws and customs than without them. Yet many of the things that he regards as advantageous (e.g. money in Xenophon, *Memorabilia* 1.6.1) presuppose organised social conventions. Moreover, it seems clear that Antiphon gave considerable thought to our collective well-being. Another work, besides *On Truth*, was *On Concord* (*homonoia*). This word means literally 'being of the same or similar mind' about things. Aristotle regarded it as common wisdom that 'civic friendship' consists in such like-mindedness (*Nicomachean Ethics* 1167b2), and the term features in the remains of other sophists such as Gorgias and Thrasymachus.

Nonetheless, the remaining fragments from Antiphon's *On Concord* stress the *difficulties* that arise when we try to arrive at a collective good or collaborate with others to pursue our own good. The longest fragment concerns the difficulties that one brings upon oneself by getting married and thereby being in a position to worry about someone's good other than your own. Children only add to our worries.

> For I, if I had a second body which needed as much care as I give to myself, could not live, considering all the trouble I give myself, what with tending to the health of my body and earning my daily livelihood, and seeing to my honour and temperance and good fame (fragment 43, in Dillon and Gergel 2003, 160).

But *On Concord* does not seem to recommend isolation as a solution either. Another relatively long fragment relates the story of a man 'who distrusted others and never helped anyone' (fragment 51, Dillon and Gergel 2003, 164). He comes to grief because the money he could have lent with interest, had be been cooperative, is instead stolen. The key to managing our social relations is prudence and temperance (which figure in both fragments 51 and 52, Dillon and Gergel, 2003, 164-5). A similar ambivalence about our social context emerges from two short fragments. In the first, Antiphon notes that man is 'the most godlike of all the beasts' (fragment 40, Dillon and Gergel 2003, 160). In another, where the setting is conversational, he says to his *companion* – 'my good fellow' – that life is nothing special but instead 'everything is small and weak and of short duration' (fragment 41, Dillon and Gergel 2003, 160).

It is hard to know how these rather different sentiments figured in Antiphon's book. One speculative answer is that Antiphon combined the perspective of Sophocles' famous chorus from *Antigone* ('Wonders are many, but none more wonderful than man ...' 332-75) with the perspective of the individual. Sophocles' chorus has no time for the person who does not honour the laws and customs (*nomoi*) of the land, thinking that such a person should be outside the community (*apolis*). We think that it is just possible that Antiphon had the audacity – the *tolma* as in Sophocles' chorus – to point out that social existence is not an unalloyed good. That *we* gain by the institution of law and custom does not mean that *I* would not gain more by ignoring it from time to time. Yet if everyone reasoned in this way, all individuals would be worse off.

This tension between individual and collective good is a familiar one in the tradition of contractualist accounts of morality. David Gauthier (1967, 469-70) takes this problem up in the context of his discussion of the problem of the prisoner's dilemma. He argues that agents who, in every individual situation, pursue their own advantage are unable to secure for themselves certain advantages that are open to persons who are not as consistent in the pursuit of their own interests. We are better off if we stick to our agreements even when it isn't individually in our interests. Yet it is surely paradoxical that we collectively have a good reason to do something that no one of us individually has a good reason to do.

We do not wish to urge the view that Antiphon went as far as to work all of this out: only that his remarks in *On Concord*, as well as his critique of *nomos*, are consistent with an appreciation of the tension between individual and collective advantage. In a sense, the perspective of individual things is common to what little we know of Antiphon's physical theorising. Aristotle (*Physics* 193a9-17; fragment 19 in Dillon and Gergel, 149) attributes to him the view that the nature of a thing consists in what Aristotle would go on to describe as its matter. Antiphon argued for this view, apparently by appeal to the following counterfactual claim: if one were to bury a bed, and if the rotting wood were to send up shoots, it would grow to be a tree, not a bed. The configuration of the bed is merely an arrangement that it has thanks to convention and craft (*tên kata nomon diathesin kai technên*) – it is really wood because that is *inevitably* how it will go on. Similarly, perhaps Antiphon thought of human individuals as natural advantage-seekers. (This is why those who renounce an advantage willingly do what is unnatural – though given enough time they too will eventually seek their own advantage.) This makes our social arrangements, which involve *nomoi* (laws and customs) that demand that we sometimes renounce an advantage, rationally problematic, if not positively unnatural. But, on the third hand, there are things we can accomplish if we share a viewpoint – we have *homonoia* – that we could not accomplish otherwise. The conjunction of these thoughts is indeed puzzling. Perhaps Antiphon himself thought that they were irresolvably puzzling, as the sole epistemological fragment from the first book of *On Truth* suggests:

> perceiving these things [i.e. the things in this book?] you will know absolutely none of them, neither the things which he who sees farthest sees with sight, nor the things which he who perceives farthest perceives with the mind (fragment 1 in Pendrick's translation (2002, 103).

In Antiphon we have the first available formulations of a reasoned critique of custom justified at least in part in terms of human nature. Some of the details of that critique and those terms are unclear or ambiguous; due to the twin effects of a scarcity of source material and the momentous effort of giving birth to a new line of argument. Antiphon's praise of nature; his explication of the relationship between advantage, pleasure, and life; his attack on law and custom ... if these seem to us to be only half finished, we should keep in mind the fact that he helped give a first, perhaps primitive, shape and form to the antithesis of law and nature: one of the most influential controversies in the history of philosophy. The lamentable lack of evidence gives rise to a corresponding need for boldness in inference and conjecture – a kind of boldness no doubt familiar to those sophists about whom we know so very little.

Notes

1. Most authors call Antiphon the Rhamnusian an orator, and we shall do likewise, in spite of the fact that he *wrote* speeches for others rather than giving them as one would expect of a *rhêtôr*.
2. So consider that Aristotle claimed, 'from the hour of their birth, some are marked out for subjection, others for rule' (*Politics* 1254a22-3). Against this backdrop one might see Antiphon's argument as a denial that slavery is natural. Note, however, that Barnes (1979, 211) is not terribly interested in this fragment, and suggests that other interpretations of it are possible.

Bibliography

Avery, H.C., 'One Antiphon or Two?', *Hermes* 110 (1982), 145-58.
Barnes, J., *The Presocratic Philosophers*, vol. II: *Empedocles to Democritus* (London: Routledge and Kegan Paul, 1979).
Dillon, J. and Gergel, T., *The Greek Sophists* (London: Penguin, 2003).
Gagarin, M., *Antiphon the Athenian: Oratory, Law, and Justice in the Age of the Sophists* (Austin, TX: University of Texas Press, 2002).
Gauthier, D., 'Morality and Advantage', *Philosophical Review* 76 (1967), 460-75.
Grube, G.M.A. and Reeve, C.D.C. (trans.), *Republic*, in *Plato: The Complete*

Dialogues, ed. J.M. Cooper and D.S. Hutchinson (Indianapolis, IN: Hackett, 1997).

Guthrie, W.K.C., *A History of Greek Philosophy,* vol. I: *The Earlier Presocratics and the Pythagoreans* (Cambridge: Cambridge University Press, 1962).

Guthrie, W.K.C., *A History of Greek Philosophy*, vol. II: *The Presocratic Tradition from Parmenides to Democritus* (Cambridge: Cambridge University Press, 1965).

Guthrie, W.K.C., *The Sophists* (= *A History of Greek Philosophy*, vol. IIIa) (Cambridge: Cambridge University Press, 1971 [first published 1969]).

Kerferd, G.B., *The Sophistic Movement* (Cambridge: Cambridge University Press, 1981).

Hardie, R.P. and Gaye, R.K. (trans.), *Physics*, in *The Complete Works of Aristotle*, ed. J. Barnes (Princeton, NJ: Princeton University Press. 1995).

Jowett, B. (trans.), *Politics*, in *The Complete Works of Aristotle*, ed. J. Barnes (Princeton, NJ: Princeton University Press, 1995).

Morrison, J.S., 'Antiphon', *Proceedings of the Cambridge Philological Society* 187 (1961), 49-58.

Ostwald, M., '*Nomos* and *Phusis* in Antiphon's *Peri Alêtheias*', in *Cabinet of the Muses: Essays in Honor of Thomas G. Rosenmeyer*, ed. M. Griffith and D.J. Mastronarde (Atlanta, GA: Scholars Press, 1990).

Pendrick, G.J., *Antiphon the Sophist: The Fragments*, ed. J. Diggle et al. (Cambridge: Cambridge University Press, 2002).

Reesor, M.E. (1987), 'The *Truth* of Antiphon the Sophist', *Apeiron* XX(2) (1987), 203-18.

Rhys Roberts, W. (trans.), *Rhetoric*, in *The Complete Works of Aristotle*, ed. J. Barnes (Princeton, NJ: Princeton University Press, 1995).

Ross, W.D. and Urmson, J.O. (trans.), *Nicomachean Ethics*, in *The Complete Works of Aristotle*, ed. J. Barnes (Princeton, NJ: Princeton University Press, 1995).

Ryan, P. (trans.), *Menexenus*, in *Plato: The Complete Dialogues*, ed. J.M. Cooper and D.S. Hutchinson (Indianapolis, IN: Hackett, 1997).

Saunder, T.J. (1978), 'Antiphon the Sophist on Natural Laws (B44 DK)', *The Aristotelian Society* NS LXXVIII (1978), 215-36.

Solomon, J. (trans.), *Eudemian Ethics*, in *The Complete Works of Aristotle*, ed. J. Barnes (Princeton, NJ: Princeton University Press, 1995).

Treddenick, H. and Waterfield, R. (trans.), *Memoirs of Socrates*, in *Xenophon: Conversations of Socrates* (London: Penguin, 1990).

Warner, R. (trans.), *Thucydides: The Peloponnesian War*, ed. G.V. Rieu (Harmondsworth: Penguin, 1954).

Woodhead, W.D. (trans.), *Gorgias*, in *Plato: The Complete Dialogues*, ed. J.M. Cooper and D.S. Hutchinson (Indianapolis, IN: Hackett, 1997).

Woodruff, P., 'Antiphons, Sophist and Athenian: A Discussion of Michael Gagarin, *Antiphon the Athenian*, and Gerard J. Pendrick, *Antiphon the Sophist*', *Oxford Studies in Ancient Philosophy* XXVI (2004), 323-36.

8

Thrasymachus

Daniel Silvermintz

Thrasymachus (the name means 'bold fighter') was renowned by his contemporaries for having innovated and perfected several rhetorical styles.[1] He has, however, won enduring notoriety for the challenge he poses to Socrates at the beginning of Plato's *Republic* by defending the superiority of injustice over justice. And although Socrates claims to have refuted Thrasymachus (*Republic* 354a, 358b, 498d), Glaucon, a fellow participant in the discussion, accuses the philosopher of being hasty in declaring his victory over the sophist: 'do you want to seem to have persuaded us or truly to persuade us, that it is in every way better to be just than unjust' (*Republic* 357b). Adopting Thrasymachus' position, Glaucon and his brother Adeimantus demand that Socrates prove the inherent goodness of justice in spite of the more apparent benefits derived from acts of injustice committed with impunity.[2] Faced with a most formidable challenge, Socrates single-handedly fights to overcome Thrasymachus' argument in a war of words that lasts for the remainder of the dialogue. This fight over ethical first principles continues to rage in our own day as Thrasymachus' position that 'might makes right' will always find vigorous defenders, be they bullies in a schoolyard or tyrants ruling rogue nation-states.

Life and contributions to rhetoric

Thrasymachus (459-400 BC) was a native of Chalcedon, though he would eventually claim Athens as his home since it was here that he gained notoriety as a teacher of rhetoric and sophistry. His fame also brought him great wealth, obtained from students eager to learn the tricks of his trade. Socrates, believing that the truth cannot be bought and sold, singles out Thrasymachus for profiting in this manner: 'or is this that art of speech by means of which Thrasymachus and the rest have become able speakers themselves, and make others so, if they are willing to pay them royal tribute?' (Plato, *Phaedrus* 266c).[3]

Although none of Thrasymachus' works survive, he made important contributions to the early development of rhetorical theory. Among the works attributed to him are a handbook on rhetoric and a collection of model passages illustrating different rhetorical styles. His pre-eminent skill, celebrated here by Socrates, appears to have been his ability to manipulate an audience by playing on their emotions:

> For tearful speeches, to arouse pity for old age and poverty, I think the precepts of the mighty Chalcedonian hold the palm, and he is also a genius, as he said, at rousing large companies to wrath, and soothing them again by his charms when they are angry, and most powerful in devising and abolishing calumnies on any grounds whatsoever (*Phaedrus* 267c-d).

In reviewing the early development of rhetoric as an art form, Aristotle is helpful both in situating Thrasymachus among the early founders of the discipline, as well as evaluating his monumental contribution:

> For it may be that in everything, as the saying is, 'the first start is the main part': and for this reason also it is the most difficult; for in proportion as it is most potent in its influence, so it is smallest in its compass and therefore most difficult to see: whereas when this is once discovered, it is easier to add and develop the remainder in connexion with it. This is in fact what has happened in regard to rhetorical speeches and to practically all the other arts: for those who discovered the beginnings of them advanced them in all only a little way, whereas the celebrities of today are the heirs (so to speak) of a long succession of men who have advanced them bit by bit, and so have developed them to their present form, Tisias coming next after the first founders, then Thrasymachus after Tisias, and Theodorus next to him, while several people have made their several contributions to it: and therefore it is not to be wondered at that the art has attained considerable dimensions (Aristotle, *Sophistical Refutations* 183b22-34).

One might consider how Thrasymachus' introduction of periodic prose substantiates Aristotle's claim regarding the effect of small contributions to an art in its infancy. With this innovation, Thrasymachus seems to have completely revolutionised prose style from its earlier form in what Aristotle terms the 'free running' style: 'By "free-running" I mean the kind that has no natural stopping-places, and comes to a stop only because there is no more to say of that subject. This style is unsatisfying just because it goes on indefinitely' (Aristotle, *Rhetoric* 1410b). In contrast to the long-winded approach adopted by Herodotus, Aristotle defines the periodic in the following manner:

> By a period I mean a portion of speech that has in itself a beginning and an end, being at the same time not too big to be taken in at a glance. Language of this kind is satisfying and easy to follow. It is satisfying, because it is just the reverse of indefinite; and moreover, the hearer always feels that he is grasping something and has reached some definite conclusion ... (*Rhetoric* 1410b).

The extent of Thrasymachus' contribution to prose style may be assessed by Aristotle's remark that hardly anyone used the 'free running' style after the introduction of periodic prose.

Justice is the interest of the stronger

Thrasymachus' violent entrance into the discussion about justice in the *Republic*, described here by Socrates, is as brutal as the ethics that he promotes:

> Now Thrasymachus had many times started out to take over the argument in the midst of our discussion, but he had been restrained by the men sitting near him, who wanted to hear the argument out. But when we paused and I said this, he could no longer keep quiet; hunched up like a wild beast, he flung himself at us as if to tear us to pieces (*Republic* 336b).

Although Thrasymachus appears to disrupt the civility of the discussion, his brutal sense of ethics motivates the dialogue's opening scene. Thwarted in his attempt to make his way home, Socrates is threatened by Polemarchus and his gang, who demand that he do as they say since they outnumber him. ' "Well, then", Polemarchus said, "either prove stronger (*kreittous*) than these men or stay here" ' (*Republic* 327c). Both by his word and his deed, Polemarchus anticipates Thrasymachus' formal definition of justice as 'the interest of the stronger (*kreittonos*)' (338c). Callicles, who is often compared with Thrasymachus, defends a similar notion of justice in the *Gorgias*. Understanding nature as nothing other than a play of forces, Callicles attempts to provide a philosophic grounding of the right of the stronger: 'But nature, in my opinion, herself proclaims the fact that it is right for the better to have advantage of the worse, and the abler of the feebler' (Plato, *Gorgias* 483d). This disturbing conception of justice is certainly nothing new in the history of Greek ethical theory. On the contrary, one finds the notion of justice upheld by both Polemarchus and Callicles to be defended across the history of Greek literature from Achilles' claim to be the best of the Achaeans to the Athenians' justification for their rule over the Melians with the claim that, 'The strong do what they can and the weak suffer what they must' (Thucydides 5.89).[4]

Appearing at first to be promoting the well established notion that 'might makes right', Thrasymachus is quick to point out that he does not mean something as naive as the belief that the physically strongest members within a society are always the most advantaged. On the contrary, Thrasymachus is advancing a much more sophisticated conception of power relations derived from his observations of different political regimes: 'And each ruling group sets down laws for its own advantage; a democracy sets down democratic laws; a tyranny, tyrannic laws; and the others do the same' (*Republic* 338e). With this simple yet astute observation of the differing systems of political governance, Thrasymachus establishes a founding principle of what will later be known as legal positivism. John Austin, one of legal positivism's leading proponents, asserts (1995, 166) that a legal system derives its authority from a sovereign power that both enacts laws and is capable of enforcing them on the rest of society through some form of sanction.

Although some versions of legal positivism are compatible with natural law theory, Thrasymachus' further articulation of his principles suggests that he supports the conventionalist position summarised here by Aristotle: 'Now, some people think that everything just exists only by convention, as whatever is by nature is unchangeable and has the same force everywhere – as, for example, fire burns both here and in Persia – whereas they see that notions of what is just change' (Aristotle, *Nicomachean Ethics* 1134b24-9).[5] Indeed, if one were to search for unchanging transcendent principles among different political systems, one might conclude along with Thrasymachus that the only natural law is that every society is a power struggle between those in power and the remainder of the population who must respect the sovereign's authority: 'In every city the same thing is just, the advantage of the established ruling body' (Plato, *Republic* 339a). Identifying the right of the sovereign as the only element of political life that is grounded in nature, the conventionalist concludes that all forms of government – be they tyrannic or democratic – are equally valid.

Like many of his fellow sophists, Thrasymachus' political thought owes a debt to Protagoras' claim that 'Man is the measure of all things' (Plato, *Cratylus* 386a and *Theaetetus* 152a; Aristotle, *Metaphysics* 1062b, quoted in Waterfield 2000, 213, 215). Thrasymachus refines Protagoras' maxim by suggesting that some select individuals, as a result of their political status, determine the system of values for the rest of the community. Moreover, Thrasymachus points out that the privileging of some faction within the community is not without consequence since this group will inevitably enact laws that serve their own interest rather than the greater good. Thrasymachus asserts: 'And they declare that what they have set down – their own advantage – is just for the ruled, and the man who departs from it they punish as a breaker of the law and a doer of unjust deeds' (*Republic* 338e). Regardless of the individual or faction that is in power, the one thing Thrasymachus is certain of is that the sovereign power will establish a system of justice that serves its own interest.

Injustice pays

Although Thrasymachus initially appeared to defend justice even if its beneficiaries are the powers that be, when pressed by Socrates he openly proclaims the superiority of injustice over justice. Rather than quelling the beast, Socrates' attempt at refuting Thrasymachus only provokes him. In this new onslaught, Thrasymachus unleashes an even more troubling formulation, amounting to nothing less than the revaluation of all traditional values.

Socrates, using some rhetoric of his own, tries to get Thrasymachus to reconsider his formulation about justice by appealing to his sense of professionalism. Just as the expert adheres to his professional training to produce the expected end product, so too, Socrates argues, should the sovereign govern for the sake of the citizens. Socrates illustrates his point here with a carefully chosen example for conceiving of the benevolent ruler: 'Then, isn't it the case that the doctor, insofar as he is a doctor, considers or commands not the doctor's advantage, but that of the sick man? For the doctor in the precise sense was agreed to be a ruler of bodies and not a money-maker' (*Republic* 342d). Certainly, no one would consider all of the unpleasantnesses that the physician must endure in his treatment of the sick to be personally beneficial. On the contrary, the physician appears to be selflessly labouring for the sick patient. If one accepts Socrates' analogy between the activities of the artisan and the actions of the just man, then it is the weaker party that is benefited by just dealings, and Thrasymachus' understanding of politics is mistaken. One would furthermore expect that Thrasymachus, as a celebrated practitioner of the art of rhetoric, would concede this point to Socrates.[6] Notwithstanding his pride in his professional abilities, the profit-seeking Thrasymachus now affirms that the artisan practises his profession only as an instrumental good requisite for his own benefit. Thrasymachus illustrates his point with no less a carefully chosen example than Socrates':

> You suppose shepherds or cowherds consider the good of the sheep or the cows and fatten them and take care of them looking to something other than their masters' good and their own; and so you also believe that the rulers in the cities, those who truly rule, think about the ruled differently from the way a man would regard sheep, and that night and day they consider anything else than how they will benefit themselves (*Republic* 343b).

And so rather than conceiving of the ruler as a physician who selflessly doctors the maladies of state, Thrasymachus contends that the ruler's concern for the citizens is not unlike the shepherd who fattens his sheep before bringing them to slaughter.

Thrasymachus' ideal tyrant is, consequently, shrewd enough to know that he must benefit the people in the short term in order to win their favour and continuing support. One now sees why Socrates had denounced Polemarchus' seemingly honourable definition of justice, 'doing good to friends and harm to enemies', as the view of a tyrant (*Republic* 336a). While the masses may be placated so as to believe that upholding justice is in their best interest, this is obviously not supported by the facts. On the contrary, Thrasymachus argues quite convincingly that injustice is more beneficial than justice:

The just man everywhere has less than the unjust man. First, in contracts, when the just man is a partner of the unjust man, you will always find that at the dissolution of the partnership the just man does not have more than the unjust man, but less. Second, in matters pertaining to the city, when there are taxes, the just man pays more on the basis of equal property, the unjust man less; and when there are distributions, the one makes no profit, the other much (*Republic* 343d-e).

Thrasymachus' reversal of values reflects the prevailing orientation of the sophists, summarised here by Aristophanes' personified character, Unjust Speech, who proclaims his superiority over the old-fashioned and stodgy values of Just Speech: 'I'll overturn the just things by speaking against them, for I quite deny that Justice even exists' (Aristophanes, *Clouds* 900). In support of the conventionalist position, Thrasymachus and Unjust Speech claim that while the advantages of injustice are undeniable, justice has no transcendent existence outside the accepted standards of the community. This assumes, as Thrasymachus here affirms, that 'The gods', understood as mere forces of nature, 'pay no attention to human affairs' (Hermias, *Notes on Plato's 'Phaedrus'* 239.21-4, quoted in Waterfield 2000, 274).

Thrasymachus' claim concerning the indifference of the gods is validated by examining the law of nature as exhibited in the animal kingdom. While almost all societies have prohibitions against murder, no statesman has ever attempted to prosecute a lion for brutally slaughtering a lamb. On the contrary, the lion is heralded as the king of the jungle for his superior ability to preserve his existence. The prudent man appeals to the law of nature rather than to the law of the land in directing his affairs. Since the only rationale for obeying the civil laws is fear of the consequences inflicted upon the transgressor, the prudent man learns to be sufficiently cunning so as to commit acts of injustice with impunity. That said, the fear of punishment by the civil authorities is sufficient for convincing most men that obeying the law is the best course of action. Recognising the obvious risks involved in petty acts of injustice, Thrasymachus qualifies his position in the following manner: 'Injustice on a sufficiently large scale is a stronger, freer, and a more masterful thing than justice ...' (*Republic* 344c). One would thus achieve the noblest life, according to Thrasymachus, only when one is beyond the law and is ruling others as a tyrant.

Legacy

Thrasymachus' cogent defence of the immoralist position synthesises many key sophistic principles. In so doing, he provides the fundamental challenge with which all succeeding ethical speculation grapples. Anyone attempting to advance a theory of natural law must contend with Thrasymachus' claim that justice is nothing other than what the sovereign declares it to be. As discussed, this understanding of justice provides an important precursor to legal positivism. Other recent intellectual movements that owe a debt to Thrasymachus' thought include social constructivism as applied in both psychology and sociology and studies of power relations found in the field of cultural studies.

Athenaeus 10.454f (quoted in Sprague 2001, 88) reports that the following epitaph was inscribed on Thrasymachus' memorial: 'Name: Thrasymachus. Birthplace: Chalcedon. Profession: wisdom.'

Notes

1. On the meaning of Thrasymachus' name, see Aristotle, *Rhetoric* 1400b, and for his contributions to rhetorical theory, see Plato, *Phaedrus* 266c; Aristotle, *Sophistical Refutations* 183b22-34; *Rhetoric* 1413a5-10; *Suda*, s.v. 'Thrasymachus' T.462; Dionysus of Halicarnassus, *On Isaeus* 20 in Dillon and Gergel 2003, 209; Quintilian, *Institutio Oratoria* III.9; Dobson 1919, 3.1.

2. At *Republic* 545a Socrates acknowledges that the entire inquiry up to this point has been an attempt to respond to Thrasymachus' argument in defence of injustice.

3. Also see *Republic* 337d where Thrasymachus demands that Socrates pay him a fee in order to receive his instruction about the nature of justice. At *Republic* 341c, 345d and 346a-347d, Socrates gets Thrasymachus to concede that the true craftsman is recognised for his technical training rather than for his engagement in the subsidiary art of making money. Compare *Republic* 450b, where a seemingly converted Thrasymachus states that he has come to hear arguments rather than to make money.

4. For discussion of the Melian dialogue in relation to Thrasymachus' thought, see Kerferd 1981, 124-5.

5. For discussion, see Strauss 1953, 81-119.

6. Also consider *Republic* 340d where Thrasymachus establishes that an artist in the precise sense is one who possesses knowledge of his subject matter and is, therefore, unerring in questions pertaining to his field.

Bibliography

Aristotle, *De Sophisticis Elenchis* (*On Sophistical Refutations*), trans. W.A. Pickard (Cambridge: Cambridge University Press, 1928).

Aristotle, *Nicomachean Ethics*, trans. M. Ostwald (Englewood Cliffs, NJ: Prentice Hall, 1962).

Aristotle, *Rhetoric and Poetics*, trans. W. Rhys Roberts and Ingram Bywater (New York: McGraw-Hill, 1984).

Austin, J., *The Province of Jurisprudence Determined* (Cambridge: Cambridge University Press, 1995).

Dobson, J.F., 'Life and Work of Thrasymachus', in *The Greek Orators* (London: Methuen, 1919).

Dillon, J. and Gergel, T. (eds), *The Greek Sophists* (London: Penguin, 2003).

Kerferd, G.B., *The Sophistic Movement* (Cambridge: Cambridge University Press, 1981).

Plato, *Euthyphro, Apology, Crito, Phaedo, Phaedrus*, trans. H.N. Fowler, Loeb edition (London: Heinemann, 1925).

Plato, *Lysis, Symposium, Gorgias*, trans. W.R.M. Lamb, Loeb edition (London: Heinemann, 1925).

[Plato], *The Republic of Plato*, trans. A. Bloom (New York: Basic Books).

[Plato and Aristophanes], *Four Texts on Socrates: Plato's Euthyphro, Apology, and Crito, and Aristophanes' Clouds*, trans. T.G. West and G.S. West (Ithaca, NY: Cornell University Press, 1998).

Quintilianus, *Institutio Oratoria*, trans. H.E. Butler, Loeb edition (London: Heinemann, 1920).

Sprague, R.K. (ed.), *The Older Sophists* (Indianapolis, IN: Hackett, 2001).

Strauss, L., 'The Origin of the Idea of Natural Right', in *Natural Right and History* (Chicago: University of Chicago Press, 1953).

Suda online: http://www.stoa.org/sol/.

Thucydides, *The Peloponnesian War*, trans. R. Crawley (London: Dent, 1910).

Waterfield, R., *The First Philosophers: The Presocratics and the Sophists* (Oxford: Oxford University Press, 2000).

9

Callicles

Louis Groarke

The overly scrupulous might wonder what Callicles is doing in a book about the sophists. We have no sure source of information for the existence of this shadowy figure outside Plato's dialogue *Gorgias* (written *c.* 380 BC). Some authors have suggested that Plato's character is mere fiction, a stand-in for some other prominent Athenian political figure (such as Alcibiades or Isocrates), or that he represents the author's autobiographical self-portrait of a younger, more dangerous self. Did Callicles exist? Was he an authentic historical figure or only a literary figment of Plato's masterful imagination?

In his dialogues Plato customarily depicts authentic historical characters interacting with Socrates. It would seem odd then that he would make an exception for Callicles. After all, this is a major figure in a major dialogue conversing with real-life historical figures. Furthermore, as E.R. Dodds, W.K.C. Guthrie, Terrence Irwin and Debra Nails all observe, Plato's individualised portrait in *Gorgias* suggests a living person, with real-life friends, lover and family. Douglas MacDowell, basing himself on what would have to be spelling mistakes in two ancient legal texts, goes so far as to suggest that Callicles was one of those executed by the infamous Thirty Tyrants (see pp. 115-17 below). Other scholars are not convinced (see Redfield 1964). It is hard to know.

On the one hand, Socrates tells Callicles that he is a lover of the Athenian *demos*, the mob or the rabble (*Gorgias* 481d-e), which might set him on a collision course with the oligarchy of the Thirty. On the other hand, Callicles' elitist political opinions and his harsh manner of expression might put him into trouble with the democracy. But whatever transpired in his personal life and whichever path his political career took, we can easily imagine that such a forceful and reckless personality would come to an evil end at the hands of his enemies. It seems likely then that Callicles was a young man with serious political ambitions who perished in the 'dirty wars' of Athenian politics after the Peloponnesian War. This violent turn of events would explain why a personality as intense and as eloquent as Plato's Callicles left no other discernible mark on ancient history.

If Callicles existed, was he a real sophist? Dodds, for example, insists that he 'certainly was not a Sophist' (Dodds 1959, 13). Guthrie claims that he was 'a wealthy and aristocratic young man, [but] no Sophist himself' (Guthrie 1969, 102). Irwin explains that he 'is a disciple of neither' the distinguished elder sophist Gorgias nor his younger colleague Polus (Irwin 1979, 110), and Nails, who points out that Callicles discredits sophists as 'worthless' (*Gorgias* 520a1), argues that there is little evidence that Callicles or his friends associated with any of the sophists (Nails 2002, 75). Still, this kind of scholarly hesitation overstates the case.

Callicles was not, in any technical sense, a sophist. But this is only to say that he did not have to teach in order to make money. Callicles was wealthy on his own account and, in any case, as he explains to Socrates, he considers the theoretical life to be little more than an adolescent preoccupation. Still, Callicles must have had some intimate association with the sophists for he welcomes an illustrious representative 'of the first generation of Sophists' (Guthrie 1969, 269) into his home. Dodds claims that his distinguished guest is only a rhetor and a clever talker, but this is unconvincing. Gorgias was clearly a sophist in a widely-accepted sense of the term: he made money by teaching rhetoric understood as the art or knack of persuasion and was notoriously unconcerned about the truthfulness of his claims. What mattered, in his mind, was not unattainable truth but power of persuasion and stylistic ornament (*Gorgias* 452e, 456b). In his discussion with Socrates, he boasts that rhetoric is the master art and the supreme accomplishment.

As a sophist, Callicles' teacher or friend Gorgias seems to have been a breed apart. Plato does not include him in the important gathering of sophists he depicts in his dialogue the *Protagoras*, and unlike some of his colleagues (Protagoras, for example), Gorgias never claimed to teach virtue (*aretê*). But this more modest approach does not detract from his professional status. As Guthrie sensibly points out, this negative claim is probably intended as disparagement of his competitors' overly grandiose self-descriptions (Guthrie 1969, 271). If, however, Gorgias may want to distance himself from the pretensions of his rivals, he remains a sophist, a paid teacher of rhetoric who focuses on opinion rather than truth. Plato's dialogue is intended to show that even sophists like Gorgias who do not claim to teach 'virtue' are a danger to the public good. Callicles' impetuous dismissal of even the most minimal moral standards is, according to Plato, the sorry consequence of Gorgias' amoral teaching methods. As Dodds explains, 'Gorgias' teaching is the seed of which the Calliclean way of life is the poisonous fruit' (Dodds 1959, 15).

In Plato's dialogue, Callicles enters fearlessly into the fray to defend Gorgias from the logical criticisms of Socrates. We naturally might assume that Callicles is an actual student of Gorgias or his younger colleague Polus. But even if he is not an actual student, Callicles typifies the kind of client the successful sophist catered to: a wealthy young man with burning political ambitions, emboldened by the flashy rhetoric of the sophists, who adopts and defends the moral and political attitudes exemplified by a certain strain of *physis*-Sophism. Callicles is a man of action, a business-man and a politician instead of an intellectual, but also an excellent and fearless defender of Gorgias. He condemns the other sophists (those who claim to teach virtue) and trumpets, in no uncertain terms, the importance of rhetoric over philosophy. His defence of the sophist art of rhetoric quickly develops into a dangerously frank account of a 'morality' based on greed, brute power, and self-interest.

In the course of their discussion, Callicles ridicules Socrates' pious embrace of orthodox morality. What most of us call morality is, he claims, an artificial convention (*nomos*) that supplants the true morality based, not on mere custom, but on nature (*physis*). Only simpletons and children take conventional morality seriously. Any clear-thinking person who hon-estly and realistically evaluates the world recognises the ultimate value of power. This is what we all want; this is what we all strive towards. So this is what is right. Might *is* right. The strong *should* lord it over the weak. The superior *should* oppress the inferior. What is good is to be able to hurt one's enemies, to take as much as one wants, to satisfy one's every whim and caprice, and to be able to resist any kind of retaliation, punishment or censure.

Callicles claims that morality is a trick that snares the strong and the naturally gifted. As he explains:

> In my opinion those who framed the laws are the weaker folk, the majority. And accordingly, they frame the laws for themselves and their own advan-tage, and so too with their approval and censure, and to prevent the stronger who are able to overreach them from gaining advantage over them, they frighten them by saying that to overreach others is shameful and evil, and injustice consists in seeking advantage over others ...This is why seeking an advantage over the many is by convention said to be wrong and shameful, and they call it injustice. But in my view nature herself makes it plain that it is right for the better to have the advantage over the worse; the more able over the less. And both among all animals and in entire states and races of mankind it is plain that this is the case – that right is recognised to be the sovereignty and advantage of the stronger over the weaker (*Gorgias* 483b-d; trans. Woodhead, 266).

Callicles, in a passage that must have inspired the later Nietzsche, eulogises the Great Man who will rise above convention and, by his independent spirit and his own resourcefulness, take the law into his own hands. The Great Law-Breaker will see through society's insidious at-tempts to condition and restrain his heroic individuality. Callicles explains:

> [Such a man will] act in accordance with the true nature of right, yes and by heaven, according to nature's own law, though not perhaps by the law we frame. We mold the best and strongest among ourselves, catching them like

young lion cubs, and by spells and incantations we make slaves of them, saying that they must be content with equality and that this is what is right and fair. But if a man arises endowed with a nature sufficiently strong, he will, I believe, shake off all these controls, burst his fetters, and break loose. And trampling upon our scraps of paper, our spells and incantations, and all our unnatural conventions, he rises up and reveals himself our master who was once our slave, and there shines forth nature's true justice (*Gorgias* 483e-484b, trans. Woodhead, 266-7).

Callicles openly admires Xerxes, the King of Persia, a sworn enemy of Greece and a symbol of unrestrained luxury and moral decadence. And he takes inspiration from a morally off-colour incident that derives from the story of Heracles' twelve labours. As Callicles describes the event, Heracles steals the oxen of Geryon (a triple-bodied monster) 'which were neither given to him nor paid for, because this is natural justice, that the cattle and all other possessions of the inferior and weaker belong to the superior and stronger' (*Gorgias* 484b-c, trans. Woodhead, 267). This then is what it means to be a Great Man. To take successfully – by hook or by crook – whatever one wants. Callicles' ecstatic praise of the all-powerful figure who places himself above the law, his unqualified enthusiasm for tyranny as the natural form of government, and his worship of brute power are deeply disturbing.

Callicles has no qualms in saying out loud what some of the darker figures in the history of politics may have secretly thought in their hearts. But Callicles thinks he is only telling the truth. We say that we refrain from unlawful activity because we want to be moral, but this is dissembling. Our public approval of morality is only a front, a wall behind which we hide our true motivations. In fact, we all want to have more than our fair share, we all want to take from the weak, we all want to impose our will on others, but we refrain because we are afraid. Morality reduces, in effect, to cowardice. When the Great Man comes, he will boldly do what the rest of us are afraid to do.

At the very beginning of his discussion with Callicles, Socrates welcomes him as a debating opponent because of his disarming candour. He declares delightedly that Callicles possesses three important qualities needed to test the truth: knowledge, good will and frankness. If Callicles has rather limited knowledge and his good will is questionable, his opinions are remarkably candid (*Gorgias* 487a.) He is not content openly to dispute Socrates' perhaps idiosyncratic philosophical beliefs. In a very real sense, he flaunts his disagreement with Greek society as a whole through his vehement disapproval of the most common moral attitudes.

The ancient Greeks believed that temperance (*sôphrosunê*) was a chief virtue. Greek culture, predating Plato, widely celebrated this characteristic trait as a successful mix of self-control, self-knowledge and moderation. Aristotle's doctrine of the Golden Mean is only one historically conspicuous way of presenting this moral insight. Callicles, on the other hand, boldly and blithely dismisses temperance as an unmanly virtue. It is a morality for weaklings. The good life requires gargantuan indulgence: great desires followed by successful attempts to appease them. What we dislike are not appetites but unsatisfied appetites. Callicles declares:

> Anyone who is to live aright should suffer his appetites to grow to the greatest extent and not check them, and through courage and intelligence should be competent to minister to them at their greatest and satisfy every appetite with what it craves (*Gorgias* 491e-492a, trans. Woodhead, 274).

His position is so extreme that one wonders if Plato is exaggerating. If, however, morality means following Nature, and if Nature gives us appetites, then the man who follows Nature will satisfy his appetites to the utmost.

Here again, Callicles believes he is only reporting what ordinary people already think. We say we refrain from excessive pleasure because this is base or ignoble, but this familiar rationale is only pretending. The truth is we lack the ability to satisfy our own desires to the utmost, so we pretend that such behaviour is bad. But the Great Man, the one who has the will and the power to do anything he wants, does not need to resort to such inveterate falsehoods. He will cultivate vast desires, so that he can experience to the full the joy of satisfying them.

Callicles has an eloquent manner of expression – there is a passionate, poetic, soul-stirring quality to his energetic defence of heroic human immorality – but logically he is no match for the seasoned Socrates, who is a master of rigorous argument. Socrates runs logical circles around Callicles' unsuccessful attempts to defend his position. Indeed Callicles grows disgusted at the game and, mid-way through the discussion, gives up. Even if Socrates can beat him at verbal sleight of hand, so what? It may be a pretty thing to argue eloquently and cleverly, but if philosophers preach a doctrine that goes against Nature, this is not momentous. On Callicles' account, Nature is more powerful than philosophy. In the final analysis, Nature is what matters.

Callicles does not begrudge philosophy its proper place in human life. He believes, in fact, that it is an essential component of a liberal education. An older man must, however, turn his attention to more serious matters. 'It is a good thing to engage in philosophy just so far as it is an aid to education, and it is no disgrace for a youth to study it, but when a man who is now growing older still studies philosophy, the situation becomes ridiculous' (*Gorgias* 485a-b, trans. Woodhead, 268).

Too much philosophy 'is the ruin of any man' (*Gorgias* 484c, trans. Woodhead, 267). Philosophy ultimately ruins a man because it directs his energies and talents away from the active life. The adult philosopher spends his time squinting at dusty books, thinking about obscure problems, and keeping to himself.

Such a man, even if exceptionally gifted, is doomed to prove less than a man, shunning the city-centre and the market place in which ... men win distinction, and living the rest of his life sunk in a corner and whispering with three or four boys, and incapable of any utterance that is free and lofty and brilliant (*Gorgias* 485d-e, trans. Woodhead, 268).

Philosophers are like adults who act like children. Anyone who persists in the practice is worthy of a whipping (*Gorgias* 485b-e).

In *Gorgias*, Callicles makes an ominous and true prediction, that a guileless innocent like Socrates will be unable to defend himself if his enemies get hold of him and drag him into court:

'And yet, my dear Socrates, – ... I am saying this out of good will toward you – do you not consider it to be a disgrace to be in [this] condition ..., you, and the others who advance even farther in philosophy? For if anyone should seize you or any others like you and drag you off to prison, claiming you are guilty when you are not, you realise that you would not know what to do, but you would reel to and fro and gape open-mouthed, without a word to say, and when you came before the court, even with an utterly mean and rascally accuser, you would be put to death, if he chose to demand the death penalty' (*Gorgias* 486a-b, trans. Woodhead, 268).

Callicles thinks that an older man who devotes himself to philosophy exchanges the useful art of political persuasion for logical niggling and theoretical speculation. No one takes him seriously. This is to divest oneself of the responsibilities and the prerogatives of Greek citizenship. It is to make oneself vulnerable; it is to die a quick death at the hands of one's enemies.

There is a kind of purposeful irony here. We know about Callicles only because Plato the philosopher wrote about him. Yet Callicles, who disappeared into the mists of time, believes that the serious practitioner of philosophy will never amount to anything. The philosopher is not a man of action; he literally does nothing. Such a person may as well erase himself from the history books. It is as if he never lived. Callicles believes that the praiseworthy man, the man who will be remembered, must be an accomplished public citizen, a mover and a shaker in the corridors of power, with a wide experience of human characters and multiform pleasures. He must be able to help his friends and hurt his enemies. And he must do this with panache! This is the good life, the glorious life, the life worth living.

If Callicles argues openly against the law, against temperance and against philosophy, there is a larger issue looming in the background. Commentators do not always notice that Callicles (along with Gorgias and Polus) defend rhetoric as a means to individual liberty (*eleutheria*), what Gorgias describes as 'the greatest blessing to man ... the greatest boon' (*Gorgias* 452d-e, trans. Woodhead, 236). After Gorgias has his turn, Polus chimes in, claiming that even Socrates would revel in liberty understood as the absolute power to do whatever he pleases. He makes fun of the philosopher: 'Just as if you, Socrates, would not like to be at liberty to do whatever seemed good to you in the state rather than not, and are not jealous when you see a man killing or imprisoning or depriving of property as seems good to him!' (*Gorgias* 468e, trans. Woodhead, 251). Callicles' panegyric to the value of absolute power is only the logical extension of this way of thinking.

Callicles is an apt symbol and a perfect representation of this negative notion of freedom. Socrates comments on his penchant for bold and free speech (*Gorgias* 492d). Of all of Plato's characters, Callicles is known for his utterly frank mode of expression. He is entirely, dangerously candid. He keeps no secrets. He speaks without any restraint. He openly praises negative liberty (*eleutheria*), along with debauchery (*truphe*) and weakness of will (*akrasia*), as the greatest of virtues (*Gorgias* 492c). What Callicles prizes is freedom understood as non-interference, as unrestrained agency. The Greek adjective '*eleutherios*' – 'speaking or acting like a freeman, free-spirited, frank' (Liddell and Scott) – comes to mind. The freeman (someone who is *eleutheros*) is the opposite of the slave; he can do and say what he wants. This is what Callicles values; this best expresses his own personal ideal of character. Callicles champions the 'liberal' pursuits (*eleutheron*) of the free citizen and pours contempt on slavish or illiberal pursuits (*aneleutheron*) such as Socratic philosophy. (Cf. *Gorgias* 485b-c). He says all this publicly, with enthusiasm, in conversation with Socrates.

We should not be too quick to dismiss such ideas as merely outrageous. Callicles' negative account is not so far off modern liberal definitions of freedom as the absence of interference. Except that modern liberalism places a strict limit on individuality. We can do what we want with our private lives, but we cannot interfere with the private lives of other people. We are held back by the no-harm principle, by the social contract, by a belief in principles of equality, tolerance, and consent. But Callicles would wonder aloud: why should we take such liberal ideas seriously? If freedom, understood as doing what we please, is most valuable, we should reject anything – modern liberalism included – that stands in the way of obtaining it. Callicles consistently follows through this line of reasoning to its logical end. He is a kind of freedom-saint, someone who does not hesitate to act according to the values he professes.

We can then describe the clash between Socrates and Callicles as a clash between two different notions of freedom. Put simply, Socrates subscribes to a positive notion of freedom as human flourishing. Freedom, for Socrates, means acting in accordance with reason. Callicles subscribes to a negative notion of freedom as the absence of obstacles. Freedom, for Callicles, means doing what one wants to do without interference. The battle between two opposing types of freedom parallels the battle between Sophism and philosophy. The sophists value rhetoric. Once we master rhetoric, we can accomplish what we want. Why? Because we can convince every one else to do our bidding. We can (as Gorgias says) make everyone else our slaves. Callicles claims that this is the road to freedom and ultimately, the road to happiness. Socrates, on the other hand, values philosophy. Once we master philosophy, we can gain knowledge of the good. Knowing the good makes us moral. Morality sets us free. This is what happiness is.

In *Laws*, Plato's Athenian sets out to demonstrate 'that unqualified and absolute freedom from all authority is a far worse thing than submission to a magistrate with limited powers' (*Laws* 698b, trans. Taylor, 1226). In Plato, however, political reality mirrors interior reality. What goes on inside the just state is analogous to what goes on inside the just individual. When we ignore reason like Callicles, we are doubly enslaved. In a reason-less state, when the law is not respected, we become enslaved to others' opinions. Even the master rhetorician is enslaved, for he has continually to flatter the mob or those presently in power in order to be successful. In a disordered psyche, when the natural authority of reason is dethroned, we become enslaved to our own appetites which come to control us. (Hence the shameful reference to catamites in *Gorgias* 494e.) So Callicles' bold new account of absolute freedom inevitably degenerates, according to Socrates, into its opposite, absolute enslavement.

Plato presents Callicles as the product of a corrupt education; he is the immoral spawn of Gorgias' morally vacuous teaching. When arguing with Socrates, the young man champions rhetoric understood as a self-sufficient guide to conduct. Socrates, on the other hand, disputes the value of rhetoric *taken by itself*. The shrewd practitioner can bend rhetoric to any end whatsoever. This is what makes this showy eloquence attractive to someone like Callicles, but it is this very lawlessness that makes it useless as a moral guide. Plato agrees with Gorgias that rhetoric alone does not lead to virtue (*aretê*). If, however, Gorgias eventually settles on the idea that his teaching is morally neutral, Plato thinks it actually worsens the individual; it turns him into an evil person like Callicles. Rhetoric gives us unlimited power and this kind of power, unaccompanied by proper moral knowledge, i.e. unaccompanied by philosophy, inevitably corrupts.

Is Callicles thoroughly evil? In Plato's eyes, Callicles is a thoroughly ignorant agent and ignorance equals vice. On the other hand, Callicles is not a pure egotist; he clearly believes the Great Man should help his friends. And he is not a pure hedonist, despite his first attempts to justify any kind of pleasure (which he eventually discounts). Callicles proposes an alternative morality. Power has, in his eyes, a moral and aesthetic attraction. It is intrinsically valuable. Domination is what counts, in the eyes of Nature, as true accomplishment. This is not an unfamiliar ethical ideal among young men and adolescent boys.

Callicles uses his flair for a well-turned phrase to defend the magnificent-stallion view of man. Biological success is moral success. The Great One is the dominant male who takes control of the herd. He beats off competitors and wins sexual gratification. Except that this movement from biology to morality seems, at first glance, logically problematic. Rachel Barney (2004, s.v. 'Callicles and Thrasymachus') claims that Callicles commits the naturalistic fallacy. He derives an 'ought' from an 'is'. He assumes that because Nature is like this, this is a good way to be. In fact, Callicles' attitude is more scientific rather than philosophical. Callicles is not trying to argue a new set of values into existence. He is truthfully describing (he thinks) what human beings already value. He is not drawing an 'ought' from nothing; he believes that there already is an 'ought' in human nature. In effect, he tells Socrates: stop arguing and look!

It is as if humanity is in a race. We are all running towards the finish line; everyone is trying to get there as fast as possible; everyone is trying to win. The slowest, who are much more numerous, teach the faster runners that it is immoral to run on ahead. They make them slow down so that everyone can cross the finish line together. But this is profoundly unsatisfying. It is clear that we all want to win; we all secretly want to cross the finish line ahead of everyone else. Callicles is not saying that we *should* value winning; he is saying that, in fact, we *do* value winning. This is just the way we are. The only way to counter Callicles' argument is to show (as Socrates attempts) that there is something wrong with his account of human nature.

Callicles' position resembles that of other immoralists such as Niccolo Machiavelli, Friedrich Nietzsche, the Marquis de Sade and Ayn Rand. His Great Man resembles Milton's Satan, Nietzsche's *Übermensch*, or Rand's John Galt. Or again, it reminds us of larger-than-life historical figures such as Hitler, Mussolini, Stalin or Mao. It is a sinister coterie. Dodds, in discussing the influence of Callicles on Nietzsche, writes:

> It is an irony of history that Plato's exposition of the ideas he meant to destroy should have thus contributed to the formidable renaissance of these ideas in our days. Yet so it is: Nietzsche was, in certain aspects of his thought, the illegitimate and undesired offspring of Plato, as the Nazis were to be in turn the illegitimate and undesired offspring of Nietzsche (Dodds 1959, 390-1).

Dodds is not entirely wrong. If, however, the Nazis found inspiration in Nietzsche, and if Nietzsche found inspiration in Callicles, Callicles himself does not subscribe to the peculiar pseudo-scientific blend of racism and eugenics that characterised National Socialism. Callicles does not argue for government by a superior, purer race. He believes in great individuals, not in great communities.

Because we do not have any independent source of information about

Callicles, we must, in the final analysis, see him through Plato's eyes. There is a symmetry at work in *Gorgias*. This is a disagreement between two men, Socrates and Callicles, who will share a similar fate. As far as we can tell, both were executed. Each warns the other of the approaching danger. One will be a martyr for virtue; the other will be a martyr for absolute freedom. One will die for philosophy; one will die for sophism. But that is where the similarity ends. It is not simply that one historical figure is remembered and that – but for Plato's account – the other would be entirely forgotten. There is also a stark asymmetry in their positions. Socrates who is finally tried and convicted for being a sophist who corrupts the youth of Athens is shown by Plato to be the one person who devotes all his energies to refuting the dangerous opinions of an interlocutor like Callicles, a young man corrupted by sophism.

Bibliography

Andokides, *On the Mysteries*, ed. with introduction, commentary and appendices by Douglas MacDowell (Oxford: Clarendon Press / New York: Oxford University Press, 1962).

Barney, Rachel, 'Callicles and Thrasymachus', *Stanford Encyclopedia of Philosophy*, 2004: http://plato.stanford.edu/entries/callicles-thrasymachus/

Guthrie, W.K.C., *A History of Greek Philosophy*, vol. III: *The Fifth Century Enlightenment* (Cambridge: Cambridge University Press, 1969).

Liddell and Scott, *Greek-English Lexicon* (Oxford: Clarendon Press, 2002).

Nails, Debra, *The People of Plato: A Prosopography of Plato and Other Socratics* (Indianapolis, IN: Hackett, 2002), s.v. 'Callicles of Acharnae' pp. 75-7.

Plato, *Gorgias*, trans. Benjamin Jowett (New York: C. Scribner's Sons, 1871).

Plato, *Gorgias*, trans. with introduction by W.C. Helmbold (New York: The Liberal Arts Press, 1952).

Plato, *Gorgias: A Revised Text*, trans. with introduction and commentary by E.R. Dodds (London: Oxford University Press, 1959).

Plato, *Gorgias*, trans W.D. Woodhead, in *The Collected Dialogues of Plato,* ed. Edith Hamilton and Huntington Cairns (Princeton, NJ: Princeton University Press, 1961).

Plato, *Gorgias*, trans. Terrence Irwin (Oxford: Clarendon Press, 1979).

Plato, *Laws*, trans. A.E. Taylor, in *The Collected Dialogues of Plato*, ed. Edith Hamilton and Huntington Cairns (Princeton, NJ: Princeton University Press, 1961).

Redfield, James, 'Review of Andokides: "On the Mysteries" by Douglas MacDowell (editor)' in *Classical Philology* 59, 4 (Oct. 1964), 286-8.

10

Critias

Sabatino DiBernardo

Critias (*c.* 460-403 BC), an aristocratic Athenian of intellectual acumen, literary, musical, athletic and oratorical skill, and, during his latter years, political aspiration, has been both heralded and demonised in the ancient Greek literary record. Most of our information regarding Critias' life comes to us from stories written by Plato (*c.* 429-347 BC), Xenophon (*c.* 427-355 BC), and Philostratus (*c.* 170-*c.* 247 AD).

Critias was born into a long line of distinguished citizens and leaders in Athens. He was the son of Callaeschrus, with connections stretching back to Solon the lawgiver (*c.* 640-560 BC) and forward to his younger second cousin Plato (Critias was first cousin to Plato's mother Perictone, as well as a cousin of Charmides). Socrates testifies to this exceptional lineage when he proclaims that Critias' philosophical and poetic skills, shared by the rest of his family, date back to Solon (Plato, *Charmides* 155a). Thus it is safe to assume that Critias received a traditional Athenian education as befitted an aristocrat, encompassing philosophy, music, literature, rhetoric and athletics, and intended to develop a cultured soul and to prepare the privileged Athenian male for civic life.

Critias first appears as an interlocutor in four of Plato's Socratic dialogues (namely *Charmides*, *Protagoras*, *Timaeus* and *Critias*). However, there has been some question as to the identity of the Critias represented in the dialogues (Critias the sophist, or this Critias' grandfather). If one accepts the argument proposed by Dorothy Stephans that the Critias of the *Timaeus* and *Critias* is actually Critias the sophist's grandfather, this would leave *Charmides* and *Protagoras* as the two dialogues in which Critias the sophist is represented. The benefits of accepting this theory are twofold: first, the genealogical discrepancies in traditional accounts of who is being referenced in the Platonic dialogues are rectified; second, it further works to absolve 'Plato of an inexcusable ignorance about his own family's history' (Stephans 1939, 5).

Regarding Critias' dealings with the sophists, he is believed to have been a student of Gorgias (*c.* 483-375 BC), who is credited with developing sophism. Critias would have had plenty of opportunity to attend Gorgias' lectures as well as those of other itinerant sophists during the fifth century. The sophists' increasing popularity was due in large measure to their pedagogical concentration on preparation of Athenian males for success in civic life – for a fee. This unheard of practice for philosophers of this period caused great consternation among other philosophers, including Socrates and, later, Plato, who could not fathom the selling of virtue/ knowledge for monetary gain. Nevertheless, the tools that the sophists taught, which included public speaking and argumentation, provided the requisite skills for those with civic and political ambitions.

Although Critias has long been considered a sophist, there have been some scholarly reservations regarding this inclusion. Of course, this question is contingent upon one's definition of a sophist and is by no means a denial of sophistic proclivities on the part of Critias. If by this term one means an itinerant, professional (i.e. paid) teacher of rhetoric and argumentation, then Critias was not a sophist. As Dillon and Gergel argue, 'Critias was not really a professional Sophist; rather, he was an Athenian gentleman, of reactionary political sympathies (very much like Callicles portrayed in Plato's *Gorgias*), who entered thoroughly into the sophistic tradition' (Dillon and Gergel 2003, 218). G.B. Kerferd suggests that Critias was 'in a sense a pupil of Socrates and other sophists rather than himself a sophist' (Kerferd 1981, 52). Notwithstanding this question of his *professional* status as a sophist, one might argue that an acceptance of the sophistic teachings would, in a broad sense, allow us to count Critias among their number. As Jacqueline de Romilly suggests, 'Even if he did not receive any payment for his lectures, he lived as an intellectual, writing treatises on constitutions, taking part in philosophical debates, and helping to spread the Sophists' ideas' (Romilly 1998, 108). Thus it is safe to assume that at the very least Critias' sophism entailed an acceptance and implementation of the rhetorical and dialectic skills in which he was trained for success in the civic affairs of Athenian political life.

Given this pedagogical relationship with Gorgias and the sophists, what is one to make of Critias' affiliation with Socrates, who had no great admiration for the sophists? It is safe to assume that an association of some significance existed between these two figures when one takes into account Critias' inclusion in the Platonic dialogues as an interlocutor of Socrates and couples this with the historical narratives provided by Philostatus and Xenophon which indicate a close, if somewhat contentious, relationship between Critias and Socrates. However, important questions surface regarding the level or depth of this affiliation. For example, to what extent was Critias' affiliation with Socrates pedagogical or personal in nature? Was Socrates simply a family friend continuing a relationship that began between Socrates and Critias' grandfather? Was Critias a *serious* student of Socrates? Or, was he simply an acquaintance on the fringes gravitating around Socrates for whatever benefits this familiarity might entail?

Although a simple resolution to questions of personal intent is a difficult undertaking, especially when removed by such an expanse of time and context, perhaps, assessing this relationship may be more a matter of degree than of kind. Nevertheless, the ancient commentators felt this connection important enough to explain, since this teacher/student relationship was to be used by Athenian politicians to impugn Socrates' character (and, perhaps, to bring charges against Socrates that would subsequently bring about his execution) based on his role as 'teacher' of Critias (who had become *persona non grata* based on his tyrannical role in the oligarchic government, as we will see).

Xenophon's account, for instance, reads as an apologia for Socrates' life and a rehabilitation of his character for posterity. And even in the case of Philostratus, writing centuries later *within* the sophistic tradition and for whom Socrates' defence was not of paramount concern, Critias does not escape unscathed. A juxtaposition of their lives is summed up in one reflective statement by Philostratus: 'it is a strange thing that he did not grow to be like Socrates, the son of Sophroniscus, with whom above all others he studied philosophy and who had the reputation of being the wisest and the most just of his times' (Philostratus, *Lives of the Sophists* I.16; Sprague 2001, 242). This suggests not only that Critias had indeed studied under Socrates but also that he did not remain within his tutelage. At some point Critias, as well as Alcibiades with whom Critias shared a close, if later damaged, bond, parted company or at least common philosophical values with Socrates.

Xenophon plunges deeper into this question with a greater sense of something real at stake – the legacy of the man he admired, Socrates. According to Stephans, Xenophon distinguished between two types of students: one 'who imitated the master and adopted his ideas, and another, like Critias and Alcibiades, who associated with him and listened to him without reflecting his mind or soul in their own' (Stephans 1939, 10-11). As previously noted, Xenophon's narrative should be placed within the context of a defence or apologia for Socrates against accusations made that he was an evil man based on his role as 'teacher' of Critias (along with another 'student' Alcibiades, both of whom had become characterised in the popular mind as tyrannical and brutal). Consequently, Xenophon's defence of Socrates establishes rather than denies an affiliation while calling into serious question the kind, quality and commitment of Critias to Socrates and his philosophical way of being. In the process of rehabilitating Socrates' reputation, we are provided with a possible glimpse into Critias' personal inclinations and politically motivated aspirations.

In *Memorabilia*, Xenophon states that Socrates' accusers claim that it was after their association with Socrates that Critias and Alcibiades 'harmed the city the most. For Critias was the most thievish, violent, murderous of all in the oligarchy, and Alcibiades the most incontinent, violent and murderous of all in the democracy' (*Memorabilia* I.2.12). Without denying the accusers' charges against these men and in no way wanting to defend them, Xenophon argues that this relationship with Socrates was instigated by self-aggrandising political pretensions and egocentric dispositions:

For these two men were by nature the most honour-loving of all the Athenians. They wished that all affairs might be conducted through themselves and that they might become the most renowned of all ... Since these two saw things and were of the sort I mentioned before, would anyone say that they yearned for his association because they desired the life of Socrates and the moderation that he had, or because they held that if they associated with him they would become the most competent in speech and action? (*Memorabilia* I.2.14-15).

Xenophon clearly questions the purity of their intentions and motivations with respect to their desire to be associated with Socrates. In order to drive this point home in no uncertain terms, Xenophon speculates that if given a choice between living like Socrates or dying, these two would rather choose to be dead, and that this was made quite evident by their actions. Moreover, when perceived that their skills were greater than others' in Athens with whom they needed to contend for political power, 'they immediately bolted from Socrates and engaged in political affairs, which was precisely the reason they had yearned for Socrates' (*Memorabilia* I.2.16). Xenophon tells a tale of a politically usurious ulterior motive that drew Critias to Socrates. Further to support his claim, Xenophon explains that this was made evident by the absence of any desire to 'attempt to converse with any others more than with those most deeply engaged in political affairs' (*Memorabilia* I.2.39). Indeed, in contradistinction to the claims being levelled against Socrates, this narrative seems to suggest that both were actually better off for their association with Socrates, notwithstanding their own personal intentions. Although both Critias and Alcibiades may have been driven by political pretensions and an excessive zeal for power, in fact moderation of temperament was the result of being in the company of Socrates.

Xenophon concludes that the primary reason for Critias' fall from grace (as well as Alcibiades') was not his association with Socrates, which actually kept his desires in check during their affiliation; rather, it was because 'they were also inflated because of their birth, conceited due to being rich, puffed up by power, and fussed-over by many human beings; and having been corrupted by all these things, they were also away from Socrates for a long time. Why is it a wonder if they became arrogant?' (*Memorabilia* I.2.25). Thus, if one is to believe Xenophon's account, arrogance, self-aggrandisement, pretensions to power and excessive pride due to family lineage, privilege and wealth all contributed to the eventual path that Critias would travel away from Socrates and into the historical record as a brutal tyrant.

But this is not the end of the story regarding the relationship between Socrates and Critias. One very important public excoriation at the hands of Socrates would forever mark Critias with anger, resentment and, ultimately, vengeance against his former associate. Xenophon recounts an

114

episode in which Socrates publicly reprimanded Critias' ignoble advances, lustful and 'swinish passion in desiring to move against Euthydemus like piglets against stones' (*Memorabilia* I.2.30). It is evident that whatever association Critias had with Socrates early in life, this did not extend into his later years when he was actively opposed to Socrates. Indeed, it is evident that Critias bore a grudge over this incident (as well as over Socrates' public statements about the murderous actions of Critias and the Thirty) that would rear its head when, during Critias' reign of terror, Socrates was brought in before the Thirty and forbidden to speak with the youth of Athens. While admonishing Socrates to obey the laws against teaching the art of speeches, Critias took the opportunity to return this long-festering slight by announcing publicly and, one would imagine, with the most moralistic inflection that he could muster, that Socrates should stay away from 'shoemakers, builders and smiths' (*Memorabilia* I.2.37) for their sake.

Whatever one may think of the means that Critias utilised to acquire his desired ends, they worked. Critias' political position in Athens as a leader of the oligarchic government known as the Thirty Tyrants (403 BC) following the Peloponnesian War is unquestioned. Unfortunately, these same unsavoury means would come back to haunt Critias long after he went to the grave. Critias' actions during his brief political tenure, which in a later historical period would come to be characterised as Machiavellian, would set the stage for his tainted legacy. Indeed, it is this period of Critias' life that would henceforth brand him in the eyes of many as an evil tyrant.

The perceptions of and accusations levelled against Critias as being tyrannical and merciless in zeal find their primary source in events surrounding the ousting of the Athenian democracy and the establishment of the new oligarchic government with Critias, who was pro-Spartan, and other anti-democratic Athenians in leadership positions (Dillon and Gergel 2003, 217). The political turmoil following the Peloponnesian War, which brought the Golden Age to a close, engendered a political rift in Athens between pro-democratic and pro-oligarchic (i.e. pro-Spartan) polities. With the Spartan defeat of Athens came a restructuring of the political arena that had to negotiate these competing political alignments.

In the midst of this political and war-weary morass, Sparta attempted to establish a sense of freedom within the Greek states from the previous imperialistic Athenian government and policies. However, whatever moderate intentions the Spartans may have entertained, this political replacement merely substituted one form of hegemonic rule for another, with Lysander the conquering commander becoming increasingly powerful and at the centre of enacting governmental policies. It had become Spartan practice to establish oligarchic rules over areas that they had conquered. This typically included a group of ten in charge of governance with a Spartan commander and army at their disposal. However, this was to change somewhat from Spartan protocol under the direction of Lysander. As Victor Ehrenberg explains:

five ephors were at first appointed (Lysias 12, 43), an unheard-of office after the Spartan model; then the decree of Dracontides formally established oligarchy. Under the pretext of aiming at restoring the 'ancestral laws', thirty men were elected to be masters of the state (Ehrenberg 1967, 344).

Critias and Theramenes were two of the most prominent among the Thirty chosen to govern. Unfortunately, the corruption of power that had brought about the downfall of Athens was beginning to infect the characteristically austere Spartans and in particular Lysander, who instituted the Thirty. Signs of this contagion became evident in the pretensions of the Thirty when they began to assume power from the local courts and instituted a vicious campaign that would lead to further violence and death for many Athenians, as a result of which this group would become branded as the Thirty Tyrants.

It was against this backdrop that Critias found himself at the centre of a political situation pregnant with possibility for those with such aspirations. However, as with any civil warfare and unrest, deeply held political allegiances were not without risk to the life of the state and individual. For Critias, the alignment with Sparta and the establishment of an oligarchy were only natural given his predisposition towards all things Spartan. For instance, in one literary fragment (*The Constitution of the Spartans*) Critias praises the moderation of the Spartans in their eating and drinking habits (which would not dull their thoughts and readiness for action), and their laughter in contrast to Athenian tendencies to excess in these areas (Dillon and Gergel 2003, 237). Some note that Critias' love for and excellence in playing the flute may also be traced to his attraction to Spartan culture (Dillon and Gergel 2003, 229), as might his commending the Spartans on everything from their clothing to their furniture to their manner of raising children. Consequently, when Athens was confronted with the Spartan army led by Lysander, Critias was among those ready and willing to take part in the new government, which was established to revise Athenian law but in actuality began their absolute rule. As Dillon and Gergel note, 'The Thirty never did revise the laws, but turned immediately to executing, first, notorious democratic troublemakers, but then, progressively, rich citizens and resident aliens ... to raise funds from confiscating their assets' (Dillon and Gergel 2003, 227). It appears that even moderate oligarchs such as Theramenes, who protested the executions of pro-democratic Athenians and was ultimately himself executed at the behest of Critias, were unsafe during this period of ever-tightening control and internal power struggles.

Philostratus tells us that Critias' role in the oligarchy was oppressive and was not above drawing upon the method of false accusation from his arsenal of political strategies (Philostratus, *Lives of the Sophists* I.16). Interestingly, Philosostratus does not revile Critias for his part in overthrowing the democracy in Athens, since he (as well as Plato early in his life) recognised that the democracy had become 'so overbearing and insolent that it would not heed even those who governed according to the established laws' (Philostratus, *Lives of the Sophists* I.16). Rather, Philostratus described Critias as an evil man based on Critias' *betrayal* of Athens due to his pro-Spartan tendencies, his blasphemous behaviour (perhaps a reference to Critias' purported complicity in the desecration of the Herms – statues of the phallic god Hermes that were thought to bring good luck – on the eve of the Sicilian Expedition by Athens in 415 BC, which marked the beginning of the end for Athens), and his culpability in brutal crimes against his fellow Athenians. Some of Philostratus' accusations against Critias were that he:

> conspicuously sided with Sparta, and betrayed the holy places to the enemy; that he pulled down the walls by agency of Lysander; that he deprived the Athenians whom he drove into exile of any place of refuge in Greece by proclaiming that Sparta would wage war on any that should harbour an Athenian exile; that in brutality and bloodthirstiness he surpassed even the Thirty; that he shared in the monstrous design of Sparta to make Attica look like a mere pasture for sheep by emptying her of her human herd (*Lives of the Sophists* I.16).

Indeed, for Philostratus, Critias' vile behaviour is even more incomprehensible and culpable given his education and his distinguished family roots. Thus, in Philostratus' opinion, Critias 'cannot be acquitted in the sight of most men of the charges that these crimes were due to his own natural wickedness' (*Lives of the Sophists* I.16).

Critias' political misdeeds, violence and impiety were even to impact on his cousin Plato, who during his youth entertained thoughts of devoting himself to a life of public service. After witnessing the unjust policies that Critias and the Thirty were pursuing, and perhaps naively thinking that 'they were going to lead the city out of the unjust life' that Athens had been living and 'establish her in the path of justice' (Plato, *Seventh Letter* 324d-325a), Plato rejected Critias' request to join him in the oligarchy and abandoned any political ambitions he may have nurtured. Plato recounts a particularly distasteful event that would instigate his disassociation from his cousin and the regime:

> Among their other deeds they named Socrates, an older friend of mine whom I shall not hesitate to call the justest man of that time. As one of a group sent to arrest a certain citizen who was to be put to death illegally, planning thereby to make Socrates willy-nilly a party to their actions. But he refused, risking the utmost danger rather than be an associate in their impious deeds. When I saw all this and other like things of no little consequence, I was appalled and drew back from that reign of injustice (*Seventh Letter* 324c-325b).

Although the historical record concentrates primarily on the negative or less than amiable characteristics of Critias' behaviour as a consequence of his political ambition, there is another side of his personality that has been overshadowed historically by his political intrigues. As an aristocratic Athenian, Critias enjoyed the privilege of exposure to a well-rounded education, which included art, music, literature, dialectics and athletics. However, exposure alone cannot account for his achievements in so many of these areas. Indeed, Critias possessed a natural ability and predisposition toward things artistic, musical, athletic and intellectual. He was known to have been an excellent flautist and a prolific writer. While the vast majority of Critias' own writings are lost to history with the exception of some fragments, his extensive authorship is widely recognised in antiquity with numerous works in prose and verse in a variety of styles attributed to him. The following are included within his literary corpus: *Constitutions* of the Thessalians, Spartans and possibly the Athenians; *Aphorisms,* didactic and praise poetry including one to his friend Alcibiades; and tragedies such as the *Tennes,* the *Rhadamanthys* and the *Pirithous.* Also, the satyr-drama *Sisyphus* is attributed to him by Sextus Empiricus who counts him among the atheists. This fragment is of particular importance in terms of attaching Critias to the sophistic tradition by way of the *homo mensura* doctrine (i.e. man as the measure of all things) as it relates to the gods. According to Sextus, Critias provides a narrative attributing the 'existence' of the gods to a discursive fabrication perpetrated by clever humans wishing to maintain civil order based on a morality that is punished and rewarded by an omniscient and omnipotent God. In the fragment from *Sisyphus* preserved by Sextus (in *Against the Physicists* I.54) Critias states:

> A time there was when anarchy did rule
> The lives of men, which then were like the beasts,
> Enslaved to force; nor was there then reward
> For good men, nor for wicked punishment.
> Next, as I deem, did men establish laws
> For punishment, that Justice might be lord
> Of all mankind, and Insolence enchain'd;
> And whosoe'er did sin was penalized.
> Next, as the laws did hold back men from deeds
> Of open violence, but still such deeds
> Were done in secret, – then, as I maintain,
> Some shrewd man first, a man in counsel wise,
> Discovered unto men the fear of Gods,
> Thereby to frighten sinners should they sin
> E'en secretly in deed, or word, or thought.
> Hence was it that he brought in Deity,
> Telling how God enjoys endless life,

Hears with his mind and sees, and taketh thought
And heeds things, and his nature is divine,
So that he hearkens to men's every word
And has the power to see men's every act.
E'en if you plan in silence some ill deed,
The Gods will surely mark it; for in them Wisdom resides.
So, speaking words like these,
Most cunning doctrine did he introduce,
The truth concealing under speech untrue ... .

In addition to this challenge to conventional wisdom pertaining to the existence of the gods, this fragment also reveals a trace of the rhetorical sophistic device of making the 'worse' argument the 'better' (or making that which is untrue true for the intended end of the one instigating the discourse). Thus Critias attempts to tell a tale of wise humans that became their own measure of truth in order to secure their desired ends.

With respect to Critias' oratorical skill, Philostratus, who was no friend of his, tells us that Critias

> abounded in brief and sententious sayings, and he was most skilful in the use of elevated language, but not of the dithyrambic sort, nor did he have recourse to words borrowed from poetry; but his was the kind of elevated language that is composed of the most appropriate words and is not artificial. I observe, moreover, that he was a master of concise eloquence, and that even when he maintained the tone proper to speech in defence, he used to make vigorous attacks on his opponent ... (*Lives of the Sophists* I.16).

Philostratus does not fail to add that due to Critias' questionable character, 'this man's wisdom and his writings are held in slight esteem by the Greeks; for unless our public utterances and our moral character are in accord, we shall seem, like flutes, to speak with a tongue that is not our own' (*Lives of the Sophists* I.16).

In closing, when one juxtaposes Critias' literary corpus and the beliefs contained therein with his political tactics, ascendancy to a position of power within Athens, and the rhetorical prowess that he wielded toward this end, it is not unreasonable to assume that he utilised the tools of the sophists well, as was to be expected of those who sought this type of education, and accomplished that which he desired. Nevertheless, for all of his abilities, talents and skills, Critias did not escape unscathed from his involvement in politics, which in the end was his undoing. Critias would himself suffer exile in Thessaly (406 BC), a fate he had meted out to others. Finally, those he had executed for their opposition to his rule were joined by Critias in May 403 BC when he died on the battlefield as a member of the Thirty.

Bibliography

Cooper, J.M. (ed.) *Plato: Complete Works* (Indianapolis, IN: Hackett, 1997).

Dillon, John and Gergel, Tania, *The Greek Sophists* (London: Penguin, 2003).

Ehrenberg, Victor, *From Solon to Socrates: Greek History and Civilization during the Sixth and Fifth Centuries BC* (London: Methuen, 1967).

Guthrie, W.K.C., *The Sophists* (Cambridge: Cambridge University Press, 1971).

Kerferd, G.B., *The Sophistic Movement* (Cambridge: Cambridge University Press, 1981).

Philostratus, *Lives of the Sophists*, trans. Wilmer Cave Wright, Loeb edition (London: Heinemann, 1922).

Romilly, Jacqueline de, *The Great Sophists in Periclean Athens* (Oxford: Clarendon Press, 1992).

Sextus Empiricus, vol. III: *Against the Physicists: Against the Ethicists*, trans. R.G. Bury, Loeb edition. (London: Heinemann, 1936; Cambridge, MA: Harvard University Press, 1987, reprint).

Stephans, Dorothy, *Critias: Life and Literary Remains,* unpublished dissertation, University of Cincinnati, 1939.

Xenophon, *Memorabilia*, trans. Amy L. Bonnette (Ithaca, NY: Cornell University Press, 1994).

Euthydemus and Dionysodorus

Geoff Bowe

Euthydemus and Dionysodorus are said to have been brothers from Chios. This island in the Aegean across from ancient Smyrna (modern Izmir) was home to the poet Simonides and reputed to be the birthplace of Homer. Like the sons of Cephalus, namely Polemarchus, Euthydemus and Lysias, who appear in Plato's *Republic*, and the historian Herodotus, Euthydemus and Dionysodorus were involved in the founding of a new Athenian colony at Thurii in Southern Italy in the 440s BC. This colonisation was led by the sophist Protagoras at the request of Pericles. After the Sicilian expedition (Athens' attempt to take Sicily in the Peloponnesian War) ended in disaster for Athens in 413, those with Athenian sympathies were exiled from Thurii, and this group of exiles included our two sophists. They are said by Plato in *Euthydemus* to have been in and around Athens for several years; they are rather old, and Socrates himself is old, which places the dialogue in the range of the last decade of the fifth century, at which time Socrates was in his sixties and these men perhaps a little older.

Most of our information about the two sophists comes from Plato's dialogue *Euthydemus*. In the nineteenth century Schliermacher assumed the dialogue to be directed at Plato's contemporary Antisthenes, a one-time pupil of the sophist Gorgias, but later a follower of Socrates and founder of the cynic sect. Indeed in *Euthydemus* (285dff.) we see Dionysodorus employing an argument of Antisthenes' about speaking falsely, which is said to be impossible, given that it is not possible to speak of what is not. Despite the fact that Socrates says that he has heard it on many occasions, and seen the idea employed by Protagoras and his followers, and in spite of the fact that Parmenides claims in his poem *On Nature* that 'you cannot speak of what is not', scholars ascribe the argument to Antisthenes. On the assumption that the dialogue is directed at Antisthenes, and that the two sophists here depicted are fictional, Euthydemus and Dionysodorus were omitted from Diels' collection of fragments of the sophists; they re-appear in Sprague's *The Older Sophists*, and more recent works on the sophists have followed suit, including recent books edited by Waterfield (2000) and Dillon and Gergel (2003).

That the two men were in fact real, and not merely an invention of Plato employed as an attack against Antisthenes, is evidenced by the fact that Xenophon discusses Dionysodorus in his *Memoirs of Socrates* (*Memora-*

bilia I.1.1), and Aristotle twice refers to an argument of Euthydemus, once in *Rhetoric* (1401a27) and once in *Sophistical Refutations* (177b12), an argument that does not come from Plato's dialogue. According to Xenophon, Socrates' assessment of Dionysodorus' skill at teaching generalship was rather inadequate and suspect. According to Aristotle, Euthydemus was known to have offered a rather silly argument to the effect that one knows there is a trireme in the Piraeus because one knows what a trireme is, what the Piraeus is and what 'is in' means. Plato also refers to Euthydemus outside the dialogue that bears his name, in a passage in *Cratylus* where Euthydemus is said to have maintained that everything always has every attribute simultaneously (386d). The evidence, scant as it is from sources other than Plato's *Euthydemus*, seems to suggest that Euthydemus and Dionysodorus were real people.

Having said that, the information we have about the two sophists outside Plato's *Euthydemus* amounts to little more than a few lines, and as such we are dependent on Plato for our knowledge of them, much as we are dependent on Plato for our knowledge of Socrates. Thus Sprague, in reintroducing Euthydemus and Dionysodorus into her canon of early sophists, must admit that it may be preferable to call the 'fragments', the bulk of which are from *Euthydemus*, 'Euthydemian' rather than attributing the ideas and arguments that Plato depicts them as employing as authentic *testimonia* of their work. Knowledge of the specific arguments of the two men is further hampered by the fact that Plato's treatment of them in the dialogue is highly farcical, ironic and directed at the nature of degenerate sophistry in general, and hence likely to be a mélange of sophistical approaches rather than a record of the specific arguments employed by the two men. It has already been remarked above that the argument about speaking falsely has been employed by others. The overlap between another argument in *Euthydemus* about whether the wise or the ignorant learn and the famous paradox in *Meno* (*Euthydemus* 275dff.; *Meno* 80e) also suggests that we are being treated to a display of stock sophistic arguments in *Euthydemus* rather than a collection of authentic thoughts of Euthydemus and Dionysodorus. Given the manner in which Plato chooses to depict the performance of the two men in his dialogue, this is not surprising. They emerge as hacks that rely on memorised set arguments, presented in such a way as to show their real skill to be that of choreography as opposed to education. We can say something about the approach of the two men, bearing in mind that we must interpret this approach through Plato, whose intention is clearly highly critical and uncomplimentary. As this chapter is meant to be an assessment of Euthydemus and Dionysodorus, it may seem odd to spend so much time discussing Plato; given our scant sources this is inevitable, and it does allow us to see how Plato regarded the two men, and what he saw as wrong with their approach, thus allowing us to build up a reasonable, if biased, picture of their activities. For while Plato does seem to have accorded sophists such as Protagoras and Gorgias some modicum of respect, the same cannot be said for his treatment of Dionysodorus and Euthydemus. I will dispense with any discussion of the literary structure of *Euthydemus*, famous for its frame of Socrates' report to Crito about his meeting with the two sophists the previous day, and instead focus on what Plato has Socrates actually report.

In the opening of *Euthydemus*, we find Dionysodorus and Euthydemus giving a display of their skills in the Lyceum, a gymnasium on the outskirts of Athens. The Lyceum was a favourite haunt of Socrates, and later became the site of Aristotle's school. Now while it is true that from a historical point of view the Lyceum would have been a likely place for itinerant sophists to give exhibitions of their skills in the hope of attracting new students, from a literary and inter-textual point of view it must have been hard for Plato to resist the connotations of the Lyceum for the pastiche of the two sophists that he is about to mount. This is worth remarking on as a reply to scholars such as Schliermacher who questioned the dialogue's authenticity on the grounds that it was a childish farce unworthy of Plato. In the first instance, one may recall the opening lines of Plato's *Euthyphro*, where Euthyphro asks Socrates why he is on the steps of the court of the King Archon, instead of his usual haunt, the Lyceum (*Euthyphro* 2a). The overture suggests that while Socrates may fare well in a place of open and fair competition, he may not fare so well in the land of forensic oratory. We shall soon see in *Euthydemus* that the display put on by the two brothers from Chios is anything but fair and open. It is, rather, sport, or play, as Socrates himself puts it – the two sophists, being asked to give a display of what they profess to teach, proceed to beguile the youth Cleinias (a relative of the notorious Athenian general Alcibiades) with verbal trickery, until Socrates wades into the argument to put a stop to it.

One of the interesting points that emerge from Socrates' introduction of Euthydemus and Dionysodorus to Cleinias in the opening scene is that Socrates has seen the two men before, but under a different guise. Socrates knows them as martial arts instructors, and also as forensic speechwriters, and introduces them as such to Cleinias, an introduction that is met with mild dismay by the two sophists, who now, it seems, have taken on a new profession, the teaching of virtue:

> So I greeted the two brothers, as not having seen them for some time; after that I said to Cleinias: 'My dear Cleinias, these two men, you know, are skilled not in little things, but in great. For they understand all about war, that is, as much as is needful for him who is to be a good general; both the tactics and the strategy of armies, and all the teaching of troops under arms; and they can also enable one to get redress in the law courts for a wrong that one may have suffered.'
> When I had said this, I saw they despised me for it, and they both laughed,

looking at each other; then Euthydemus said: 'No, no, Socrates, we do not make those matters our business now; we deal with them as diversions.'

At this I wondered and said: 'Your business must be a fine one, if such great matters are indeed diversions to you; so I beseech you, tell me what this fine business is.'

'Virtue, Socrates', he replied, 'is what we deem ourselves able to purvey in a pre-eminently excellent and speedy manner' (*Euthydemus* 273c-d).

Presumably the two brothers would have preferred to be introduced as professors of virtue, as it would be in their business interests for their reputation as such to have preceded them. The fact that this is an art that they have just recently 'perfected' and the fact that they claim to be able to impart virtue quickly and easily to all and sundry for a fee is bound to raise eyebrows, and indeed the whole jack-of-all-tradesmanship of these characters indicates what Plato would have us make of these men. They are charlatans, hustlers out to cash in on whatever seems most profitable. Socrates, ironically or not, praises the men's skill at martial arts to Cleinias. Given the circumstance, one suspects that Socrates is being ironic in this praise, an assumption which is strengthened somewhat when one considers that the report of Dionysodorus' skill in teaching generalship in Xenophon's *Memorabilia* is directed at the shallowness of the instruction given:

'...tell us the first lesson [Dionysodorus] gave you in generalship.'

'The first was like the last,' he replied; 'he taught me tactics – nothing else.'

'But then that is only a small part of generalship. ... Well and good, provided that he taught you also to distinguish the good and the bad men. If not, what have you gained by your lessons ...'

'I assure you he didn't; so we should have to judge for ourselves which are the good men and which are the bad.'

'But,' said Socrates, 'did he teach you only the disposition of an army, or did he include where and how to use each formation?'

'Not at all.'

'And yet there are many situations that call for a modification of tactics and strategy.'

'I assure you he didn't explain that.'

'Then pray go back and ask him. If he knows and has a conscience, he will be ashamed to send you home ill-taught, after taking your money' (*Memorabilia* III.1.5-11).

On the surface, the way in which Socrates describes the sophists' treatment of Cleinias in *Euthydemus* shows that the two are disputatious and show little regard for the truth. They make a spectacle of the boy, employing set arguments grounded in double meanings and verbal ambiguities designed to confound and confuse an interlocutor, all to the cheers and laughter of a band of admirers. Plato conveys the sense of the spectacle of a doomed gladiator falling again and again to the cheers of a bloodthirsty audience. The vivid description of the carnival-like atmosphere generated by the showmanship of the two brothers can be seen in the following passage, wherein Cleinias' initial claim, that it is the foolish and not the wise who learn, is contradicted by stock sophistical argumentation:

> When he had thus spoken, all those followers of Dionysodorus and Euthyde-mus raised a cheer and a laugh, like a chorus at the signal of their director; and before the boy could fairly and fully recover his breath Dionysodorus took up the cudgels and said: 'Well now, Cleinias, whenever your writing-master dictated from memory, which of the boys learnt the piece recited, the wise or the foolish?'
> 'The wise,' said Cleinias.
> 'So it is the wise who learn, and not the foolish: hence the answer you gave just now to Euthydemus was a bad one.'
> Thereupon arose a great deal of laughter and loud applause from the pair's adorers, in admiration of their cleverness; while we on our side were dismayed and held our peace. Then Euthydemus, observing our dismay, and seeking to astonish us still further, would not let the boy go, but went on questioning him and, like a skilful dancer, gave a twofold twist to his questions on the same point: 'Now, do the learners learn what they know, he asked, or what they do not?'
> Then Dionysodorus whispered to me again softly: 'Here comes a second one, Socrates, just like the first.'
> 'Heavens!' I replied: 'Surely the first question served you well enough.'
> 'All our questions, Socrates,' he said, 'are like that; they leave no escape' (*Euthydemus* 276b-e).

As Euthydemus is questioning Cleinias, his brother Dionysodorus keeps a running side-commentary on how the arguments are destined to defeat Cleinias, that he has no escape, whispering his remarks to Socrates, who is less than impressed. The two brothers are depicted as working in tandem, picking up each other's cues and playing with Cleinias as if tossing a ball to and fro in a highly choreographed display of confounding verbal eristic.

Some scholars have approached *Euthydemus* as Plato's attempt to list, systematically or unsystematically, sophistical arguments, arguments that were to be rendered more systematically by Aristotle in his *Sophistical Refutations*. However, as Thomas Chance has argued quite convincingly, we gain more insight into the dialogue if we focus on the role that protreptic or exhortation to virtue plays in it, examining the dialogue on its own terms, independently of the question of the specifics of the sophistical argumentation that places the focus of Plato's intention on the nature of philosophical protreptic (Chance 1992, passim).

Protreptic in Plato is often ignored, which is a shame insofar as a better understanding of it yields a better understanding of Plato's philosophy in general, and grants deeper insight into why it is that Plato gave the name 'sophist' the negative connotation it presently has. In addition to the idea that the sophist is a *banausos*, someone who 'sells himself', the kind of 'education' offered up by Euthydemus and Dionysodorus is mere show-manship that should not be taken seriously. But if they are not to be taken seriously, we are left with a deeper philosophical question as to why Plato took the time to address them. This seems to be the force of Crito's remarks in *Euthydemus* itself, which suggest that the readiness to engage in discussion with such people before a large company is worthy of reproach (*Euthydemus* 305b). Read a certain way, *Euthydemus* delves into a deeper danger of sophistry, one that Plato goes to great lengths to distinguish from philosophy. For on the surface there is much similarity between the methodology of Euthydemus and Dionysodorus and that of Socrates. Both sides employ eristic arguments, both quibble with words, both use a question-and-answer method that points up contradictions in their inter-locutors' beliefs. The difference between the sophistic employment of these tools and the way that Socrates employs them is the direction to which the result points. That is, in the case of our two sophists in *Euthydemus*, once the show is over, we are left wondering what the next step is. What is the point of merely confounding an opponent once the applause and cheers have died? Plato is striving, it seems, to show that there is no point. That this is the point to which Clitophon is brought at the end of the curious dialogue that bears his name (*Clitophon* 408e), and that *Clitophon* is one of few Platonic works that mentions protreptic explicitly will be of signifi-cance for the deeper target of Plato's assessment of Euthydemus and Dionysodorus.

For Socrates has asked the two sophists to give a demonstration of how to exhort a student to take up the study of virtue, and to take it up with them. That is, Socrates has asked the two sophists to show how they would convince someone who was unaware of the need to seek instruction in virtue that it is indeed necessary. Socrates even offers what he says is a rudimentary and amateurish protreptic discourse, in order to elicit from the men what he expects will be a more professionally polished and convincing version of the same. This of course is not forthcoming, and the sophists lapse into more and more absurd and untenable 'sophisms', evoking the ire of Cleinias' lover Ctesippus and making them appear more and more ridiculous, amateur and shallow in contrast to the sincere if rudimentary goals of Socrates' philosophical protreptic.

Since Demetrius of Phaleron (born *c.* 350 BC), it has generally been thought that Platonic protreptic is implicit, the intended result of Socratic elenchus (questioning or cross-examination) and *aporia* (the confusion resulting from elenchus) procedures that is not explicitly spoken. That the Socratic method, in its fundamental outlook and aim, is explicitly or implicitly the exhortation to the care of the soul is borne out by Socrates' own assessment of his Apollonian mission in the *Apology*, by Alcibiades' drunken encomium on Socrates in *Symposium*, and by Clitophon's com-plaints in *Clitophon*. Even in *Meno*, a dialogue which has resonances with

11. Euthydemus and Dionysodorus

Euthydemus, as has already been observed, Socrates explicitly suggests that the goal of *aporia* and indeed of the theory of recollection offered to Meno are protreptic in intention and meant to offer an alternative to the arguments of eristic debaters.

In short, what *Euthydemus* points out is that in the degenerate sophistry represented by the two brothers from Chios, there is no profit to be had in terms of wisdom, and as Socrates himself puts the point in the course of the dialogue, no profit can come from any skill that does not employ wisdom. But wisdom, in the final analysis, is commensurate with the care of the soul, and it is precisely this that Euthydemus and Dionysodorus, professed experts in virtue, fail to grasp. Education, as Socrates tells us explicitly in his *Republic*, is not imparting knowledge by pouring sight into blind eyes – as many professional educators think that it is (*Republic* 518b-c). This seems to be intended as a reproach to the irate candour of Thrasymachus, who earlier offers to pour his argument into Socrates' soul in order to make him understand – Socrates emphatically refuses (*Republic* 345b). This difference in approaches, grounded as it is in the assumption made explicit in *Euthydemus*, that protreptic is an integral prerequisite to instruction in virtue, and that education is not merely the imparting of a skill, is a point that is suggested at many places in the Platonic corpus. Socrates in *Symposium,* on touching Agathon's cloak, laments that knowledge cannot be imparted by physical contact (*Symposium* 175d). Meno, the pupil of Gorgias, is someone who wants knowledge to be handed over to him on a plate, and Clitophon suffers from the same ailment in his demand that Socrates tell him what justice is. In short the limitation of Euthydemian sophistry is such that it fails to grasp the true nature of education, the true value of philosophy, the importance of protreptic, and the patience and time needed to master virtue.

That Plato would go to great pains to point this out, whether as a response to Isocrates, as many have suggested about the unnamed critic at the end of *Euthydemus,* or as a general statement of the Platonic approach to education, or perhaps more plausibly as a defence of Socrates against charges of sophism in the court of Athens or the court of public opinion, casts Dionysodorus and Euthydemus in sharp relief.

Bibliography

Adam, J., *The Republic of Plato* (Cambridge: Cambridge University Press, 1902).

Aristotle, *Rhetoric*, in *The Complete Works of Aristotle,* ed. J. Barnes (Princeton, NJ: Princeton University Press, 1984).

Aristotle, *Sophistical Refutations*, in *The Complete Works of Aristotle,* ed. J. Barnes (Princeton, NJ: Princeton University Press, 1984).

Chance, T.H., *Plato's Euthydemus: Analysis of What Is and Is Not Philosophy* (Berkeley: University of California Press, 1992).

Dillon, J. and Gergel, T., *The Greek Sophists* (Harmondsworth: Penguin, 2003).

Plato, *Cleitophon*, trans. R.G. Bury, Loeb edition (London: Heinemann, 1929).

Plato, *Cratylus*, trans. H.N. Fowler, Loeb edition (London: Heinemann, 1926).

Plato, *Euthydemus*, trans. W.R.M. Lamb, Loeb edition (London: Heinemann, 1962).

Plato, *Euthyphro*, trans. H.N. Fowler, Loeb edition (Cambridge, MA: Harvard University Press, 1999).

Plato, *Meno*, trans. W.R.M. Lamb, Loeb edition (London: Heinemann, 1924).

Plato, *Symposium*, trans. W.R.M Lamb, Loeb edition (London: Heinemann, 1924).

Michelini, A., 'Socrates Plays the Buffoon: Cautionary Protreptic in "Euthydemus" ', *American Journal of Philology* 121, 4 (Winter, 2000), 509-35.

Slings, S.R., *Plato: Clitophon* (Cambridge: Cambridge University Press, 1999).

Sprague, Rosamond Kent, *The Older Sophists* (Indianapolis, IN: Hackett, 2001).

Waterfield, R., *The First Philosophers*: *The Presocratics and Sophists* (Oxford: Oxford University Press, 2000).

Xenophon, *Memorabilia*, trans. E.C. Marchant, Loeb edition (London: Heinemann, 1923).

12

Isocrates

Doug Al-Maini

Isocrates of Athens (436-338 BC) was a contemporary of Plato (429-347 BC), although Isocrates was both born earlier and lived longer than the famous philosopher. Growing up in a wealthy family (his father Theodorus made a fortune in flute production), Isocrates received a fine education, with reports coming down to us of his studying with some of the famous intellectuals of the day, most probably with Gorgias, although Protagoras and Socrates are also mentioned as figures with whom Isocrates spent time. The family fortune was destroyed by events following the Peloponnesian War, and Isocrates was forced to write speeches for use in the law-courts in order to earn a living. He continued to write speeches for the rest of his adult life, although he eventually rejected his early courtroom speeches in favour of more politically and educationally oriented work. As a result of these later speeches, Isocrates has come to be known as one of the 'Ten Attic Orators', a canonical list of men who encapsulate the great rhetorical achievements of Athens.

Public speaking was very important to Athenian political life and to Classical Greek culture in general (Vernant 1982, 46-50); oratory is the name we give to examples of discourse that are made with the intention of educating or persuading people on some matter. Isocrates is best known for his contribution to this area of Athenian culture. Aristotle famously divides oratory into three categories: *judicial*, which covers all speeches concerned with the courts; *deliberative*, which is concerned with proper planning generally and which finds its civic example in the oratory that takes place in the Assembly; and *display*, which can be understood to include every oration not belonging in an obvious way to either the judicial or deliberative categories (*Rhetoric* 1.3). More helpfully, display (*epideictic*) speeches are orations that do not call for a specific action on the part of the audience, but rather are meant as depictions of oratorical skill or as amusements of some sort. It is to the last category, display pieces, that Isocrates made his greatest contributions.

Isocrates' fame as a speechwriter was such that he was able to open a school in Athens sometime around 392 BC (there are reports that, having been forced to flee Athens in 404 because of the Peloponnesian War, he established a school of rhetoric on the island of Chios at an earlier time). Education is a common theme in Isocrates' work, and it is important to realise that Isocrates characterised himself as a teacher of philosophy and his school as a school of philosophy. Isocrates established his school before Plato set up the Academy, and though it is Plato's school that tradition associates with the origins of institutionalised higher learning, Isocrates would dispute this claim. The two schools competed with each other, and it is clear that some of Isocrates' work is meant both to defend his own understanding of what philosophy consists of and to castigate other, more theoretically-based, notions of philosophy that are championed by Plato, among others. So we see that Isocrates, as well as being a speechwriter, also has some right to the title of philosopher.

The fees charged at his school are now thought to have been very high, and are one source of the fortune he amassed. Life at the school was devoted to preparing for participation in civic affairs, and this meant being able to engage in public discourse. Isocrates could with some justification claim to be a trainer of speakers and politicians generally, developing his students' skill at composing effective arguments intended to persuade juries and assemblymen. Indeed, he worried that he would be known as someone who is 'able to make the weaker cause the stronger' (Isocrates, *Antidosis* 313), invoking the famous description of Protagoras the sophist. Furthermore, Isocrates is at home in the tradition of the sophists who extol pan-Hellenic virtues. In other words, Isocrates champions the attitude of Greeks thinking of themselves primarily as Greeks, as opposed to the non-Greeks who surrounded them (such as the Persians and the Egyptians), and possibly even more so than as citizens of any particular city or polis. These descriptions of Isocrates' activities, charging high fees for teaching others how to make clever speeches, pan-Hellenism, and especially the ability to invert the relative power of arguments are the hallmarks of a sophist.

However, Isocrates takes great pains to distance himself from the sophists. An early speech of his, entitled *Against the Sophists*, contains these lines:

> Indeed, who can fail to abhor, yes to contemn, those teachers, in the first place, who devote themselves to disputation, since they pretend to search for truth, but straightaway at the beginning of their professions attempt to deceive us with lies? (291).

It is fair enough to perceive in this castigation similarities with Hamlet's mother Gertrude who protested too much, and one question that arises when trying to understand the life of Isocrates is whether or not he is a sophist. It has been argued that Isocrates 'left several premises of the sophistical tradition intact while challenging some of its methods and results' (Poulakos 1995, 113). If this is true, then we can see why Isocrates was worried about being interpreted as a sophist, full stop: such a perspective would prevent Isocrates from preserving what he thought was worthwhile in the sophists' enterprise. In this chapter I wish to explore this question of whether or not Isocrates qualifies as a sophist and what the arguments are on either side of the case.

Because of the breadth of Isocrates' endeavours, in order to confront this question it will be useful to set the category of sophist off against the related terms of philosopher and speechwriter. As this brief introduction has shown, Isocrates has some reason to be considered as a member of all three of these professions. I hope that the notion of what a sophist is will become clearer by means of this comparison, and that seeing how Isocrates both conforms to and breaks the conventions of these three professions will give us both a better understanding of his life and a better appreciation of the other figures in this book. In any event, it is worth exploring Isocrates as a figure who exists on the fringes of the category of 'sophist': he provides an excellent test case that shows where the borders between sophist, philosopher and speechwriter lie, and this is because of the way he combines his moral life with his chosen professional activities.

To begin with, then, we shall approach Isocrates as a philosopher, a perspective which, as we have seen, he himself was inclined to adopt. Famously, the word 'philosophy' itself comes to us from ancient Greek, combining the words *philos* meaning 'love' and *sophos* meaning wise. A philosopher is thus a lover of wisdom, and the overlap between our two categories of philosopher and sophist is apparent from their etymology: they both are concerned with wisdom. The names also indicate a certain humbleness on the part of the philosopher that the sophist does not share; thus the philosopher is only a lover of wisdom. Indeed, if we are to accept the assertion of Socrates in Plato's *Symposium* that all love is a desire for something of which one is in need, then philosophers are as good as admitting that they do not have wisdom (Plato has Socrates defend this claim about love being a lack of something at *Symposium* 200a-c), while the sophist professes actually to be a 'wise one'. By Isocrates' time, the name 'sophist' had some disrepute attached to it (e.g. Plato, *Meno* 91c), but it had not by any means become simply a pejorative term; rather it is better to understand the term 'sophist' as taking on both positive and negative connotations. It seems that at this point in history the meaning of the term 'philosopher' is still vague enough to be open to clarification. Indeed, recent scholarship has indicated that establishing a clearer meaning for the word 'philosophy' was 'a valued prize well worth contending for' among the intellectual elite of this time, and Isocrates was one obvious competitor (Ober 1998, 251n.7; see also Nightingale 1995, 13-41).

Isocrates provides an indication of how he feels the word philosophy should be understood in his speech, *Antidosis*. Scholars interpret the speech as representing the formation of a new genre in the field of oratory, being a subtle blend of two court trials, one historical and the other fictional. The historical trial was a case brought against Isocrates for proper payment of civic responsibilities. In Athens at this time the wealthy were required to finance certain activities of the state, such as outfitting warships and sponsoring plays at religious festivals. These financial burdens were called 'liturgies'. If a wealthy person who had been called on to provide a liturgy could find another citizen who was not providing an equivalent outlay to the state, then that second person could be brought to trial by the first and forced to take on the liturgy in question or to trade properties with the accuser. A challenge of this sort was called an 'antidosis', and it seems such a case was successfully made against Isocrates. Apparently, Isocrates was surprised by the lowness of his standing in Athenian society that this case revealed, and so he set about writing the *Antidosis* to make some defence of himself. The fictitious case, then, and the true subject of Isocrates' speech, is the charge 'that I corrupt young men by teaching them to speak and gain their own advantage in the courts contrary to justice' (*Antidosis* 316). It is with this obvious reference back to the trial of Socrates in mind that we should understand Isocrates' definition of philosophy.

In the *Antidosis* Isocrates states:

> Since it is not in the nature of man to attain a scientific knowledge by which, once we possess it, we would know what to do or say, I consider those men wise who are able by means of conjecture to hit upon, for the most part, what is best; and I call those men 'philosophers' who are engaged in the studies from which they will most quickly achieve this kind of wisdom (*Antidosis* 271).

Isocrates makes several points in this passage, two of which are important to our study. The first is his characterisation of wisdom: Isocrates places clear limits on the extent of human comprehension, and since 'scientific knowledge' concerning how to behave is impossible, wisdom becomes the ability to discern what is most likely to be the best conduct. This is a position that Isocrates maintains throughout his life: the *Antidosis* is a relatively late work, written when he was 82 (*Antidosis*, 312) but in *Against the Sophists*, one of his earliest speeches (*Antidosis* 193 tells us that this speech was written 'at the beginning of my career'), he writes that sophists pretend to be able to provide knowledge that assures achieving one's goals in the public arena, and this is 'making greater promises than they can possibly fulfil' (*Against the Sophists* 291).

This stance is perfectly in keeping with the etymological concerns of the word philosophy that were raised earlier. One of the most fiercely contested issues among intellectuals of the time was the possible extent of human wisdom, and whether humans are capable of a degree of knowledge that guarantees a stable, happy and prosperous society and individual. Isocrates comes down firmly on the side of interpreting human knowledge as being useful to these pursuits, but not providing the universal guarantee that some thinkers might envision. For example, in *Against the Sophists*, he writes

> For myself, I should have preferred above great riches that philosophy had
> as much power as these men claim; for, possibly, I should not have been the
> very last in the profession nor had the least share in its profits. But *since it
> has no such power*, I could wish that this prating might cease (*Against the
> Sophists* 11; emphasis added).

That level of wisdom, says Isocrates, lies beyond human capacity. Readers
of the *Antidosis* who are primed to see reflections of Socrates in the
charges will also notice here an overlap of Socrates' misgivings concerning
human knowledge. Socrates goes to great pains to point out the impoverished nature of human knowledge, contrary to our usual inflated self-
evaluation (Plato's *Apology* gives an eloquent defence of this position).
Isocrates, in attacking the sophists for claiming to know more than they
actually do (indeed, Isocrates goes so far as to claim that, in his opinion,
they profess to a knowledge that is not even possible), reflects Socrates'
activity, challenging people to substantiate their beliefs. Taking Socrates
as the paradigm case of a philosopher would thus seem to support
Isocrates' claim to be listed among the philosophers.

The second point to underline in this passage from *Antidosis* 271 is the
emphasis of philosophy's relationship to useful action. Isocrates writes
about the necessity of actually applying studies and learning to the
practical problems of life, and he castigates anyone whose concept of
philosophy does not have a pragmatic end (see also *Antidosis* 183-4). On
this matter, Isocrates is quite willing to trot out examples of his own
former students who have gone on to be successful in the public arena,
such as Timotheus, proving the utility of Isocrates' endeavours (*Antidosis*
131-9). More important is his own case: the goal of the *Antidosis* is to prove
Isocrates' good effect on the youth of Athens and hence avoid the penalty
of the charges. In this way he shows the practical value of his pursuits and,
if we are to accept his definition of the term, of philosophy. For Isocrates,
philosophy consists of studies that most quickly and efficiently lead citizens to a point where they are ready to engage in their political
responsibilities. There are, according to Isocrates, pretenders who claim
to be providing a philosophical education, but there is a basic problem
when the course of studies remains too esoteric and never rejoins the world
of practicality. Other so-called professors of philosophy

> who are skilled in disputation and those who are occupied with astronomy
> and geometry and studies of that sort ... benefit their pupils not so much as
> they profess. ... Most men see in such studies nothing but empty talk and
> hair-splitting, for none of these disciplines has any useful application either
> to private or to public affairs ... I do not, however, think it proper to apply
> the term 'philosophy' to a training which is of no help to us in the present
> either in our speech or in our actions, but rather I would call it a gymnastic
> of the mind and a preparation for philosophy (*Antidodis* 261-6).

The need to promote the relevance of philosophy to life is actually not as striking as it might seem at first, as it is a common enough theme among those who wrote on the nature of philosophy. For example, at *Gorgias* 521d Plato has the philosopher Socrates say, 'I think that I am one of very few Athenians, not to say the only one, engaged in the true political art, and that of the men today I alone practise statesmanship.' Far from being impractical, Plato is famous for having proposed that philosophy is the only essential element to politics. Indeed, other thinkers such as Plato are quick to point out the practical benefits of studying philosophy, but they tend not to see this as the only reason to engage in philosophy. Rather, philosophy and wisdom are understood as ends in their own right, and are good to have in and for themselves, as well as for other benefits that they might bring. Isocrates sets his own account apart through the extent to which his view of philosophy turns away from being an actual love of wisdom. Those who study abstraction and knowledge purely because they love to have knowledge are not, according to Isocrates, philosophers. Wisdom, as an end in itself, is not the goal of Isocrates' philosopher, and it is this position that is problematic if we are to understand Isocrates as a philosopher himself.

Seeing Isocrates with this rather utilitarian view of philosophy may seem to be a further reason to cast his lot in with the sophists. Sophists came to be regarded suspiciously because of a perception that their wisdom served the sole purpose of personal profit. On this reading, sophists are not to be trusted because their motives are never for the common good. Proof of this attitude towards the sophists is grounded in the realisation that sophists might be able to train their pupils to win their case in arenas of public discourse, no matter what position was being advocated. For example, sophistic training in rhetoric raised the possibility of winning a trial purely because of facility with argumentation, regardless of where matters stand in terms of justice. Similarly, good, sophistically trained speakers can be supposed to have an advantage in the Assembly where public policy is formulated, and this to the detriment of the interests of their fellow citizens. Thus sophists may possibly undermine the foundations of consent-based politics, where dialogue and debate in the Assembly are expected to produce a course of action that is best for the whole city, and not just the interests of a limited few. If a citizen gained in oratorical skill to the point of being able to control the goings-on in the Assembly through the power of persuasion (a power the sophists commonly advertised themselves as being able to provide), then those people have effectively consolidated their own power within the city, turning a democratic Assembly (in the case of Athens) into a tyranny.

It is not the place of this chapter to answer problems concerning the viability of the sophistic agenda within an open political system. Certainly there are many responses that the sophists could make in response to these fears, not the least of which is the claim that there is no necessary connection between rhetorical skill and unabated self-interest. Be that as it may, the possibility of the use of rhetorical skill for purely selfish ends, or worse, in order to exploit others, remains a dangerous aspect of the sophistic movement. Partly, this concern is a response to the itinerant nature of the early sophists' lives; apart from Antiphon of Athens, all the early sophists were chronic wanderers, taking up residence wherever they could make financial gain. Even in the case of Antiphon, one could not say that he does not see the value of approaching the world with a narrowly individualistic and selfish attitude. Furthermore, sophists are famous for amassing fortunes from their profession, and one is left with the image (false or not) of a sophist coming to a town, bleeding it dry of money, and leaving it in no better shape for being introduced to sophistical education. Thus it is easy to see why the sophists are criticised for being too selfish in outlook, and lacking a patriotism or allegiance to a home city that the Greeks consider a basic component of life. The claim of making the weaker argument appear stronger comes back to haunt the sophists at this point, for it is difficult to hear this slogan without finding something morally discreditable in it.

Against this, we see Isocrates brandishing his patriotism. The glory and goodness of Athens is another theme that runs throughout Isocrates' career, and it can be interpreted as a foil to the other aspects of his life that align him with the sophists. 'I am sure that all men would acknowledge that our city has been the author of the greatest number of blessings, and she should in fairness be entitled to the hegemony', wrote Isocrates in his early work *Panegyricus* (100). He was deeply committed to Athens, and often enough his speeches were written with the purpose of giving political advice to the city. And while Isocrates left Athens during the civil strife that enveloped Athens at the end of the Peloponnesian War, he returned when it was safe to do so, and remained a proud citizen of the city till the end of his days. No travelling from city to city for him, selling his rhetorical wares to those who might pay a high price. Instead Isocrates stayed at home, combining his ability to make a living at rhetorical instruction with an active interest and involvement in civic affairs. Isocrates put the welfare of Athens at the forefront of many of his speeches, and we might understand him as seeing his own benefit as coinciding with that of the city itself, something any good citizen ought to do.

One further argument can be made for doubting a full identification of Isocrates as a sophist and it is based on his contribution to the intellectual advancements that the sophists achieved. The accomplishments of the sophists in what we would call the humanities are many; for example, Protagoras gives us a theory of relativism that undermines the great Greek essentialists for generations to come and which is debated still in moral philosophy, Gorgias is the first to point out explicitly the degree to which oratorical facility must be considered in assessing the stability and inclusiveness of a political system based on discourse, and Antiphon outlines a powerful individualistic theory of human nature. If we place Isocrates beside these figures, we do not find a corresponding commitment to intellectual innovation. In a way the reasoning here is similar to the justification behind not wanting to label Isocrates a philosopher because of his unwillingness to engage in a love of wisdom for its own sake. On this matter the sophists and the philosophers stand together, participating in the intense intellectual growth of the period.

If we see shortcomings in identifying Isocrates as a philosopher or as a sophist, he is more obviously at home under the heading of speechwriter. Here Isocrates did make valuable contributions to his field, both in its technical development and in its place in Greek culture. Without Isocrates' contributions, rhetoric and oratory would be much poorer. One clear advancement he gave to the art of speechwriting was the injection of hiatus avoidance into his speeches; 'hiatus' refers to the practice of placing a word that begins with a vowel sound after a word that ends with a vowel sound; the effect of Isocrates' concern to avoid hiatus is to give the speech a more natural and flowing sound when it is recited or even read in private. Following up on this observation, we see Isocrates was careful everywhere to make sure that no unnecessary clashes or artificiality arose during the pronunciation of his work. This aspect of his technical facility in the construction of speeches has had wide influence; even Plato took it up as a rule of composition. Isocrates also moved Greek speechwriting more generally towards a natural style. Prior to Isocrates, oratory as an art was dominated by the style of Gorgias, an affected and artificial way of speaking. This can be a highly effective strategy, especially as it sets itself off from mundane speech and thus seems somewhat more appropriate to the high political purpose speech serves for Athenians. It is even possible that such a style was a necessary phase for rhetoric to go through in establishing itself. Isocrates is the figure who brought rhetoric back to a more common mode of talk, arguably helping to remove some of the elitism in political discourse and bringing it closer to being a tool of the masses.

Isocrates wrote his speeches by and large for private consumption. True, his earliest works were forensic, meaning they were to be used in court, and he has speeches concerned with the unity of Greece that may have been recited in public, but it is generally accepted that most of his orations were intended for private audiences, perhaps at small gatherings. Indeed, some of his works appear to be too long to be read out in public, and are probably meant to be read only (Too 1995, 48). In this way he engaged in a more direct relationship with his audience, a 'one on one' meeting, rather than the old image of an orator speaking to a crowd. Thus Isocrates was part of a generation that took advantage of the growing literacy of the Athenian population. While a high degree of illiteracy among citizens can help to emphasise the oral nature of political discourse (and this is especially true of the early history of the polis), as a population becomes more and more literate, the possibilities of authors being able to circumvent the actual speaker of a speech and engage an audience directly through writing becomes more and more viable (Thomas 1989, passim). Isocrates was a speechwriter who took advantage of this shifting ground of the Athenian citizenry, and his ability to keep speechwriting in tune with cultural developments that are happening more generally is another aspect of his contribution to the field. These observations all combine to show Isocrates standing at the forefront of the practice of speechwriting. His somewhat suspicious attitude towards learning and abstraction should cause some doubt concerning his philosophical claims, but his heartfelt devotion to his home city and concern for the actual betterment of his fellow citizens exclude him from the usual understanding of what a sophist is; his real home is among the writers who are trying to effect some change in their polity through persuasion.

Bibliography

Guthrie, W.K.C., *The Sophists* (New York: Cambridge University Press, 1971).

Isocrates, trans. G. Norlin, vol. II, Loeb edition (London: Heinemann, 1929).

Jaeger, W., *Paideia: The Ideals of Greek Culture*, trans. from the German manuscript by Gilbert Highet, vol. III (New York: Oxford University Press, 1944).

Kerferd, G.B., *The Sophistic Movement* (Cambridge: Cambridge University Press, 1981).

Mirhady, D. and Too, Y.L. (trans.), *Isocrates I* (Austin, TX: University of Texas Press, 2000).

Nightingale, A., *Genres in Dialogue: Plato and the Construct of Philosophy* (Cambridge: Cambridge University Press, 1995).

Ober, J. *Political Dissent in Democratic Athens*, vols I-III: *Intellectual Critics of Popular Rule* (Princeton: Princeton University Press, 1998).

Poulakos, J., *Sophistical Rhetoric in Classical Greece* (Columbia: University of South Carolina Press, 1995).

Thomas, R., *Oral Tradition and Written Record in Classical Athens* (Cambridge: Cambridge University Press, 1989).

Too, Y.L., *The Rhetoric of Identity in Isocrates* (Cambridge: Cambridge University Press, 1995).

Vernant, J.-P., *The Origins of Greek Thought* (Ithaca, NY: Cornell University Press, 1982).

The *Anonymus Iamblichi* and the *Double Arguments*

Patricia O'Grady and Daniel Silvermintz

The *Anonymus Iamblichi* and the *Double Arguments* are sometimes, although not always, treated together. Dillon and Gergel (2003) placed them together in one chapter; Sprague (1972) grants each title a dedicated chapter.

The two works are often grouped together because they are both anonymous, written not many years apart, following the period of the great sophists who are the topics of this book. They are otherwise unrelated works which will be treated separately here in this single chapter.

THE *ANONYMUS IAMBLICHI*
Patricia O'Grady

The *Anonymus Iamblichi* was preserved by Iamblichus of Chalcis (c. AD 250-325) in his *Protrepticus* (*Exhortation to Philosophy*). It was written in the late fifth or early fourth century BC (Cole 1961, 156). Authorship is variously ascribed to 'a known author' (Guthrie 1969, 314), 'an unknown ... sophist' (Dillon and Gergel 2005, 310) and 'an unknown writer' (Sprague 1972, 271). Because the material is unacknowledged, many scholars have attempted to trace the work to an author or to various authors of the fifth century. Following a discussion of the text of the *Anonymus Iamblichi*, I will return to the question of possible authorship.

The text consists of seven sections, each with a number of subheadings. Anonymus commences: 'In whatever field of endeavour one wishes to achieve the very best results, whether it be wisdom, courage, eloquence, or excellence', thereby listing characteristics which are necessary to achieve 'success in life': this is the overall theme of the work. Anonymus then tells us how to achieve this rare state. The first requirement is 'good natural endowment' which, as Anonymus admits, 'may be credited to chance' while the other elements 'are already in the power of the man himself' (Sprague 1972, 271): they are eagerness for noble things, willingness to work hard, to commence these studies when one is young and to persevere with them for a long time. Anonymus does not limit natural ability to the upper class, so we see that anyone, by chance or good luck, be they of high or low birth, could have the good fortune to be born with natural ability.

'But if even one of these things is absent, it will not be possible for him to carry anything through to the supreme excellence, but if he has all of these, whatever he may attempt will not be surpassed' (Sprague 1972, 272). Apart from having natural ability, Anonymus lists qualities that he considers essential for achieving success in life, but they are supreme, matchless qualities. The first of these matchless qualities or virtues is that one must embrace the noble things, that is, honourable, meritorious qualities. Then there is the need for constant industry and endless perseverance.

Anonymus declares that these attributes are absolutely essential. Clearly then, the person would be exceptional, striving to attain perfection. It is not possible to attain virtue in a short time. It must be brought 'to fruition over a long time and with great care' (Sprague 1972, 272) and would be a remarkable undertaking and a life-long endeavour. But, in any case, a person who has suddenly and in brief time become wealthy, wise, good or manly is not readily received (Sprague 1972, 273). Almost inevitably, envy and resentment come into play.

Those are the qualities that Anonymus enumerates and explains in section 1 of his text. The remaining six sections also deal with aspects of succeeding in life: the acquisition of a good reputation; using one's abilities 'for good and lawful purposes'; self control which includes rising above 'the love of money'; not to 'seek to preserve one's life with dishonour'. One should pursue justice and strive for moral excellence – it is in these two matters that most people lack self-control (Sprague 1972, 273-4).

In section 3.3-4, Anonymus discusses the acquisition of virtue. The text reads:

> Again, we must consider by what kind of speech or action a man who desires complete virtue would become best. He would become this if he benefited as many people as possible. But if anyone benefits his neighbours by gifts of money, he will be forced to be nasty again if he collects the money. … he could not bring together such an abundance that his resources would not fail while he is making gifts and presentations. Then, too, this second disadvantage is added after he has collected the money, if, having been rich, he becomes poor and has nothing, although he once had possessions (Sprague 1972, 273).

I will return to these lines later. Anonymus continues with a discussion about mankind's need to live in communities, and consequently, the necessity for law and justice. Here we recognise a clear similarity to Protagoras' *Great Speech* (see Chapter 3, T3), which also describes man's need to live in communities because he is unsuited to living a solitary existence.

Anonymus next engages in a discussion on obedience to the law. He lists the many benefits which accrue as a result of living by the law, and the evils which befall lawless societies. With the latter, there is a lack of trust between people creating a state of affairs which results in external war and internal discord. Abiding by the law is best, not only for individuals, but is one of the great benefits in communal life. A lawful society ensures conditions of trust and civility, so that life would be pleasant and free of anxieties. In the following sections Anonymus amplifies these many benefits. Then in Part 6 he pronounces:

> Law and Justice are kings among men ... If a man should possess all the required characteristics; invulnerable, not subject to disease, free from emotion, extraordinary, and hard as adamant in body ... in fact there could not be such a man ... (Sprague 1972, 275) (see fragment 30 below).

Obedience to law leads into the final part of Anonymus' treatise, Part 7, which is the longest of all the parts and continues the discussion of law. Under point 12, the final point, Anonymus analyses tyranny, describing it as 'an evil of such proportions, [which] arises from nothing else than the non-observance of law' and explaining the conditions under which tyranny is able to develop (Sprague 1972, 277-8).

Anonymus makes thirty-four references to, and discussion of, topics such as law, law and justice, and obedience to the law, all this in a work that is just over two thousand words in length.

The ideal about which Anonymus writes is the acquisition of virtue. The entire work is advice on how to attain virtue in order to live a good life. The Greek ideal of a good life is totally distinct from the current ideas of a 'good-oh' life which is one of pleasure, extravagance and self indulgence. Virtue (*aretê* in Greek) encompasses the qualities of goodness, excellence, manhood and valour. In a moral sense *aretê* particularly applies to virtue and goodness. In Homer virtue encompassed the so-called manly qualities such as bravery (*Iliad* XX.411), and of women, qualities such as Penelope's excellence (*Odyssey* II.206). It is in the latter sense that we still employ the word; the meaning still pertains to moral virtue.

Anonymus not only offers advice on leading a good life, and the tangible benefits that are then enjoyed, but describes the disadvantages of a lawless life. He never advocates behaviour which is morally corrupt, or which brings harmful or ruinous consequences to a person or to his polis. He promotes a life-style that is an ideal that could be attained only through living an austere life, so much so that it would become an impractical ideal. It is not a life-style for the faint-hearted. From the description of that tough, demanding life-style the idea of a superman has arisen but, as Anonymus adds, 'a man of steel, a person of adamant' is an impossibility (Sprague 1972, 275; Guthrie 1969, 74).

A.T. Cole believes that the original work was compiled by Anonymus in the late fifth or early fourth centuries BC. Cole traces the material from

13. The Anonymus Iamblichi and the Double Arguments

Possible transference of ideas to Iamblichus
(after Cole 1961; dates BC unless otherwise stated)

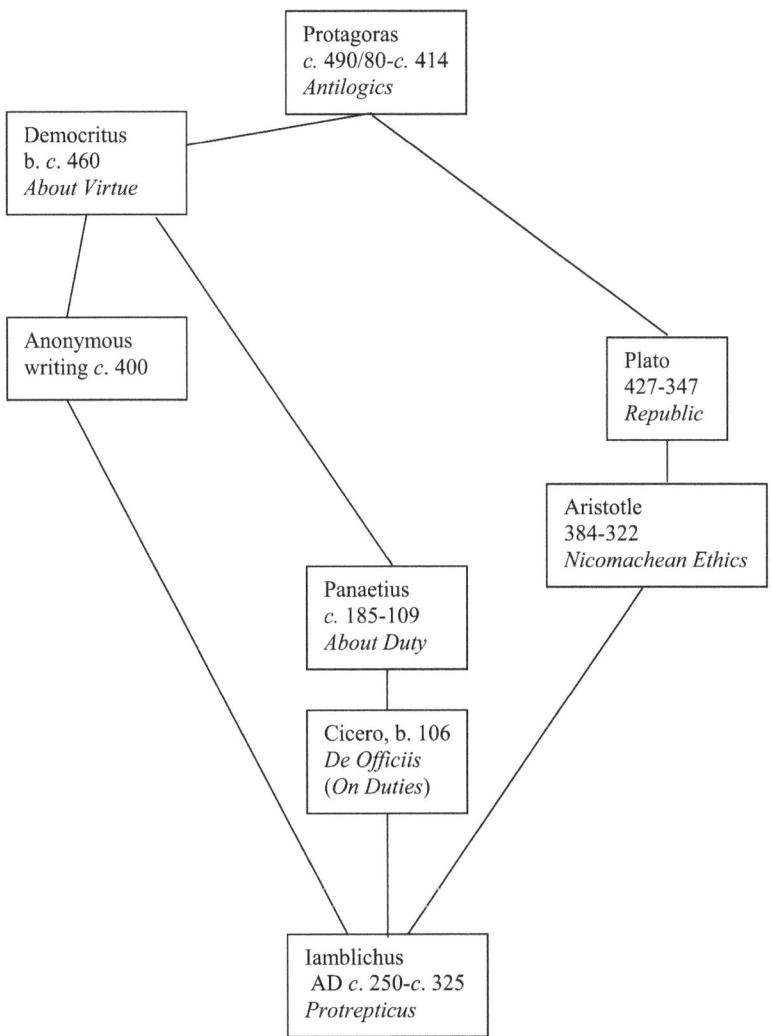

Protagoras (born between 490 and 480, died *c.* 414, but dates of his birth and death are uncertain) to Democritus (born *c.* 460 BC) then to Anonymus (*c.* 400 BC) and then, about six hundred years later, to Iamblichus (AD *c.* 250-*c.* 325). Another line traces Anonymus from Protagoras to Democritus, then to Panaetius (*c.* 185-109 BC) and to the *De Officiis* of Cicero (born 106 BC). A third line leads from Protagoras to the *Republic*[1] of Plato (427-347 BC) (Cole 1961, 156). Virtue and justice were common themes of the times, and of Plato. We associate them very much with Socrates and with Plato who amplified them. As a Neoplatonist, Iamblichus would have been familiar with Plato's work.

There are clear similarities between passages in Panaetius and Cicero's *De Officiis* (e.g. II.xv.52; III.iv.17). In III.ii.7, Cicero states: 'Panaetius, then, has given us what is unquestionably the most thorough discussion of moral duties that we have, and I have followed him in the main – but with slight modifications.' Cicero acknowledges Panaetius on many other occasions (III.ii.8-9; II.xvii.60; II.x.35).

Guthrie describes the *Protrepticus* of Iamblichus as 'unacknowledged borrowings from earlier philosophers as one may see from its incorporation of word-for-word extracts from the *Phaedo* [of Plato]' (Guthrie 1969, 314). Because the *Anonymus* is embedded in the *Protrepticus* one might expect it too to be borrowing from 'earlier philosophers'. Now several of the sophists were, indeed, also philosophers, and present-day commentators observe similarities between the work of the sophists and the content of the *Anonymus*. Themes common to many of the sophists and to Anonymus include the debates on law and order, their attention to the teaching and/or the pursuit of virtue, and their development of language. Their attention to constructing and extending language was advantageous to the sophists in their teaching, but also of benefit to society.

As a 'tentative choice of authorship' Dillon and Gergel (2003, 311) favour Protagoras and his *Great Discourse*. Others who are suggested as possible authors are Hippias of Elis,[2] Antiphon of Rhamnus and Critias. Guthrie (1969, 314-15) wrote that 'He could well be some pupil of Protagoras acquainted with the teaching of other Sophists and with Socrates, and probably not himself a professional Sophist.'

E.R. Dodds offers an interesting view:

A measure of the swift decline in confidence is the changed tone of the Sophist known as '*Anonymus Iamblichi*' who shared Protagoras' belief in nomos [law or convention] and was perhaps his pupil. Writing, we may guess, in the later years of the Peloponnesian War, he speaks in the despondent voice of one who has seen the whole social and moral order crumble about his head (Dodds 1951, 197n.27).

Still in relation to authorship and date, de Romilly wrote:

Although the identity of this writer is not known, it is unanimously agreed that he must have been writing during the Peloponnesian War, and most scholars believe him to have been a Sophist, although some identify him as Democritus. As to which Sophist he might be, many names have been put forward, with a slight preference for either Hippias or Protagoras (de Romilly 1992, 168-9).

In addition to those three writers, de Romilly (1992, 169n.6) adds

'Prodicus, Critias, Antiphon, Antisthenes, Theramenes, and others too' as possible authors.

Iamblichus does not enlighten us with the identity of the author; perhaps even he did not know:

> and [he] does not even signal that it is not by him, ... and scholars are unanimous in believing that these words [in the collection] date from the Sophistic period of the fifth century. The anonymous author shows himself, in a rather tedious fashion, to be a utilitarian democrat, and a champion of law and order, whose virtues he sings at some length ... (Waterfield 2000, 301).

If we accept that Anonymus produced this intriguing work during the latter part of the Peloponnesian War or soon after, we can understand that his writing was a result of his disillusionment. They were tragic times for Athens. The glorious days of the most famous of all democracies were gone. We may accept that the author probably:

> lived in an Athens where he saw its culture flowering, he witnessed the construction of the Parthenon, a period where art and sciences, particularly the literary arts, oration and rhetoric blossomed; there existed an unprecedented level of intellectual curiosity, a questioning of superstitions and conventions, and a belief in progress (adapted from Usher 2005, 112).

Then the democracy came crashing down. Although there seemed little about which to be optimistic, Anonymus put forth his recipe for attaining the good life and also listed the evils that could befall those who failed in the endeavour to practise virtue.

The ideas that Anonymus promotes proceed in a logical, commonsense, well organised style. I believe it to be the work of a discerning, concerned thinker and a talented writer. One could hardly describe Democritus as despondent: he was known as the 'laughing philosopher', but Democritus cannot be excluded from the possibilities. Perhaps the strongest possibility is that the work originated with Protagoras, then passed down to Democritus, then one branch went to Anonymus and to Iamblichus. We should not omit the sophists as sources, all of whom were writers whose works were, in all likelihood, still available.

Who borrowed from whom is unknown. In about 400 BC there was considerable material, from the sophists and others, from whom Anonymus may have borrowed ideas or text. The lives of Protagoras and Anonymus may have overlapped, but where Anonymus' manuscript lay for the period of about seven hundred years between Anonymus and Iamblichus is unknown.[3] If Anonymus was not himself a philosopher, he certainly chose philosophical passages from his sources, be they sophist or not.

There is no convincing argument supporting Democritus as the author.

He could have been acquainted with the Athenian sophists and with Socrates. In the fragments of Democritus listed below one may discern similarities to Socratic ideas.

Diogenes Laertius attributes seventy titles to Democritus; these cover a wide range of topics and show Democritus to have been a prolific writer (Diogenes Laertius IX.46-9). Of particular interest to us is one called *Concerning Goodness* or *Of Virtue*. The work is no longer extant but we do have a large number of fragments; although they are probably snippets from his larger works, we have no way of knowing where they originated. Three hundred and nine fragments are recorded (Freeman 1948, 24-34). Most but not all relate to ethics; Democritus had a wide range of interests; biology, mathematics, geometry, music, ethics and, with Leucippus, constructed an atomic theory 'with wide-ranging implications that have reverberated down to the present day' (Chalmers 2005, 117). There is 'a number of reasons for believing that Anonymus was no less a figure than Democritus' (Cole 1961, 127), but Cole is not convincing.

Following are a few of the fragments that relate to the attainment of a good life and those which seem to be of significance when viewing Democritus as a source for Anonymus (Freeman 1948, 98-120).

> 30 Zeus considers all things and he knows all and gives and takes away all and is King of all.

It is interesting to observe Anonymus' comment 'Law and Justice are kings among men' (Sprague 1972, 275). We should remember that the ancients were much closer to the gods than we are and afforded them greater responsibility. For instance Cole declares that fragment 30, cited above, 'shows that Democritus regarded the idea of divinity as somehow related to that of kingship' (Cole 1967, 203).

> 40 Men find happiness neither by means of the body nor through possessions, but through uprightness and wisdom.

> 59 Neither skill nor wisdom is attainable unless one learns.

> 62 Virtue consists, not in avoiding wrong-doing, but in having no wish thereto.

> 119 Men have fashioned an image of Chance as an excuse for their own stupidity. For Chance rarely conflicts with Intelligence, and most things in life can be set in order by an intelligent sharpsightedness.

> 175 But the gods are the givers of all good things, both in the past and now.
> ...

> 176 Chance is generous but unreliable. ...

242 More men become good through practice than by nature.

252 One must give the highest importance to affairs of the State, that it may be well run; one must not pursue quarrels contrary to right, nor acquire a power contrary to the common good. The well-run State is the greatest protection, and contains all in itself; when this is safe, all is safe; when this is destroyed, all is destroyed.

287 Communal distress is harder than that of individuals; for there remains no hope of assistance.

304 I alone know that I know nothing.

We are immediately reminded of Socrates' (469-399 BC) belief that all he knew was that he knew nothing. This is not the sort of comment Protagoras would make but it may be that Democritus' text was also a compilation of ideas gathered from other sources, and not necessarily his own views.

All the selected fragments display marked similarities to the ideas and values of the sophists about whom we have read in the preceding chapters, and to the pleas in the *Anonymus Iamblichi*.

It seems clear that some of the fragments attributed to Democritus relate views that were not those of Protagoras, but we do not have Protagoras' writings and we do not know the content of Democritus' book, *Concerning Goodness* or *Of Virtue*. One cannot, then, make claims connecting Democritus' views with those of Protagoras with any certainty.

Another possible connection leads from Democritus to Panaetius and then to Cicero. Panaetius was a Stoic philosopher who was head of the Athenian Stoa for about twenty years until his death in 109 BC. Besides being a Stoic, he was an eclectic so his interest in Anonymus' text is well justified. Democritus would have been a 'natural model' for Panaetius:

[Democritus'] doctrines could not but strike Panaetius as embodying in unusual degree that balance between the claims of man's public and private existence – of politics and philosophy – to recreate which was one of the principal aims of the Middle Stoa (Cole 1961, 156).

I turn to a well-known passage from Aristotle's *Nicomachean Ethics* (1109a):

But to be angry with or give money to the right person, and to the right amount, and at the right time, and for the right person, and in the right way – this is not within everybody's power and is not easy; so that to do these things properly is rare, praiseworthy, and noble.

This brings us back to section 3.3-4 quoted above from the Anonymus text, and the similarity between the two. Aristotle may have borrowed the ideas from Anonymus, and he could have done so without acknowledging his source. That would not be unusual for the times. Iamblichus may have taken the ideas from Aristotle and incorporated them into his text, the *Anonymus Iamblichi*. This complexity does nothing towards diminishing the confusion that is inherent in the question of sources and borrowings – it does lead us into further thought but, probably, another dead end.

Anonymus Iamblichi is not a set of commandments. It consists of guidelines which not only provide for the virtuous behaviour one should practise if one is to achieve the virtuous life, but also list the consequences if one does not live by those principles and values. They may be seen as both a remedy for the ills that had overwhelmed Athens during the Peloponnesian War and an appeal to the population to heed the advice.

Reading Anonymus now and applying him to our own society and to current world events we recognise aspects of the treatise. All are fine principles from which society would benefit. Anonymus has provided values for individual living, and for avoiding external conflict. He has presented it in a relatively clear-cut manner, certainly when compared with some of the wordiness of a number of other works.

The various fragments show the ideas that were prevalent at the time, and are more than mere homilies. The pursuit of virtue figured in the earliest Greek literature and philosophy, and continues to rank highly in philosophical and sociological debates and at various levels right through society: when a child exclaims 'That's not fair!' the issue is virtue. It is crucial to most of society, relating as it does to justice, whether it be to delivering justice or withholding it.

The author may never be identified; nor is it possible to know which author borrowed from whom, nor where the material lay between the seven hundred years that elapsed between Anonymus and Iamblichus, or in the five hundred years between Democritus and Cicero. The question of authorship is intriguing, but the answer continues to elude scholars. As Cole concludes (1961, 150) 'a final solution to the problem is perhaps impossible'.

Notes

1. See especially *Republic* IV, 428b; *Republic* X, 600c.
2. De Romilly states that 'there is a slight preference for either Hippias or Protagoras' (2002, 169n.6).
3. Readers endeavouring to unravel the mystery of authorship of *Anonymus Iamblichi* will find guidance in the paper and references of Cole (1961). See also previous note.

Bibliography

Chalmers, Alan, 'Democritus' in *Meet the Philosophers of Ancient Greece*, ed. Patricia O'Grady (Ashgate: Aldershot, 2005).

Cicero, *De Officiis*, trans. Walter Miller, Loeb edition (Cambridge, MA.: Harvard University Press, 1961).

Cole, Andrew Thomas, 'The *Anonymus Iamblichi* and his Place in Greek Political Theory', *Harvard Studies in Classical Philology* 65 (1961), 127-63.

Cole, Thomas, *Democritus and the Sources of Greek Anthropology* (Cleveland: Western Reserve University Press, 1967).

Dodds, E.R., *The Greeks and the Irrational* (Berkeley: University of California Press, 1951).

Freeman, Kathleen, *Ancilla to the Pre-Socratic Philosophers: A Complete Translation of the Fragments in Diels, 'Fragmente der Vorsokratiker'* (Cambridge, MA: Harvard University Press, 1948).

Romilly, Jacqueline de, *The Great Sophists in Periclean Athens*, trans. Janet Lloyd (Oxford: Clarendon Press, 1992).

Sprague, Rosamond Kent (1972), *The Older Sophists* (Columbia: University of South Carolina Press).

Usher, Mathew, 'Thucydides' in *Meet the Philosophers of Ancient Greece*, ed. Patricia O'Grady (Aldershot: Ashgate, 2005).

THE *DOUBLE ARGUMENTS*
Daniel Silvermintz

Double Arguments, one of the few surviving works of the sophistic movement, is by an anonymous author about whom we know almost nothing. Written in the Doric dialect, the nine brief chapters treat common sophistic concerns relating to ethics, politics and epistemology. The work was originally believed to have been composed in the late fifth century because of its reference to Athens' defeat in the Peloponnesian War in 404 BC as a recent event of history (*Double Arguments* I.8); however, passages in the text that directly respond to several Platonic dialogues, in particular Plato's *Theaetetus*, *Meno*, *Protagoras* and *Hippias Major*, suggest composition in the early to mid fourth century (Robinson 1979, 34-41). The title is taken from the first two words of its opening sentence (I.1): 'Double arguments (*dissoi logoi*) are put forward in Greece by those who profess philosophy concerning the good and the bad', and identifies the sophistical method of antilogic as the author's primary mode of inquiry. Rather than refuting one of the two positions and reconciling the contradictory claims about ethics, the author advances his position in antilogical fashion by arguing on behalf of both sides of the debate. Some scholars have suggested that since the latter chapters of *Double Arguments* depart from the structure and method employed in the opening chapters, the work represents notes compiled from lectures on various topics and should not be read as a unified piece (Levi 1940, 292; Robinson 1979, 54-73; Kerferd 1981, 54; Dillon and Gergel 2003, 319). Alternatively, one might consider how the complexities of

147

the ethical and political notions explored in the early chapters of the work set the stage for the latter chapters in which the sophist is defended as a legitimate teacher of virtue (VI, IX) and whose expertise is necessary for the proper governance of cities (VII, VIII). *Double Arguments* merits careful study, not merely because it is one of the few surviving works of the sophistic movement, but as a masterful use of the antilogical method in defending a nuanced version of ethical and epistemological relativism.

The antilogical method

G.B. Kerferd (1981, 59-67, 85) has identified the antilogical method as the defining characteristic pervading all sophistic thought. The significance of this claim can be fully appreciated only when one considers the radical challenge posed by antilogic to the prevailing approach adopted in the history of philosophy. Aristotle, who defines the dominant method for at least the next two thousand years of philosophic thought, asserts the principle of non-contradiction as the absolutely indisputable first principle of all inquiry: 'Obviously it is impossible for the same man at the same time to believe the same thing to be and not to be' (*Metaphysics* 1005b). In contrast, antilogic affirms contradiction by 'causing the same thing to be seen by the same people now as possessing one predicate and now as possessing the opposite or contradictory predicate' (Kerferd 1981, 61).[1] There is no doubt that the philosophic tradition, critiqued by postmodern thinkers as logocentric, would be quite different had a line of investigation been pursued in which contradiction was affirmed.[2]

Although the idea of competing truth claims is evident in every dispute, Protagoras is recognised as the first thinker to have consciously developed the contentious character of knowledge into a method. Diogenes Laertius writes with regard to Protagoras' first principles, 'He was the first to declare that there are two possible positions on every question, opposed to each other; and indeed he was the first to present arguments along these lines' (DK 80A12, quoted in Dillon and Gergel 2003, 3). Echoing the prevailing Greek sentiment that strife, whether in an athletic competition, dramatic contest, or between craftsmen in the marketplace, is beneficial, Protagoras contends that one strengthens an argument by pitting it against the opposing viewpoint. He would thus train his students by having them adopt the position that is originally perceived as weaker in order to show how it might be strengthened and possibly even more persuasive than the opposing position (Aristotle, *Rhetoric* 1402a; DK 80B6b). While consideration of opposing arguments may serve to make one a more critical thinker, Philostratus indicates how training in the antilogical method could be employed for unscrupulous ends: 'The Athenians when they observed the too great cleverness of the Sophists, shut them out of the law-courts on the ground that they could defeat a just argument by an unjust, and that they used their power to warp men's judgement' (Philostratus, *Lives of the Sophists* 11).

The contrasting arguments of ethical thought

The author of *Double Arguments* begins the treatise by laying out the perennial debate between those who defend ethical absolutes and those who defend ethical relativism. The first school of thought may be identified with the approach inaugurated by Socrates' search for non-contradictory definitions of ethical terms and further developed by Plato's theory of a transcendent realm of unvarying forms. The opposing position is that upheld by the sophists, most notably Protagoras' claim in the human measure fragment that all reality is relative to the perception of the individual and his community (DK 80B1; Plato, *Cratylus* 386a and *Theaetetus* 152a; Aristotle, *Metaphysics* 1062b). Following the antilogical method, the author successively defends the relativistic and the absolutist positions; however, one should note a revealing passage in which he shows his true conviction: 'I myself side with the latter opinion' (*Double Arguments* I.2). Moreover, the author's defence of the absolutist position reduces oppositional ethical notions to nothing more than their linguistic correctness – the good, noble, just and their opposites are true for the speaker at the moment at which he utters them (I.11).

The author frames the central dispute of the treatise by asserting that the absolutists contend that notions such as good and bad, noble and base, just and unjust, true and false represent mutually exclusive opposites while the relativists conceive that the same thing may at one time be good for one and bad for another, noble for one and base for another, just for one and unjust for another, true for one and false for another. He begins each of the successive chapters by defending the relativist position, drawing on examples that emphasise the contingency of each of the oppositional notions with reference to the individual's perspective and cultural identity. While feasting, drinking and having sexual intercourse may be enjoyable for the healthy, these same activities are painful for those in a state of infirmity (I.2).[3] Likewise, these same things are deleterious for the addict, but beneficial to the merchant who traffics these wares (I.3). Advancing the notion even further that one man's misery is another's fortune, the author cynically asserts the most extreme of his examples: 'And death is bad for those who die, but good for undertakers and gravediggers' (I.3). And lest one think that the problem of perspective only afflicts the human condition by placing stock in a divine realm of transcendent absolutes, the author notes that the war between the gods and the giants was good for the gods, but bad for the giants (I.10). Having shown through numerous examples that the same things are good for some and bad for others, the author now attempts to argue the opposing side by showing that the previous argument does not allow us to exchange good for bad as if they were the same thing. If this

149

were the case, then we would be justified in doing bad to our loved ones rather than good (I.12) and in reckoning no difference between the fortune of the beggar and that of the king (I.15). Although the argument concludes by affirming that the good and the bad are distinct from each other, the author admits that he cannot tell us what the good is (I.17) leaving us to conclude with the relativists that the good is nothing other than something perceived by an individual at a given time and place.

The poet Pindar says that 'custom is king of all' (Herodotus 3.38). This sociological fact acknowledges that there is no transcendent set of beliefs, but rather each city has its own distinct laws, institutions and practices. Despite the variability of cultural practices, the norms within a community are as binding as the king's decree. The author of *Double Arguments* goes even further when suggesting the following thought experiment:

> And I think, indeed, that if someone should order all men to bring into one heap everything that each of them regards as shameful, and then to take from the collection what each of them considered to be fine, not a thing would be left, but they would all divide up everything, because all men do not hold the same views (II.18).

Drawing on comparative study of different cultural practices, the author of *Double Arguments* brings multiple examples to suggest that norms do not merely differ from each other, they are often polar opposites. For example, while the Greeks judge incest to be an abominable act, the Persians regard sexual relations with one's family members as legitimate (II.15). Noble and base are determined by doing the right things at the right time (II.20) and the significance of a cultural practice is not refuted even if it is judged in contradictory ways by different cultures.

Defending the sophists as teachers of virtue

Socrates contends throughout the *Meno* that virtue is not teachable. In support of this, one need only consider how many parents have tried to raise good children and failed. Having first considered Socrates' arguments and having established in the previous chapters that ethics are nothing other than the cultural norms of a community, the author of *Double Arguments* legitimates the professional claims of the sophists by defending the teachability of virtue. Just as one learns the language spoken in the community in which one is raised, so too does one learn the ethical norms that are sanctioned and prohibited (VI.12).[4] While even the simpleton will achieve enough proficiency to communicate, the student who applies himself under the tutelage of a teacher of the art of speaking well, namely one of the sophists, can become a master rhetor. The sophist is proven to be the wise man who is capable of navigating the cultural norms so as to know the right way to act in any given situation (*Double*

Arguments VIII.1-2). With knowledge of all things, the sophist is the one best equipped to advise both individuals and cities.

Notes

1. One should note that antilogic does not violate the principle of non-contradiction as both acknowledge that either the same man at different times or different men at the same time may affirm contradictory claims. The significant difference between the two approaches is, therefore, whether one chooses to reconcile contradiction or affirm it. See Aristotle, *Metaphysics* 4.4-5 responding to those who attempt to deny the principle of non-contradiction.

2. For a most valuable discussion of the history of the antilogical method and an attempt to revive it as a contemporary pedagogical practice, see Mendelson 2002.

3. Cf. Plato, *Theaetetus* 159b-e.

4. Cf. Plato, *Protagoras* 327a-e.

Bibliography

Aristotle, *Metaphysics*, trans. W.D. Ross (Oxford: Clarendon Press, 1924).

Aristotle, *Rhetoric and Poetics*, trans. W.R. Roberts and I. Bywater (New York: McGraw Hill, 1984).

DK = Diels, Hermann and Kranz, Walther, *Die Fragmente der Vorsokratiker* (Zurich: Weidman, 1985). This work is in Greek and German. Translations are given by Dillon and Gergel (2003).

Dillon, J. and Gergel, T. (eds), *The Greek Sophists* (London: Penguin, 2003).

Herodotus, *The History*, trans. D. Grene (Chicago: University of Chicago Press, 1988).

Kerferd, G.B., *The Sophistic Movement* (Cambridge: Cambridge University Press, 1981).

Levi, A. (1940), 'On Twofold Statements', *American Journal of Philology* 61 no. 3 (1940), 292-306.

Mendelson, M., *Many Sides: A Protagorean Approach to the Theory, Practice, and Pedagogy of Argument* (Dordrecht: Kluwer, 2002).

Philostratus, *Lives of the Sophists*, trans. W.C. Wright, Loeb edition (London: Heinemann, 1981).

Plato, *Laches, Protagoras, Meno, Euthydemus*, trans. W.R.M. Lamb, Loeb edition (London: Heinemann, 1924).

Plato, *Theaetetus, Sophist*, trans. H.N. Fowler, Loeb edition (London: Heinemann, 1921).

Robinson, T.M. (trans. and ed.), *Contrasting Arguments: An Edition of the* Dissoi Logoi (New York: Arno Press, 1979).

14

Minor Sophists

Trevor Curnow

The term 'Minor Sophists' is used here to cover a number of individuals, most of them very obscure. Indeed, the attribution of minor status to them is largely the consequence of how little we know about them. In some cases it may be deserved, but in others it may not. Those covered by this chapter lived in the period from when the sophists first emerged in the early fifth century BC to the middle of the first century AD. After that the period known as the Second Sophistic begins, which is a subject that falls outside the scope of this volume. Many minor sophists are nothing more than names mentioned in passing by various authors, often of a significantly later period. Some of these authors are better known than others and it may be helpful to begin with a brief overview of them.

When thinking of the sophists, the philosophical mind naturally turns to Plato (c. 424-348 BC) for the simple reason that a number of his dialogues feature or were named after sophists. Although he would not have known the very earliest sophists (Protagoras of Abdera, for example, died around the time Plato was born), he was a contemporary of many others. However, the sophists around whom Plato constructed some of his most famous dialogues, such as Gorgias, can scarcely be regarded as minor. In fact, as a source of information about the minor sophists, Plato is relatively unhelpful. Although a number of works of Isocrates (c. 436-338 BC), one of Plato's contemporaries, survive, he mentions few sophists by name. However, his *Antidosis* is a useful account of how some of them pursued their profession in his time. He was also the author of a work entitled *Against the Sophists*. The title is explained by the fact that he did not regard himself as a sophist, although many others have done so.

More is to be gleaned from the works of Aristotle (384-322 BC). His *Rhetoric* constitutes an early and surviving handbook on the subject, while his *Sophistical Refutations* also contains some interesting insights. *Rhetoric* is particularly useful for the early history of the subject, although the names mentioned in that context lived well before Aristotle's time and he knows them only second-hand and by repute.

After the time of Aristotle, there is a long break in significant primary sources until the first century BC when there is a major flurry of activity. Cicero (106-43 BC) produced a number of relevant works, in particular *On Invention, Brutus, The Orator* and *On the Orator*, although between them they yield surprisingly few names. The opposite is the case with the elder Seneca (*c.* 50 BC-*c.* AD 40) whose *Declamations* list one name after another. A contemporary of Seneca was Dionysius of Halicarnassus (*c.* 60-*c.* 7 BC) whose *On the Ancient Orators* is a useful source of information. In the first century AD Quintilian (*c.* 35-c. 95) wrote his *The Orator's Education*, a textbook on rhetoric that listed and commented on a number of other authors on the subject. Suetonius (*c.* AD 70-*c.* 160), better known for his lives of the Caesars, also wrote about other famous people. Some of the surviving fragments deal with rhetoricians, although most of those he wrote about lived well before his own time. His close contemporary, Plutarch of Chaeronea (*c.* AD 46-*c.* 120) also mentions a number of sophists in his collection of essays known as *Moralia*, especially in his *Lives of the Ten Orators*, although most of his references are historical and he sheds relatively little light on his contemporaries.

Flavius Philostratus was probably born in around AD 170 and was responsible for *Lives of the Sophists*, a major source of information whose narrative stretches from the time of Plato up to his own. Diogenes Laertius mentions some sophists in passing in his *Lives of Eminent Philosophers*, written perhaps in the early fourth century AD. The *Lives of the Philosophers and Sophists* by Eunapius (AD 346-*c.* 414) covers a shorter time span, having little to say about anyone who lived before the third century AD. Finally, mention must be made of *Suidas* or *Suda*, an encyclopaedia that was compiled in around the tenth century AD. Although invaluable in some ways, its reliability is patchy.

The problem of reliability is compounded by the fact that exactly what constituted a sophist is itself a contentious point on which opinions vary, and the meaning of the term itself changed over time. With the minor sophists we often lack adequate information to come to an independent judgement on whether they were sophists or not, whatever criteria for being a sophist are employed. In some cases all we know about them consists of a single comment that lacks corroboration. Consequently it is entirely possible that some of 'the minor sophists' were never really sophists at all.

As professional educators at a time when education was traded as a commodity, the sophists obeyed the law of supply and demand. There was no system of state education so they made a living by selling to those who could afford to pay for it whatever it was that they wanted: the sophists followed both money and trends. Skill in debating was something many people wanted, paying premiums in both the political and the legal arenas. It is therefore no surprise to find that sophists were often associated with the teaching of rhetoric, the so-called 'art of persuasion'. For this reason, some regard the first sophists as Corax and Tisias, both from Syracuse in Sicily, who are said to have formalised some of the basic principles of rhetoric in the early fifth century BC. Because 'Corax' could be a nickname (it means 'crow') and because the stories of the two are difficult to disentangle, it has been suggested (Cole 1991) that Corax and Tisias might have been one and the same person. In any event, it is Tisias who is said to have taught another Sicilian, Gorgias of Leontini (*c.* 485-*c.* 380 BC) and Lysias (*c.* 445-*c.* 380 BC), an Athenian with Sicilian connections. It is also possible, although less sure, that he taught Isocrates. Through his pupils, and in particular through Gorgias, the new ideas about rhetoric made their way to Athens. They were not only transmitted orally but it seems that Corax and/or Tisias also produced a textbook on the subject.

According to Cicero (*Brutus* xi.46), drawing on a now lost book on rhetoric by Aristotle, the work of Corax and/or Tisias came out of a situation when there were many disputes about property ownership in Syracuse. This locates the origins of rhetoric as it developed in Sicily in a specifically legal and competitive context. What emerged was a formal and systematic approach to the subject that could be set down, taught and learnt. A strong emphasis seems to have been laid on how to make the weaker case appear stronger since success in a legal dispute is about winning rather than about being right. Lysias practised this new art in Athens, but his interests were at least as much political as legal and he was a keen supporter and advocate of the democratic cause. Polus of Acragas (modern Agrigento in Sicily) was a pupil of both Gorgias and Licymnius of Chios, who himself seems to have been taught by Gorgias, although precisely who was a student of whom is not always clear. As with many of the minor sophists, precise dates for both Polus and Licymnius are lacking, making it difficult to resolve confusions over such matters.

There was also another line of development that may have contributed to the emergence of the sophist. Plutarch of Chaeronea tells of a certain Mnesiphilus who was an advisor to Themistocles (*c.* 525-*c.* 460 BC), the celebrated Athenian statesman and naval commander. Mnesiphilus was 'neither an orator nor one of the so-called natural philosophers'. Instead, he was versed in 'a combination of political acumen and practical intelligence, which had been handed down in unbroken succession from Solon, as though it were a set of philosophical principles. His successors combined it with various forensic techniques and transferred its application from public affairs to the use of language and were termed Sophists' (Plutarch, *The Rise and Fall of Athens* 78). What Plutarch seems to be identifying here is a certain kind of shrewdness or sense of realpolitik. Sophists like Protagoras may represent the next stage of this line of development, but with the added twist, according to Plato (*Protagoras* 349a), that he was the first to charge for his services and to call himself a sophist. His interests were also more philosophical than political, although Diogenes Laertius (IX.50) credits him with producing a new constitution for Thurii in southern Italy. Phaleas of Chalcedon perhaps more obviously belongs in this group. He was probably an older contemporary of Plato and is discussed at some length by Aristotle in the second book of his *Politics* (II.7) where he is shown to have been involved at least in the theory and perhaps also in the practice of drafting constitutions.

These two lines of development, rhetoric and realpolitik, came together in Athens in the fifth century, with the opportunities afforded by a democratic state and the rewards offered by a rich one. The resultant mixture prospered there for well over a hundred years. Because the aim of those studying with sophists was usually in order to succeed in some area of public life, few students of sophists actually aimed at becoming sophists themselves. Many became practitioners of oratory rather than teachers of it or of anything else. One exception was Antimoerus of Mende: in *Protagoras* (315a) Plato makes it clear that this particularly talented pupil of Protagoras hoped to follow in his master's profession.

Of the other names of minor sophists already mentioned, Licymnius was celebrated mainly as a poet, although he also wrote a technical work on rhetoric. Polus also wrote a work on rhetoric and Socrates is said to have read it (*Gorgias* 462b). In *Rhetoric* (1400a) Aristotle also mentions a Callippus and a Pamphilus as authors of handbooks of rhetoric, but nothing else is known about them. The fact that they all wrote handbooks on rhetoric suggests that they may well have been professional teachers of the subject. Polus at least is positively identified as a sophist by Philostratus (I.13). Lysias may have taught rhetoric for a few years around the end of the fifth century BC.

The names of a number of other people connected with rhetoric and the sophists are sprinkled throughout the works of Plato. Some, like the wealthy Callias (*c.* 450-*c.* 367 BC) and Meno (*c.* 423-400 BC), are simply students or followers of sophists rather than sophists in their own right. Others, such as Archinus of Coele, Cephalus of Syracuse and Epicrates of Cephisia may have studied and practised rhetoric but not taught it. The dates for all of these is uncertain, but they were all born in the fifth century BC and all except Cephalus lived on into the fourth. A more problematic case is a contemporary of theirs, Evenus of Paros, who was certainly a teacher. It is not clear exactly what he taught but it is apparent that he charged for his services. In *Apology* (20a) he is presented as the teacher of Callias' children. A poet and a scholar of rhetoric, he may have been a sophist, although Plato never calls him one and in *Phaedo* (60c-61c) suggests he is a philosopher. In *Phaedrus* (267a) he is credited with the invention of certain rhetorical techniques, such as innuendo, that operate in an indirect way. Another difficult case is Damon of Oe (*c.* 485-414 BC), a pupil of Prodicus. He was also a teacher, perhaps of music, and may have acted as a political adviser to Pericles (*c.* 495-429 BC) in much the same way as Mnesiphilus earlier had to Themistocles. Again, he is never explicitly referred to as a sophist.

Two people known to have taught rhetoric in Athens in the fifth and fourth centuries BC were Polycrates (440-370 BC) and Aspasia (*c.* 470-*c.* 400 BC). Polycrates composed rhetorical exercises and wrote speeches as

155

well as a host of minor works. There was a tradition that he wrote a speech to be delivered at the trial of Socrates, but most think it unlikely. Aspasia was the unofficial consort of Pericles and taught rhetoric to both him and Socrates.

Socrates himself admits in *Gorgias* (465) that it is not entirely easy to distinguish the teacher of rhetoric from the sophist. Philostratus points to a different problem. Discussing Eudoxus of Cnidus (*c.* 390-*c.* 340 BC), he comments that he was often regarded as a sophist 'because his style was ornate and he improvised with success' (*Lives of the Sophists* I.1). Eudoxus was perhaps the best known mathematician of his time as well as an astronomer and geographer. He does not conform to the standard picture of a sophist, yet according to Philostratus he and a number of others were regarded as sophists because of their eloquence and style. Two of them, Leon of Byzantium and Dias of Ephesus, both seem to have studied under Plato at the Academy. Little is known about Dias, but he seems to have been active politically. According to Philostratus (I.3), it was his powers of persuasion that led Philip of Macedon to undertake a military expedition in Asia in 337 or 336 BC, his motive in doing so being to relieve some of the pressure Philip was putting on the Greek states. A similar story is told of Leon (I.2) who is supposed to have persuaded Philip not to attack his home city of Byzantium in 340 BC. In both cases it was evidently their persuasive arts that caused them to be identified as sophists, although there is no indication that either followed the profession of sophist.

Leon's older compatriot Theodorus of Byzantium is sometimes regarded as a sophist. He wrote a handbook on rhetoric and was renowned for his eloquence. In *Phaedrus* (266e) Plato recognises his inventiveness by calling him *logodaedalus*, literally a 'Daedalus of words'. However, Aristotle criticises him in *Rhetoric* (1414b) for inventing unnecessary technical distinctions where none exist in reality, a criticism he also levels at Licymnius of Chios. Theodorus seems to have written a number of works and may be presumed to have taught rhetoric.

Although Aristippus of Cyrene (*c.* 440-*c.* 399 BC) is generally thought of as a philosopher, Diogenes Laertius (I.65) regarded him as a sophist because he accepted payment for his services. According to Diogenes, he had been a pupil of Socrates and was the first of his pupils to set himself up on a professional basis. When he sent Socrates a share of his earnings, the money was returned. Aristippus is often regarded as the founder of the Cyrenaic school of philosophy. The school preached an extreme form of hedonism and Aristippus took great pleasure in pleasure. Antisthenes of Athens (*c.* 446-*c.* 366 BC), another pupil of Socrates at one time, is also sometimes regarded as a sophist. However, although he studied with Gorgias and possibly other sophists as well, he is more often regarded as one of the founders of Cynicism and the austerity of his later life stands in contrast to the relative opulence of the sophists.

Bryson of Heraclea Pontica was a contemporary also sometimes regarded as a sophist although, like Eudoxus, his main interests were in mathematics. However, he certainly studied language and Aristotle at least (*Rhetoric* 1405b) seems to regard him as a sophist. He argued that there is no such thing as bad language because 'coarse' words mean exactly the same thing as their more refined alternatives. Polyxenus was a student of Bryson and Diogenes Laertius (II.76) suggests that he, too, followed the career of a sophist.

Some sophists are relatively easy to locate within their correct historical and cultural contexts because of their connections with better known individuals. However, this is not always the case. Two particularly difficult examples are Xeniades and Lycophron. Xeniades came from Corinth and if he was a sophist may have been one of the first since he was praised by Democritus of Abdera, which suggests he was probably older than Protagoras. He argued that everything was false (Sprague 2001, 29), which in some ways makes him look like a very early Sceptic. However, although the only known mention of him comes from the works of Sextus Empiricus, a Sceptic of the second and third centuries AD, the position Xeniades takes is actually a dogmatic one since it argues for a particular viewpoint whereas the Sceptics questioned every viewpoint.

The surviving evidence concerning Lycophron is a little more extensive, but still consists only of a handful of references to him scattered around the works of Aristotle and his commentators (Sprague 2001, 68). He is specifically identified as a sophist on more than one occasion. He may have been a student of Gorgias, although this is unclear. Unfortunately the quotations and opinions attributed to him are so fragmented as to yield little sense of what he actually thought or taught. He evidently interested himself in a variety of problems, including that of knowledge, but it is impossible to reconstruct a coherent outlook, let alone a career.

In the cases of Herodicus of Selymbria and Miccus the position is different. There is clear evidence that both of them were teachers and Herodicus is explicitly identified in *Protagoras* (316d-e) as a sophist. However, what they taught lay far from the interests normally associated with the sophists. Miccus, who was a friend of Socrates, taught wrestling while Herodicus seems to have taught physical fitness in a more general way. One of his pupils was Hippocrates of Cos (*c.* 469-399 BC?), recognised as the first great physician, and Herodicus is said to have discovered the effects of diet on health. Two other contemporaries, Agathocles (*c.* 470-433 BC) and Pythoclides of Ceos are also identified in *Protagoras* (316e) as belonging among the sophists. Both were musicians and Agathocles, at least, taught music as well. In his *Poetics* (16, 17) Aristotle refers to someone called Polyidus as a sophist. From the context it is not entirely clear who is meant but he may also have been a musician and a poet.

In his *Lives of Ten Orators*, Plutarch refers to another teacher, Sophilus, as a sophist (832C). Sophilus was the father of Antiphon of Rhamnus.

However, it seems that he taught only young children at a very elementary level. As a consequence most exclude him from the list of the sophists, as they were generally associated only with what can be regarded as specifically higher education.

Although it was pointed out earlier that the pupils of the sophists did not generally seek to become sophists themselves, a number of those who studied with Isocrates are thought to have done so. Those most likely to have pursued careers as sophists from the available evidence are Cephisodorus, Metrodorus, Philiscus of Miletus, Isaeus, Lacritus of Phaselis and Theodectes (*c.* 375-334 BC), also from Phaselis. Cephisodorus wrote a technical work on rhetoric that strongly criticised Aristotle. Metrodorus taught Theocritus of Chios and Isaeus probably taught Demosthenes (384-322 BC). Demosthenes went on to become one of the most famous of Greek orators and one of his speeches was composed for a legal action against Lacritus. Theodectes, a poet and friend of Aristotle's, wrote a handbook on rhetoric in both verse and prose as well as over fifty tragedies. Theocritus of Chios is generally reckoned to have been a sophist himself although he, like his compatriot and opponent Theopompus of Chios (*c.* 378-*c.* 320 BC), was perhaps primarily an historian. Theopompus caused a stir in philosophical circles by suggesting that Plato had borrowed extensively and without acknowledgement from the works of Antisthenes and Aristippus in writing his dialogues.

Although many pupils of Isocrates became celebrated in one way and another and the approach to rhetoric that he advocated and taught came to be regarded as authoritative, this did not happen without opposition. Alcidamas of Elaea was a pupil of Gorgias and opponent of Isocrates who wrote his own handbook of rhetoric. Anaximenes of Lampsacus, tutor for a while to the future Alexander the Great, may also have produced a handbook of his own. The Athenian statesman Aeschines was probably a pupil of Alcidamas. Defeated in debate by Demosthenes in 330 BC, he retired to Rhodes where he became a teacher of rhetoric, presumably in the style of his earlier teacher.

By the time this happened, the Greek world had changed greatly. At the battle of Chaeronea in 338 BC Philip II of Macedonia had defeated the combined forces of Athens and Thebes. This, followed by the brief reign (336-323 BC) of his son Alexander the Great, marked the end of classical Greece and the onset of the Hellenistic age, which is usually taken to have lasted until 31 BC when Augustus became the sole ruler of the Roman domains. The end of classical Greece was also the demise of classical democracy, and the available political outlets for the skills taught by the sophists shrank accordingly, although legal disputes could always be reckoned to continue. However, those who overthrew and conquered the Greek states politically nevertheless respected their culture such that it continued to exert an influence for centuries afterwards. One of the areas in which Greek ideas continued to hold sway was in that of education, and it is impossible to understand the next stage in the history of the minor sophists without understanding the form this education took.

Education was essentially a private affair, hence the demand for the sophists. The earliest stage of education involved learning to read and write, followed by a secondary stage when grammar was the main concern. During the fifth and fourth centuries BC the general foundations of higher education were developed and these evolved into a system that was to remain remarkably stable almost until the end of the ancient world itself. Rhetoric and philosophy established themselves as the pre-eminent subjects. Philosophy came to be taught mainly under the combined aegis of the great schools (the Academy, the Lyceum, the Stoa and the Garden of the Epicureans) and for obvious reasons those who taught in them were regarded as philosophers. While, as has been seen, the early sophists taught a number of different subjects, they subsequently became identified much more closely with rhetoric. 'Rhetorician' and 'sophist' came to be virtually synonymous with each other. As rhetoric came to be seen as the alternative to philosophy, so those who taught it came to be seen as the alternatives to philosophers, namely sophists. However, for reasons that are not at all clear, the sophists did not found durable schools in the way the philosophers did. It may be that there was a simple reason for this: while the philosophers continued to disagree with each other, the rhetoricians came to offer an increasingly standardised product based on ever fewer handbooks. They could teach it wherever they wanted to, and there was plenty of demand for it which meant that many made a good living out of it. When Rome took over the main elements of the Greek approach to education, the future of the sophists and rhetoric was assured for a few more centuries. Rhetoric and philosophy had both taken hold in Rome by the middle of the second century BC and the practical preferences of the Romans ensured that rhetoric was the more popular of the two.

From the period between 338 BC and 161 BC, the year in which alarmed Roman traditionalists temporarily banished both philosophers and rhetoricians from their city, few sophists are known. Some regard Demetrius of Phalerum (*c.* 350-280 BC) as a sophist because he wrote on rhetoric and may have had some pupils from time to time, but he was primarily a politician. Philostratus (I.19) mentions the names of Ariobarzanes of Cilicia, Xenophron of Sicily and Peithagoras of Cyrene without saying when they taught, only that they came after Aeschines. It may be that they belong to this time. When the sophist Abas lived is not known at all and perhaps he practised his profession during this same period. Posidonius of Olbiopolis is another who may have lived at this time, although opinions are divided on his most likely dates. Similarly, a book entitled *On Style* written by someone called Demetrius is assigned by some to the third century BC, but others put it somewhat later. Some have attributed it to Demetrius of Phalerum, but this is now generally rejected. A certain Bion of Syracuse, author of some works on rhetoric, may also have come from this time.

With the advent of the second century, the clouds begin to lift again. The expulsion of the rhetoricians in 161 BC is adequate evidence of their presence and significance, and those seeking to play a leading role in public life were evidently making increasing use of their services during this time. Two of the first names known are those of Diophanes of Mitylene and Menelaus of Marathus, the teachers of Tiberius and Gaius Gracchus respectively. Both Tiberius (*c.* 164-133 BC) and Gaius (154-121 BC) achieved fame as politicians and social reformers. The resistance they encountered in their attempts to effect social change doubtless gave them ample opportunities to exercise their rhetorical skills.

There was also an important development in the technical literature of rhetoric. Some time during the second century BC Hermagoras of Temnos produced a new handbook which from that time on became the standard work on the subject. It has not survived, but Cicero's *On Invention*, which has, is based on it. Nothing is known about Hermagoras himself apart from the fact that he seems to have set up his own small school in Athens. A contemporary, Apollonius of Alabanda, sometimes known as Apollonius Malakos, had a school in Rhodes. Cicero (*On the Orator* xix) mentions a Menedemus who taught in Athens in the late second and early first century BC, while Quintilian makes several references to an otherwise unknown Athenaeus who wrote a book on rhetoric at around the same time Hermagoras wrote his.

Diophanes, Hermagoras, Apollonius and Menedemus were all Greek and it is not until the early first century BC that Roman teachers of rhetoric emerge, along with a Latin literature on the subject. If not the first, then certainly one of the first Roman teachers was Lucius Plotius Gallus, one of whose pupils was Cicero, who went on to become not only an accomplished speaker but also the author of some important works on rhetoric. Gallus himself had a setback when he was banned from teaching in 92 BC, but the tide of events was moving in his direction. The first Latin work on rhetoric comes from the same period, its author an otherwise unknown Antonius. The statesman and soldier Pompey the Great (106-48 BC) had at least one Roman teacher, Lucius Voltacilius Plotus, while Marcus Epidius taught both Mark Antony (83-30 BC) and Augustus (63 BC-AD 14). However, the picture was by no means entirely a Roman one. When in *Brutus* Cicero mentions his own teachers of rhetoric from time to time, many of them are still Greek: Demetrius the Syrian, Menippus of Stratonicea, Dionysius of Magnesia, Aeschylus of Cnidus, Xenocles of Adramyttium and Apollonius Molon. He mentions two other teachers of rhetoric, Pammenes and Lucius Coelius Antipater. Pammenes was a Greek who taught Marcus Brutus. Antipater had been a teacher of Gaius Gracchus, but he was better known as an historian.

At least one of the teachers in Rome during the first century BC came from Alexandria. Timagenes seems to have first arrived in Rome as a prisoner and subsequently set up his own school of rhetoric there. One of his pupils, Asinius Pollio of Tralles, later took over the school. Timagenes was also an historian and the author of a number of works. Philoxenus is said to have been another sophist from Alexandria teaching in Rome at this time, although his area of pre-eminence seems to have been grammar rather than rhetoric.

Although never able to compete on equal terms with Alexandria, Pergamum had also become a major centre of learning. Apollodorus of Pergamum wrote a new handbook on rhetoric there during the first century BC. It was written in Greek but one of his Roman students, the senator and poet Gaius Valgius Rufus, translated it into Latin and wrote some further works of his own on rhetoric, grammar and medicine. Augustus was another of Apollodorus' students for a while. Another Latin work on rhetoric, known as *Ad Herennium* (*To Herennius*) was produced during the same century. Some have attributed it to Cicero, others to someone called Cornificius, but neither attribution is certain and more than one Cornificius has been suggested.

Theodorus of Gadara and Potamo of Mitylene were also active sophists in Rome during the first century BC. Although of humble birth, Theodorus had the distinction of teaching the future emperor Tiberius. He was a prolific author writing on various aspects of language, such as dialects and pronunciation, as well as on history.

An important source of information on rhetoric and teachers in the later part of the first century BC is Seneca the Elder. In his later years he wrote a book for his children in which he recalled the great orators and teachers of his younger days. By this time the teaching of rhetoric in Rome made extensive use of 'declamations', which usually took the form of composing speeches to be made at imaginary trials. Not all who composed these taught rhetoric, and unfortunately it is not known how many of the nearly sixty 'declaimers' mentioned by Seneca could be regarded as sophists in any way. However, a few of the names he mentions are worthy of note. Caius Albucius Silus wrote a handbook on rhetoric. Marullus, the teacher of Seneca, was clearly a sophist, as was Marcus Porcius Latro, a fellow student who went on to become a teacher of rhetoric in his own right before committing suicide in AD 4. Dionysius of Halicarnassus, originally from Asia Minor, moved to Rome in around 30 BC and taught rhetoric there. He was a prolific author and substantial portions of his writings survive, although relatively few of them deal with rhetoric. His works were often cited by Quintilian.

In many ways, Quintilian stands at the end of a tradition and it is appropriate to end this historical overview with him, although it would be unfair to characterise him as a 'minor' figure. The movement known as the Second Sophistic began during his lifetime and he stood against it. The sophists of the Second Sophistic paid a great deal of attention to ornamentation, and Quintilian felt they were more interested in style than substance.

The story told in this chapter began with the names of Corax and Tisias and legal disputes in Syracuse. After their time the use of rhetoric developed in both the legal and the political arenas, and those who sought to advance their careers in one or both of these arenas sought out those who could train them in the necessary skills. For obvious reason political debate flourishes best in an open democratic society where winning an argument or a debate can have real results. When dictatorship takes hold, public debate tends to descend into either redundancy or flattery. The Macedonian conquest was a setback for political oratory in Greece just as the end of the Republic was for it in Rome. The legal arena almost always remained open for business but offered limited opportunities in a less litigious age. One reaction was for rhetoric to retreat to irrelevance and the practice of rhetorical skills for their own sake, and this sometimes happened. Sometimes it was the sophists themselves who did all that was required to give themselves a bad name without the need for any adverse propaganda.

As I indicated at the beginning of this chapter, the 'minor' status of many of 'the minor sophists' is simply a matter of our ignorance of them, and many of the names that have appeared on the pages of this chapter are little more than names. But, as I hope has been shown, if they are individually minor, nevertheless collectively they constitute a significant body of people stretching over many centuries. While we are never likely to know the full contribution they made to the history of Western thought, their names at least deserve to be known even if most things about them have long been forgotten.

Bibliography

Aristotle, *Art of Rhetoric*, trans J.H. Freese, Loeb edition (London: Heinemann, 1959).

Aristotle, *On Sophistical Refutation* and *On Coming-To-Be and Passing-Away*, trans. E.S. Forster, Loeb edition (London: Heinemann, 1955).

Aristotle, *Poetics*, in *Classical Literary Criticism*, trans. P. Murray and T.S. Dorsch (Harmondsworth: Penguin, 1965).

Aristotle, *Politics*, trans. C.D.C. Reeve (Indianapolis, IN: Hackett, 1998).

Bowen, James, *A History of Western Education*, vol. I: *The Ancient World: Orient and Mediterranean* (London: Methuen, 1972).

Cicero, *Brutus* and *Orator*, trans. G.L. Hendrickson and H.M. Hubbell (London: Heinemann, 1962).

Cicero, *De Inventione, De Optimo Genere Oratorum, Topica*, trans. H.M. Hubbell, Loeb edition (London: Heinemann, 1949).

Cicero, *On Oratory and Orators*, trans. J.S. Watson (Carbondale: Southern Illinois University Press, 1970).

Clarke, M.L., *Rhetoric at Rome* (London: Cohen and West, 1953).

Cole, Thomas, 'Who was Corax?', *Illinois Classical Studies* XVI (1991), 65-84.

Curnow, Trevor, *The Philosophers of the Ancient World: An A to Z Guide* (London: Duckworth, 2006).

14. Minor Sophists

Diogenes Laertius, *Lives of Eminent Philosophers*, vols I and II, trans. R.D. Hicks, Loeb edition (London: Heinemann, 1958, 1959).

Dionysius of Halicarnassus, *Critical Essays*, trans. S. Usher, 2 vols. Loeb edition (London: Heinemann, 1974, 1985).

Eunapius, *Lives of Philosophers,* in Philostratus, *Lives of the Sophists* and Eunapius, *Lives of Philosophers*, trans. W.C. Wright, Loeb edition (Cambridge, MA.: Harvard University Press, 1921).

Guthrie, W.K.C., *The Sophists* (Cambridge: Cambridge University Press, 1971).

Isocrates, *To Demonicus, To Nicocles, Nicocles or The Cyprians, Panegyricus, To Philip, and Archidamus*, trans. G. Norlin, Loeb edition (London: Heinemann, 1928).

Isocrates, *Areopagiticus, On the Peace, Panathenaicus, Against the Sophists, Antidosis*, trans. G. Norlin, Loeb edition (London: Heinemann, 1929).

Kennedy, George A., *The Art of Persuasion in Greece* (London: Routledge and Kegan Paul, 1963).

Kennedy, George A., *Classical Rhetoric and its Christian and Secular Tradition from Ancient to Modern Times* (Chapel Hill: University of North Carolina Press, 1980).

Marrou, H.I., *A History of Education in Antiquity*, trans. G. Lamb (Madison: University of Wisconsin Press, 1982).

Nails, Debra, *The People of Plato: A Prosopography of Plato and other Socratics* (Indianapolis: Hackett, 2002).

Philostratus, *Lives of the Sophists*, in Philostratus, *Lives of the Sophists* and Eunapius, *Lives of Philosophers*, trans. W.C. Wright, Loeb edition (Cambridge, MA.: Harvard University Press, 1921).

Plato, *Gorgias*, trans. W. Hamilton (Harmondsworth: Penguin, 1960).

Plato, *The Last Days of Socrates*, trans. H. Tredennick (Harmondsworth: Penguin, 1969).

Plato, *Phaedrus* and *Letters VII* and *VIII*, trans. W. Hamilton (Harmondsworth: Penguin, 1973).

Plato, *Protagoras* and *Meno*, trans. W.K.C. Guthrie (Harmondsworth: Penguin, 1956).

Plutarch, *Moralia*, vol. X, trans. H.N. Fowler, Loeb edition (London: Heinemann, 1960).

Plutarch, *The Rise and Fall of Athens*, trans. I. Scott-Kilvert (Harmondsworth: Penguin, 1960).

Quintilian, *The Orator's Education*, trans. D.A. Russell, 5 vols, Loeb edition (Cambridge, MA: Harvard University Press, 2001).

[Seneca] The Elder Seneca, *Declamations*, trans. M. Winterbottom, 2 vols, Loeb edition (London: Heinemann, 1974).

Smith, William, *Dictionary of Greek and Roman Biography and Mythology* (1867). http://www.ancientlibrary.com/smith-bio/ (accessed 20 November 2006).

Sprague, Rosamond Kent (ed.), *The Older Sophists* (Indianapolis: Hackett, 2001).

Suda online. http://www.stoa.org/sol/ (accessed 20 November 2006).

Suetonius, vol. II, trans. J. C. Rolfe, Loeb edition (London: Heinemann, 1959).

15

Was Socrates a Sophist?

Christine Farmer

There is not really a single definition of 'sophist' on which all are agreed, and which includes all those who have been called by this term. According to one definition, the sophists were a class of professional teachers; but this view excludes the historian Thucydides and the poet Euripides, who are often referred to as sophists. Another view defines them according to their ideas and areas of interest; yet they were not a philosophical 'school', and there was no discrete 'doctrine of the sophists'. It can be broadly stated that those referred to as sophists shared a general scepticism about the possibility of certain knowledge or ultimate truth, and in some cases denied the existence of an objective truth outside the minds of men. Also, that they concentrated on the everyday contingency of living, admitting a relativism with respect of law and belief, since they upheld that such things were not god-given and eternal, but only man-made, mutable and variable from place to place. This view was understandable since, unlike the Athenian Socrates, the majority of sophists were foreigners with no allegiance to traditional Athenian values. Perhaps the one thing they all had in common was a belief in the teachability of *aretê* ('excellence' or 'virtue'), and all sophists who taught gave classes in public speaking and rhetoric: the effective use of language to persuade or influence others, a skill much in demand in fifth-century Athens.

Our sources for the sophists and for Socrates (469-399 BC) are for the most part one and the same. While the sophists wrote many treatises, these mainly survive as fragments, and we rely on summaries or references to their work made by others. Chief among these was Socrates' follower and their ideological opponent, Plato. Socrates, by comparison, wrote no philosophy, preferring to engage others in ongoing philosophical debate, rather than convey a finished thesis in written form. Our major sources for what Socrates did and thought are the dialogues of his friends Plato and Xenophon, and a depiction of him in a comic play by Aristophanes which deals with sophistry as a subject. Lastly, the ideas of Socrates and the sophists were examined by the philosopher and philosophical historian Aristotle, who forms a fourth important source.

Our earliest source for the question of Socrates as a sophist is Aristophanes, who produced his play *Clouds* in 423 BC, when Socrates was in his mid-forties and Aristophanes in his thirties. This comic play is our only major source on Socrates written in the early part of his life, by someone who was neither a close friend nor a follower, hostile in tone, and therefore considered by many to be relatively unbiased. It is also the only major source which refers to 'Socrates the sophist', and depicts him as firmly belonging to the sophistic movement, whichever definition one chooses.

In *Clouds*, Aristophanes parodied the 'new ideas' prevalent at the time, and attacked the sophists for giving instruction which went against the gods, and teaching all-comers how to argue successfully that it was for example morally 'right' for a son to beat his father (Aristophanes, *Clouds* 1421ff.). Socrates is parodied as chief sophist, an out-of-touch and atheistic stargazer spouting nonsense about the universe while hanging from a basket. He heads a school called the *phrontisterion* ('think tank'), and exacts fees in exchange for teaching a corruptible public the use of rhetoric to escape one's creditors.

The question is, how accurate a picture of what the historical Socrates did and thought can be established from a reading of a comic play, the aim of which was to make the public laugh and to win a prize by popular vote? All humour needs at least a grain of truth or it will not work, but Old Comedy is well known for exaggeration for comic effect, and for sacrificing reality to fantasy and the needs of the plot. An example of this is in Aristophanes' *Lysistrata,* where a 'sex-strike' by the wives of Athenian soldiers brings an end to warfare, while conveniently ignoring the existence of prostitution. And there is no reason to suppose that *Clouds* represents anything other than an appeal to popular prejudice concerning intellectuals in general and the sophists in particular, in order to raise a laugh.

It was convenient for dramatic effect that Aristophanes should unite many aspects of the 'new thought' in the person of a single character. In many ways Socrates was the perfect choice for this. He was a well-known figure about the city, physically unusual by all accounts, with an ungainly walk and the habit of going about without a cloak or sandals. In the public mind he no doubt fitted the picture of a 'typical intellectual', and was referred to in that sense in several comedies during his lifetime. According to Plato, Socrates commented, when on trial for his life in 399 BC, that far from being an accurate depiction of himself, *Clouds* simply reflected popular opinion and the slanders which were to be repeated against him for decades (Plato, *Apology* 18b; 19b-c). Socrates went on to defend himself against the specific suggestions that he had made serious enquiries into natural physics, had 'made the weaker argument defeat the stronger', or taught either of those things to others (*Apology* 19b-c).

But how far can we trust Plato's account? Socrates was on trial for his life, and faced charges of impiety, and corruption of the youth of Athens. In fact it is probable that Socrates was brought to trial because his existence had become politically inconvenient, and that the true reasons behind his trial could not be stated because of a political amnesty in force at that time. In the mind of the public, Socrates was associated with his friends and one-time associates Critias and Alcibiades: young men who had gone on to become implicated in infamous acts of sacrilege, even treason. Similar charges of atheism and corrupting the young had been successfully brought against intellectuals before Socrates. The question of whether or not he was 'a sophist' suddenly became important, and to an extent it is for this reason that the question is debated today.

The popular conception of Socrates as a sophist continued long after his death. Aeschines in 345 BC referred to him as 'Socrates the sophist' and 'teacher of Critias', in a public debate fifty-four years after his execution (Aeschines, *Against Timarchus* 173). This argument could not have been used successfully had it not still been the common perception of Socrates. It was against this popular conception that Socrates' friends and associates sought to defend him, as well as to preserve his memory. His followers wrote many dialogues in which Socrates was a major character but only those of Plato and two by Xenophon survive. Both these men were about forty-five years Socrates' junior, and knew him perhaps for only the last decade of his life.

The stated aim of Xenophon's *Memorabilia* was to defend his former friend from what he saw as the unjust charges for which he had been executed. Like Aristophanes, Xenophon (born between 430 and 425 BC, died after 355) was no philosopher, but a soldier and gentleman. As such he is less useful on Socrates' philosophical stance than Plato, but provides a description of his habits, beliefs and interests which contrasts markedly with Aristophanes' picture of the man.

Aristophanes had shown Socrates charging for his knowledge, and we know that the sophists became extremely wealthy by taking fees (Plato, *Meno* 91d). Socrates, by contrast, paid no attention to his own status, wealth or physical appearance, preferring to go about poorly dressed and unshod, a fact parodied by Aristophanes (*Clouds* 356). Xenophon states explicitly that Socrates never charged fees for his time, nor 'taught' anyone, but rather benefited his friends by the example of his character, actions and conversation (Xenophon, *Memorabilia* I.3.1). Xenophon's Socrates compares teaching knowledge to all comers for a fee with prostitution, and called the sophists 'prostitutors of wisdom' (I.6.13-14).

Socrates and his friends were by contrast, says Xenophon, 'useful to *one another*', reading texts and sharing useful extracts, engaged in a common search for knowledge (I.6.13-14). This image of Socrates as 'fellow-seeker' rather than teacher is one we also receive from Plato's dialogues, discussed below. We certainly see no evidence in either Xenophon or Plato of anything resembling the 'think tank' of Aristophanes. But formal schools of philosophy, such as Plato's Academy and Aristotle's Lyceum, were not to appear in Athens until after Socrates' death. The teaching of the sophists probably took place in circumstances not very different from the gatherings attended by Socrates and his associates: informal meetings both public and private, such as the symposia. These were drinking parties, which were devoted to conversation but sometimes lapsed into intemperate behaviour. Indeed Plato shows Socrates along with all the major sophists and politically hungry young men, socialising within the same circles, if not always on friendly terms. An example of this is in Plato's *Protagoras*, in which Plato is keen to show a young and still-uncorrupted Alcibiades moving out of the influence of Socrates and into that of the sophists. On the charge of 'corrupting the young', Socrates said that if anyone who associated with him had gone on to become either a good or a bad citizen, he himself could not be held responsible, since he had never promised to teach, or ever taught, anything to anyone (*Apology* 33a-b).

Far from charging a fee, Socrates says that he was pleased to speak to and debate with anyone willing, and Plato has Socrates refute outright the charge of taking fees in his *Apology* (19d). Plato also explained Socrates' reasons for not charging: that if one charged a fee, one was obliged to teach. Socrates believed that not everyone was ready for his particular method of joint-enquiry into truth. His theory was that one had to first 'conceive' an idea in one's own mind, and that he, Socrates, could then help one to 'give birth' to the thought. Far from being able to teach others, Socrates stated that like all good midwives, he himself was barren, i.e. he had no wisdom of his own to impart (Plato, *Theaetetus* 150, 151b). Those whom he thought lacking in ideas of their own, he sent to the sophists, who were more suited to help them (151b). And in a reference no doubt to Alcibiades, he claimed that others had left him prematurely, and had consequently 'suffered a miscarriage' of their ideas through bad company (151b). This metaphor of the miscarriage of ideas is likely to have been used by Socrates himself, since it not only appears in Xenophon and Plato, but was also parodied in *Clouds* (133ff.).

Turning from the definition of sophist as 'professional teacher' and to the subjects they taught, we see that in *Clouds*, Socrates is portrayed as having an interest in natural phenomena, and especially in their explanation without reference to the gods as causative forces. The play sees Zeus replaced by the notion of Vortex or 'awhirl' (380-1), a reference to the intellectual atheism of the fifth century; a result of the Presocratic enquiries into natural science in the previous generation. Such subjects were typically explored and taught by sophists including Hippias, Prodicus, Gorgias and Protagoras.

Sources other than Aristophanes show Socrates as uninterested in these matters, and certainly never having taught them. The first part of Xenophon's *Memorabilia* is largely concerned with refuting the idea of Socrates as an atheist, and there are many references in Plato which support this contention, most strongly stated in the *Apology* (23d). Now Socrates did not deny ever having been interested in the natural sciences, but his interest came early in life and was soon discarded, and undertaken only for personal interest. We learn this from Plato's *Phaedo* (96-8), in which Socrates explains how he had once been interested in the work of the Presocratic Anaxagoras, but had become disillusioned with that philosopher after he failed to live up to his promise of explaining the guiding principle of the universe as 'mind'. From then on, Socrates concentrated on matters of ethics rather than natural philosophy. We hear the same from Xenophon, who stated that Socrates did not speculate on the nature of the universe, since there was so much in ethics which had not yet been explored, and that matters of heaven were beyond human comprehension (*Memorabilia* I.1.11-13). Now Plato and Xenophon were of course at pains to defend their former friend from accusations which had led to his execution, and so we may suspect them of bias. But Aristotle also said that Socrates concentrated on ethics and the moral virtues and ignored the physical universe (*Metaphysics* 13, 1078b), and as we shall see shortly, Aristotle was a relatively unbiased source. Indeed, it is to the philosophers Plato and Aristotle that we turn for a fuller discussion of the ideas and methods of Socrates, and to see how these differed from those of his contemporaries in Athens.

Plato was born in 427 BC, and we do not know when he met Socrates. But if they had met when Plato was eighteen, Socrates would have been in his sixties, and their acquaintance can have lasted only a decade. Plato developed the dialogue as a vehicle for showing Socrates' ideas and his method of philosophising through debate. However, they were not intended to be verbatim records of actual historical conversations between Socrates and his interlocutors, but rather to illustrate both sides of a philosophical argument. In addition, Plato used Socrates as a 'mouthpiece' for his own more developed philosophy. Living and working for a further fifty years after Socrates' death, Plato built on the work of his former master to develop his own theories, such as the 'Theory of Ideas', which he intended as a final response to the scepticism and relativism of the sophists.

At the same time, Plato may have modified the arguments of the sophists with whom he shows Socrates conversing, for the sake of making a philosophical point. However, it is unlikely that in doing this, Plato strayed too far from the truth of their position, since at the time he was writing much of their work was still extant. While Plato was often hostile in his treatment of the sophists, he was by no means always unsympathetic to the philosophical position of individual sophists (e.g. Protagoras). On balance, we cannot accept uncritically the evidence presented by Plato either as concerns Socrates, or his interlocutors.

A less biased source is Aristotle, who wrote a remarkably even-handed history of philosophical thought down to his time. Born in 384 BC, fifteen years after Socrates' execution, Aristotle of course never met the earlier philosopher. Having no particular reason to defend Socrates or his work, Aristotle criticised his ideas on more than one occasion. And while Aristotle accused some sophists of bad reasoning and deception, and of teaching for money a wisdom 'not real but apparent' (Aristotle, *Sophistical Refutations* 164b25-165a19), he nevertheless treated their arguments fairly, and in some cases defended their philosophical position against Socrates.

Aristotle studied for more than twenty years in Plato's Academy, and with access to the works of his philosophical predecessors and Plato himself, he is our best source for distinguishing Socrates' thought from that of his student, a difficulty known as the 'Socratic Question'. It is from Aristotle that we learn that the Theory of Forms, voiced by Socrates in the dialogues, was actually the work of Plato and his followers, who gave the simple definitions of Socrates a 'separate existence' and named them 'Forms' (*Metaphysics* 1, 987b1; 13, 1078b).

Aristotle states that two innovations could fairly be ascribed to Socrates: inductive reasoning and a search for general definitions of key moral virtues (*Metaphysics* 13, 1078b27). Inductive reasoning implies a 'leading on' of the mind from particular to universal examples. In this method, examples of a particular virtue are collected and examined to discover the common quality which makes them either, for example 'courageous' or 'lawful' or 'good'. This accords with what we learn of Socrates' method, known as the *elenchus*, from Plato's dialogues, in which we see Socrates in search of the definition of particular moral concepts such as 'the good', 'justice', 'courage' and 'virtue'.

A typical dialogue begins with Socrates adopting a position of ignorance with regard to the meaning of a particular virtue. This is called 'Socratic irony' (from the Greek *eironeia*: 'pretended ignorance'), and was adopted by Socrates not merely for effect, or the purposes of debate. Socrates always claimed ignorance of any wisdom, and said that it was only the assumption of bystanders, who observed him revealing another's deficiency of knowledge, that he himself was 'wise' on any subject (*Apology* 23a-b). Socrates invites his interlocutor, who claims knowledge of a particular virtue, to provide examples of it, in order that Socrates may learn its nature. Each of the examples offered are then examined, sometimes upheld, and sometimes discarded in the light of a counter-example offered by Socrates which renders the original example invalid or otherwise unsuitable. The aim is always to discover the common quality which is shared by all the accepted examples. In this way, Socrates and his interlocutor proceed towards a 'general definition' of the virtue thus examined.

A good example of this is in Plato's *Meno*, where Socrates asks Meno, who has studied *aretê* under the sophist Gorgias, if he can give him a definition of this virtue, so that he may recognise it and act accordingly. Meno proves unable to give a single definition of *aretê*, and can only provide what Socrates calls a 'swarm of excellences', saying what is *aretê* for a man, for a woman, for a slave, and so on (*Meno* 79b-c). But Socrates was not content with this response, since it seemed to suggest that Meno had no true knowledge of the virtue, but could only recite Gorgias' list of practical examples. This, for Socrates, illustrated the difference between real knowledge, and that taught by the sophists. Interestingly, Aristotle preferred Gorgias' method to that of Socrates, and insisted that while universal definitions were useful for scientific terms, they were not applicable in the moral field (*Politics* 1, 1260a24-8). Perhaps it was for this reason that almost all the dialogues end without a general definition being found.

Despite the often negative conclusion of the dialogues, the failure to find a definition, Socrates remained optimistic that one was nevertheless possible, if one searched in the correct way. There is an important distinction to be made between 'Socratic ignorance' and the outright scepticism of the sophists, though to the casual observer they might not always have appeared distinct. Socrates was no relativist, and believed in the existence of absolute moral values. Similarly, Socrates' focus on definitions no doubt appeared similar to Prodicus' interest in the form and gender of nouns, and this similarity enabled Aristophanes to conflate the sophistic position with that of Socrates for the sake of his comedy. But unlike Prodicus, Socrates wasn't interested in the meaning of the words themselves, but in the underlying eternal concepts in which he believed, and which may be defined by groups of words or a definition.

For Socrates, an important part of the search for knowledge was ridding the mind of false or inconsistent beliefs, and highlighting where beliefs were based on circular arguments or led to absurd conclusions. Socrates' offering of counter-examples in debate was intended always to expose an error in reasoning, and had the aim of identifying the 'true' from the incorrect example. Plato contrasts this with the sophistic use of anti-logic, the aim of which was to negate any position put forward, whether or not it was true, and render an opponent ultimately incapable of further verbal response (*Euthydemus* 272a7-b1). Socrates expressly denied that his purpose in refuting an argument had any aim other than an honest investigation into 'truth' (*Charmides* 166c-d). Plato in his later work specifically warned that rhetoric could be used for either purpose, and that one of its dangers was a conclusion that since one can prove others wrong and be proved wrong oneself, that therefore nothing is true (*Republic* 540b-d). Plato therefore warned that rhetoric should only be taught to those over thirty, as more mature men were unlikely to descend into relativism (*Republic* 539b9-d1).

But the mental confusion and uncertainty felt by those reduced to speechlessness by a sophist cannot have felt very different from the 'torpification' expressed by Meno as a result of Socrates' questioning on his conception of *aretê*. Meno complains that his 'soul and tongue are numbed', and that he no longer knows what he thought he knew (*Meno* 79e-80b). This is a perfect description of the *aporia*, which was a critical part of the process of Socratic *elenchus*, and was parodied in *Clouds* where Socrates reduces Strepsiades to a state of confusion (790ff.). Socrates' aim, however, was not to end the debate, but to reach a point at which one had discarded all erroneous thought, and could thence proceed to the 'truth'. At this point in the *Meno*, rather than consider the debate 'won' and his interlocutor silenced, Socrates proceeds to expound the theory that all true knowledge is a 'recollection' or 'un-forgetting' (*anamnêsis*) of truths known to the immortal soul. In the form given in this dialogue, the theory is almost certainly Plato's. But the point remains that for Socrates, a negative result does not lead to relativism and a rejection of the possibility of knowledge.

At the beginning of the *Meno* Socrates stated that not only does he not know what *aretê* is, but that he has no idea how, or even whether, it can be taught (70a). It was Socrates' belief that in order to be able to teach a virtue, one ought to be able to define it. In many of the dialogues, Plato shows Socrates questioning sophists who claim such knowledge, and say they can teach it to others. In the *Protagoras,* Socrates shows that this sophist holds conflicting opinions on the nature of the virtue which he claims to be able to impart to others. Now Plato had some sympathy with Protagoras' position, but in other cases, sophists subjected to the *elenchus* ended up expressing a perhaps understandable anger as a result of Socrates' questioning. An example of this is in the *Republic*, where Thrasymachus claims that Socrates intended to shame him by asking questions only in order to refute them, and by demanding clear definitions which Socrates himself was unable to deliver (336b-d; 337e). It is not surprising, then, that Socrates at his trial talked of a 'bitter and persistent hostility' held against him, which arose as a result of his investigations (*Apology* 23a-b).

Socrates had an ultimate purpose behind his search for definitions, and the aim was practical. As Aristotle said, Socrates used logic in order to determine how we should live (*Metaphysics* 13, 1078b). Socrates believed that if we know what 'justice' is, then we can be sure to act justly and we can know how to vote in the courts when asked whether someone has acted justly. If we can define 'virtue' then we will know how to conduct our lives with excellence. For Socrates, knowledge and virtue were the same thing. He argued that one would not do the wrong thing if one knew what the right thing was, or that 'no one sins deliberately' (Plato, *Protagoras* 351-8). Xenophon said that for Socrates, 'justice and all the rest of virtue was knowledge' (*Memorabilia* III.9.5.). And Aristotle also states: Socrates believed that 'virtue is knowledge', i.e. it is the same thing to know what is justice as to be just in one's actions (*Eudemian Ethics* 1216b6-8), and that no one acts against what one believes to be 'best', and therefore one acts wrongly only out of ignorance (*Nicomachean Ethics* 1145b21-7). However, as before, Aristotle criticised this extension by Socrates of theories applicable to the sciences into the moral realm. While we can learn about architecture and thus become 'an architect', it does not follow that we become 'just' because we understand 'justice', just as we do not become 'healthy' simply by knowing what health is (*Eudemian Ethics* 1260a).

Socrates' belief in timeless and unchanging moral virtues was essentially different from that of the sophists, who argued that what was 'right', 'virtuous', or 'just' was relative to a situation, and even that there was no ultimate 'good' outside human convention (*nomos*). In some cases they held that what was 'good' or 'right' depended only on one's ability to convince another of one's argument or position. On the whole, the sophists favoured 'natural law', *physis*, over *nomos*. Thrasymachus, for example, argued that what was 'right' was what was right for the dominant or 'stronger' class (Plato, *Republic* 338c), and that it is natural and 'good' for one to further one's position even by unlawful acts if necessary: 'injustice pays and justice doesn't' (348c). But not all sophists were of this opinion. Protagoras thought that the rule of law was necessary for the survival of civilisation, and that mankind, left to its own devices, would destroy itself. While his famous dictum 'man is the measure of all things' sounds extremely relativistic, Plato has him argue that while there may be no such thing as objectively 'right' or 'wrong' conduct, one could distinguish acts which were more or less profitable or useful. It was this profitable conduct or 'aptitude for civic life' which Protagoras claimed to be able to teach.

Similarly, Socrates believed in the 'good' as that which was beneficial or useful. But unlike Protagoras, Socrates differentiated the 'good' from the 'pleasurable' or immediately beneficial. He pointed out that what is pleasurable now, for example over-eating, is often not in one's own long-term interests; and what may be unpleasant now, for example bad-tasting medicine, may prove to be advantageous in time (Plato, *Protagoras* 351-8). For Socrates, what mattered was *enlightened* self-interest, and said that while one may escape damage, and even prosper, in the short term by evading the law, the outcome for one's soul may be unfortunate. This contrasts markedly with the picture of Socrates we saw in the *Clouds* who offered to teach errant youths how to escape their creditors.

In fact, Socrates believed that life was not worth living if one did not ask repeatedly of oneself and others what was the *real* good for man, and what was the excellence or *aretê* which would lead one to that good. The well known quotation which prescribes an unmatched ethical avowal to which all should aspire appears in the *Apology* (38):

> I say again that daily to discourse about virtue, and of those other things about which you hear me examining myself and others, is the greatest good of man, and that the unexamined life is not worth living.

His view was that one must do the 'right thing', even if it seems unpleasant or contrary to one's immediate gain or political expediency. He said that the happiest man is the just man, and that injustice never pays better than justice (Plato, *Republic* 354). As an example of this, Xenophon stressed that Socrates put his life in danger more than once because he preferred to uphold Athenian law than carry out illegal orders from the oligarchs

15. Was Socrates a Sophist?

(*Memorabilia* I.1.17-19). And there is perhaps no greater example of Socrates acting in a way which he believed was ultimately right, rather than in the interests of immediate gain, in that he refused to escape execution when the opportunity presented itself, preferring instead to drink the hemlock. Any other action would have been a betrayal of his personal beliefs and mission.

A reply to the question, 'Was Socrates a sophist?' relies on our ability to define what a sophist was, and to say how far Socrates fits this definition. This in turn depends on the nature and preservation of our sources. That the question arises at all is due at least in part to the fact that Socrates was executed on charges which associated him with the sophists, and coloured the content of the dialogues which form some of the main sources for the philosophy of the period.

Socrates had no interest in many of the subjects which engaged the sophists. He did not think that *aretê* could be taught, but believed that real knowledge came from within. He denied teaching at all, and denounced the sophistic practice of teaching wisdom for a fee, saying that he himself had no wisdom to impart, and preferring the role of fellow-seeker and, at most, midwife to the birth of wisdom in others.

Faced with the same intellectual problems as the sophists, he rejected their sceptical and relativist conclusions, and continued to believe in a truth beyond the everyday world of changing appearances, and in the ability of the human mind to attain real knowledge of that truth. But he understood that this idea could no longer be based on tradition and religion, but that a logical philosophical foundation had to be found, and therefore searched for definitions of moral terms in an almost scientific manner. His use of rhetoric and counter-argument in debate was not, as with the sophists, undertaken in order to persuade, or to win an argument, but in pursuit of real knowledge. In this respect he is the epitome of Plato's 'true philosopher' (*Republic* 490a-b), living his life in an authentic search for a truth in which he believed, and dying without compromising his ideals.

Bibliography

Aeschines, *Against Timarchus*, trans. N. Fisher (Oxford: Clarendon Press, 2001).

Aristophanes, *Clouds*, trans. K. Dover (Oxford: Clarendon Paperbacks, 1989).

Aristotle, *Eudemian Ethics*, trans. M. Woods (Oxford: Clarendon Press, 1992).

Aristotle, *Metaphysics*, trans. H. Lawson-Tancred (Harmondsworth: Penguin Classics, 1988).

Aristotle, *Nicomachean Ethics*, trans. R. Crisp (Mineola, NY: Dover Publications, 1988).

Aristotle, *Politics*, trans. T.A. Sinclair (Harmondsworth: Penguin Classics, 1994).

Aristotle, *On Sophistical Refutations*, trans. E.S. Forster and D.J. Furley, Loeb edition (London: Heinemann, 1955).

Plato, *Apology* and *Phaedo* in *The Last Days of Socrates*, trans. H. Tredennick (Harmondsworth: Penguin, 1969).

Plato, *Charmides*, trans. T.G. and G.S. West (Indianapolis: Hackett, 1986).

Plato, *Euthydemus*, trans. R. Kent Sprague (Indianapolis: Hackett, 1993).

Plato, *Meno* and *Protagoras*, trans. W.K.C. Guthrie (Harmondsworth: Penguin, 1956).

Plato, *The Republic*, trans. D. Lee (Harmondsworth: Penguin, 1987).

Plato, *Theaetetus*, trans. M.J. Levett (Indianapolis: Hackett, 1990).

Xenophon, *Memorabilia*, trans. Amy L. Bonnette (Ithaca, NY: Cornell University Press, 2001).

Plato: The Sophist

Paul Groarke

The distinction between Socrates and the sophists seems to have its principal origins in Plato's dialogues. The following chapter argues that Plato introduced this distinction for rhetorical reasons, in defence of Socrates. This does a disservice to the sophists.

The word 'sophist' has different senses. In one sense, the word is no more specific than the word 'teacher' or 'philosopher'. In another sense, it may refer to someone who has mastered the art of rhetoric. The irony is that Plato seems to be a sophist in both senses of the word. This is more readily apparent to those outside philosophy, such as I.F. Stone, a journalist, who writes that the dialectic in the dialogues is full of 'much the same verbal trickeries that [Socrates] attributed to the Sophists' (Stone 1988, 83).

The literary critic Northrop Frye takes a similar position and openly calls Socrates a sophist. In *Words with Power*, he sets out three arguments in Plato that the sophists are not true philosophers (Frye 1990, 14). The first is that the sophists were concerned with rhetoric, rather than dialectic, and trained people 'to speak effectively in law courts and assemblies' (Frye 1990, 13). Frye finds this difficult to accept: it is Socrates' skill in rhetoric, he suggests, that distinguishes him from lesser figures. The second argument is epistemological. This concerns the general view of Protagoras that things are relative. The third is that the sophists seek payment for their teaching.

The distinction that Plato makes between Socrates and the sophists can be found in the political realities of the time. When the Peloponnesian War reached its end in 404 BC, the Spartans installed an oligarchy under the Thirty Tyrants (see Chapter 10, pp. 115-17), who were led by the notorious Alcibiades (*c.* 450-404 BC), grandson of Alcibiades the Elder. Pericles was the guardian of the younger Alcibiades, who was the intimate and pupil of Socrates.

Plato's relative, Critias (*c.* 460-403 BC), was another leader of the Thirty Tyrants, and was described by Benjamin Jowett as a student of Socrates (Jowett 1953, I, 369). The period of the Thirty Tyrants degenerated into a reign of terror: estates were confiscated, opponents were summarily executed; and thousands were banished from the city.

The trial of Socrates took place in 399 BC, after democracy was restored.

Although an amnesty had been proclaimed, it was a time of reckoning. And since it was the younger men of Athens who played the leading role in the upheaval, there was a natural desire to blame those who had influenced them. This appears to explain the charges against Socrates, who was prosecuted for impiety, and for corrupting the morals of the young.

The real source of the charges seems to be that Socrates taught the young men of Athens to question the legitimate sources of authority. A good deal of the literature on the trial nevertheless suggests that the real accusation was that Socrates was a sophist. Legally, this is a question of reputation, and it seems significant that Socrates was depicted as a sophist, not merely in Aristophanes' *Clouds* (performed in 423 BC) but in plays by Callias, a playwright not to be confused with the Callias who appears in the *Protagoras*; Eupolis, a comic poet whose first play was produced in 429 BC; and Teleicleides, another successful playwright of comedy.

The three arguments that Frye sets out can all be traced to Plato, who separates 'true philosophers' and sophists, and tries to rebut the charges against Socrates. None of the arguments is particularly successful. The weakest is simply that the sophists charge fees for their services. In Plato's *Sophist*, the Eleatic stranger sets this out as a defining attribute of the profession (223a).

This is easily misunderstood in a money-economy. Stone suggests that Plato's scorn for the payment of fees represents nothing more than the prejudices of the aristocrats in Athens, who paid their teachers by providing them with room and board (Stone 1988, 41f.). This is in keeping with Socrates' proposal, after his conviction, that the state should provide him with free meals in recognition of his public services: 'And if I am to estimate the penalty fairly, I should say that maintenance in the Prytaneum[1] is the just return' (Plato, *Apology* 37a1).[2] Plato has no difficulty with the idea that Socrates should be compensated for his services.

From a legal perspective, this goes nowhere. It is difficult to see how a distinction between those who take money and those who receive other benefits can be maintained in a courtroom. People can be paid in many ways. The argument in the dialogues is that the sophists' desire for payment inevitably corrupts them. This is hardly worthy of an answer, however. We cannot assume that the sophists were dishonest, merely because they were paid. It would follow that a university professor, to use an obvious example, cannot be a true philosopher.

There is more going on here. Socrates and Plato seem to be trying to re-define the notion of a teacher, in postulating that the payment of fees is an essential factor in the relationship between the sophists and their students. In Plato's *Apology*, Socrates says that he is not a teacher and does not 'take money' (19d8). The two conditions are identified with each other. The rhetorical strategy behind his position can probably be traced to the allegation that he had influenced the young, since this would have been relatively easy to establish against a teacher. This seems disingenuous: how can we characterise the relationship between Socrates and Plato as anything other than a relationship between a teacher and a student?

The idea that Socrates was not a teacher runs against the fact that his form of dialectic was a recognised form of pedagogy. Elizabeth Asmis and Gary Alan Scott argue that the Socratic method was a 'development' of a technique invented by the sophists (Asmis 1992, 340) and was not particular to Socrates (Scott 2002, 154f).[3] There is also Socrates' use of allegories, metaphors and analogies to explain important concepts. These are the ways of a teacher. The most famous example is probably the story of the cave in the *Republic*, where Socrates suggests that the objects we perceive are only shadows of the eternal, unchanging Forms (7.514a-17b). In the *Theaetetus*, he uses the metaphor of a man who enters an aviary and takes a ring-dove, instead of the pigeon he is seeking, to try and explain how the mind errs (199b).

There is also a discernible body of teaching in the historical account. Socrates teaches that evil comes from our ignorance of the good (Plato, *Meno* 77e), and that those who know good will pursue it. He teaches the doctrine of anamnesis, which holds that our knowledge, particularly of mathematical principles, is a recollection from a previous existence (*Meno* 81d). He explains sexual love, in the *Symposium*, as an expression of our longing for immortality (206e-207a). This body of teaching goes beyond philosophical issues, since Xenophon's memoirs of Socrates canvass more mundane topics, like the management of a household.[4]

Plato's *Apology* ignores all of this and depicts Socrates as a man, unlike the sophists, who merely asks questions. This is a calculated rhetorical move, which insulates him from the charge that he was the teacher of Critias, as his accusers alleged, and influenced the young. There is some dispute as to the authenticity of Plato's record of the trial: it is suspicious that the case for the prosecution is missing, and his *Apology* seems heavily tailored. Still, some of the *Apology* has the ring of authenticity, such as the fact that Socrates interrogates Meletus (26c6), and implicitly asserts his superiority.[5]

The real issue is simply that the position in the dialogues is dubious. Socrates, Plato and Aristotle all played the educational role that is attributed to teachers, in ancient Greece and elsewhere. Plato himself gave public lectures and founded the Academy.[6] The reason why the question of fees becomes so significant is that it seems to add some plausibility to a very implausible claim, which is that Socrates was not a teacher. This is not convincing. As G.B. Kerferd puts it: 'The fact that [Socrates] took no payment does not alter his function in any way' (Kerferd 1981, 57). Socrates himself, in Xenophon's account, finds it an amazing thing that he is 'being prosecuted' on a capital charge 'because I am adjudged by some people supreme in what is man's greatest blessing, – education ...' (Xenophon, *Apology* 1.21).

177

The reality is that it is not clear that any compensation is necessary, to make Socrates a teacher in the ordinary sense of the word. The issue of fees seems to have been invented by Plato and does not appear to have raised questions in the minds of ordinary Athenians. Stone quotes Aeschines, in *Against Timarchus* (1.173), where he declares that his fellow citizens put Socrates to death: 'because he was shown to have been the teacher of Critias ...' (Stone 1988, 178).[7] The success of Plato's rhetoric, in spite of this, is remarkable. The modern philosophical literature studiously avoids the statement that Socrates was a teacher and uses terms like 'associate' to describe his relationship with his followers (Brickhouse and Smith 1994, 166-70).

The second argument that Frye sets out is that the sophists are sceptics. Protagoras taught that knowledge is relative. This adds an element of uncertainty to everything we know, and means that what we take for knowledge is only a kind of belief. It is usually assumed that this goes against Plato's theory of the Forms, as expressed by Socrates in the *Republic* (as cited above). The suggestion is that our apprehension of the Forms – sometimes called the Ideas – does not admit of any uncertainties. They are exactly what they present themselves to be.

It is hard to know Socrates' position. The argument that Plato can be distinguished from the sophists on this basis, however, does not fare that much better than the argument regarding fees. Richard Robinson wrote in the 1950s that Plato had abandoned the theory of the Forms by the time he wrote the *Theaetetus*, the major source of his later epistemology (Robinson 1950, 5). This seems to be the right position.[8]

An examination of the *Theaetetus* suggests that Plato shares the sophists' scepticism. As David Bostock writes, the first part of the dialogue is clear enough. The proposal is that knowledge is to be found in true belief, rather than perception. Socrates then suggests that knowledge is true belief, with a *logos*: that is, with 'the addition of an "account",' or 'a "working out of the reason"' (Bostock 1991, 268). The dialogue then founders. Socrates seems to confuse knowing with mere thinking.

This is a fundamental error: knowledge is not a matter of thinking of something; it is a matter of thinking something that is true. The concept of a justified true belief – the standard philosophical formula for knowledge – requires some external reference. As soon as we introduce the idea of truth, we need something to refer to, in order to determine whether a given belief is true.

This is only a short step away from an empirical view. The reference that is needed to determine the truth of a statement can be found in the Forms; but it can also be found in the 'world' to which the statement refers. Robinson argues that this explains the significance of the reference to the witness in the *Theaetetus*. The importance of the legal account is that it requires external justification.

The passage to which Robinson refers is worth a closer look:

SOCRATES: When, therefore, judges are justly persuaded about matters which you can know only by seeing them, and not in any other way, and when thus judging of them from report they attain a true opinion about them, they judge without knowledge and yet are rightly persuaded, if they have judged well (*Theaetetus* 201b9-201c2).

There is a sense in which this is true; and a sense in which it is not. A judge's statement of facts is, strictly speaking, an opinion. Socrates nevertheless overstates his position.

SOCRATES: And yet, O my friend, if true opinion in law courts and knowledge are the same, the perfect judge could not have judged rightly without knowledge; and therefore I must infer that they are not the same (*Theaetetus* 201c4-7).

The missing observation is that the judge has knowledge of the evidence and his true belief is a justified true belief. This does not displace the philosophical point entirely. Socrates' position is that 'knowledge' refers to a kind of cognition that is necessarily true. Since it cannot be said that the judge's belief is necessarily true, it accordingly remains opinion.

There are linguistic complexities here, however, that Socrates did not appreciate. Once a judge has found the facts of the case, the law holds that they must be taken as true. They are therefore a proper subject of knowledge. A judge is entitled to say, on sentencing: 'we *know* that the accused did these things, and he has to be sentenced on that basis'. The statement of facts is 'known', in law, not merely by the judge and the parties, but by the whole world.

The distinction that Socrates draws between the judge and the eyewitness is fallacious. A judge is relying on the evidence in the same way that the eyewitness is relying on his perceptions, and the reality is that the judge's belief is often more reliable. The accurate statement is that the witness believes he saw something; but witnesses are often mistaken and his belief is mere opinion. It is not possible to say, in the narrow sense in which Socrates is using the word, that the witness 'knows' what happened.

The problem is that we do not use the word 'know' (or its Greek equivalent) in the way that Socrates suggests. The statement that we know something is a deductive conclusion, which says very little about the way we apprehend the relevant thought or proposition. We cannot say that we 'know' Socrates questioned Meletus without asserting that this statement corresponds with what occurred in ancient Athens. This requires some kind of reference, which is always open to error.

Socrates implicitly acknowledges this when he suggests that we may be dreaming, or in a state of madness (*Theaetetus* 158b8, 158d9). This is a special case, and is really more of an hypothesis than a credible objection to our use of the word 'knowledge'. It nevertheless demonstrates that it is impossible to eradicate all of the uncertainty from our beliefs. This does not diminish if we accept Plato's earlier epistemology, since our experience of the Forms is open to the same criticism. We might be deluded.

The point is that the sophists are right. Everything is relative and in the face of competing opinions, we need to examine the evidence and see which is more justified. This brings in a legal standard. All we have are probabilities, and at some point, the probability that a belief is true is high enough to treat it as a certainty. This is all we mean by 'knowledge'.

Socrates has no response to this kind of argument. Late in the *Theaetetus* he says:

> SOCRATES: The truth is, Theaetetus, that we have long been infected with logical impurity. Thousands of times have we repeated the words 'we know' and 'do not know', and 'we have or have not science or knowledge', as if we could understand what we are saying to one another, so long as we remain ignorant about knowledge ... (196d11-e5).

This is pure bravado. Socrates suddenly asserts that he and Theaetetus do not know what it means 'to know' when the entire conversation proves otherwise. Socrates and Theaetetus 'know' what knowledge is: the problem lies in providing an account of it.

This draws our attention to the most significant feature of the *Theaetetus*, which is simply that it fails. Socrates is unable to provide a satisfactory account of knowledge. It is hard to believe that this is Plato's error: it does not seem plausible to suggest that he would write a dialogue which demonstrates the failure of his own views, or that he would allow competing views to succeed. The more likely explanation is that he accepts the conclusion that Socrates reaches at the end of the dialogue: we do not know what knowledge 'is'. This is the position of the sophists.

The third argument concerns the practice of rhetoric. Frye's answer to the argument that Socrates devoted himself to dialectic, in contradistinction to rhetoric, is that the two arts do not exclude each other. It is Plato who introduces a categorical division between the two forms of argument or inquiry, in order to distinguish Socrates from the sophists.

This takes us back to the trial of Socrates. It is difficult to determine the extent to which the prosecution relied on the allegation that Socrates was a sophist. The idea nevertheless seems implicit in the affidavit from the prosecution, which supposedly stated that Socrates 'makes the worse appear the better cause, and teaches the aforesaid doctrines to others' (Plato, *Apology* 19b6). There are reasons to believe, however, that it was Socrates – or Plato, writing many years later – who made this into such a prominent issue in the trial.

This in keeping with the normal dynamic in a courtroom. One of the first rules in any defence is to re-define the trial in the terms chosen by the defence. Plato accordingly turns, like a shrewd lawyer, on the sophists.

There are a number of reasons why the effort to condemn the sophists and their teaching was a more effective legal strategy than a simple contravention of the charges. The primary reason – if one accepts that Socrates was essentially charged with teaching Critias – is that there was no real defence. There seems little doubt that popular sentiment after the restoration of democracy was against Socrates and the only hope of the defence was to engage the attentions of the jury on another issue.

The sophists were an easy scapegoat, all round. The idea that most of the sophists were foreigners, who had become wealthy at the expense of ordinary Athenians, had aroused widespread jealousy and resentment. As Benjamin Jowett put it, in his introduction to Plato's *Sophist*:

> There is nothing surprising in the Sophists having an evil name; that, whether deserved or not, was a natural consequence of their vocation. That they were foreigners, that they made fortunes, that they taught novelties, that they excited the minds of youth, are quite sufficient reasons to account for the opprobrium which attached to them (Jowett 1953, III, 328).

There is also the practical fact that the sophists were not present and could not defend themselves.

The actual mechanics of the trial would have lent itself to this kind of strategy. The Athenian jury, made up of 500 citizens, was more like a crowd than a modern jury, and must have operated on its emotions.[9] The rhetorical skill in such a defence is apparent in the fact that it builds on the case in the affidavit for the prosecution, which invokes the popular prejudice against the sophists on in its own behalf. Although there were legitimate complaints against the sophists, both sides seem to have been promoting a popular caricature of the sophists to their own advantage.

There is more than a hint of demagoguery here. This is the worst kind of psychological simplification, which creates a class of people for the purpose of channelling the hostility of the people. The unpleasant reality is that Plato had an interest in furthering the xenophobia in this caricature of the sophists, since Socrates' identity as an Athenian could not be questioned. This also explains why Plato makes so much of the fact that the sophists sought payment for their services. It is not that the payment is particularly significant, in itself. It is that it provides an easy way of distinguishing between Socrates and the class of teachers that Plato is attacking.

The real issues that arise in this context are moral issues. It seems clear that Plato was a psychological tactician and a realist. Instead of openly acknowledging that the term 'sophist' – referring to a class of teachers – could easily be applied to Socrates, he chose to work with the prejudices of the time, and even augment them. A good part of the defence of Socrates in the dialogues is merely that the sophists were contemptible. The popular prejudice was justified.

The most troubling feature of Plato's position is that it is sly, in exactly the way that he alleges the sophists are sly. Socrates describes rhetoric as 'clever dealing' and a kind of flattery; mostly because it is careful not to challenge the views of listeners (Plato, *Gorgias* 463a-b; and see *Sophist* 223a). Elsewhere, he says that the art of the sophists is 'an art of deception' (*Sophist* 240d). The problem is that these kinds of criticisms can all be levelled at Plato, whose defence of Socrates is remarkable primarily because it does not address the accusations against him. The most likely reason for this is that Socrates had no real defence.

It was Plato who wanted to turn the question whether Socrates was a sophist into the major issue in the trial. Having done so, he needed to define who the sophists were in way that excluded Socrates. This explains why he exaggerates the fact that Socrates did not take money. Rhetorically, he needed stark, seemingly irrefutable facts, to separate Socrates from the sophists. The irony is that he needed this kind of fact because his immediate argument – that Socrates was not a teacher, and did not influence Critias – was so implausible. This is accordingly where Plato's *Apology* is the least trustworthy.

The story that unfolds in the dialogues is a political rather than a legal drama. Socrates was an obvious target for would-be politicians, or those who wanted to even the score with the preceding regime. The trial of Socrates was a show trial and there was scapegoating on both sides. I have suggested elsewhere that the Athenian legal system had not developed to the point where it was capable of functioning independently of the politics of the time. The political issue in the trial was whether Socrates would submit to the new democracy.

Socrates' answer on this issue is little more than a rebuke. He baits the jurors and invites them to convict him.[10] The egotism in Plato's portrait of Socrates has been overlooked in the haze of adulation that obscures the philosophical account. Perhaps it takes a trial lawyer to see the egotism in Plato's portrait of Socrates. The theory of the Forms is telling, since Socrates' fundamental claim is that he knows the absolutes. The argument in the *Apology* is really that he is above criticism. The defence is that he is the wisest of men.

This defence naturally rests on the premise that Socrates is quintessentially different from other would-be philosophers. Plato accordingly belittles his intellectual rivals. This obscures the legal question posed by the trial, which was whether Socrates was the teacher of Critias and in some way responsible for corrupting him. The rhetorical issue that Plato introduces in lieu of this simply falls away when it is properly examined. If we accept Plato's own view, and the generalities inherent in the word, there seems no reason why Plato cannot be called a sophist. Plato was himself a teacher, skilled in rhetoric, who eventually distanced himself from epistemological absolutes.

The trial of Socrates seems central in explaining why Plato introduces the distinction in the first place. This seems the proper place to leave the subject. Socrates' appetite for philosophical inquiry, his fearlessness, his equanimity in the face of death, all bear witness to his strength of character. As soon as we accept Plato's narrative, however, which asserts that Socrates is completely singular and essentially alone among his contemporaries in pursuing 'true philosophy', we have fallen victim to the rhetoric of the defence. This debases the philosophical accomplishments of his contemporaries.

Notes

1. Greek cities historically had a building called a *prytaneum* (from a word meaning 'chief' or 'first'), in which the chieftain probably lived. The building would have had a central hearth and was considered the home of the community. This became the city hall in Athens, where the *prytaneis*, the city's democratic executive, held meetings. It contained a public hall in which foreign dignitaries, eminent citizens, and the victors at the Olympics were fed. Socrates is suggesting that he is entitled to the same reward.

2. All of the translations from Plato are taken from *The Dialogues of Plato* (4th edition), translated by Benjamin Jowett with Analyses and Introductions (Oxford: Clarendon Press, 1953).

3. Socrates seems to acknowledge this in the *Sophist* (230a-231a), when he discusses the art of admonition.

4. In Xenophon's *Economics*, for example, Socrates advocates tidiness (3.2). There is important philosophical material in Xenophon's account, though much of it is disputed. One of the chapters in the *Memorabilia* provides an account of natural law (4.4.12). More adventuresome students might want to consult Calder (2002), which contains additional sources from antiquity.

5. There are a few ancient sources which seem to suggest that Socrates did not speak at the trial (Calder, 2002, 221-32), but this may simply speak to the fact that he did not present a recognised defence.

6. Plato founded the Academy in 387 BC after he returned to Athens from various travels. It took its name from a grove of olives left to the city by Akademos, one of the city's heroes. The Academy survived for nine hundred years and is often considered Europe's first university.

7. The best and most reputable source of this and other classical texts is probably the catalogue of Greek and Latin material in Gregory Crane (ed.), *The Perseus Digital Library*, available online at:
http://www.perseus.tufts.edu/cache/perscoll_Greco-Roman.html

8. This remains a major topic in the literature. See Adalier, for example, who discusses the issue at length and argues that the model of judgement in the second part of the *Theaetetus* fails precisely because it neglects the Forms (Adalier 2001, 4f.). His article contains a bibliography of relevant sources.

9. For a reliable account of the legal system and the use of juries in ancient Athens, see Allen 2003. One of the popular misconceptions regarding Socrates is that drinking hemlock was a form of execution. This is a mistake: those prisoners who could afford the hemlock were allowed to commit suicide in order to spare themselves a slow death by crucifixion.

10. There is a convenient analysis of Socrates' rhetoric and its political implications at Ober 2006.

183

Bibliography

Adalier, Gokhan, 'The Case of *Theaetetus*', *Phronesis* 46, no. 1 (February 2001), 1-37.

Allen, Danielle S., 'Punishment in Ancient Athens', in Adriaan Lanni (ed.), 'Athenian Law in its Democratic Context' (2003) (Center for Hellenic Studies On-line Discussion Series: Athenian Law), available at:
http://chs.harvard.edu/chs/athenian_law

Asmis, Eliza, 'Plato on Poetic Creativity', in Richard Kraut (ed.), *The Cambridge Companion to Plato* (Cambridge: Cambridge University Press, 1992), 338-64.

Bostock, David, *Plato's Theaetetus* (Oxford: Clarendon Press, 1991).

Brickhouse, Thomas C. and Smith, Nicholas D., *Plato's Socrates* (New York: Oxford University Press, 1994).

Calder, William M. III et al., *The Unknown Socrates* (Wauconda, IL: Bolchazy Carducci, 2002).

Crane, Gregory, ed., *The Perseus Digital Library*, available at:
http://www.perseus.tufts.edu/cache/perscoll_Greco-Roman.html

Frye, Northrop, *Words with Power: Being a Second Study of the 'Bible and Literature'* (Markham, ON: Viking, 1990).

Kerferd, G.B., *The Sophistic Movement* (Cambridge: Cambridge University Press, 1981).

Ober, Josiah, 'Gadfly on Trial: Socrates as Citizen and Social Critic' (2006) (Center for Hellenic Studies On-line Discussion Series: Athenian Law), available at:
http://chs.harvard.edu/chs/athenian_law

[Plato] *The Dialogues of Plato*, trans. Benjamin Jowett with Analyses and Introductions), 4th edition, vol. I (Oxford: Clarendon Press, 1953).

Robinson, Richard, 'Forms and Error in Plato's *Theaetetus*', *Philosophical Review* 59, no. 1 (January 1950), 3-30.

Scott, Gary Alan, *Does Socrates Have a Method? Rethinking the Elenchus in Plato's Dialogues and Beyond* (University Park: Penn State University Press, 2002).

Stone, I.F., *The Trial of Socrates* (Boston: Little, Brown, 1988).

Xenophon, *Conversations of Socrates*, trans. Hugh Tredennick and Robin Waterfield, edited with new material by Robin Waterfield (Harmondsworth: Penguin Classics, 1990).

Were the Sophists Philosophers?

Trevor Curnow

Were the sophists philosophers? On the face of it this is a simple question. For centuries the sophists and the philosophers have been opposed to each other rather than identified with one another. Apart from when they show up in some of Plato's dialogues, most philosophers have simply ignored them as irrelevant. The high esteem in which Plato has come to be held has led to his verdicts on the sophists being accepted almost without question. However, there are at least three reasons why the question is worth asking. In the first place, the variety that existed among the sophists themselves means that any simple answer to the question stands a chance of turning out to be *too* simple. Secondly, the question itself may be too simple. It can be interpreted in at least two different ways. Interpreted one way it is equivalent to asking, 'According to what people understood by "philosopher" in their own time, were the sophists philosophers?' Interpreted another way it can mean, 'According to what people understand by "philosopher" in our time, were the sophists philosophers?' And thirdly, as we find out more about the sophists, then the evidence on which the answer rests changes, requiring it to be reconsidered. All of these questions will be explored here in one way and another.

The starting point of any answer to the question must be the time in which the original sophists lived. The period in which the group of people loosely known as the older sophists lived and worked lasted from around 460 to 380 BC. Unfortunately, very little evidence about them survives from that time, and a substantial portion of what there is comes from Plato (*c.* 429-348 BC) who must generally be treated as a hostile witness. In many cases he is also the principal witness, but fortunately he is not the only one, so it is possible to reconstruct at least some of the context in which his texts are to be understood.

One of the elements of this context is how the meaning of the Greek word *sophistês* changed over time. The meaning that is now generally attached to 'sophist' is one that emerged during the fifth century BC. From having the general sense of a wise person, who might display wisdom in any one of many different ways, it increasingly came to have the much narrower sense of a professional educator. However, it could only carry such a meaning when professional educators themselves had come into existence. Although the attribution is disputable, Protagoras of Abdera

185

(*c.* 490-420 BC) is often regarded as the first. After studying philosophy in his home town with his compatriot Democritus, he moved to Athens where he amassed a significant personal fortune by charging for the educational services he provided to the rich over a period of thirty years or more. Also in Athens at that time were Socrates (469-399 BC) and the playwright Aristophanes (*c.* 448-*c.* 380 BC). Aristophanes' satire on the sophists, *Clouds*, was first performed in 423 BC when all three of them were alive. It may be noted that although Plato has often been blamed for giving the sophists a bad name, Aristophanes was well ahead of him in this regard. When *Clouds* was written, Plato had barely been born.

Curiously, to modern eyes, it is Socrates who is the butt of Aristophanes' humour in the play. It is evident that Aristophanes sees little if anything to choose between Socrates and the sophists. Indeed, his choice of Socrates suggests that he may have regarded him as the worst of the lot. Socrates is joined in the play by two further characters, True Logic and False Logic, who represent philosophy and sophistry. Unfortunately, while True Logic makes it clear that he stands for traditional virtues such as Justice and Moderation, he mentions no names. As a result, it is not clear whom Aristophanes regards as the genuine philosophers with whom the sophists are unfavourably contrasted. This is a pity because it is an important issue. If Socrates is regarded as one of the sophists rather than a philosopher, why? And if he is not regarded as a philosopher, who is?

In a famous and often quoted line in his *Tusculan Disputations* (V.4.10-11), Cicero said that Socrates 'was the first to call philosophy down from the heavens ... and compel her to ask questions about life and morality and things good and evil'. The idea that *all* the philosophers before Socrates had asked questions *only* about the heavens is an obvious over-simplification. The Pythagoreans at least were keenly interested in 'questions about life', for example. Nevertheless it is widely accepted that Socrates was instrumental in pushing philosophy in a significantly new direction and it is notable that after his time a number of schools grew up that claimed to preserve his heritage in one way or another. Later historians of philosophy have come to talk about his predecessors collectively as the Presocratics, thus establishing the life of Socrates as a watershed in that history. But if Socrates really did push philosophy in a significantly new direction, then it is scarcely surprising that some people questioned whether what he was doing counted as philosophy at all. Rather than seeing him as an innovator who was transforming philosophy, those of a more traditional mindset (such as Aristophanes) might instead see him as someone who simply failed to meet the criteria for being a philosopher.

Those now commonly referred to as the Presocratics were a very mixed group of people and it could be argued that the only things holding them together are that they shared a particular period of history and a common language. Thales and his fellow philosophers from Miletus were interested in the natural world. Pythagoras founded a religious movement. Heraclitus wrote obscure verses in which he described a world that was constantly changing. Parmenides tried to persuade people that change was impossible and movement never happened. It could certainly be argued that they all took an interest in metaphysics in one way or another (which seems to be the implication of Cicero's observation), but that shared interest led them in a variety of different directions.

Perhaps this was inevitable. Whether or not he actually coined the term, people seemed to start talking about 'philosophy' around the time of Pythagoras, and 'philosophy' means 'the love of wisdom'. However, because there was no single understanding of what wisdom was, there was also no single thing to love or pursue or one single way in which to love or pursue it. Wisdom could mean many things and be understood in many different ways. As evidence of this one has only to look at the various lists of the Seven Sages of ancient Greece. It is difficult, if not impossible, to identify anything that they all had in common. The notion of what a philosopher was therefore remained importantly open. Because most philosophers seemed to have at least some interest in metaphysics, this might be regarded as an identifying feature, but it can be questioned whether it was ever genuinely a necessary condition for being a philosopher, let alone a sufficient one.

It is sometimes forgotten that the Presocratics were not only philosophically diverse but also geographically dispersed across the ancient Greek world. It was not until the fourth century BC that Athens became an important philosophical centre. It is said that Anaxagoras of Clazomenae (c. 498-428 BC) was the first philosopher to take up residence there. Clazomenae was in western Asia Minor, and Anaxagoras seems to have followed in the older philosophical footsteps of Thales and the Milesians. (Miletus and Clazomenae lay less than a hundred miles away from each other as the crow flies.) Because of the limited and ambiguous evidence available, there are disagreements over when he arrived in Athens, when he left there and why, but during his time there he is said to have taught Archelaus of Athens, who in turn taught Socrates. Anaxagoras wrote a book on the nature of the world, containing what we would now regard as a mixture of physics and metaphysics. It is not clear that Archelaus ever wrote a book on the same subject, but it was certainly his main area of interest. It would be entirely understandable if Aristophanes took these two people based in Athens during his lifetime as his paradigmatic philosophers. If he did, it would scarcely be surprising if he thought of Socrates as being something different.

However, there are many different ways of *not* being a philosopher, and being a sophist is only one of them. There is therefore the further point to consider: why did Aristophanes regard Socrates as a sophist? In *Clouds*, it is made clear, partly through the role of False Logic, that one of the things Aristophanes associated the sophists most closely with was argumentation. This is supported by what is known about the interests the early sophists took in rhetoric. However, an interest in argumentation was scarcely new and hardly sufficient to distinguish the sophists from earlier philosophers. Although the Presocratics might sometimes resort to assertion or poetic evocation, it could hardly be said that they were collectively ignorant of the ways of argument. The manner in which Anaximenes of Miletus (sixth century BC) constructed his metaphysical theory and the ingenuity with which Zeno of Elea (early fifth century BC) spun his paradoxes indicate that they possessed sharply analytical minds. What might have distinguished the sophists and Socrates from such earlier philosophers, however, was the way in which they used argument to arrive at uncertainty rather than at positive conclusions, at nothing rather than something. This suggests one reason why Aristophanes felt able to group them together.

A belief in the importance of definitions is perhaps another area in which Socrates and the sophists most obviously broke new ground. Plato's early dialogues, generally reckoned to be the most authentic in their portrayal of the historical Socrates, are full of demands for definitions and critical demolitions of them. Although firm dates for these dialogues are elusive, the very earliest of them may date to around 390 BC. It is known that at least some of the sophists took a serious interest in language in a variety of ways, and they came to acquire a reputation for hair-splitting. It is not necessary to go back to the fifth or fourth centuries BC to find people who take a delight in such things being dismissed as clever but ultimately petty quibblers. Similar criticisms were levelled against those philosophers in the twentieth century who emphasised the importance of conceptual analysis and who constantly saw problems of philosophy as actually being problems of language once they were understood correctly.

On the other hand, some of those who came after Socrates and the sophists and who took a similar interest in argument and definition managed to retain the title of philosopher without too much trouble. The school of Megara founded by Euclides, a friend of both Plato and Socrates, produced a number of dialecticians without it being suggested that they were simply a group of sophists. It might even be argued that philosophy itself moved further in this direction after the time of Socrates, making the sophists, if anything, philosophers ahead of their time rather than no philosophers of any time. Certainly, during the remaining centuries of antiquity, when the major philosophy schools held sway, their followers were often engrossed in highly technical debates that relied hugely on complex argumentation and precise definition.

One of the groups that sprang up at least partly in the wake of Socrates was the sceptics, although they never seem to have constituted a formal school apart from the time when Plato's Academy was dominated by those under the influence of scepticism during the third and second centuries BC. Pyrrho of Elis (*c*. 360-*c*. 270 BC) was generally regarded as the founder of Greek scepticism, which was also sometimes known as Pyrrhonism as a result. However, various remarks scattered throughout book IX of Diogenes Laertius' *Lives of Eminent Philosophers* suggest that Pyrrho had his predecessors, although the picture that emerges is far from clear. One possible interpretation of the confused and sometimes contradictory evidence links Pyrrho through a line of teachers directly back to Protagoras, while another links him with Metrodorus of Chios who may have studied under Democritus of Abdera at the same time as Protagoras.

The historical evidence is insufficient to draw any remotely firm conclusions, but the idea that the sceptics and sophists were perceived as in some sense kindred spirits is not difficult to understand. On the one hand, 'Protagoras was the first to say that on every issue there are two arguments opposed to each other' (Sprague 2001, 4), and on the other, according to Sextus Empiricus (second/third century AD), 'The Sceptical ability is the ability to set in opposition appearances and ideas in any manner whatsoever' (Inwood and Gerson 1997, 303). The sceptics took arguments for uncertainty as their stock in trade and made them the basis of their whole philosophy. Some saw the tendency of sophists to argue both sides of a case with equal zeal and equal lack of genuine conviction as an exercise in cynicism (in the modern sense of the word). However, the sceptics regarded the idea that there was a counterargument for every argument as a genuine revelation that, if persisted with, could lead to tranquillity. If truth is terminally elusive, then the only rational strategy is to give up the search for it.

It is interesting to note that although the sceptics were generally taken seriously as philosophers, some ancient historians of philosophy such as Hippobotus (second or first century BC) denied scepticism the status of a genuine philosophical school because, like the sophists, the sceptics taught no positive doctrine. However, the challenges of the sceptics were influential in shaping how philosophy developed after the time of Socrates because the different schools felt the need to defend themselves against the criticisms of their teachings articulated by the sceptics.

But if the sceptics were regarded as philosophers, why weren't the sophists? What genuine differences were there between them? It may be worth exploring here the difference between anti-dogmatism and relativism. The principal concern of the ancient sceptics was with knowledge of the true nature of things. Their position, as long as they were consistent, was not that such knowledge was impossible, because that would have been to make a dogmatic statement. Instead, they claimed that as a matter of fact they never found themselves fully persuaded by any arguments concerning the true nature of things, concerning how things really were as opposed to how they appeared to be. The truth, if it existed, was elusive. That did not make truth itself a vacuous concept, although for practical purposes it obviously had very limited value. On the other hand, one of the objections to the sophists seems to have been that they moved, pragmatically at least, in the direction of relativism and towards the idea that truth was a sufficiently flexible concept to be tantamount in practice to a vacuous one. This seems to lead in the kind of direction in which it may be necessary to go in order to understand why the sophists were rejected as philosophers. Unlike the sceptics, who played the philosophical game to win, with an aggressive and in many ways unorthodox strategy, the sophists did not play the game at all. Or rather, they played a different game. Their interests, and those of their clients, lay elsewhere.

Indeed, it is in their interests rather than in their doctrines that such unanimity as existed among the sophists can be found. So far, the sophists have been discussed as if they were some kind of homogeneous group, but they were far from that. They certainly did not share a common doctrine, although many shared some basic elements of a common outlook, which at least tended towards relativism and scepticism. What they taught varied, although rhetoric became an increasingly dominant and constant part of it. As professional educators they were paid for their work, and their clients generally sought them out because they thought they could enhance their chances of success in civic life through acquiring the skills they taught. One of the recurrent criticisms of them made by the philosophers was that while philosophers valued truth, the sophists valued expediency, and this constituted a significant difference between them (and between True Logic and False Logic, in *Clouds*). The sophists were also criticised for the simple fact of charging fees for their teaching. While the sophists may never knowingly have undersold themselves, it is not clear how much importance should be attached to this. It is always easy for those who do not have to work for a living to look down on those who do, and old money frequently holds new money in contempt. More significantly, perhaps, it could be argued that while the sceptics taught a genuinely philosophical way of life with tranquillity as its aim, the sophists simply used argumentation as a means to gaining short-term pragmatic advantage. While philosophers were concerned with knowing, the sophists were concerned with winning.

But perhaps it is not as simple as that. At the beginning of his *Nicomachean Ethics*, Aristotle observes that everyone seeks the good life, but that people disagree on what the good life is. It seems safe to assume that no one went to the sophists or philosophers in pursuit of a worse life. Happiness, in one form or another, ran through the teachings of the schools that followed Socrates. In this regard, the philosophers and the sophists were in the same line of business, and it is even said that for a time Antiphon of Rhamnus ran a kind of philosophical consultancy where people with problems could go and help to have them resolved. From this perspective, the main difference between the sophists and the philosophers was that the sophists thought of happiness primarily in terms of wealth and success in public life. But if, as Aristotle thought, they were wrong to do so, then it might be argued that they were bad philosophers, but that is not the same thing as not being philosophers at all.

190

17. Were the Sophists Philosophers?

To some extent, the question of whether or not the sophists were philosophers resolved itself over time. Philosophy and rhetoric became established as the two main areas of higher education and they were provided by philosophers and sophists respectively. However, it is important not to project a later clarity back onto an earlier confusion. In the time of Socrates and Plato, ideas concerning what it was to be a philosopher and what it was to be a sophist were both changing. In the end the confusion was at least partly addressed by establishing a line of demarcation that separated the two: part of what it meant to be a philosopher was not to be a sophist and part of what it meant to be a sophist was not to be a philosopher. The earlier, more general meaning of 'sophist' disappeared while the meaning of 'philosopher' changed because of the influence of Socrates. The way in which philosophy was taught was also changing. By the end of the fourth century BC Athens had become home to four institutions that would dominate the teaching of philosophy for centuries to come. The first, Plato's Academy, was founded in around 385 BC. This was followed by the Lyceum of Aristotle, the Stoa of Zeno of Citium and the Garden of Epicurus. Being a philosopher became increasingly closely connected with being a member of one of these schools. Moreover, being a 'philosopher' or a 'sophist' also increasingly became a matter of self-identification. The view taken towards sophists by philosophers was not one that was universally shared, and it should not be assumed that the title of sophist was universally shunned.

However, during the time of Plato and Socrates many of these factors did not apply, or did not apply to a significant extent. The relatively clear division of labour that emerged after their time meant that in due course it became relatively easy to distinguish sophists from philosophers. During their time, it was not. The surviving writings of Protagoras are not lacking in philosophical content, and if Aristophanes could openly and clearly identify Socrates as a sophist, that fact has to be acknowledged and made sense of rather than ignored.

But were the sophists philosophers in terms of how we understand 'philosopher' today? There are good reasons for saying at least some of them were. An obvious sticking point can be easily removed. While the sophists of the fifth and fourth centuries BC were castigated by their contemporary opponents for their professionalism, this is no longer a problem. Philosophers of the present day are not expected to work for nothing, and having to do so is more likely to be seen as a sign of failure than of success!

Furthermore, if teaching a way of life is what philosophers are meant to do, then most contemporary teachers of philosophy fail this test. In important ways the scope of philosophy has shrunk over the centuries and perhaps nowhere is this more evident than in this particular regard. Even those who work in the areas of philosophy that are most relevant to everyday life, such as ethics, are likely to confine their attentions to a few particular problems rather than address life in general. It might be argued that in recent decades, existentialism has been the philosophical movement that has most resembled ancient philosophy in articulating an outlook on life as a whole. But even in that case it is not obvious that any or many of the existentialist philosophers of the twentieth century *lived* existentialism in the way that, for example, Epicurus lived Epicureanism. However, even if the existentialists are given the benefit of the doubt, the prevailing image of the twentieth-century philosopher in the English-speaking world (whether unfairly or not) is more likely to be that of the disputatious pedant, bearing a considerable resemblance to the stereotypical sophist. It may also be noted that modern philosophy is generally held to have begun with the work of Descartes (1596-1650), and that one of its distinctive characteristics is a modern form of scepticism. In ancient philosophy, scepticism was the philosophical school that had most in common with the sophists.

Just as ideas about what it meant to be a philosopher or a sophist changed during the time of Plato and Socrates, so they have continued to change since then, to the point where there is a very substantial overlap. Although most philosophers have little interest in the subject of rhetoric, skills in argumentation are nevertheless highly valued. The ability to take an argument apart and expose its weaknesses is a significant part of what is taught in university philosophy departments today. In an age where scepticism is a powerful force, truth becomes elusive and so argument becomes mainly critical. More than that, as both the sophists and the sceptics of old showed, the sustained critical use of argument can itself serve to undermine belief in truth. This is one of the reasons why traditionalists such as Aristophanes viewed the sophists with such suspicion; they were perceived as dangerous because a society that lost confidence in the validity of its values and beliefs might dissolve into anarchy. But philosophers who terminally and irrevocably disagree with each other can also undermine a society's belief in truth. Indeed, it was the very fact that the philosophers disagreed so drastically with each other on so many issues that both the sophists and the sceptics exploited so cleverly to their advantage.

However, even if modern philosophers have become more like the sophists of old in many ways, it is interesting to note that whereas in Athens between the middle of the fifth century and the middle of the fourth century BC those keen to make their mark in public life sought out the sophists, few who are interested in carving out a political career in today's democracies seem to think that studying philosophy is the way forward. On the other hand, it is also interesting to note the number who come to politics through the legal profession, one of the very few areas in modern life where rhetorical skills are particularly valued and developed.

To conclude, the aim here has been to show that the question 'Were the sophists philosophers?' is not a simple one, and neither is its answer. In the time of Socrates it was by no means always clear what it meant to be either a sophist or a philosopher. If the line of demarcation was unclear, then it was also unclear who stood on which side of it and who straddled it. Things became clearer in time, but the clarity also revealed a significant degree of overlap as some of the skills developed by the sophists became valued within philosophy. In the modern era, the practice of philosophy has come to resemble the practice of the sophists of old in a number of ways to an extent that might have horrified Socrates and Plato, let alone Aristophanes.

Bibliography

Aristophanes, *Plays*, vol. I, trans P. Dickinson (Oxford: Oxford University Press, 1970).

Aristotle, *Nicomachean Ethics,* trans. C. Rowe (Oxford: Oxford University Press, 2002).

Barnes, Jonathan, *Early Greek Philosophy* (Harmondsworth: Penguin, 1987).

Cicero, *Tusculan Disputations*, trans. J.E. King, Loeb edition (London: Heinemann, 1945).

Curnow, Trevor, *The Philosophers of the Ancient World: An A-Z Guide* (London: Duckworth, 2006).

Diogenes Laertius, *Lives of Eminent Philosophers*, trans. R.D. Hicks, Loeb edition (London: Heinemann, 1958 and 1959).

Inwood, Brad and Gerson, L.P., *Hellenistic Philosophy*: *Introductory Readings*, 2nd edition (Indianapolis: Hackett, 1997).

Nails, Debra, *The People of Plato: A Prosopography of Plato and Other Socratics* (Indianapolis: Hackett, 2002).

Sprague, Rosamond Kent (ed.), *The Older Sophists* (Indianapolis: Hackett, 2001).

Law against Nature?

Andrew Shortridge

Both fragments and testimonia reveal the sophists' deep interest in ethical and political theory, and particularly in the question of the grounds and legitimacy of laws, of the relationship between *nomos* ('law' or 'convention') and *physis* ('nature', sometimes transliterated as *phusis*). Study of *nomos* and *physis* does not originate with the sophists; both directly and under the guise of cognate terms, *nomos* and *physis* were the subject of sustained intellectual attention from the beginnings of philosophic inquiry. However, it is in the study of *nomos* and *physis* considered as ethical concepts that the sophists made a significant contribution to ethics.

After a short examination of some of those thinkers who discussed *nomos* and *physis* prior to the sophists,[1] I turn to previous scholars who have argued that conflict and antagonism are integral to comprehending how the sophists understood the relationship between law and nature. I survey several scholarly accounts of sophistic ethics in which the antagonism of law and nature is given centre stage and used as the first principle from which to account for all of sophistic ethical theorising. Of particular importance here is Guthrie (1971), who gives perhaps the most sustained and detailed account of sophistic conceptions of *nomos* and *physis*, arguing that law and nature are, for the sophists, antithetical to one another, 'opposed and mutually exclusive' (Guthrie 1971, 55). Along the way, some portions of those more forceful or influential sophistic analyses of 'law and nature' are examined. This is done both to demonstrate first-hand some arguments about the role of nature and the legitimacy of law in ethical theory, and also to provide source material by appeal to which we can ask what sort – or sorts – of antagonism the sophists envisaged as characterising relations between law and nature, and, therefore, evaluate which of the later scholarly accounts of the sophistic ethics best captures, displays, and explains the thoughts of these powerful and controversial thinkers.

Western philosophy begins with Thales and the Milesian tradition of inquiry into 'nature'. Barnes (2001, xiv-xxv) argues that in conducting their speculations, the Milesians developed four concepts: *kosmos* ('the cosmos', or, 'the order thereof'); *archê* ('principle'); *logos* ('account'); and *physis* ('nature'). The work of the poet Hesiod contains myths about cosmic origin, and the first use of '*physis*' is in Homer's *Odyssey* (10.303): the originality of Milesian discussions of nature lay in the absence of appeals to the divine (Lloyd 1982, 16). Aristotle called the Milesians '*physikoi*' or '*physiologoi*', since they gave accounts of *physis*. They attempted to account for the plenitude of the universe by discovering the substance from which all other things arose, but there was wide disagreement as to which substance was responsible – Thales thought water, Anaximenes air, and Anaximander blamed 'the Boundless' (*to apeiron*).[2] Aristotle suggests that an understanding of *physis* involved both an identification of the substance or substances that underlie the cosmos, and some understanding of the principles by which that substance produced or transformed into the cosmos:

> There must be some nature – either one or more than one – from which, being preserved itself, the other things come into being. But as to the number and form of this sort of principle, they do not all agree (*Metaphysics* 983b17-27, in Barnes 2001, 11).

There is much debate today about what the Presocratic thinkers thought was actually explained by an account of *physis*: did an account of nature explain the origins of the universe, the processes of change and development in the universe, or the end result of that change – or some combination thereof?[3] Sophistic appeals to *physis* seem to be a part of explaining the political condition of mankind; focussing on human nature, rather than on the cosmos as a whole, the sophists were surely influenced by Hippocratic writings.

Ionians sought to explain the whole cosmos in terms of *physis* – often, though not always, being a single substance or operating on a single principle. In contrast, the Hippocratics seem to understand *physis* to mean 'constitution', and used 'nature' to identify what was common. However, the exact target, that which shares 'what is common', was variable – one could sensibly speak of the *physis* of a man, or of all men, or of a hand or an organ, or of a river or a place (see Beardslee 1918, 31-9; also Hankinson 1998, 51-69). Beardslee explains the difference between Ionian and Hippocratic speculation thus: the Ionians sought to explain the cosmos, and thought that the world's plenitude was best explained by appeal to some underlying substratum – *physis* – which was prior to and explained the constitution of things. The Hippocratics use 'nature' to refer to 'the constitution produced by the mingling of the elements, not the elements that are mingled together' (1918, 33). So, the proper treatment for epilepsy – the 'sacred disease' – involved understanding that epilepsy 'has a nature (*phusis*) and an occasion (*prophasis*)' (*The Sacred Disease*, trans. Jones, in Hankinson 1998, 53, sec. 65); treating a fracture, no doctor needs to theorise about how best to bind or sling an arm, 'for the patient himself holds out the arm for bandaging in the position impressed on it by conformity with nature' (*Fractures*, trans. Withington, in Lloyd 1986, 279).

'Nature' identified what was medically normal, but *nomoi* could just as easily run counter to normal behaviour as they could accentuate it.

The Hippocratic author of *Airs, Waters, Places* explains the behaviour of 'the inhabitants of Asia' – probably Turks, perhaps also Persians – by explaining the distinguishing aspects of their own nature and the climate and locale where they dwell. 'Such things seem to me to be the cause of the feebleness of the Asiatic race, but a contributory cause lies in their customs' (*Airs*, sec. 16, in Lloyd 1986, 160) – they are ruled by kings, and monarchy makes men less rather than more warlike.[4] Similarly, the Europeans are more warlike because of their physiology, climate, and custom (*Airs*, sec. 23, in Lloyd 1986, 167). The direction of entailment here is unclear: are a people governed in some particular way because of their *physis*? Or is some aspect of their *physis* reinforced or emphasised by some particular *nomos*, as climate can reinforce or alter at least some of the tendencies of nature?[5] Explanatory appeals to *nomos* and *physis* could involve the two concepts running counter to or reinforcing one another.

Ancient sources indicate various attitudes towards *nomos*:

> The term *nomos* and the whole range of terms that are cognate with it are always prescriptive and normative and never merely descriptive – they give some kind of direction or command affecting the behaviour and activities of persons and things ... (Kerferd 1981, 112) .

Nomos is systematic, always the product 'of some intentional assignation or deliberate practice, though not necessarily one that can be ascribed to specific acts and specific originators' (Long 2005, 415). Laws prescribe: but do they always prescribe rightly?

In the *Sisyphus* fragment – attributed to either Critias or Euripides – the origin of laws is said to lie with men: human life was chaotic, good went unrewarded and vice unpunished, so 'men introduced / The restraint of law, so that justice would be the tyrant / Of the human race, the master of abuse / And the punisher of any transgression' (in Waterfield 2000, 305-6). Some 'shrewd and clever' fellow goes on to convince his compatriots that the gods exist, witness to every injustice: there lies the origin of law, and of some ways of encouraging law-abiding behaviour. Presumably, the speaker is the wicked, wily Sisyphus. We ought to treat his words with caution, but we need not infer that this account of the origins of law implies a criticism: it suggests that 'it is vitally important that we have *nomoi*, and that they have some authoritative backing, even if this is based on a fiction' (Bett 2002, 252).

Antigone, in Sophocles' play of that name, ignores the lawful commands of Creon: 'Your wisdom appealed to one world – mine, another' (Sophocles, *Antigone* 628). Although Aristotle interpreted this as an appeal to 'what is just and unjust in accordance with nature' (*Rhetoric* 137b4-11, in Kerferd 1981, 113), later scholars argue that this is not a straight contrast of *nomos* against *physis*, but of *nomos* against unwritten law, the *nomima*, divinely-inspired rules which are separate from positive law (see Guthrie 1971, 75-9, 117-31; also Ostwald 1973). Clearly, the laws could be criticised in various ways: but why did the sophists and their contemporaries focus such critical attention on the laws to begin with? With an expansion of the horizons of the world came recognition that 'things could be otherwise': the Presocratic speculations fostered an enthusiasm for intellectual inquiries in general. This inquisitive spirit focussed on the diversity of laws, their legitimacy and their basis, at least in part due to 'the anthropological survey of cultural diversity and the developmental account of human civilisation' (Kahn 1981, 106) that was so popular.[6] Another spur to criticism of the laws came from the growth of religious scepticism. Religion was one of cornerstones of civic law: the counterpart to burgeoning agnosticism or atheism was an agnosticism concerning the legitimacy of the law (Guthrie 1971, 56).

Clearly, both *physis* and *nomos* could adopt subtleties of meaning, whether alone or contrasted with one another. Beardslee (1918, 70) identifies four sets of connotations that the two terms took when contrasted with one another. First – and understandable, particularly in light of Hippocratic diagnoses – is the contrast of *physis* as the normal behaviour of constitution of a thing, with *nomos* as erratic or unusual behaviour. The second contrast is of self-moving things against things that are moved by external forces. Third is the contrast of one's character against one's training or upbringing – the opposition of *nomos* to *physis* is the progenitor of the contrast, familiar from psychology, of nature to nurture. Finally, *physis* and *nomos* are associated with reality and opinion. It is in this last sense that Democritus contrasts *nomos* and *physis*, denying the reality of hot and cold, bitter and sweet, and of colour: 'By convention sweet and by convention bitter [etc.] ... in reality atoms and the empty' (in Barnes 2001, 208) It is a short step from denying the reality of various perceived phenomena to denying that the perception of moral qualities was grounded in anything real. Morality is simply a matter of taste, as Crassus implies in Kubrick's *Spartacus* (1991, restored version) when he draws an analogy between sexual morality and dietary preference: 'Do you consider the eating of oysters to be moral, and the eating of snails to be immoral? ... my taste includes both snails and oysters.' If the report by Diogenes Laertius is trustworthy, Archelaus was the first thinker to take this step.

> He said that there are two causes of generation, hot and cold, and that animals were generated from mud. And that things are just or ignoble not by nature but by convention (*Lives of Eminent Philosophers* II.16, in Barnes 2001, 199).

Guthrie argues that this comic, clumsy juxtaposition by Diogenes of ethical theory with biological science nonetheless reveals the close connection between 'evolutionary physical theories and theories of the conventional origin of morality and law' (1971, 58). Speculative inquiries had led up to this point: people wanted to know what made the law legitimate; convention and nature could be understood as being in conflict and hostile to one another. The sophists were perhaps the first thinkers to explore and analyse this significant and powerful insight, that law and nature might be dissonant or incompatible.

So the sophists viewed *nomos* and *physis* as being opposed to one another, and, reading the various different ways that this conflict or opposition could be played out, scholars have mapped the various positions in ethical and political theory to which different sophists seem committed. Hence, Beardslee argues that 'on the basis of the distinction between phusis and nomos the sophists were divided into two schools, Naturalists or Physiocrats ... and the Humanists ...' (1918, 76-7). Gill (1995, 72-5) argues that there were four ancient positions on the role of nature in politics: that there was a gap between human desires and the moral order; second, the claim that some natural *diktat* justified absolute ruthlessness in action, by men and by states; a third group sees 'human nature [as] such that we can only survive and lead tolerable lives by framing legal rules and by developing ethical attitudes'; finally, some thinkers argued that those laws and attitudes were products of contractual agreement, usually implicit, between individuals. There are many ways to unpack this conflict of *nomos* and *physis*; no matter how many positions can be articulated out of this conflict of law and nature, scholars view the hostility of law and nature, the conflict or antagonism between them, as fundamental and foundational to sophistic ethics. One attempt to chart the terrain of sophistic ethical discourse will be considered in detail: the tripartite model developed by Guthrie (1971, 55-134).

Aristotle argues that the widest range of rhetorical ploys that force opponents to commit themselves to paradoxical statements are those 'which depend on the standard of nature and convention' (*Sophistical Refutations* 173a7ff.). Presumably the sophists were familiar with such tactics: Guthrie argues, as I read him, that the sophists not only appealed to opposed notions of law and nature, but thought that law and nature were actually opposed to one another. Guthrie argues that the *nomos-physis* antithesis was invoked particularly in ethical arguments, and that 'once established, [the antithesis] led to very different estimates of the relative value of *physis* and *nomos* in the moral and political field' (1971, 58). He identifies three broad categories of sophistic ethic.

First are the *conventionalists* who saw in *physis* only the brutal original condition of mankind. Through the slow application of will and intellect, men raise themselves to a civilised condition. This civilising process can include the development of language, agriculture, carpentry, augury, and other skills: it of course includes the development or invention of *nomos*. The laws are conventional *qua* unnatural: but their value relies on their being unnatural, since all that nature gave to man was hardship and penury. Guthrie finds in Protagoras' speech (Plato, *Protagoras* 320c-328d) the greatest example of the conventionalist ethic. (Other sources of conventionalist sentiment include Aeschylus' *Prometheus Bound*, the choral ode on Man in Sophocles' *Antigone*, and the *Sisyphus* fragment, all three of which are cited by Guthrie (1971, 79ff.).) In the speech, Protagoras uses myth and argument to tell how the city first began and now survives. Men could not live together until Zeus granted them the civic virtues of shame (*aidôs*) and justice (*dikê*) as the foundation for friendship and law; fathers pay greatest attention to educating their sons in virtue; every citizen teaches every other to be virtuous; the courts, laws and education likewise serve the same function. Guthrie argues that Zeus' decree 'stands for what in the non-mythic anthropologies (and in Protagoras' mind) was the work of time, bitter experience, and necessity', and says that Protagoras makes two clear points: every civilised person possesses some degree of virtue, but virtue is not innate (1971, 66). *Nomos* is not natural, but it is good: this is the essence of the conventionalist position.

Guthrie's next category includes all of the *realists*. The realist ethic is espoused especially by Thucydides, and by Thrasymachus (Plato, *Republic* book I) and Glaucon (*Republic* book II, 359cff.). The realists think that neither law nor nature is wholly positive or negative, though they are wholly opposed to one another. The two conditions, say realists, are best viewed through the lens of self-interest and necessity: this gives realism a somewhat amoral tone. Realism's first claim is that the *nomoi* (attempt to) constrain the selfish natural desires (*physis*) of men. Such restraint produces an eventual benefit for some individual: the party benefiting might be the ruler of the city, 'the stronger', or even those who are too weak to pursue their own advantage successfully when alone, as in Glaucon's contractual account. Guthrie (1971, 84-8) points to those instances in Thucydides' *History* where the parties indicate that pious appeals to justice 'lack teeth' in the face of the pursuit of interest (*to sumpheron*) or necessity (*anagkê*). For instance, in discussing appropriate punishments for the rebellious Mytileneans, both Cleon – making the case for slavery and atrocity, and Diodotus – making the case for restraint (Thucydides 3.37-50, in Gagarin and Woodruff 1995, 108-18) – justify their arguments by claiming that their preferred course of action aligns with the Athenian interest. Questions of justice are collapsed into questions of interest, or set to one side as irrelevant. Thrasymachus' argument takes a similar course: 'the infallible or ideal ruler is ... the one who legislates unerringly *in his own interests*' (Guthrie 1971, 95). Guthrie calls Thrasymachus a 'disillusioned moralist' railing against hypocrites, whose main aim is to show that the idea of justice is empty or vacuous – the just man is a fool, since his acts benefit another. Every person actually acts in their own interest, and he who is lawmaker makes laws to that end – this is the beginning and end of *nomos*, hence Thrasymachus' disillusionment.[7]

Realists think of *physis* as self-interest: *nomos* is the command, obedience to which aids another person – the ruler, the stronger. When obedience to *nomos* is not in the interest of an individual, it is swept aside, as the Athenians swept talk of justice to one side in their debates about the proper fate of the Mytileneans. It is neither right nor wrong that men pursue their self-interest, whether by creating laws or ignoring them – that's just the way things are.

Guthrie calls the final category *antinomianism*: it differs from realism in arguing that it is right and proper to ignore or reject *nomos* in favour of *physis*. The boldest antinomian must be Callicles, with his spirited criticism of *nomoi* and praise for the 'law of nature', the *nomos physeôs*. Guthrie suggests that Callicles represents 'a somewhat stylised presentation of the doctrine "might is right" in its most extreme form' (1971, 102). Callicles describes the strong man who embodies this doctrine as being like a lion cub, who is cowed and de-clawed by society:

> But if a man arises endowed with a nature sufficiently strong, he will, I believe, shake off all these controls, burst his fetters, and break loose. And trampling upon our scraps of paper, our spells and incantations, and all our unnatural conventions, he rises up and reveals himself our master who was once our slave, and there shines forth nature's true justice (Plato, *Gorgias* 483e-484b).

Physis stands for the imperative of nature, that each man exert himself as best as he is able, in whatever way he sees fit – and the devil may take the hindmost! This 'natural law' is constrained and opposed by *nomos*, the conventions of the weak, who would subdue and stupefy the strong man, who would otherwise be king. Inasmuch as he could be king, Callicles seems committed to the view that he ought: for he is suited *by nature* to ruling over the weak.

Under the guise of appealing to a contrast of *nomos* and *physis*, Guthrie argues that the sophists could appeal to various cognates and associated meanings of 'nature' – as savagery, or self-interest, or strength and the moral imperative to be strong – and 'law' – as the illegitimate ties of the weak over the strong, or a reification (in the form of a command) of some act that is advantageous to the lawmaker, or as a civilising institution that makes life possible and worthwhile. We have seen some of the ways in which these accretions of meaning are the products of earlier speculations and inquiries conducted by the Presocratics, Hippocratics, and others. What is perhaps unique to sophistic appeals, according to Guthrie, is that *nomos* and *physis* are antithetical to one another.

It is, of course, possible to construct a map of sophistic ethical theories that has more than three placeholders. Guthrie admits as much, arguing that the division of sophistic ethics into three groups is 'convenient' (1971, 60). It seems that regardless of the number of ethical theories that sophistic inquiries might yield, Guthrie is committed to each of them viewing *nomos* and *physis* as antithetical to one another, no matter how 'law' and 'nature' are conceived of and understood. But is this 'antithetical' view correct? For instance, Protagoras says that the virtues are not by nature, but by choice (Plato, *Protagoras* 323c): does it follow that the virtues must be 'by convention'? Antiphon the sophist seems to draw a strong contrast between advantage and disadvantage: should we infer that this is a contrast of *nomos* and *physis*? Glaucon's account of the origins of society seems to make it natural both to create conventions and also natural to violate them: how is the antithesis invoked here?

Guthrie undertakes an immense task: to survey the diverse inquiries of a disparate group of intellectual freelancers and innovators, and to discover those basic premises common to the inquiries that are shared by them all. Cherniss (1935) criticised Aristotle's exegesis and analysis of the Presocratics, which was so biased as to make most of his predecessors into proto-Aristotelians, since Aristotle read into Presocratic sources ideas and concepts that were foreign to the original authors. Cherniss' argument is also marshalled against philosophers who do not sufficiently appreciate the effects of Aristotle's efforts on later scholarly studies of the Presocratics. Inasmuch as we are historians of philosophy, the situation must be a little different – Aristotle read the Presocratics into his wider vision and project of 'what philosophy is', whereas an account of sophistic conceptions of *nomos* and *physis* need not aim at such an overarching goal. A historian might simply wish (as much as is possible) to 'tell it like it is', and in the telling might appeal to different models and schema that show the common themes and commitments underlying various diverse phenomena. The different ways of approaching the past have different virtues and associated risks. Making models, one risks overlooking subtle differences between individuals who are grouped *together*; studying individuals in isolation, one risks failing to see the trends and intellectual movements that give shape to the historical period. In what ways does Guthrie's model of a *nomos-physis* antithesis help or hinder our understanding of the sophists? How should 'the sophists' be identified as a group, and so distinguished against the backdrop of the intellectual milieu that characterised late fifth-century Greece? Such questions can be best answered by returning to the sophistic sources and testimonia themselves; this does not prevent us from categorising sophists by affinity and antipathy. We could study individual sophists very closely, or study them as a philosophical movement, looking for family resemblances. We need not think that these two approaches are antithetical to one another, but it is not clear that they are perfectly compatible.[8]

Notes

1. I shall not discuss the connections between law, nature, and justice (*dikê*): on these topics, see Long (2005), Barker (1964).

2. An absence of anything but fragments from Milesian writings forces interpreters to be very cautious: see Cherniss (1935), also O'Grady (2002), Lloyd (1982).

3. On this, see Naddaf (2005).

4. Compare this with the condition of free men, discussed in this Hippocratic text and also by Demaratus, in his paean to Law, as recorded by Herodotus (7.105, cited in Guthrie 1971, 69).

5. For instance: 'When the weather changes often, abnormalities in the coagulation of semen are more frequent than when the weather is constant. A variable climate *produces a nature* which is coupled with a fierce, hot-headed and discordant temperament, for frequent fears cause a fierce attitude of mind whereas quietness and calm dull the wits' (*Airs*, sec. 23, in Lloyd 1986, 167, emphasis added).

6. On ancient anthropology and accounts of the development of civilisation, see Guthrie (1957), Havelock (1957), and Naddaf (2005).

7. Note that Thrasymachus' argument is quite complex, and Guthrie admits (1971, 92n.1) that his interpretation is 'a minority view and others have much to be said for them'.

8. During the writing of this piece Dirk Baltzly provided me with both encouragement and constructive criticism, for which I am very grateful.

Bibliography

Aristotle, *Sophistical Refutations*, trans. W.D. Ross, in *The Complete Works of Aristotle*, vol. I, ed. J. Barnes (Princeton, NJ: Princeton University Press, 1995).

Barker, Sir E., *Greek Political Theory: Plato and his Predecessors* (London: Methuen, 1964; first published 1918).

Barnes, J. (trans. and ed.), *Early Greek Philosophy* (London: Penguin, 2001, revised edition; first published 1987).

Beardslee, J.W. Jr., *The Use of* phusis *in Fifth-Century Greek Literature* (Chicago: University of Chicago Press, 1918).

Bett, R., 'Is There a Sophistic Ethics?', *Ancient Philosophy*. 22(2) (2002), 235-62.

Cherniss, H., *Aristotle's Criticism of Presocratic Philosophy* (New York: Octagon Books, Inc., 1935).

Diogenes Laertius, *Lives of Eminent Philosophers*, trans. R.D. Hicks, Loeb edition (London: Heinemann, 1972).

Gagarin, M. and Woodruff, P. (eds), *Early Greek Political Theory: From Homer to the Sophists* (Cambridge Texts in the History of Political Thought, ed. R. Geuss and Q. Skinner) (Cambridge: Cambridge University Press, 1995).

Gill, C., *Greek Thought* (New Surveys in the Classics, vol. XXV) (Oxford: Oxford University Press, 1995).

Guthrie, W.K.C., *The Sophists* (Cambridge: Cambridge University Press, 1971; first published as *A History of Greek Philosophy*, vol. III., part 1, 1969).

Hankinson, R.J., *Cause and Explanation in Ancient Greek Thought* (Oxford: Oxford University Press, 1998).

Havelock, E.A., *The Liberal Temper in Greek Politics* (London: Jonathon Cape, 1957).

Kerferd, G.B., *The Sophistic Movement* (Cambridge: Cambridge University Press, 1981).

Kubrick, S., *Spartacus* (Universal Pictures, restored ed., 1991; first released 1960).

Lloyd, G.E.R., *Early Greek Science: Thales to Aristotle* (London: Chatto and Windus, 1982; first published 1970).

Lloyd, G.E.R. (ed.), *Hippocratic Writings*, trans. J. Chadwick, W.N. Mann, I.M. Lonie and E.T. Withington (London: Penguin, 1986).

Long, A.A., 'Law and Nature in Greek Thought', in *Cambridge Companion to Ancient Greek Law*, ed. M. Gagarin and D. Cohen (Cambridge: Cambridge University Press, 2005).

Naddaf, G., *The Greek Concept of Nature* (SUNY Series in Ancient Greek Philosophy, ed. A. Preus) (New York: SUNY Press, 2005).

O'Grady, P., *Thales of Miletus: The Beginnings of Western Science and Philosophy* (Aldershot: Ashgate, 2002).

Ostwald, M. (1973), 'Was There a Concept *agraphos nomos* in Classical Greece?', in *Exegesis and Argument: Studies in Greek Philosophy presented to Gregory Vlastos*, ed. E.N. Lee, A.D.P. Mourelatos and R. Rorty (Assen, The Netherlands: Koninklikje Van Gorcum and Comp. B.V., supplemental volume 1 to *Phronesis*, 1973).

Plato, *Gorgias*, trans. and ed. T. Irwin (Oxford: Clarendon Press, 1979).

Plato, *Protagoras*, trans. and ed. C.C.W. Taylor, revised edition (Oxford: Clarendon Press, 1990; first published 1976).

Plato, *Republic*, trans. and ed. C.D.C. Reeve (Indianapolis: Hackett, 2004).

Sophocles, *The Three Theban Plays: 'Antigone', 'Oedipus the King', 'Oedipus at Colonus'*, trans. R. Fagles (London: Penguin, 1982).

Thucydides, *History of the Peloponnesian War*, trans. Rex Warner (Harmondsworth: Penguin, 1954).

Waterfield, R. (trans. and ed.), *The First Philosophers: The Presocratics and the Sophists* (Oxford: Oxford University Press, 2000).

The Sophists and Natural Theology

George Arabatzis

The 'naked heads'

The philosopher and orator Themistius (born in Paphlagonia in the fourth century AD) wrote that his beloved Socrates at some time expressed himself as 'mostly irreverent and far from his usual piety and somehow close to Prodicus of Ceos, Protagoras from Abdera and Gorgias of Leontini and to other naked heads who proclaim themselves wise among the Greeks' (*Orations: Erotikos*, 161d-162a); in another of his speeches Themistius speaks of Prodicus as a guarantor of piety, but this second passage (349b) is considered spurious. Leaving aside the open question of Socratic piety, Themistius, by his reference to Protagoras, Prodicus and Gorgias, follows a long series of lists of the atheists of antiquity which, together with the above sophists, includes people such as the poet Diagoras Melius (fourth century BC), the philosopher Theodorus of Cyrene (third century BC), and the philosopher Euhemerus of Messena (340-260 BC); Themistius' triad of atheists is added to other similar triads. Cicero (106-43 BC) includes Protagoras, Diagoras Melius and Theodorus of Cyrene (*On the Nature of the Gods* I.2); Philodemus (first century BC) writes of Prodicus, Diagoras and Critias (*On Piety* 112); Plutarch (AD *c*. 46-120) includes Theodorus, Diagoras and Hippo (*On Common Conceptions* 31); pseudo-Plutarch gives Diagoras, Theodorus and Euhemerus (*On the Opinions of the Philosophers* I.7); like pseudo-Plutarch, Galen (AD 130-200) includes Diagoras, Theodorus and Euhemerus) in his list (*On the History of Philosophy* 35,4-5); Aelian (AD *c*. 170-235) names Hippo, Diagoras and Herostratus (*On the Nature of the Animals* VI.40); Minucius Felix (who flourished between AD 200 and 240) includes Theodorus, Diagoras and Protagoras (*Octavius* 8,2-3); the Christian Father of the Church, John Chrysostom (fourth century AD), names Protagoras, Diagoras and Theodorus (*Discourse on Epistle to the Corinthians 1,* 4,5,) and Libanius (fourth century AD) gives Anaxagoras, Protagoras and Diagoras (*Declamations 1: Apology of Socrates,* 153-4). For an account of these triads of atheists see Pease 1968, 120, note.

During the long period from the fourth century BC to the fourth century AD and beyond, covered by the above writers, charges of atheism were based on: (1) the absolute denial of the existence of gods; (2) the denial of the established gods in favour of foreign cults; (3) the denial after critique of the accepted gods followed by the introduction of more adequate conceptions of the divine against, for example, animism, anthropomorphism or polytheism. We should not ignore, of course, the case of simply calumnious accusations (see E. Derenne, 1930; Pease 1968, 120-3). The epithet 'naked head', used by Themistius, is a reference to Plato's *Phaedrus* (237a) where we see Socrates covering his head when he deceptively speaks about love in the impious manner of Lysias (*c.* 450-*c.* 380 BC) before proceeding to an apology of manic Eros. Eventually, 'naked head' came to mean the impious. Like the pagan Themistius, Christian writers such as Gregory Nazianzenus of Cappadocia (third century AD) and John of Damascus (AD *c.* 650-*c.* 750) made use of this appellation when referring to atheists or to heretics. The originality of Themistius lies elsewhere, namely in the fact that he proposed a triad of atheists consisting of some of the principal sophists of antiquity and that he explicitly and exclusively linked sophistic thought to impiety. His testimony aligns with the typical perception of the sophists as atheists and tends also to assimilate the sophistic to the rhetoric of orators such as Lysias, an hypothesis worthy of examination.

The sophists and religion

The sophists were not unaccustomed to thinking about religion, and in their theories we find some of the most interesting and original ideas about religious phenomena. Antiphon (Sprague 1972, 231) and Thrasymachus (Sprague 1972, 93) seem not to accept divine Providence. Critias, if the *Sisyphus* fragment is really by him and not by Euripides, related religious feeling to primal fear of the gods (Sprague 1972, 259-60): in reality, it was a wise human invention intended to form a society obedient to moral law. But in the end, it seems that Themistius' triad refers to the most interesting sophistic statements about religion, those of Protagoras, Prodicus and Gorgias.

Protagoras wrote (independently or as a part of a greater work) a book entitled *On the Gods*, and in a famous fragment (Sprague 1972, 20) stated that we cannot have a solid opinion about the existence or non-existence of the gods. His position is best described as agnostic or aporetic (doubting or inconclusive), and his inclusion in the group of atheists is problematic. It seems that in antiquity Protagoras was one of the few to advocate an intermediate position between arguments for and against the existence of gods (Gigon 1985, 431). Nevertheless, if the relevant testimony is true, this theoretical subtlety did not help him to avoid exile. In a poem by the Sceptic philosopher Timon of Phlius (*c.* 320-230 BC) we read: '... they made up their minds to make ashes of his books because he put it in writing that he did not know nor could he perceive what or who the gods are ...' (Sprague 1972, 10). Philostratus (*c.* AD 200) says that Protagoras' unorthodox position was formed under the influence of Persian seers:

I think it was from his Persian instruction that Protagoras derived the
unorthodox view that one cannot say whether the gods exist or not; for the
[Persian] magi acknowledge the gods in their secret rites but try to do away
with the public belief in divinity, since they do not wish to give the impression that their power is from that source (Sprague 1972, 6).

In Plato's *Laws* (X, 889e), the atheists do not accept a natural justice, a
position very close to that of Protagoras in *Theaetetus* (167c, 172b, 177d).
It has been argued that his rejection of the possibility of knowledge about
the gods is 'scientific' and, furthermore, that his agnosticism is a form of
individualistic approach to the religious phenomenon: 'if, in spite of this,
Protagoras could still devote an entire treatise to the problem of the belief
in God, he must have been satisfied with a somewhat lesser degree of
certainty as his work progressed ... "I am unable to discover" (whether the
gods exist or not) ... With these words he restricts the scope of his sentence
about the impossibility of knowing the gods, and makes it an expression
of an individual opinion' (Jaeger 1947, 189). Protagoras' theology had a
remarkable influence on later thinkers; the title *On the Gods,* for the first
time attested in Protagoras, appears also in Speusippus, Xenocrates,
Theophrastus, Straton and Theodorus of Cyrene. It is probable that the
book was concerned with (a) proofs for and against the existence of gods
and (b) problems arising from the gods' outer form. As for (a), some
Protagorean arguments can be traced through Aristotle and Carneades;
as for (b), Cicero and Sextus Empiricus offer aporetic arguments about
anthropomorphism which may go back to Protagoras himself. In examining the question of the existence of gods, Protagoras must have taken
under consideration the following arguments: the *consensus humani gene-
ris* (general agreement); the cosmic order; the appearance of gods as
humans according to the tradition. It has been said that the religious
agnostic attitude of Protagoras is to be explained by his general feelings
toward certain and objective truth (see Gigon 1985).[1]

Prodicus, who is also remembered for his interest in etymology, is the
sophist whose theory seems to correspond better to the term 'natural
theology'. The theory says that the gods of folk theology do not exist but
that primitive man out of admiration deified the fruits of the earth and
virtually everything that supported his subsistence (Sprague 1972, 83). It
has been argued that Prodicus' originality is not limited to the identification of gods with nature's gifts but should be perceived as a twofold
epistemological rupture with previous conceptions: first, he ascribed to the
divinities human origins, not merely human characteristics, and, second,
he placed the deification process on the anthropological level and not on
the mythological-religious one (Henrichs 1984, 145); in this last regard, his
position is very close to Critias'. Heinrichs summarised Prodicus' position
as follows:

19. The Sophists and Natural Theology

In the beginning, there was nature and there was man. Soon primitive man came to realize that in order for him to survive he had to depend on nature. Therefore he stood in awe of those things on which he was most dependent, such as sun and moon, rivers and fruits of the earth, and what else he deemed vital for his continued existence. When the time had come for mankind to give everything its proper name, they agreed to refer to the various benefactions of nature which they admired as 'gods', and began to worship them. Gradually as human wit entered into competition with nature and human individuals distinguished themselves as inventors of new means of survival and as benefactors of mankind, this nomenclature was extended to include them too, so that they were likewise called 'gods', with their personal names like Demeter and Dionysos retained for individual identification, and they were worshipped as such (Henrichs 1975, 111).

Prodicus' theory met with striking success among the Athenian intelligentsia. A passage in Euripides' *Bacchae* (274-85, on Demeter and her gifts to humanity) proves his influence on the tragic poet. We see also traces of his theory in Aristophanes' *Clouds* (577, 611). It seems that Prodicus' natural theology influenced the Stoics and notably Persaeus, a pupil of Zeno and an active political figure before and around the middle of the third century BC. It has been suggested that Persaeus' views on theology were partly adopted by Chrysippus (c. 280-207 BC) (Pease 1968, 261). It is said that Prodicus' influence extended to Cleanthes (331-232 BC) as well (Jaeger 1947, 179). We perceive the extent of Prodicus' influence in the way Jewish and Christian writers continually urge against pagan gods the objection that the idols represent dead men and pagan temples are the tombs of the dead. This raises the real question whether the cult supposed by Prodicus was posthumous or already active during the life of the men/deities. Concerning the relation of Prodicus to Protagoras in *Suidas* (Sprague 1972, 71), there is a note that Prodicus was Protagoras' disciple. It is possible that Prodicus, by giving an anthropological explanation of the origins of religion, has prolonged the neutrality of the Protagorean position or even carried to extremes the sceptical or atheistic element in Protagoras' thought. On the other hand, if for Protagoras the question of the existence of gods is beyond the principle 'man the measure of all things', then Prodicus' theory which attributes the creation of deities to humans themselves is explicitly contrasted to that of Protagoras.

Themistius' inclusion of Gorgias in his group of atheists is surprising. A probable contribution of Gorgias to sophistic religious scepticism and to atheism in general is his aporetic stand on being which was also applied by the atheists to the actual being of gods, as we see in Plato's *Laws* X, 885b. Beyond that, there is not much we can tell about a 'natural theology' in Gorgias. Nevertheless, there is a passage where he offers a historical outline related to the divine and especially to incantations to the gods leading to the discovery of the positive and negative power of words. In this way, he moves from divinity to a *technê* or skill, that of rhetoric:

Sacred incantations sung with words are bearers of pleasure and banishers of pain, for, merging with opinion in the soul, the power of the incantation is wont to beguile it and persuade it and alter it by witchcraft. There have been discovered two arts of witchcraft and magic: one consists of errors of souls and the other of deceptions of opinion (Gorgias, *Helen* B 11(10); Sprague 1972, 52).

Gorgias' historical model gives an account of the fall from god-inspired use of language to a use that can induce error and deception. It is doubtful whether this fall was the subject of disapproval by the 'justificator of rhetorical deception' that Gorgias is said to be (it is probably for this reason that Themistius attributed to him the title 'naked head'); while for Prodicus, it is doubtful whether his description of the origins of religion is that of a fall. In any case, it seems that for Prodicus the constitution of language predated the creation of the gods.

Enlightenment?

When we refer to sophistic agnosticism, atheism or religious scepticism, we should wonder whether the univocal, transcultural reading of the name 'God' is legitimate. The question of natural theology in our Christian era goes back to Eusebius (AD 260-339) (*Preparation for the Gospel* 3,15,1) who claimed that 'the poets are making myths about gods and the philosophers are making natural theology', or to Augustine (AD 354-430) who stated (*City of God* 4,27) that the pagans distinguished three kinds of gods, 'one of the poets, another of the philosophers and another one of the statesmen'. In the *City of God* 6,5, Augustine quotes Varro (116-27 BC) for a threefold division of theology: 'mythical, mainly that of the poets; natural, that of the philosophers; and civil, that of the people'. The theology of the poets was, from as early as Xenophanes (*c.* 500-428 BC), contrasted with that of the philosophers, and later, with that of state religion (see Aëtius, *Opinions of the Philosophers* 1,6,9, reflecting Stoic views, perhaps of Posidonius). Natural theology is usually distinguished from revealed theology in the following way: natural theology is irrelevant to confirming or refuting the existence of gods, which is precisely Protagoras' stand; this aporetic position amounts to what is called theological non-naturalism. All *bona fide* statements of revealed theology have to make an appeal to natural theology; faith must venture into language since we cannot believe in something without our (fragmented and fragmenting) account of reality (see Matthews 1964). Another important distinction is the threefold partition of theology into folk theology or popular cult, intellectual theology of the religious scholars, and mystical theology that accomplishes the immediate access to the divine.

The sophists are often considered as the representatives of a first Enlightenment (Guthrie 1971, 48). In this regard, are we to suppose that their presumed atheism was a part of a movement against the Athenian *ancien régime*? In the case of Prodicus, if gods are people's invention, is natural theology a folk theology? What we probably see in Prodicus is a distinctive intellectualist trend: by explaining folk theology, he clearly distances himself from it. The relation of the divine to utility was an established characteristic of Greek culture,[2] and for this reason, it is hard to perceive Prodicus' theory of religion as the exclusive expression of a pragmatic utilitarianism which in turn would appear as the hallmark of sophistic enlightenment. It has been argued that Prodicus' theory led to worship practices such as the Isis aretalogies (epigraphical records of the goddess's deeds) in the Hellenistic period (first or second century AD) (see Henrichs 1984). If this hypothesis is exact, it would mean the transformation of an intellectualist stand into popular cult. The connection of rational attitudes to worship should not sound strange to our modern ears, if we remember the cult of reason in eighteenth-century France. Seers and prophets of classical Athens, such as Teiresias of the Euripidean drama *Bacchae*, have been recently referred to as 'theological sophists' for knowing that their magic had to 'make some concessions to rationalism': Plato's Euthyphro was a 'theological sophist' like Teiresias; Lampon, another theological sophist, was associated with the Thurii pan-Hellenic colony plan of Pericles, together with Protagoras (see Roth 1984). We should not perceive here some abdication from the spirit of sophistic 'Enlightenment', especially if we keep in mind the religious and mystical aspects of the often-called 'atheistic' Enlightenment of the eighteenth century.

The crucial element here is the problem of the Good. Xenophon (fourth to third centuries BC) states (*Memorabilia* IV.3.13-14) that Socrates did not discourage the search for God but merely advised men to infer the existence of God from his works rather than to wait, perhaps vainly, for a theophany. Aristotle strongly dissociated gods from practical virtues, but through the contemplative life (*theôria*) that he promoted and the felicity that *theôria* promised (*Nicomachean Ethics* X), he offered a genuine solution to the lack of practical virtues in gods. In Prodicus, gods possess practical virtues; in fact, for him, practical virtues make gods. The relation of utility to the divine, commonly admitted by the Greeks, found an echo in the sophists' interest in the practicalities of a successful social life, reflected also in the fact that their teachings were offered for money to the young sons of the wealthy and the noble. But why did Protagoras withdraw himself from turning the weaker theological argument into a stronger one, since this was not incompatible with rhetoric? His aporetic position shows that the sophistic philosophical stand is stronger than a mere expression of rhetorical skill. It is possible that sophistic religious boldness had to do with the widening of the generation gap in the Athenian upper class and the ambitions of strong young men entering the political scene at Athens (Ehrenberg 1968, 331-2). It is often said that the sophists inaugurated the sociological reading of religion. Can we conclude from this that the sophistic critique evicts the existential or intuitional factor? On a sociological level, the sophistic position was attached to the subjectivism of the noble young men taught or even patronised by the sophists. These young men had a critical attitude towards the traditional piety of their fathers; yet they were more consenting to the folk-theology or the religious mentality of the people that they were aiming to govern. The fact that the existence of God in Western thought is often confirmed or refuted by evidence derived from man's experience of the world (Hutchison 1958, 939) sounds very close to the sophists' theological subjectivism. Yet the individualistic element should be counterbalanced by another general trend. In order to achieve a fuller understanding of Prodicus' theology, we should not ignore the importance of language which gave humans the ability to name and thus to create gods (Henrichs, 1975, 111-12). The path that leads Greek thought from myth [*mythos*] to reason [*logos*] must be traced with greater distinction: the sophists do not make a science of religion but rather actualise in the present the effects of religion: explanatory impasse, social utility, rhetorical proliferation.

The sophists, language and the divine

A comparison of sophistic natural theology with the Stoic theory of natural religion may be useful here. The strong historical link between the two theories lies in the position held by Persaeus. This was very similar to that of Prodicus, but Persaeus was a political man and it is probable that his interest in sophistic natural theology had the same origins as that of the young noble Athenians. What the sophists have in common with the Stoics is empiricism and nominalism; yet the former could have subscribed neither to a dogmatism like that of the latter nor to a cosmological apology for deity. It is typical of the Stoics that when they refer to Critias' theory the adverse aspects of the heavenly phenomena (Sprague 1972, 260) are completely suppressed. For the sophists and in the limits of the distinction between convention [*nomos*] and nature [*physis*] religion lost its natural basis so that we cannot speak of a natural God as the Stoics did. In this sense, the natural theology of the sophists is a *theological non-naturalism* and the term 'natural theology' refers neither to a *physis*/nature as a sum of complex phenomena exterior to humans nor to some intrinsic essence of man, but more probably to certain enduring rules common to all men before the enactment of laws that varied from people to people. Speaking metaphorically, the natural law of sophistic natural theology is a common law. The sophists must also be distinguished from the Stoics on the level of expression, for the latter were applying an allegorical method[3] while the former favoured an etymological and historical approach.

This remark introduces us to the question of the relation between language and the divine in the sophists. Prodicus' theory is also a process of *naming* gods and in this respect it manifests the non-naturalism of speech. In recent times we have witnessed the creation of two schools regarding the study of sophistic thought: the 'Foundationalists' and the 'Anti-foundationalists'. The Foundationalists believe that there are certain basic principles of knowledge beyond mere opinion. For the Anti-foundationalists, all knowledge is an interpretation, implicated in the norms of an institutional community; applied to sophistic thought, Anti-foundationalism appears very close to sophistic rhetoric. In fact, the Anti-foundationalists tend to identify metaphysics or ontology with Foundationalism and rhetoric with Anti-foundationalism (Consigny 1996, 255). If the Anti-foundationalists' position is taken under consideration the questions to be asked comprise the following: does sophistic thought rely on a set of strong principles or are sophistic views relativistic accounts producing a kind of interpretative vertigo effect? Does sophistic discourse contribute to the impossibility of its own evaluation? In the case of religion, how principled or circumstantial is sophistic natural theology? In other words, is sophistic natural theology a coherent theory or a polemical stand?

It seems appropriate to refer here to Nietzsche, who at the end of the nineteenth century proclaimed the death of God. Nietzsche was extremely interested in sophistic thought and was focusing his attention almost exclusively on Protagoras and Gorgias. According to him, the sophists express the Greek fighting (agonistic) spirit, but the importance given to the polemic tone goes hand in hand with the sophistic assertion that there is no naturalness of language. All language is rhetorical figuration in view of an *agon* (conflict or dispute): in Protagoras it is the competitive *agon*; in Gorgias, the artistic *agon*. In this, the sophists follow the main characteristics of Greek religion. The Greek archaic conception of religion marks a difference between Greek polytheism and the other ancient polytheisms. Greek gods represent a general system wherein the force of one divinity is limited only by the force of another. The distinctions between sacred and profane and transcendence and immanence concerning gods do not account for Greek polytheism, which is focused on the notions of force, order and disorder and on anthropomorphic figuration.

The sophists, according to Nietzsche, regard rhetoric as universal in its application and at the same time 'possess the courage of all strong spirits, to know their own immorality'. However, they also make a critique of egoism because there is no permanence to the ego: sophistic immoralism is quite different and even contrary to selfishness (see Consigny 1994). Does this mean that in Protagoras' phenomenalism the affirmation 'phenomena are true' equals 'phenomena are good'. For Nietzsche, the sophists evict truth from morality and do not accept it as a good in itself. The question whether religious feeling is still personal and fundamental in Protagoras' phenomenalism, even if gods are human constructions, makes stronger the need for a theory that can fill the gap between sophistic relativism about the causes of the existence of deities and the sophistic subjectivism that supports such causes. The man-measure principle allows for some knowledge and a way to control the flux of experiences. The aporetic position concerning gods signifies the permanence of the tension between concept and phenomenalism in religion. Neither concepts nor phenomena are the property of religion or anti-religion but both can serve religious or anti-religious purposes. Plantiga (1999, 11-12) sees in Protagoras and his man-measure principle the source of one of the three major intellectual movements of philosophical credos, the 'critical antirealism' that later found a successor in Kant's criticism; the other two are 'perennial naturalism' and 'Christian philosophy'. Perennial naturalism refers to the eternity of natural objects; critical antirealism to the force of the subject; and Christian philosophy to a true humanism. If we leave the question of Christian philosophy aside, it seems that the sophists have contributed greatly not so much to the sceptical but to the subjectivist approach to the divine. There is nothing natural in sophistic 'natural' theology other than that the concept of the divine is a possibility of so-called human nature.

A brief note on Plato, the great detractor of sophists, is needed here: in the tenth Book of the *Laws,* to which we referred earlier, we notably perceive a first effort to prove the existence of God (Taylor 1934, 51). Plato's metaphysics is supported by the position that the philosopher could not or should not content himself with phenomenalism. Likewise, we should conceive his religious stand partly as an answer to the tension created by sophistic natural theology between religious scepticism and religious individualism; a tension which, for the sophists, finds an issue but not a solution on the level of language. In order to understand better the sophistic natural theology we should extend our thoughts beyond Platonic metaphysics and its impact on Christian theology.

Notes

1. Following Gigon, I will not refer to the Protagorean myth of Plato's *Protagoras* (320c-323a; Sprague 1972, 24-7), first because it is doubtful whether it is by him, and second because this narration is not properly theological but a myth about the origins of civilisation (*Kulturentstehungsmythos*, see Müller 1976, 312).

2. See Aeschylus, *Prometheus Bound* 613; Polybius, *The Histories* 34,2,8; Aëtius, *Opinions of the Philosophers* 1,6,2.

3. Kahn (1997, 261) speaks of a later allegorical use of the sophistic natural theology by the Stoics.

Bibliography

Consigny, Scott, 'Nietzsche's Reading of the Sophists', *Rhetoric Review* 13/1 (1994), 5-26.

Consigny, Scott, 'Edward Schiappa's Reading of the Sophists', *Rhetoric Review* 14/2 (1996), 253-69.

19. The Sophists and Natural Theology

Derenne, E., *Les procès d'impiété intentés aux philosophes à Athènes au Ve et au IVe siècles avant J.-C.* (Paris-Liège: Vaillant Carmanne, 1930).

Ehrenberg, V., *From Solon to Socrates* (London: Methuen, 1968).

Gigon, Olof, 'Il libro "sugli dei" di Protagora', *Rivista di Storia della Filosofia* 40/3 (1985), 419-48.

Guthrie, W.K.C., *The Sophists* (Cambridge: Cambridge University Press, 1971).

Henrichs, Albert, 'Two Doxographical Notes: Democritus and Prodicus on Religion', *Harvard Studies in Classical Philology* 79 (1975), 93-123.

Henrichs, Albert, 'The Sophists and Hellenistic Religion: Prodicus as the Spiritual Father of the ISIS Aretalogies', *Harvard Studies in Classical Philology* 88 (1984), 139-58.

Hutchison, John, 'The Uses of Natural Theology. An Essay in Redefinition', *Journal of Philosophy* 55/22 (1958), 936-44.

Jaeger, W., *Theology of the Early Greek Philosophers* (Oxford: Oxford University Press, 1947).

Kahn, Charles H., 'Greek Religion and Philosophy in the Sisyphus Fragment', *Phronesis* 42/3 (1997), 247-62.

Matthews, Gareth B., 'Theology and Natural Theology', *Journal of Philosophy* 61/3 (1964), 99-108.

Müller, Carl Werner, 'Protagoras über die Götter', in Carl Joachim Classen (ed.), *Sophistik* (Darmstadt: Wissenschaftliche Buchgesellschaft, 1976), 312-40.

Pease, A.S. (ed.), *Cicero, De Natura deorum* (Darmstadt: Wissenschaftliche Buchgesellschaft, 1968).

Plantiga, Alvin, 'Augustinian Christian Philosophy', in G.B. Matthews (ed.), *The Augustinian Tradition* (Berkeley, Los Angeles, London: University of California Press, 1999), 1-26.

Roth, Paul, 'Teiresias as Mantis and Intellectual in Euripides' *Bacchae*', *Transactions of the American Philological Association* 114 (1984) 59-69.

Sprague, Rosamond Kent (ed.), *The Older Sophists*, a complete translation by several hands of the fragments in *Die Fragmente der Vorsokratiker* edited by Diels-Kranz with a new edition of Antiphon and Euthydemus (Columbia: University of South Carolina Press, 1972).

Taylor, A.E., *The Laws of Plato* (London: Dent, 1934).

Can Virtue Be Taught?

Glenn Rawson

One of Plato's liveliest Socratic dialogues, the *Protagoras*, stages a debate between the greatest philosopher and the greatest sophist of their time, with other leading sophists in the audience. The debate concerns Protagoras' own specialty: the teaching of 'virtue' or *aretê*, a crucial term in ancient Greece that involves both moral goodness and human greatness. Protagoras and Socrates end up with oddly overlapping intellectual positions: Socrates contends that virtue is not something that's taught, though he believes that all of virtue is essentially a kind of knowledge. Protagoras denies that all virtues are forms of knowledge, though he maintains that they are in fact commonly taught, and taught especially well by himself. This historical fiction was composed some forty or fifty years after its dramatic setting, but its colourful and inconclusive portraits are probably roughly correct. (Most scholars consider Protagoras' main speech there a paraphrase or imitation of his original writings, which have not survived.) These men were debating in new ways what was already an ancient theme. But since sophists won their fame and wealth through public speeches and private courses on matters social and ethical, and since these new professionals were often suspected as charlatans, old questions about virtue and teaching were a persistent element in the sophists' environment.

The sophists and Socrates gave new life to such traditional subjects with their especially intellectual approaches. Their innovative verbal arts included the beginnings of grammar, rhetoric and logic, and though the sophists were not generally interested in Socrates' attempts to *define* virtues, the best of them used their new kinds of speeches and reasoning to explain and advocate traditional virtues in a spirit of reform and progress. In spite of some important disagreements, Socrates and the major sophists were all elaborating traditional Greek themes about human nature and society, justice and happiness. Broadly they agreed that successful communities and lives require civic virtues like justice and moderation; that cultivating those virtues requires some kind of moral education; and that moral education requires natural talents and practical training in addition to verbal instruction. Their own contributions concerning virtue were basically intellectual and theoretical, no matter how much their theories might emphasise the role of practical training. The same is true of later philosophers such as Plato and Aristotle, who were after all much influenced by these sophists.

Ancient ideals of virtue and justice

When Socrates asks Protagoras what he offers prospective students, Protagoras replies that he can make them better each day, and better not in some technical skill or specialised subject but in a quite general human virtue:

> my subject is good judgment [*euboulia*]: in private matters, so he may best manage his own household, and in public matters, so he may be most capable in the city's affairs, both in action and in speech (*Protagoras* 318e-19a).

This bold promise of success in human activity generally, of private and public excellence in word and deed, is Protagoras' professional formulation of the traditional ideal of *aretê*. Ever since the earliest Greek literature, *aretê* is a central ideal and basic motivator, embracing goodness and greatness, as an excellent human being and as an outstanding member of a human community. Protagoras calls his version the art of the citizen (319a), political virtue (322e, 324a), and man's virtue (325a). His promise about being 'most capable in the city's affairs, both in action and in speech' attracts the ambitions of wealthy young men to win power and honour in Greek politics, with effective public speaking in law courts and assemblies. It is the fifth-century political descendent of the *aretê* pursued so memorably by the epic heroes – such as Achilles and Odysseus in Homer's *Iliad* and *Odyssey* – who were literally cult figures in their hometowns as well as cultural icons throughout Greece. Homer was composing three centuries before Protagoras, working his poetic art and moral vision on stories that were much older still. His heroes strive for greatness, and constantly compete for honour, not only in the deeds of war and sport but also in persuasive and appropriate speech. Odysseus was especially recognised for his speaking abilities, and even the greatest warrior Achilles, who was enjoined by his father

> always be excellent, and be superior to others (*Iliad* XI.784)

was trained for that purpose by his personal mentor Phoenix

> to be a speaker of words and a doer of deeds (*Iliad* IX.443).

These slogans express an ideal of aristocratic education in the centuries leading to our sophists: to win honour and power through *aretê*, the manly virtues of courage, strength and skill, both in action and in speech. Such competitive virtues were thought to constitute greatness in a man, the way that beauty and fidelity were the virtues of his wife, speed the virtue of his horses, and fertility the virtue of his land.

But sophists also drew from another deep current in Greek culture, which prized modest good sense or self-restraint (*sôphrosunê*) and justice (*dikaiosunê*). Hesiod, who was second only to Homer in antiquity and authority, made justice and humble hard work the theme of his *Works and Days*. He describes a former Golden Age without competition for honour or any other kind of strife; for his own bleak times, he values only that competition which inspires honest toil to earn a good living. His *Theogony* ranks Justice (*Dikê*) as a goddess, daughter of Zeus and divine Right Rule (*Themis*). In Hesiod's vision, Zeus rewards justice with peace and prosperity, and justice even distinguishes humans from mere animals (*Works and Days* 274ff.):

> Dear Perses, take this to your heart:
> listen to justice and forget all violence.
> That's the lawful way of life that Zeus assigned for men.
> Fish and beasts and birds of the air may eat
> each other; among them is no justice.
> But humans he gave justice, which proves to be much better.

Homer's honour-loving heroes do not identify justice and self-restraint as part of their virtue or *aretê*; but on the whole Homer shares Hesiod's love of these more cooperative virtues. While the *Iliad* and *Odyssey* worked their ethical legacy largely through glorious episodes of honour-seeking competition, their plots as wholes celebrate something different: Achilles' friendship with Patroclus and his return to civilised compassion, Odysseus' enduring heart of reverence and the harmony of spirit he shares with his wife. Homer even agrees that justice suits human nature: when Achilles predicts his great outrages against Hector, he calls himself a lion and a wolf rather than a man (XXII.250-67, 337-54); and Odysseus' brutish enemy the Cyclops is less than human because he lacks law and justice (*themis*, IX.105-15).

The combination of these two ideals, harmonious justice and competitive manly *aretê*, shaped Greek ethics and politics for centuries. Generations of poets and philosophers gradually internalised both *aretê* and justice as matters of mind and character (*psychê*), rather than merely of actions and material goods. And they gradually incorporated civic virtues like moderation and justice as part of human virtue or *aretê* itself. Most sophists agreed, joining the tradition of the legendary Seven Sages, the Delphic oracle, and many works of Greek theatre and history, which constantly warn that wrongheaded pursuit of *aretê* leads to *hubris* – the boundary-breaking arrogance and violence that is the opposite of moderation and justice.

Learning virtue: teaching, training, and nature

Such constant exhortations to virtue testify to the difficulty of properly learning it, and here too the sophists add their voices to an ancient chorus. Even the earliest poetry, as it explores and celebrates human virtue, acknowledges the necessity and the limits of moral education. In the *Iliad*, when Phoenix reminds Achilles of his training in good words and deeds, he is trying to persuade Achilles back to a more honourable, less destructive path – but Achilles doesn't listen. The *Odyssey* foregrounds the late education of Odysseus' son, whose good nature deplores the *hubris* of his mother's suitors, but fails to produce good leadership in the absence of a good role model. And Hesiod's teachings in the *Works and Days* are framed as corrective lessons to his brother, who has fallen to the point of stealing Hesiod's inheritance after wasting his own. Hesiod implores (293ff.):

> Best is the man who sees all for himself,
> perceiving what's better in the future and in the end.
> And good is the man who listens to good advice.
> But he who neither sees for himself nor takes to heart
> what he hears from another – that is a useless man.
> So you, Perses, *born* of good blood, remember what I *tell* you,
> and *work*!

Centuries later, the sophists' educational theories face the same challenge of combining verbal teaching with natural abilities and personal effort – but in a different kind of social environment.

In the generations after Homer and Hesiod, the somewhat feudal aristocracies developed into sophisticated governments with civic centres and citizens' rights. A kind of people's assembly was typical even in the aristocratic 'dark ages,' convened at the nobles' discretion to serve their own agenda. But as populations and economies grew, assemblies grew in size and influence. Groups that had been subjects of the traditional noble families earned increasing shares of political power. Laws were written down for public view, and participation in real decision-making spread out from the nobles to other landholders and to those who earned through trade and industry. Some of these independent city-states became democracies – most notably Athens, where elections and lotteries and pay for public service effectively extended political rights to even the poorest citizens (but not to slaves or women). Any male citizen in Athens could serve as councillor and magistrate and judge, and formally address the whole assembly. Other city-states, with broad or narrow oligarchies, had greater restrictions on citizenship and citizens' rights, but often with corresponding kinds of assemblies and courts requiring effective public speaking. This is the social and political background to the professional success of the sophists in teaching their verbal arts. While old aristocratic families still often dominated politics (and athletics and priesthoods and social prestige generally), now their traditions of winning honour for *aretê* were pursued largely through political debate, in arguments about justice and good sense no less than in speeches about competitive greatness. Many now paid sophists to teach them how to do it effectively. In principle that success would be taught to anyone who could afford the classes.

So in part, debates about whether *virtue* can be *taught* were implicitly debates about whether the upper classes should have to share political power with lower classes. Some denied that virtue was the sort of thing that could be taught as sophists taught things: to anyone who can pay their fees and succeed in their courses. Even before such travelling teachers existed, great poets spoke for the waning aristocracies, lamenting the diffusion of traditional privileges among *nouveaux riches*. When Theognis famously pronounced that

> teaching will never make a base man noble (437-8)

these loaded terms refer at once to moral qualities and social class. And Pindar, just before the age of the sophists, proclaimed (*Ninth Olympian Ode* 100-3):

> What comes by nature is always best.
> But many strive for fame with virtues merely taught.

He too is supporting the aristocratic notion that real virtue comes through 'nature' by being born into the right families. These poets also praise teaching in the sense of personal mentoring and training within the privileged group (Theognis 33-6, 69-72; Pindar, *Tenth Olympian* 16-21). But they emphasise inherited nature to preserve that distinction over others who have won political and social concessions. By contrast, sophists' claims to teach all customers were seen as continuing the process that undermined the old order. It's no accident that they were most successful at Athens, in the thoroughly political atmosphere of the radical democracy recently established there.

However, if this new profession of teaching political skill was in principle progressive, the sophists' expensive courses were in effect exclusive, full of the sons of the very wealthy. So in addition to the elitist resistance from traditionalists about aristocratic personal mentorship, there was popular resentment for perpetuating class privilege by teaching rich boys to manipulate crowds with fancy talk. To top it off, other intellectuals like Socrates offered their own versions of both kinds of criticisms. So their undeniable commercial success and cultural influence was attended by disapproval and fear. Underlying it all was a common concern for the overwhelming importance of justice and the other virtues about which the sophists spoke so powerfully. The social upheavals of the Peloponnesian

War highlighted the vulnerability of civic virtues, and if the sophists' exclusive clientele suggested a lack of real seriousness about justice, their intellectual focus suggested disdain for what matters more: training from an early age to be a man of good character. But we shall see that various leading sophists show genuine interest in (1) advancing that moral training through their public addresses and private seminars, and (2) exploring all the elements of moral education that were implicit since Homer and Hesiod: inherited nature (*physis*), personal effort and practical training (*meletê, askêsis*), and verbal teaching (*didachê*).

Four sophists on the teaching and learning of virtue

Many classical authors concerned themselves with moral education, including playwrights, historians, statesmen and philosophers beyond those we call sophists, but most were somehow influenced by sophists. Specific debate about whether virtue can be taught is most explicit in just two sources: the schematic summaries in the anonymous *Dissoi Logoi*, and the more philosophical representations in Plato's *Protagoras* together with parts of his *Meno*. But the teachings of many of the sophists implicated and affected the teaching of virtue. Here I survey the relevant remains of four leading sophists. Protagoras was first and most important, but their careers overlapped and interacted. Since Protagoras' influence on later philosophers is clearest, I discuss Protagoras last. (I use evidence from Plato broadly and cautiously, and especially when it resonates other sources.)

Gorgias allegedly called himself an orator but not a sophist (a point highlighted in Plato's *Gorgias* but ignored in other dialogues). He claims to make men powerful speakers while denying that he teaches them virtue (*Meno* 95c). Yet Gorgias spoke powerfully *about* virtue in public gatherings throughout Greece, and his professional displays included answering questions about any subject whatever (*Gorgias* 447c-8a, *Meno*, 70b-c). He taught the same young men who studied virtue with other sophists. So his denial of teaching virtue may have been occasional and strategic, perhaps a marketing ploy against his commercial rivals. In Plato's *Gorgias*, when Socrates presses the point that Gorgias teaches men to be persuasive about justice and injustice, Gorgias concedes that he will teach them what justice is if they don't already know, though he shouldn't be held responsible for their speeches and actions (456c-60d).

But the real Gorgias may have believed that in a sense virtue cannot be taught at all. One of his compositions argued (if partly in fun) that nothing really exists, and if something did exist we couldn't know it, and if we could know it we couldn't communicate it. About virtue in particular, he would 'define' it only by enumeration, with different kinds of qualities for different kinds of people (Aristotle, *Politics* 1260a14-28; Plato, *Meno* 71cff.). So he probably believed that there is no essential truth about virtue to be learned as a matter of theory, but he may have believed that students become virtuous through the *practice* of making good speeches about noble ideals. That was the professional theory of his influential student Isocrates, and a memorial statue at Olympia claimed that 'no man yet has found a fairer art than Gorgias, to train the soul for contests of virtue'. Although Aristotle reports that Gorgias' students learned by memorising and imitating his speeches, the few models that survive are not exhortations to virtue.

Gorgias seems to have developed a theory that persuasive speaking effects its power independently of truth. He aimed at a new art of prose that works like poetry, moving its audience with quasi-metrical rhythm and balance, striking metaphors, and rhyme. In this connection, he noted that tragedy (important public poetry in Greek life) produces a kind of deception 'in which the deceiver is more just than the nondeceiver, and the deceived is wiser than the nondeceived' (Plutarch, *On the Fame of the Athenians* 5). Was he thinking only of aesthetic suspension of disbelief, or also of possible moral effects? His *Encomium of Helen* 'demonstrated' playfully that since we live by opinion rather than knowledge, speech persuades with another form of the same power exercised by physical compulsion. In any case, Gorgias was loosely 'teaching virtue' whether he admitted it or not – in the tradition of helping young men win honour from their peers and others. That was the allure of his promise to make them powerful speakers.

Hippias, in the next generation, pursued a career like that of Gorgias: while travelling as ambassador throughout Greece, he gave private classes and public displays with open question-and-answer sessions, using the kind of florid style that Gorgias introduced. But Hippias also went further. He attempted expertise in all arts, theoretical and practical. If Gorgias tried to be persuasive about all kinds of subjects without having to understand them, Hippias tried to learn all things through wide-ranging study and personal experience. Plato portrays him as boastful and over-confident, but even so his curiosity and talents must have been remarkable. He performed at public festivals in clothes and shoes and jewellery made by himself, and he taught mathematics, astronomy, music, poetry, history and genealogy. Among it all, he gave special attention to virtue, trying to encourage noble pursuits through inspiring literature. In addition to writing his own tragedies (Plato, *Hippias Minor* 368c-d), Hippias delivered speeches on ethical themes in traditional poetry. For example, he argued that Homer makes Achilles a much better man than Odysseus, and he added an episode to the Trojan saga in which Nestor teaches the orphaned son of Achilles about honourable activities and noble customs. We don't know how good his stories were, as no ancient sources preserve or discuss them in any detail.

Hippias was among the first to teach a broad antithesis between the claims of nature (*physis*) and those of custom or law (*nomos*) – and here he contributes to a momentous development in ethical debates. Earlier literature mentions divine and unwritten laws that have priority over human conventions, but Hippias alleged some kind of general opposition between conventional and natural laws. This kind of antithesis would later be used in various ways, sometimes even serving crass hedonistic egoism, as with Callicles in Plato's *Gorgias*. But Hippias represents the more humane general trend among sophists, privileging nature over convention to promote unity among men (at least among intelligent men) and to advocate harmonious reconciliation. That is the spirit in which he offers to mediate between Socrates and Protagoras in Plato's *Protagoras* (337d-e). Hippias' belief in the justice of universal, unwritten laws is reported by Xenophon too (*Memorabilia* IV.4). His ideal of a natural kinship, immune to artificial social boundaries, suggests that his stories about virtuous practices were intended as lessons for everyone everywhere.

Prodicus is often cited for his attention to fine distinctions among related terms. Plato parodies him with a speech distinguishing four pairs of ethical terms in just a few sentences (*Protagoras* 337a-c), and suggests that his attraction to fine distinctions misses the point of some ethical discussions (341e-42a, 358d-e). Yet Plato knew the importance of speaking precisely about virtues and vices, and there is something positive in his suggestion that some who aren't prepared for Socrates' exercises in definition should first study with Prodicus (*Theaeteus* 151b). The great historian Thucydides, who denounced the opportunistic perversion of ethical terms during the Peloponnesian War, was thought to have learned something from Prodicus (Marcellinus, *Life of Thucydides* 36; see Sprague, 74).

Prodicus had a striking theory about the origin of religion, in which humans first worshipped the parts of nature that were useful in their struggle to survive. Some considered this atheistic and corrupting, but Prodicus shows his support for social virtues in his rhetorical display on 'The Choice of Hercules'. He invented this tale, in which Virtue and Vice compete for the attention of the young Hercules with opposed speeches advocating different paths of life: one of easy selfish pleasure and apparent beauty; the other of hard work and generous service that eventually leads to genuine friendship, honour and satisfaction. The rhetorically polished original is lost, but the rough paraphrase recorded by Xenophon (*Memorabilia* II.1) is enough to glimpse a heavy-handed lesson for impressionable young minds. The theme of the 'Choice', and the focus upon struggle and survival in the theory of religion, follow the path of Hesiod's *Works and Days*, emphasising above all the role of hard work in achieving virtue. *Protagoras* (339e-42a) associates Prodicus with poetry by Simonides (*c.* 556-*c.* 468) about how hard it is to become good. That is the main point delivered by his Virtue personified, though she begins by noting Hercules' inherited good nature and she also mentions the need for expert teachers. The speech of Virtue itself, like the whole 'Choice of Hercules' debate, has *its* role in moral education as verbal instruction: encouraging precepts and reasons in favour of taking the more difficult path.

Protagoras. We have detected, in the remains of three major sophists, various explorations of teaching, training and nature in moral education. Now we are prepared to appreciate the work of Protagoras, which influenced all the others. Few direct quotations survive from this versatile intellectual pathfinder. He is now most famous for two striking claims:

> Man is the measure of all things: the being of what is and the nonbeing of what is not[1] (Fragment 1; see Plato, *Theaetetus* 152a, *Cratylus* 385e; Waterfield 2000, 213).

> Concerning the gods I cannot know that they exist or that they do not exist, or what form they might have. Much prevents knowing it: its obscurity, and the shortness of human life (Fragment 4; Diogenes Laertius IX.52; Dillon and Gergel 2003, 21).

But more to the point of our survey, he argued in a *Great Speech* that

> teaching requires natural talent and practice ... one must start learning young (Fragment 3; Waterfield 2000, 219).

Since the original contexts of all these lines are lost, we confront an apparent conflict: general scepticism and relativism about gods and 'all things' versus a practical realism about good education. But some scholars argue that the 'man-measure doctrine' need not imply a radical form of relativism; it could be about a kind of relative judgments that is compatible with a substantial measure of realism in science and education. (See for example the treatments by Kerferd and Woodruff.) In any case, our survey must include the debate in Plato's *Protagoras*, where Protagoras argues that real virtue is taught and learned by everyone throughout life – an argument that beautifully elaborates the quotation from the *Great Speech*.[2] That argument includes a defence of democratic assemblies, which suits Protagoras' association with the great Athenian democrat Pericles, and the fact that he wrote the laws for the democratic, pan-Hellenic settlement of Thurii. So I accept the main speech in the *Protagoras* as reconstructing Protagoras' own views, and ignore here the less reliable evidence in Plato's *Theaetetus,* which is our earliest source for the relativism of Fragment 1 above. Anyone interested in classical debates about teaching virtue must study the *Protagoras* (especially 316b-328c).

In that dialogue, when Protagoras promises to make his students good men and good citizens, Socrates explains why he doubts that virtue is taught. He cites two widely experienced facts with powerful implications:

(1) the Athenian assembly allows *anyone* to give advice on good politics and civic virtue – though it requires special qualifications for advisers on teachable technical matters, and (2) many citizens who are widely considered virtuous fail to teach their children virtue – though they do have them taught many things that are less important but clearly teachable. To Socrates these facts indicate both that virtue is not taught and that no one believes it can be taught. Protagoras disputes both inferences, explaining that (1) the Athenian system actually assumes that every adult does possess a substantial measure of virtue, since the whole city has been *teaching* and *training* them in virtue since childhood, and that (2) the sons of virtuous men sometimes turn out to be relatively vicious, though never completely vicious, because differences throughout society in *natural talents* affect how well each individual learns the virtue that the whole society teaches.

Protagoras' speech is a rich combination of story and argument, building on traditional mythology and full of suggestive ideas about the origins and basic machinery of civilisation. According to Protagoras, that machinery includes much in the way of moral education. He details a broad range of civic education that sustains justice (*dikaiosunê*) and respect (*aidôs*) and modest self-restraint (*sôphrosunê*). This lifelong education takes place in word and deed (325d), including all manner of 'practice and training and teaching' (323d), from children's stories to higher education, and from correction of children to punishment of criminals. It involves character formation through music, exercise, and imitation of good heroes along with explicit verbal instruction. All of this renders *specialist* teachers of virtue unnecessary, and it shows that 'people do not believe that virtue is just natural (*phusei*) or spontaneous, but that it is taught (*didakton*), and comes to those who get it through practice (*epimeleia*)' (323c-d). Nonetheless, Protagoras recommends his own special brand of teaching as a rare opportunity to continue our education in virtue to greater heights – just as those who already speak Greek well should welcome a chance to perfect it (327e-28a). Many people were suspicious of such claims, and of the sophists' new verbal arts and general intellectualism. But here and in his *Great Speech*, Protagoras' verbal instruction is informed by thorough awareness of its dependence on broad practical training in the formation of good character.

The speech in the *Protagoras* also incorporates reflection on human nature, explaining civic virtue as a kind of second nature for human beings. Elaborating on the traditional tale of Prometheus stealing fire from the gods, Protagoras explains that the fire represents technical skills, which he associates with language and toolmaking. These correspond to other animals' wings and claws and hides. Protagoras' story adds that when Zeus saw these humans trying to live together but destroying each other, he sent them justice and respect, so they could have peace and friendship. Unlike Prometheus' technical skills, justice and respect were distributed in some measure to all humans, since living together depends on it. While its cultivation requires teaching and training, it is more basic and universal than the variable customs of different societies. 'It is necessary that each have some share in justice, or not be among human beings' (323b-c). So Protagoras, like Socrates, rejects the aristocratic notion that only certain families have a proper capacity for virtue. Differences in natural ability at *all* levels of society are what explains why children of prominent citizens often turn out useless or bad. But all normal humans are born with a natural capacity for justice, and everyone raised in civilisation develops at least some measure of it (327c-e).

The legacy of the sophists on the teaching of virtue

So we discard the old prejudice that sophists were all radical relativists or amoral opportunists. The best sophists were contributing much to early philosophy, and helped shape the ethical philosophies of Socrates, Plato and Aristotle.

When Plato has Socrates praise Protagoras' speech, it isn't just sarcasm; he doesn't dispute any of its main points as they continue the debate. Apparently Socrates' famous '*technê*-analogy,' comparing and contrasting virtues with the knowledge embodied in technical skills, was already practised by Protagoras (321d, 322b-d). Though Protagoras rejects Socrates' particular brand of ethical intellectualism – that virtue is essentially knowledge, such that knowing what's right entails doing it – both of their approaches express the confidence in progress through reasoning that characterised the work of all the early sophists.

The new kinds of theory in Plato's *Republic* go much beyond the reasonings of Socrates or any of the sophists. But there was an ancient rumour that most of Plato's *Republic* was already contained in a work by Protagoras (Diogenes Laertius III.37, 57). However that unlikely notion came about, Plato himself suggests Protagorean influence by incorporating the elementary education he had already attributed to Protagoras: organising the child's daily life as a constant lesson in virtue, moulding character through imitation, play and punishment, and the rhythms of good music and exercise. In Plato's thinking, these measures prepare youths for complete virtue by forming well-ordered minds that can recognise the transcendent source of good order itself.

When Aristotle rejects the transcendent orientation of Platonic higher education, he maintains the emphasis on early habituation to good character. His masterfully detailed theory of virtues retains a roughly Protagorean shape: (1) we are born with a natural capacity for virtue – and for vice, though human nature and society really require the virtue; (2) virtues of character are instilled by practical training, involving imitation, punishments and rewards; (3) this training is completed through intellectual teaching and study. Aristotle's intellectual virtue of 'practical wisdom' (*phronêsis*) is much like Protagoras' 'good judgment' (*euboulia*) three generations back: a general skill in public and private words and deeds, which is necessary for flourishing in a civilised society, and which completes the ordinary course of education in virtue.

Notes

1. *pantôn chrêmatôn metron estin anthrôpos, tôn men ontôn hôs estin, tôn de ouk ontôn hôs ouk estin.* 'Man is the measure' is the standard translation. I prefer 'the human being is the measure', which better preserves an ambiguity in *metron estin anthropos*: does he mean each individual human, or humans collectively?

2. Compare also Fragment 11: 'Education doesn't sprout in the soul if one doesn't go very deep.'

Bibliography

Aristotle, *The Politics*, trans. T.A. Sinclair, revised T.J. Saunders (Harmondsworth: Penguin, 1981).

Dillon, John and Gergel, Tania, *The Greek Sophists* (Harmondsworth: Penguin, 2003).

Diogenes Laertius, *Lives of Eminent Philosophers*, trans. R.D. Hicks, Loeb edition (London: Heinemann, 1925).

Gagarin, Michael and Woodruff, Paul, *Early Greek Political Thought from Homer to the Sophists* (Cambridge: Cambridge University Press, 1995).

Guthrie, W.K.C., *The Sophists* (Cambridge: Cambridge University Press, 1971).

Hesiod, *Theogony* and *Works and Days*, trans. M.L. West (Oxford: Oxford University Press, 1988).

Homer, *The Iliad*, trans. Richmond Lattimore (Chicago: University of Chicago Press, 1951).

Homer, *The Odyssey*, trans. Richmond Lattimore (New York: Harper Perennial Classics, 1999).

Jaeger, Werner, *Paideia*, trans. Gilbert Highet (Oxford: Oxford University Press, 1939-45).

Kahn, Charles H., 'Pre-Platonic Ethics', in Stephen Everson (ed.), *Companions to Ancient Thought* 4: *Ethics* (Cambridge: Cambridge University Press, 1998).

Kerferd, G.B., *The Sophistic Movement* (Cambridge: Cambridge University Press, 1981).

Plato, *Complete Works*, ed. John M. Cooper (Indianapolis: Hackett, 1997).

Plutarch, *Moralia*, vol. IV, trans. F.C. Babbit, Loeb edition (London: Heinemann, 1936).

Shorey, Paul, 'Phusis, Meletê, Epistêmê', *Transactions of the American Philological Association* 40 (1909), 185-201.

Sprague, R.K. (ed.), *The Older Sophists* (Indianapolis: Hackett, 2001).

Waterfield, Robin, *The First Philosophers: The Presocratics and the Sophists* (Oxford: Oxford University Press, 2000).

Woodruff, Paul, 'Rhetoric and Relativism: Protagoras and Gorgias', in A.A. Long (ed.), *The Cambridge Companion to Early Greek Philosophy* (Cambridge: Cambridge University Press, 1999).

Xenophon, *Memorabilia, Oeconomicus, Symposium, Apology*, trans. E.C. Marchant and O.J. Todd, Loeb edition (London: Heinemann, 1923).

The Case against Teaching Virtue for Pay

Geoff Bowe

One point that scholars unfailingly make in talking about the sophists is that they took pay for instruction.[1] Plato himself refers to the earnings of the sophists no less than thirty-one times (Harrison 1964, 191n.44). Xenophon and Aristotle also make frequent reference to the fact that the sophists take pay. At his trial and elsewhere in Plato and Xenophon, it is emphasised that Socrates did not, and it would seem that the practice of taking pay for teaching is regarded with a disdain meant to separate Socrates from the sophists. This is significant, for one may well question precisely how Socrates differs from the sophists, especially when we recall that both the sophists and Socrates are interested in questions of virtue, both have youthful followers, and that Socrates was tried and executed on charges that certainly associated him with the practice of sophistry.

Is there anything more to sophistry than merely teaching for pay? Long ago the utilitarian philosopher Henry Sidgwick asked of the sophists most familiar to us from Plato:

> What is the common characteristic of these persons, as presented by Plato? – besides that of receiving pay, which must surely be considered an accident rather than a property of any class of teachers (Sidgwick 1872, 294).

Despite the obvious motivation of people like Plato and Xenophon to establish a distinction between Socrates and the sophists, the question remains: 'what, *philosophically*, is wrong with the practice of teaching for pay?'

In this chapter I will focus on several factors that have contributed to the pejorative light that has been cast upon the sophists' practice of teaching for pay. These factors include certain cultural and contextual prejudices regarding wage earning and citizenship, as well as moralistic arguments that levy the charge of charlatanism against the sophists. This charge of charlatanism relies heavily on the claim that the sophists attempt to teach something that cannot be taught, namely virtue, but it is important to see why and in what context virtue is thought not to be teachable in the manner of the sophists; this context ultimately amounts to the philosophical systems of Plato and Aristotle, whereby virtue is seen as something natural and objective (a *physis*) and hence outside the purview of relativistic sophistry wherein virtue ought to be conceived as something artificial and subjective (a *nomos*). My suggestion is that something natural needs to be acquired organically and over a long period of time, whereas something artificial might be constructed and conveyed much more easily. If the sophist sees virtue as artificial, he also sees it as freely and quickly distributable for a fee. Finally, I want to suggest that there is a deeper philosophical argument that suggests, in a way that is consistent if not commensurate with the foregoing considerations, predilections and prejudices, that forced attempts to supply rhetorical skills to those not naturally disposed to virtue, is seen by Plato and Isocrates to have monstrous results, results that harm both pupil and sophistic teacher alike. The sophist who must sacrifice his freedom by accepting whoever pays the fee also sacrifices his soul.

Culture, context and citizenship

Some scholars have suggested that the invidious remarks about teaching for pay do not represent a successful critique of the sophists (see Corey 2002). While such defences may serve to exculpate teaching for pay in some contexts, I think that they do not adequately address the philosophical opposition to the practice of sophistry in the ancient Greek context. One of the things that I have in mind here is Xenophon's report of Socrates' claim that teaching for pay imposed upon one's freedom:

> Nor again, did [Socrates] encourage love of money in his companions. For while he checked their other desires, he would not make money himself out of their desire for his companionship. He held that this self-denying ordinance insured his liberty. Those who charged a fee for their society he denounced for selling themselves into bondage; since they were bound to converse with all from whom they took the fee. He marvelled that anyone should make money by the profession of virtue, and should not reflect that his highest reward would be the gain of a good friend (Xenophon, *Memorabilia* I.2.5-7).

What I take to be the philosophical import of the sophists 'selling themselves into bondage' will be the focus of the last part of this chapter, but initially, and in order to make sense of the contextual implications of this remark, some background work is necessary. We may begin with a passage that overlaps to some degree with the one just quoted. In what follows Xenophon tells of Socrates' rejoinder to the sophist Antiphon's scoffing criticism that Socrates does not take pay. Socrates' response bears out several relevant cultural attitudes:

> Antiphon, it is common opinion among us in regard to beauty and wisdom that there is an honourable and a shameful way of bestowing them. For to offer one's beauty for money to all comers is called prostitution; but we think

it virtuous to become friendly with a lover who is known to be a man of honour. So is it with wisdom. Those who offer it to all comers for money are known as sophists, prostitutors of wisdom, but we think that he who makes a friend of one whom he knows to be gifted by nature, and teaches him all the good he can, fulfils the duty of a citizen and a gentleman ... (*Memorabilia* I.6.13).

It is important to remember that Athenians of the late fifth and early fourth centuries did carry a prejudice against wage-earning in general, and as such the sophist would immediately be regarded with some disdain as a wage-earner. The words of Gomperz are appropriate here:

The Greek view of life was at times aristocratic. Their respect for wage-earning stood even lower than in other slave-owning communities ... An especial reproach attached to the employment of intellectual labour for the benefit of someone who paid for it; this was regarded as degradation, as a yoke of servitude that was voluntarily assumed (Gomperz 1901, 417).

Now it is quite likely that Gomperz's observation regarding 'a yoke of servitude that was voluntarily assumed' finds its impetus in the very evidence that Xenophon here and elsewhere provides us with, that Socrates criticised the sophists as selling their freedom much like a prostitute. This however has the ring of sneer more than philosophical argument. What I want to suggest later is that there is a deeper implicit philosophical orientation and rationale at work in Xenophon's observations, one that takes on an important philosophical significance in light of the ethical approaches of Plato and Socrates. Before that, however, it is useful to reflect a little more carefully on the last part of the Xenophon passage quoted above: 'we think that he who makes a friend of one whom he knows to be gifted by nature, and teaches him all the good he can, fulfils the duty of a citizen and a gentleman ....'

The sophists, for the most part, were itinerant teachers – foreigners – who did not hold citizenship in the cities where they taught. Xenophon's comment about citizenship is borne out by the subtext of Socrates' remark in the *Apology* that young men will of their own choice ignore the free company of their own citizens in order to interact with sophists:

Yet I think it is a fine thing to be able to teach people as Gorgias of Leontini does, and Prodicus of Ceos, and Hippias of Elis. Each of these men can go to any city and persuade the young, who can keep company with anyone of their fellow citizens they want without paying, to leave the company of these, to join with themselves, pay them a fee, and be grateful to them besides (Plato, *Apology* 19e-20a).

Note that Socrates mentions the cities from which these men hail, and note that none of them hails from Athens. The idea that virtue is something that one would charge for, instead of being obligated to distribute freely as a well-meaning citizen, must have been highly problematic to Socrates. One suspects that there is a significant rhetorical move being made here by stating the home states of these famous sophists. They are not Athenian citizens, and as such have neither the same investment in nor obligation to Athenian citizens as Socrates has. Socrates' own refusal to leave his prison cell to roister up in Thessaly – as he puts it in *Crito* – shows his deep respect for his Athenian citizenship; he will not prostitute himself by living out his remaining days in a foreign land (Plato, *Crito* 53d-54a). When, at his trial, Socrates asks Meletus who it is that instructs the young in virtue, one must assume that Meletus' answer is the one that Socrates expects, and most likely agrees with:

> Tell me, my good sir, who improves our young men? – The laws.
> That is not what I am asking, but what person who has knowledge of the laws to begin with? – These jurymen, Socrates.
> How do you mean Meletus? Are these able to educate the young and improve them? – Certainly.
> All of them, or some but not others? – All of them.
> Very good, by Hera. You mention a great abundance of benefactors. But what about the audience? Do they improve the young or not? – They do too.
> What about the members of Council? – The Councillors, also.
> But Meletus, what about the assembly? Do the members of the assembly corrupt the young, or do they all improve them? – They improve them.
> All the Athenians, it seems, make the young into fine good men …
>
> (Plato, *Apology* 24e-25a)

The answers that Socrates expects and elicits imply that good citizens improve the youth. Socrates is a citizen, not an itinerant foreigner who takes money for teaching. At the same time we cannot ignore Socrates' frequent critiques of Athens in the *Apology* and elsewhere despite his remarks in the same text as an appeal to the virtues of citizenship. In the same vain, despite his remarks on obligation to the laws of Athens in *Crito*, there is no doubt that Socrates was as much a critic of Athens as Plato was. Yet we must remember that while Plato may have been highly critical of Athens and all of her institutions,[2] the fact remains that the deep cultural connections between virtue and citizenship are pointedly made by setting aside discussions with foreigners in Book I of the *Republic* to set the quest for justice on a new course with Plato's Athenian brothers, Glaucon and Adeimantus. The quest for virtue is a task for kith and kin, not something to be purchased from those with no connection to or investment in the state. For Aristotle too, virtue is inextricable from citizenship, an idea that is borne out by his famous statement that a man with no *polis* by nature and not simply as a result of ill luck is either a beast or a god (*Politics* 1253a).[3]

A further point about the itinerant nature of sophists warrants reflection. Isocrates, although his aim is to show that the life of Gorgias, his one-time teacher, was far from opulent, has indicated that the sophist from Leontini had no property, paid no taxes and bore no family expenses (Isocrates, *Antidosis* 155). This is ironic to say the least, insofar as Isocrates' remark comes up in his *Antidosis*. An *antidosis* is a challenge whereby one tasked with financing and overseeing a state service as a form of paying taxes may challenge another citizen to take on the burden, or exchange property with him (Christ 1990, 147-69). Isocrates' *Antidosis* is the author's own defence of his life's work, one prompted by his surprise at learning, as a result of such a contest, that his reputation among his fellow citizens was not as honourable as he had thought. One can't help but think – although again this is not Isocrates' point – that Gorgias and other non-tax-paying sophists may have been perceived as parasitic upon the communities from which they obtained their wealth, whether that wealth was opulent or moderate. In short, the fact that the sophists were men who had abandoned citizenship (that which Socrates would rather die than do (Plato, *Crito* 54b-d)), intellectual freedom, and responsibility to their state for a life of wage-earning itinerancy places them in a highly questionable light.

Much more may be said by way of the context and implications of citizenship, the possible perception of the sophists as parasites, their lack of investment in the state and the general disdain for wage-earning. These speak to the cultural, not the philosophical, and while the two can hardly be extricated one from the other, it is the charges that speak to differences in philosophical orientation with which I am primarily concerned in what follows. I will treat of these charges under two main heads, the first being the general charge of charlatanism, namely that the sophists teach little of real value, and the second being what I consider the more philosophical way of interpreting Xenophon's report of Socrates' claim that the sophists are not free men.

Charlatanism

As for the charge of charlatanism, we may start with a remark made by Aristotle in *Sophistical Refutations* (165a). According to Aristotle, a sophist is a quack who teaches apparent knowledge, passing it off as real: 'For the art of the sophist is the semblance of wisdom without the reality, and the sophist is one who makes money from an apparent but unreal wisdom'. One may further reflect on the following passage from the *Metaphysics*:

> Dialecticians and sophists wear the same appearance as the philosopher, for sophistry is Wisdom in appearance only, and dialecticians discuss all subjects, and Being is a subject common to them all; but clearly they discuss these concepts because they appertain to philosophy. For sophistry and dialectic are concerned with the same class of subjects as philosophy, but

philosophy differs from the former in the nature of its capability and from the latter in its outlook on life. Dialectic treats as an exercise what philosophy tries to understand, and sophistry seems to be philosophy; but is not (*Metaphysics* 1004b).

Two things are important here. The first is that philosophy is superior to sophistry since sophistry pretends to be able to deliver what philosophy really can. The second thing to note is that Aristotle here identifies philosophy with a certain choice of life. While he says that this is how philosophy differs from dialectic, the distinction may equally be said to apply to the difference between philosophy and sophistry. For what Aristotle is getting at is the idea that philosophy is a commitment to a way of living, and is not merely a way of *earning* a living. Sophistry may appear to furnish a good life, but it is not as capable or as real in terms of its approach to virtue, or in terms of the nature of instruction that is bought and sold in the short term.

Whether one should be able to charge for real instruction in the good life is a different question. Fees were not charged by Plato or Aristotle in the Academy or the Lyceum, but of course both of their founders were wealthy. We should bear in mind that Aristotle's remarks above focus not on the selling of knowledge, but the *pretension* of knowledge. In some of Plato's dialogues, Socrates may be taken as implying that if someone *could* impart knowledge, they ought to be able to charge for it. In the *Gorgias*, for example, Socrates has no truck with selling knowledge of some things, but not virtue (519b-521a) (cf. Blank 1988, 10). In the *Cratylus* Socrates claims that he himself even paid for a course from the sophist Prodicus on the nature of names (384b-c). Now perhaps Socrates merely wanted to see what Prodicus was on about. Perhaps Socrates was being ironical or even condescending in paying for the lecture. One might even speculate that Socrates really did no such thing, but that his remark, to the effect that he could only afford the cheap version of the course and thus is ill informed on the nature of names, is merely another rhetorical swipe at the sophistic practice of teaching for pay. If this is merely rhetorical sniping, we might read into the remark the charge of charlatanism. Yet if Socrates did in fact attend a course by Prodicus, would he not implicate himself in perpetuating the practice of sophistry by paying for Prodicus' course? One is reminded of the *Euthydemus*, where Crito issues a veiled chastisement of Socrates for arguing with such men in public (305b). In other words if we are moralistically strict here, we might think that Socrates' paying a fee to Prodicus actually indicates that he sees nothing morally wrong in paying for some things. At the same time, the fact that Socrates' ignorance about the nature of names is due to his poverty – he could not afford entrance to Prodicus' full course, and would have been or was turned away from it due to lack of funds – suggests that the sophist is more interested in money than education, and as such his commitment to education is rendered suspect.

The above remarks show what an interpretive landmine Socratic in-sinuation is, but also how useful it can be in parsing Socrates' real orientation. Consider another example of this kind of insinuation. In Plato's *Apology* Socrates says he learned from Callias, a man who spent more money on sophists 'than everyone else put together', that the sophist Evenus of Paros possessed the art of teaching virtue for a fee of only five minas. What Socrates then says needs to be parsed: 'I thought Evenus a happy man, if he really possesses this art, and teaches for so moderate a fee. I would pride and preen myself if I had this knowledge, but I do not have it, gentlemen' (*Apology* 20c).

Now it seems clear enough that Socrates is being sarcastic in the first sentence, and that he does not believe that Evenus possesses knowledge of virtue, and again we see the sneer at teaching for pay. It seems fair to say that Socrates does not really believe that the sophists have divine wisdom regarding virtue; they are human, and as Socrates famously states in his trial, next to divine wisdom, human wisdom is all but worthless (*Apology* 23b).[4] Yet the second sentence is difficult. Is Socrates here saying that if one did possess knowledge, it would be acceptable to charge for it? Of course Socrates merely says that he would be proud to possess such knowledge. But might not the implication here be that Socrates would do just what Evenus does in fact do, that is teach for pay, if he truly possessed knowledge? Socrates' own inability to teach, because he professes ignorance, is one thing that prevents him from teaching for pay, but is it the only thing? I suspect that helping others, where education is (as far as Plato is concerned) perhaps the greatest form of help one could offer, ought not to be the sort of thing that is restricted by monetary considerations.[5]

Might not part of this outlook also explain the disdain for teaching for pay? Might not that outlook also incorporate a disdain for money as an important part of the true account of virtue, and of the obligation of a citizen and a good man to converse and exemplify virtue as a matter of course? In other words a friend or citizen gives freely what a merchant charges for. A friend cares for his friend whereas the merchant (qua merchant) is indifferent to anyone but a potential or returning paying customer. Friendship and citizenship are lifelong endeavours, but itiner-ant sophistical teaching is touted as a short-term business transaction. Grote's reflections on philosophical friendship and teaching are worth recalling here, to the effect that Socrates:

> assimilated the relation between teacher and pupil to that between two lovers or two intimate friends, which was thoroughly dishonoured, robbed of its charm and reciprocity, and prevented from bringing about its legitimate reward of attachment and devotion, by the intervention of money payment (Grote 1907, 315).

Such an intimate relationship is not likely to be the kind that can be developed or acquired through a course of paid instruction, but rather suggests a more attached and longer commitment than paid instruction would furnish. Moreover, the contractual nature of teaching for pay does not seem to require any assessment of the capacity of the pupil. This would seem to be Isocrates' primary concern. For while Isocrates did take pay for instruction, he emphasises that virtue can be taught only to those naturally predisposed to such instruction:

> I consider that the kind of art which can implant honesty and justice in depraved natures has never existed and does not now exist, and that people who profess that power will grow weary and cease from that vain pretension before such an education is ever found. (Isocrates, *Antidosis* 274).

Isocrates' charge here is that those who would profess to teach virtue to the depraved are trying to teach something incapable of being received, and as such those who take money for such teaching are charlatans. Isocrates' own approach involves the teaching of pupils with natural potential to speak well on pan-Hellenic themes worthy of discourse, through which a virtuous character may be refined. One may also recall the diatribes in which Isocrates rails against those like Euthydemus and Dionysodorus who claim to be able to teach virtue to all comers more quickly than any other (Plato, *Euthydemus* 273d). Teaching virtue is not as simple as teaching the alphabet, or providing specific responses to all of life's contingencies, but rather the cultivation of a mind equipped with certain natural abilities to have sound judgment and persuasive speech (Isocrates, *Against the Sophists* 10). Plato would say that the kind of character formation and education extends to an internal psychic harmony and life-long commitment to education within a correctly ordered state, and that not merely education, but every aspect of the state must be reformed. In other words, for both Plato and Isocrates, though they differ in many respects, acquiring virtue is not like acquiring fast food but rather akin to a lifelong regime of diet and exercise.

Relativism

The prerequisite of natural dispositions to virtue espoused by Isocrates, or integrative approaches to virtue like Plato's, point in the direction of a conception of virtue as something natural, objective and fixed. One might intuitively observe that while the sophists are often associated with relativism, philosophers like Plato and Aristotle were concerned with a quest for a higher truth. The idea of a relativistic sophist charging for teaching virtue would certainly have been troublesome to philosophers who believed virtue to be natural, not artificial. The artificial nature of justice, conceived by Thrasymachus as the will of the stronger party

(Plato, *Republic* 338c), stands in sharp contrast with the Platonic/Aristotelian perspective, where justice is a *physis*, not a *nomos*.[6] Plato, who believes that moral education of citizens is the responsibility of philosopher-kings who know the true nature of virtue and have no interest in taking pay, fears a relativistic sophistry that runs so counter to the core of his own approach to education and virtue. Aristotle's approach to practical virtue involves imitation of the virtuous and the formation of habit in virtue of that imitation; in so far as practical virtue is relative to the situation, practical wisdom is needed to determine the golden mean, the appropriate response to a given situation. For Plato, to be virtuous is to *know* virtue, to imitate the Form of virtue. For Aristotle, to be virtuous is to *know the exemplar* of virtue, to imitate the virtuous man. To this we may also add the position of Isocrates that the cultivation of a persuasive speaker requires virtuous behaviour on the part of that speaker, so that men will respect what he has to say. In all three approaches, there is an underlying assumption that one must either know virtue as form or exemplify or emulate virtuous activity in word and deed in order to be virtuous. The charge of charlatanism against the sophists would then more specifically lie in the fact that they are neither exemplars nor do they know or believe in a fixed or objective form of virtue. As such they cannot teach it. Isocrates rhetorically suggests:

> But what is most ridiculous of all is that [sophists] distrust those from whom they are [to receive money for instruction in virtue] – they distrust, that is to say, the very men to whom they are about to deliver the science of just dealing – and they require that the fees advanced by their students be entrusted for safe keeping to those who have never been under their instruction (Isocrates, *Against the Sophists* 5).[7]

Isocrates, like Plato, believed that education is not that easy, and that it is not simply a matter of imparting knowledge from teacher to student. One must be working with a student of the right natural endowment and capacity for virtue, and even then, for Isocrates, there is no guarantee of how the student will turn out.

Psychic health, freedom and harm

I turn now to what I believe to be the deeper philosophical case against the sophistic practice of teaching for pay, and where I think the real harm lies regarding the practice. In what follows I will attempt to suggest that the harmful effect of teaching those who are not predisposed to virtue but may nonetheless requisition such instruction with a fee, is an effect harmful not only to the pupil, but to the teacher as well. That Plato did not conceive of teaching as the mere imparting of knowledge from teacher to student, is borne out in a wealth of passages in Plato's dialogues. Consider the contrastive outlook of Thrasymachus whose offer of pouring an argument into Socrates' soul at *Republic* 345b is pointedly contrasted with the assessment of education as turning the mind in the right direction at the beginning of *Republic* VII (581b-d):

> Education isn't what some people declare it to be, namely, putting knowledge into souls that lack it, like putting sight into blind eyes ... education is the craft concerned with ... this turning around, and with how the soul can most easily and effectively be made to do it. It isn't the craft of putting sight into the soul.

Now there may have been sophists who could in fact teach, and in some cases they are actually defended to a degree by Plato and by Isocrates. This 'defence' nonetheless leads to my second point about the deeper philosophical meaning in Socrates' claim that the sophists' freedom is restricted. In order to illustrate what I take to be that deeper meaning, we ought to consider Socrates' assessment of the career of Protagoras in the *Meno* and Plato's famous assessment of sophists in the *Protagoras*. What Socrates says about Protagoras at *Meno* 91dff. is instructive. Protagoras made a great deal of money, and no one ever complained that his teaching was faulty. Socrates implies that just as a cobbler would be put out of business if his work were unsatisfactory, Protagoras could not have been successful for forty years if his work were unsatisfactory.

Isocrates makes a similar claim about his own teaching in the *Antidosis*, in a passage heavily indebted to Plato's *Apology* (33d-34b):

> I am far from being a corrupter of our youth. For if I were guilty of this ... you would see the fathers and relatives of my pupils up in arms, framing writs and seeking to bring me to justice. But instead they bring their sons to me and are ready to pay me money, and are rejoiced when they see them spending their time in my company ... (*Antidosis* 240-1).

In these passages dealing with corrupting pupils; there is no complaint about the selling of knowledge at all, simply the denial that there were in fact pupils who were corrupted. Now whether or not the former pupils of sophists *should* have sought tutelage from sophists and be satisfied with their purchases is a wholly different question, and one that Socrates addresses with a great deal of eloquence in the *Protagoras*. When the young Hippocrates kicks at Socrates' door early in the morning begging for Socrates to introduce him to the great sophist of Abdera, Socrates offers this warning:

> we must take care, my good friend, that the sophist, in commending his wares, does not deceive us, as both merchant and dealer do in the case of our bodily food. For among the provisions, you know, in which these men deal, not only are they themselves ignorant of what is good or bad for the body,

since in selling they commend them all, but the people who buy from them are so too, unless one happens to be a trainer or a doctor. And in the same way, those who take their doctrines the round of our cities, hawking them about to any odd purchaser who desires them, commend everything that they sell, and there may well be some of these too, my good sir, who are ignorant which of their wares is good or bad for the soul; and in just the same case are the people who buy from them, unless one happens to have a doctor's knowledge here also, but of the soul. So then, if you are well informed as to what is good or bad among these wares, it will be safe for you to buy doctrines from Protagoras or from anyone else you please: but if not, take care, my dear fellow, that you do not risk your greatest treasure on a toss of the dice. For I tell you there is far more serious risk in the purchase of doctrines than in that of eatables. When you buy victuals and liquors you can carry them off from the dealer or merchant in separate vessels, and before you take them into your body by drinking or eating you can lay them in your house and take the advice of an expert whom you can call in, as to what is fit to eat or drink and what is not, and how much you should take and when; so that in this purchase the risk is not serious. But you cannot carry away doctrines in a separate vessel: you are compelled, when you have handed over the price, to take the doctrine in your very soul by learning it, and so to depart either an injured or a benefited man. (*Protagoras* 313d-314b).[8]

This passage betrays a mild condescension and mistrust directed at merchants of food and drink, perhaps corroborating our earlier remarks about a general disdain for wage-earning. Second, and more importantly, Socrates claims that some sophists may be unaware of, or indifferent to, the harmfulness of their wares. We should remember the claim that no one was unhappy with the wares they bought from Protagoras, and the similar remarks of Isocrates about himself and Gorgias. At the same time we should note that this remark in the *Protagoras* is not directed at Protagoras, but to *some* peddlers of doctrines, who may be unaware whether what they sell is helpful or harmful. Two other things should not be missed here. The issue emphasised is not with selling *per se*, but with the potential danger to the buyer of what is being sold. And the danger is all the more to be avoided in those too inexperienced to know the difference between good and bad instruction.[9] One cannot help but recall Socrates stepping in to save the young Cleinias from the hands of the sophists from Chios in *Euthydemus* (277d). That the youth imitate the method of elenchus or pseudo-elenchus indiscriminately and to the detriment of philosophy is something that Socrates remarks upon in the *Apology* (23c) and the *Republic*, from which the following remark is taken (539b):[10]

For I fancy you have not failed to observe that lads, when they first get a taste of disputation, misuse it as a form of sport, always employing it contentiously, and, imitating confuters, they themselves confute others. They delight like spies in pulling about and tearing with words all who approach them.

Now Isocrates had maintained that a little bit of instruction in disputation or even captious argument might aid to sharpen the mind, but is serviceable only as a propaedeutic to thinking well and more clearly about more important practical matters, matters about how to live a life of excellence (*Antidosis* 266). To substitute philosophy for one of its sparring techniques is dangerous, and it is the youth who imitate without understanding who are most unable to recognise the difference. The problem about teaching for pay, it would seem, is that the sophist may have to accept youths who have the money to pay for his tutelage, whether the prospective student has the maturity or intellectual capacity to learn from him or not. This recalls Isocrates' position that natural capacity for virtue is a prerequisite for instruction. Grote quite rightly points out that it was not the sophist who implanted corrupted morality.

> These young men wanted political power. To gratify ambition was their end and aim. But this was an aim which the Sophists did not implant. They found it pre-existing, learnt from other quarters; and they had to deal with it as a fact (Grote 1907, vol. VIII, 320n.2).

Grote goes on to say that for every man with a predisposition to misemploy the tools imparted by the sophists for the purposes of deceit, there would be another with the ability to expose such deception. Yet the fact remains that for a student with a grasping disposition, one who lacks maturity, natural ability and a predisposition to virtue, and the sophist takes him on, the sophist, far from instilling or helping virtue to flourish in the pupil, may actually ruin him.

Now one may claim, as Gorgias does in the dialogue that bears his name, that the teacher is not responsible for the misuse of the skills he imparts (*Gorgias* 457c) and this is an idea that Socrates to some degree would agree with, with the caveat that he himself does not teach, yet the new danger of deception in words as opposed to deeds represented the threat of the persuasive power of tyranny, the ability to engineer wrongful executions and deliberate deceptions – dangers that are specific to argumentation, forensics and oratory, and not as evident as misuses of practical skills. Here the potential for harm enters the equation. Speaking from the philosophical perspective of Plato, a person who harms, and benefits from that harm, and is not punished for so doing, becomes the most lamentable of men. Herein, I believe, lies the deeper philosophical implication of the bondage of the sophist who takes pay for his instruction. Socrates argues with some vigour in the *Republic* (335e) that it is never just to harm anyone, a position he maintains with equal vigour in the *Crito* (49d). Socrates concludes famously in the *Gorgias* – notably in the context of a critique of persuasive oratory – that the unpunished criminal is the most hapless of men (479e). Hence it is possible to argue that should the sophist, who is *obliged* to take pay for instruction, ruin the soul of a youth not suited for such instruction, he will be harming his pupil and himself. For by Plato's lights, if he who harms goes unpunished, he is most hapless. Just as the tyrant cannot escape the conditions that his tyranny creates, neither can the sophist escape the conditions that his sophistry creates. Socrates' apparently sneering claim that the sophist is most unfortunate in having his freedom restricted now takes on a more philosophical tenor. The inept sophist can be *forced* to corrupt the souls of the youth by taking pay for his services, and by logical extension, is condemned to a life of misery himself. According to Isocrates, such men 'inflict most injury upon their own students' (*Helen* 7).

How forcefully does Thrasymachus argue his position in the *Republic*, knowing that his reputation as a wise teacher, and hence his very livelihood, is on the line? How calmly and freely does Socrates argue, knowing that he will not lose wealth or reputation in a quest for the truth, and that such a quest can only benefit him? How often does Socrates remind his interlocutor that he will gladly be refuted in the interest of truth? How indentured is the sophist who must fight in word and deed to save face in front of paying or potentially paying clientele? (*Gorgias* 457c-458b). The sophist is not merely owned by his student, he is owned by his argument as well. The servitude to which Xenophon refers extends beyond merely having to take on whomever can pay, and encompasses a servitude to arguments that one may not believe, and ultimately to a life of servitude to a corrupted soul, one that must profit through lack of freedom to discriminate between those capable of instruction and those who are not. Those who are not capable of virtue, if given the appropriate arsenal, threaten to force Athens into tyranny rather than liberate her through education.

Conclusion

The foregoing considerations serve to highlight several aspects that seem to have contributed to the negative reputation of sophistry in ancient Greece. The cultural/contextual considerations are not specifically philosophical; rather they seem to reflect certain prejudices about wage-earning and citizenship. Charges of charlatanism, inconclusive to the extent that claims of the impossibility of teaching virtue are inconclusive, are nonetheless uncomplimentary in the face of the fact that if virtue could be taught, it ought to be taught for free by respectable citizens. In strict philosophical circles, the idea that virtue is something natural and objective contributes to the sense of charlatanism attributed to relativistic teachers who would teach that which philosophy considers natural within relativistic frameworks. On a more specific level, what Plato regards as all important, namely psychic health and the avoidance of harm and harming, turns the faulty practice of virtue instruction to unprepared students into a morally corrupt activity that harms the student and enslaves the instructor. Unlike Socrates, who associates with whomever he wishes, the practice of teaching for pay ensnares the sophist into a most precarious and indentured occupation.

Notes

1. Just a few recent examples include J. Dillon and T. Gergel, *The Sophists*, (Harmondsworth: Penguin, 2003), xiii, xviii; D. Corey, 'The Case Against Teaching for Pay: Socrates and the Sophists', *History of Political Thought*, 23:2 (2002), 189; R. Waterfield, *The First Philosophers: The Presocratics and the Sophists* (Oxford: Oxford University Press, 2000), xxvi; A. Nehamas, *Virtues of Authenticity* (Princeton: Princeton University Press, 1999), 111; J. De Romilly, *The Great Sophist in Periclean Athens* (Oxford: Oxford University Press, 1992), 4-5; S. Jarratt, 'The First Sophists and the Uses of History', *Rhetoric Review*, 6:1 (1987), 68; G.B. Kerferd, *The Sophistic Movement* (Cambridge: Cambridge University Press, 1981), 25; W.K.C. Guthrie, *The Sophists* (Cambridge: Cambridge University Press, 1971), 35; E.L. Harrison, 'Was Gorgias a Sophist?', *Phoenix* xviii:3 (1964), 185, 190-1; to which we may add G. Grote, *A History of Greece*, vol. VIII (London: Everyman, 1907), 314.

2. I am reminded here of the observation of Benjamin Jowett, that 'The great enemy of Plato is the world, not exactly in the theological sense, yet in one not wholly different – the world as the hater of truth and lover of appearance, occupied in the pursuit of gain and pleasure rather than of knowledge, banded together against the few good and wise men, and devoid of true education. This creature has many heads: rhetoricians, lawyers, statesmen, poets, sophists. But the sophist is the Proteus who takes the likeness of all of them; all other deceivers have a piece of him in them. And sometimes he is represented as the corrupter of the world; and sometimes the world as the corrupter of him and of itself' (B. Jowett, *The Dialogues of Plato*, vol. IV (Oxford: Oxford University Press, 1871), 287.

3. Presumably Aristotle has slavery in mind here, but all the better insofar as sophistry has been presented by Xenophon and Plato as a kind of intellectual servitude.

4. Note the remark at the end of the *Meno* (100b): 'It follows from this reasoning, Meno, that virtue appears to be present in those of us who may possess it as a gift from the gods.'

5. To Plato this might seem as obvious as it would to the average Canadian that health care is a universal right.

6. Grote (1907, vol. VIII, 346n.3) notes that those who argue that the sophists deny the naturalness of rights are wrong-headed in their approach. Callicles in *Gorgias*, for example, is asserting a natural right of sorts, one which is superior to legislative rights. This does little, however, to assuage the fear that legislative justice à la Thrasymachus in the *Republic* is diametrically opposed to an approach to legislative justice that attempts, in a pre-Thomistic way, to model itself on natural principles of justice. Now while Grote is right to point out that Callicles is not a sophist and that his anticipation of Nietzsche's 'Overman' is not a doctrine that a sophist bent on cultivating a clientèle in Athens would speak publicly, I am not convinced that there are any grounds for denying that the position attributed to Thrasymachus in *Republic* I is something that Thrasymachus may have said (Grote, 352). For many people hold the position, or something like it, according to Glaucon and Adeimantus in *Republic* II.

7. Cf. *Gorgias* 519c; Blank 1988, 9; E.J. Power, 'Plato's Academy: A Halting Step

Towards Higher Learning', *History of Education Quarterly* iv.3 (1964), 155-66. Of course as far as we know, only the practice of Protagoras, who took payment only upon the satisfaction of his client at the end of a course of instruction, is an exception (Aristotle, *Nicomachean Ethics* 1164a).

    8. Cf. *Gorgias* 464b-466a.

    9. Cf. Blank 1988, 9.

    10. Cf. A. Nehamas, *Virtues of Authenticity* (Princeton: Princeton University Press, 1999), 114.

Bibliography

Aristotle, *Metaphysics*, trans. H. Tredennick, Loeb edition (London: Heinemann, 1979).

Aristotle, *Politics*, trans. T.H. Sinclair (London: Penguin, 1966).

Aristotle, *Sophistical Refutations*, in J. Barnes (ed.), *The Complete Works of Aristotle* (Princeton: Princeton University Press, 1984).

Blank, David, 'Socrates vs. Sophists', *Classical Antiquity* iv (1988), 1-49.

Christ, M.R., 'Liturgy Avoidance and *Antidosis* in Classical Athens', *Transactions of the American Philological Association* 120 (1990), 147-69.

Corey, D., 'The Case Against Teaching Virtue for Pay: Socrates and the Sophists', *History of Political Thought* xxiii: 2 (2002), 189-210.

Gomperz, T., *Greek Thinkers,* vol. I (London: John Murray, 1901).

Grote, George, *History of Greece*, vol. VIII, Everyman edition (London: Dent, 1907).

Isocrates, *Antidosis*, trans. G. Norlin, Loeb edition (London: Heinemann, 1929).

Isocrates, *Against the Sophists*, trans. G. Norlin, Loeb edition (London: Heinemann, 1929).

Plato, *Apology*, trans. H.N. Fowler, Loeb edition (London: Heinemann, 1999).

Plato, *Euthydemus*, trans. W.R.M. Lamb, Loeb edition (London: Heinemann, 1962).

Plato, *Gorgias*, trans. W.R.M. Lamb, Loeb edition (London: Heinemann, 1925).

Plato, *Protagoras*, trans. W.R.M. Lamb, Loeb edition (London: Heinemann, 1924).

Plato, *Republic*, trans. G.M.A. Grube and C.D.C. Reeve (Indianapolis: Hackett, 1992).

Sidgwick, H., 'The Sophists', *Journal of Philology* viii (1872), 288-307.

Xenophon, *Memorabilia*, trans. E.C. Marchant, Loeb edition (London: Heinemann, 1923).

22

The Relevance of the Sophists Today

Seamus Sweeney

Just as 'Stoic' and 'Epicurean' are now used in ways quite different from their original meaning, 'sophist' is hardly ever used in its original sense of a lover of wisdom. 'Sophist' is, even now, a term of abuse. Sophistry has come to mean casuistry, the use of cleverness to justify the unjustifiable, to defend the indefensible, 'to make the weaker argument the stronger'. As previous contributors have written, most of our knowledge of the sophists is derived from the writings of their opponents. And from what we can re-assemble of their teachings and writings, there was far more to the sophists than the cheap charlatanry the name evokes now.

It is not difficult to find examples of the use of 'sophist' as a term of abuse today. For instance, the Catholic apologist Peter Kreeft writes:

> Socrates made a point that he never took a fee for his teaching. (Neither did Jesus.) This proved that he was not one of the Sophists, who sold their minds as a prostitute sells her body. ... The Sophists approached wealthy Athenians with this reasonable solicitation: 'Our minds are full – full of clever rhetorical tricks to confuse juries – and our purses are empty. Your purses are full and your minds are empty. Let's make a mutually profitable exchange. Grease our palms with your silver, and we will oil your brains with our wisdom.' Many wealthy Athenian parents were paying expensive tuition to Sophists to tutor their children without examining what product they were buying. Just change one word in that sentence – 'Athenian' to 'American' and you see that the more things change, the more they stay the same (Kreeft 2002, 28).

Aside from the accuracy or otherwise of Kreeft's passage – Aristophanes' play *Clouds* (which was first performed when the sophists such as Protagoras, Gorgias, Hippias, Prodicus and Antiphon were alive and practising their craft) alone suggests that concerns about 'what product [wealthy Athenian parents] were buying' abounded – it is clear that 'sophist' is, putting it mildly, a strongly loaded term. One can hardly think of a more derogatory comparison than likening a philosopher to a prostitute. Clearly there is an agenda here that goes beyond sober historical and philosophical consideration of the sophists. That the sophists still attract such attention is further testament to their relevance today. As the Kreeft passage illustrates, passions are still excited by the sophists, and the parallels that

241

can be drawn between fifth-century Athens and today's intellectual climate inflame these passions further. 'Relativism' – a trait often associated with some sophists, especially Anaxagoras – for instance, was decried by Pope Benedict XVI almost immediately on his accession. G.B. Kerferd in *The Sophistic Movement* writes that 'the modernity of the problems formulated and discussed by the sophists in their teaching is indeed startling', and goes on to give a lengthy list of these problems which informs the discussion below. And as Kerferd also illustrates, every thinker who has dealt with the sophists – from Grote to Hegel to W.K.C. Guthrie to Mario Untersteiner – has revealed as much about their own preoccupations as about the sophists. Our approach can hardly be any different.

T.S. Eliot once remarked that really profound influence is invisible. It is difficult to ascertain exactly how much Plato and Socrates influence Western thought, because their influence is so pervasive, and it may seem peculiar to ascribe huge influence to the sophists, whose name has been so traduced, whose writings are available only in fragments or in the reports of their opponents. Nevertheless, not only is the study of the sophists illuminating for its own sake, it also provides insights into the modern world.

The sophists brought tremendous intellectual excitement and glamour to Athens. The anxiety evident in *Clouds* is that young men would be distracted from dreams of horses and martial glory and into a world of, at best, useless speculation and, at worst, logical hair-splitting that would allow them, literally and figuratively, to beat their betters. All was up for grabs for the sophists, from the nature of reality itself to the nature of the good to the existence of gods. For traditionalist Athenians, it was a confusing time. There is a way of thinking of the history of ideas as a series of reactions and counter-reactions – Reformation and Counter-Reformation, Romanticism and Neo-Classicism, Postmodernism versus Modernism. One might see the Socratic movement and the sophists as being in a similar opposition. Of course, all these developments derive from the other and each depends upon the other. Socrates and the sophists were not mutually exclusive camps. Aristophanes' portrayal of Socrates in *Clouds*, for instance, is very clearly of a sophist. And the intellectual excitement which the sophists kindled in Athens surely had much to do with Socrates setting himself up as a philosopher, and with Plato, at later date,[1] writing his dialogues.

Not least of the reasons that the sophists are relevant today is their effect upon Socrates and Plato. Alfred North Whitehead once called Western philosophy a series of 'footnotes to Plato', and even the most ardent anti-Platonist will admit to his incalculable influence. One of the reasons Plato wrote his dialogues was in response to the sophists. Partly this was as a result of the sheer excitement and intellectual ferment generated by the sophists. Partly this was as a reaction to the common confusion of Socrates with the sophists, and Plato's desire to clarify the distinctions.

22. The Relevance of the Sophists Today

One of the direct ways in which the sophists are relevant today is that they were the first to put a monetary value on education; they were the first professional educators. In Plato's *Hippias Major* Socrates remarks that Gorgias 'by giving exhibitions and associating with the young, he earned and received a great deal of money from the city' and that Prodicus 'in his private capacity, by giving exhibitions and associating with the young ... received a marvellous sum of money' (282d).

Who, reading Socrates' comments on Gorgias and Prodicus, does not think of today's intellectual heavyweights, touring the world to impart their wisdom for a high fee? The sophists' innovation of seeking payment for tuition is the first appearance of an idea now so pervasive that we take it for granted. Today it is taken almost entirely for granted that teachers require payment. Education is an expensive business, and perhaps governments and administrators sometimes wish that the sophists had been more thoroughly opposed in this regard. One could argue that advances of all kinds – cultural, technical, scientific – have depended on the wider dissemination and prolongation of education, and this would be impossible without professional teachers. We live, in this quite pragmatic sense, in a world created by the sophists.

Indeed, one could argue that the sophists are relevant for purely pragmatic reasons. They laid the foundations for rhetoric, which would be polished further by the Romans and underlie the craft of orators and communicators up to our own day. The fragments of Gorgias may seem at times risible, with their clogged, dense, grand style – nevertheless who can resist the odd flourish such as the alliteration, assonance, isocolon, triple rhyming, homoeoteleuton and other peculiarly named features of rhetoric that characterise *The Encomium of Helen*? Management books have been published which cite Pericles, Alcibiades and other luminaries of the Athenian fifth century as exemplars. The pragmatically minded sophists would love to be thus immortalised, and who knows if some enterprising philosopher may undertake such a project.

Be that as it may, the real excitement and relevance of studying the sophists today is in getting to grips with their own ideas and with their influence on the ideas of others. 'The sophists' most revolutionary innovation was, precisely, that, faced with nature, they set up teaching to counteract it and considered that virtue could be learned by attending their classes.' So wrote Jacqueline de Romilly (2002, 45), and the problem of nature versus nurture, as it is invariably dubbed today, is a very old one that troubled the Athenians with a peculiar intensity. We see it in Thucydides, in the comparison between the courage of the Athenians – portrayed by Thucydides as deriving from reason, from expertise and from experience – and that of the Spartans, portrayed as 'natural' and traditional. We see it in Euripides' play, *Hecabe*, when Hecabe, wife of Priam of Troy, learns of the slaughter of her daughter, and after a few rather perfunctory words of grief launches into a meditation on this very question:

243

How strange, that bad soil, if the gods send rain and sun,
Bear a rich crop, while good soil, starved of what it needs,
Is barren, but man's nature is ingrained – the bad
Is never anything but bad, and the good man
Is good: misfortune cannot warp his character,
His goodness will endure.
       Where lies the difference?
In heredity or upbringing? Being nobly bred
At least instructs a child in goodness; and this lesson,
If well learnt, shows him by that measure what evil is.
                              (Vellacott 1963, lines 593-603)

Plato's *Protagoras* is devoted to the dispute between Socrates and Protagoras on this particular issue, virtue – although both agree that virtue can be taught, Socrates doubts Protagoras' breezy self-confidence on the issue.

Again, this is an issue that has huge implications not only for education but also for wider political economy. Our improved knowledge of genetics in the last hundred years has given the problem a new acuity. Nevertheless, in this as in many fields one can get the impression from contemporary media coverage that all this is a new problem, which only our time has had to face. Nothing could be further from the truth, as the example of the sophists illustrates.

Whatever one's own beliefs on the issue of nature-nurture, and whatever science may or may nor tell us about it, one must concede that the sophists have, from a practical point of view, won the argument. Prior to the sophists, the idea that *aretê* or excellence was inborn and therefore unteachable was universal. Therefore aristocratic birth alone qualified one for rule. If Protagoras' self-confidence in his ability to teach virtue seemed dubious to Socrates, who was after all sympathetic to the essential point, imagine how shocking it must have been to Athenians more in thrall to notions of aristocratic virtue.

To say that we, in the West, live in pure meritocracy is obviously not entirely accurate. Nevertheless, we live in societies where aristocracy, if it survives, is generally seen as a charming historical footnote rather than an active, influential force. The idea that some groups or classes simply shouldn't be educated because it is a waste of time has all but disappeared, from public discourse at least. This is a recent phenomenon – until historically very recently the education of women was a controversial issue. It is also one that is completely uncontroversial now. The notion that we should not provide universal education up to and including at least secondary level is one that would be repugnant (and politically suicidal) today. Yet it is one that was argued passionately in previous eras. Thus another reason the sophists are of great interest is because they were the first ideologues of meritocracy, and we live in the West in societies that, nominally and in many ways practically, are meritocracies.

22. The Relevance of the Sophists Today

In all spheres, the sophists challenged the orthodoxy of their time as radically as any intellectual movement since. One of the most resonant – and most famous – sophist maxims is Protagoras' 'man is the measure of all things'. What better summary of postmodernism, or theories of social constructivism? Of course (and, of course, entirely appropriately), the saying is open to many interpretations.

One of the most intriguing speculations on the sophists is that perhaps the texts that we have – the fragmentary, the epigrammatic – do actually reflect what the sophists might have written. Their emphasis on oratory and the spoken word might suggest that texts for them were essentially prompts. We should also remember that Protagoras might have been directly talking about oratory or politics – that the listener, or the voter in the assembly, was the measure of all things, the only true judge of how well a speech went.

Nevertheless, 'man is the measure of all things' is one of the key maxims in the history of ideas. No longer was some kind of divine judgement seen as overriding human reason and perception. 'Man is the measure of all things' is a catch-phrase of at least some degree of relativism. 'Relativism' has become a loaded term, just as 'sophist' has, because of its connotations of a kind of 'anything goes' approach to morality and ethics. This is rather unfair. At its most basic, relativist thinking and relativist sayings such as Protagoras' remind us that there is more than one way of seeing things. This leads me to consider another crucially relevant factor in thinking of the sophists' relevance today – their role in the development of the scientific method.

The Presocratics are called both the first philosophers and the first scientists. This, of course, is because of their inquiring minds and readiness to challenge explanations that depended solely on divine action. Nevertheless, a modern reader often finds the sophists more familiarly 'scientific' than the Presocratics. This is because of the Presocratics' tendency to expand speculation into explanation, and to engage in what we would call metaphysics. The sophists are more recognisable ancestors of modern scientists because of their scepticism, their refusal to accept simple explanations, and their great pragmatic bent. There are many ways of defining the scientific method, but an unprejudiced search for alternative explanations for any given event or observation is one of its cardinal features.

'Making the weaker argument the stronger' is of course one of the phrases with which the sophists were abused. At first glance this is entirely explicable – it has very direct suggestions of a sort of confidence trick, a justification for wrongdoing. Yet on reflection, one must not forget that 'the weaker argument' may conceal the best answer. The querying approach of the sophists forces one to examine apparently sound arguments and justifications, and thereby perhaps discover their soundness to be illusory.

If the meritocratic vision of the sophists has gone towards shaping the modern world, the scientific method they helped create has changed it utterly. From a purely technological point of view, the triumph of science is perhaps obvious. Probably the surest proof of this triumph is how much we take for granted – email, air travel, antibiotics – all these innovations are the product of the rigorous scepticism that the sophists praised. On a deeper level, the sceptical, querying cast of mind of the sophists is now the cast of mind of modern, Western humanity; querying dogma, querying authority, querying received wisdom, querying religion.

The reader will have his or her own opinion as to whether this is a good thing. Nevertheless their influence is obvious. It would be inaccurate to call the sophists the first atheists or agnostics; nevertheless they do provide the first evidence of an ideology of atheism. Prodicus' explanation for belief in gods was that men deify those things such as fire and the sun and bread that are important for human life. Critias, who is not regarded as a sophist as such but was allied with their thought, believed that the gods were invented by authorities to foster the belief among ordinary people that everything was witnessed, and therefore to discourage law-breaking. Again, whatever one thinks of these arguments as such, they foreshadow the various attempted explanations for the existence of religion from atheistic-tending intellectuals from Freud and Durkheim to Richard Dawkins.

So to summarise: there is a liberating sense to a lot of what the sophists did. Their rejection of dogma and pragmatism is refreshing and immediate to modern minds. There is also a sense of accessibility, a sense that for all the piles of academic papers and wells of ink expended on scholarly argument, any interested, curious reader can respond to the sophists on something like equal terms. It does not depend on a knowledge of ancient cosmology or theology, but on a willingness to accept the fragmentary nature of the sources and engage with the ideas as they stand.

We live in an academic climate increasingly dissatisfied with the received view of the ancient world – hence the explosion of the interest in the Hellenistic period, traditionally seen as a rather inglorious epoch between the achievements of the fifth-century Athens and the rise of Rome. This scepticism also applies to fifth-century Athens itself, and to those usually seen as villains in a story of heroic Great Men existing in a world of pure mind. Few in academia at least would paint the sophists as the deceitful intellectual prostitutes of Kreeft's account above.

Furthermore, in the past there was a tendency to see the work of scientists and philosophers as proceeding in a sort of vacuum, isolated completely from society. Modern scholarship is generally impatient with this sort of view. We realise now the importance of an awareness at least of the times that ideas were formulated. Like other ideas, this can be taken to extremes, and sometimes one might think that the ideas themselves were secondary or trivial, compared to economic organisation or social conditions. However there is much to be gained from considering the kind of society in which the sophists operated. In the space of a few decades, Athens went from one small polis among others, a community not all that far in spirit or in fact from its agrarian roots, to the cosmopolitan cultural capital of Greece.

Phenomena that are familiar to any observer today – the flight from the land to the cities, the increasing footlessness of urban life, its disconnectedness from traditional roots – were all in evidence at the time. The sophists' advent was partly a reaction to the times, to an age when the traditional pieties seemed in question and everything was in flux. This is such a moment around the world, especially in rapidly industrialising countries such as India and China. Perhaps it is always thus.

In the West around the time of the end of the Cold War, there was a widespread sense of having reached 'the end of History', that the great questions had been decided and all that was left was the gradual dissemination of Western liberal democracy across the world. Subsequent events have made a mockery of this optimism. As it always is, this is a world where 'everything is in flux', as Heraclitus, one of the sophists' predecessors observed. It is why the sophists – sceptical, playful, practical, questioning – have continuing relevance today.

Note

1. Plato was born in about 429 BC and lived until 347. He was present at Socrates' trial in 399 BC but was not present at Socrates' execution. He was greatly affected by the condemnation and execution, and we may accept that he recorded the events of the day which resulted in his *Apology*, which is mainly a description of Socrates' defence. He was about thirty years old at the time. The *Apology* is considered to be one of Plato's earliest works.

Bibliography

Dillon, John and Gergel, Tania, *The Sophists* (Harmondsworth: Penguin, 2004).

Howatson, M.C., *The Oxford Companion to Classical Literature* (Oxford: Oxford University Press, 1989).

Kerferd, G.B., *The Sophistic Movement* (Cambridge: Cambridge University Press, 1981).

Kreeft, Peter, *Philosophy 101 by Socrates: An Introduction to Philosophy via Plato's Apology* (New York: Ignatius Press, 2002).

Romilly, Jacqueline de, *The Great Sophists in Periclean Athens*, trans. Janet Lloyd (Oxford: Clarendon Press, 2002).

Vellacott, Philip, trans., *Euripides' Hecabe* (Harmondsworth: Penguin Classics, 1963).

Waterfield, Robin, *The First Philosophers: The Presocratics and Sophists* (Oxford: Oxford University Press, 2000). References to texts attributed to the sophists are to this volume.

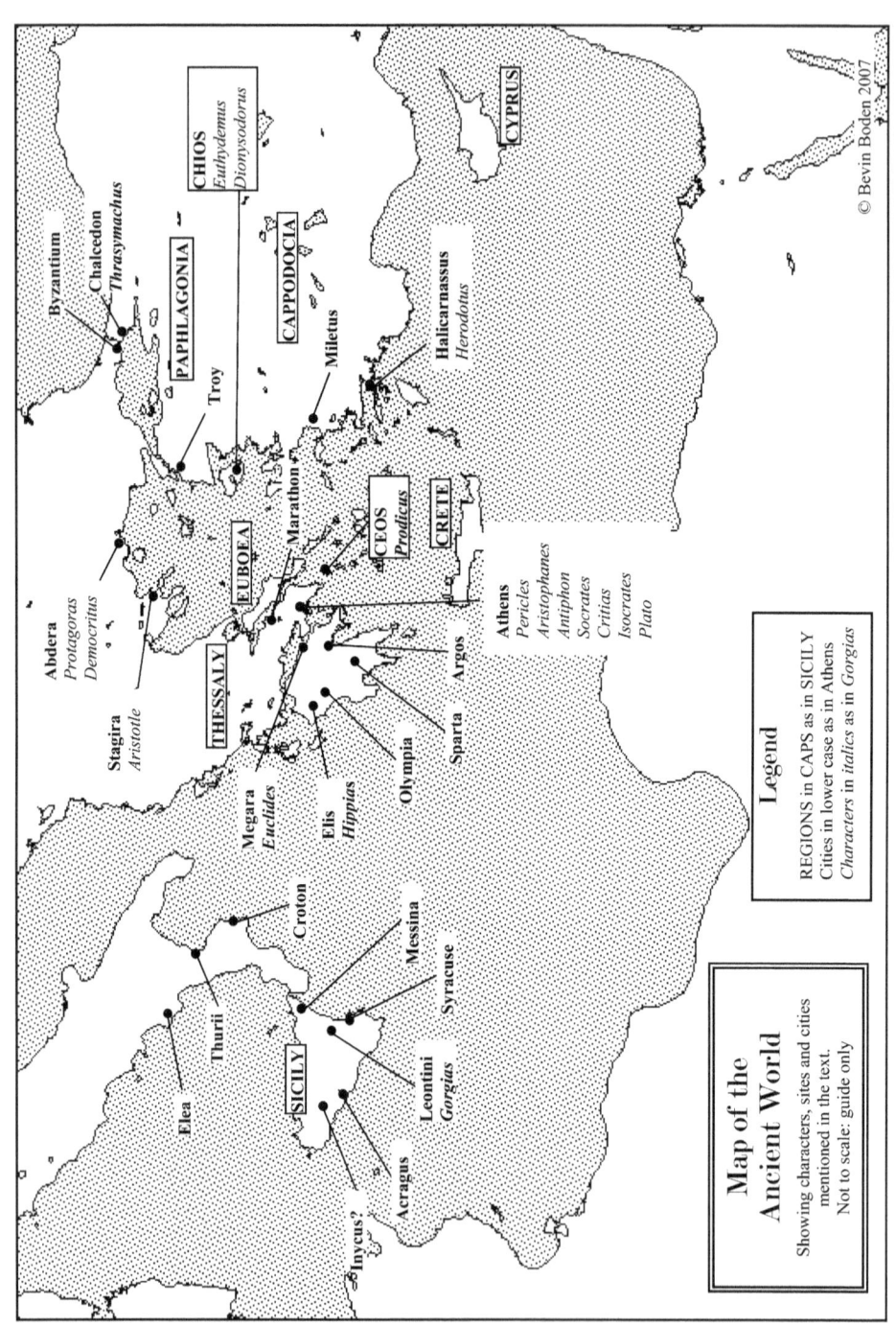

Map of the
Ancient World

Showing characters, sites and cities
mentioned in the text.
Not to scale: guide only

Legend

REGIONS in CAPS as in SICILY
Cities in lower case as in Athens
Characters in *italics* as in *Gorgias*

© Bevin Boden 2007

CHIOS
Euthydemus
Dionysodorus

CYPRUS

CAPPODOCIA

PAPHLAGONIA

Byzantium
Chalcedon
Thrasymachus

Troy

Miletus

Halicarnassus
Herodotus

Abdera
Protagoras
Democritus

Stagira
Aristotle

THESSALY

EUBOEA

Marathon

CEOS
Prodicus

CRETE

Athens
Pericles
Aristophanes
Antiphon
Socrates
Critias
Isocrates
Plato

Argos

Sparta

Olympia

Elis
Hippias

Megara
Euclides

Croton

Thurii

Elea

Messina

Syracuse

Leontini
Gorgias

Acragas

Inycus?

SICILY

Index